THE PRENTICE HALL LATIN READERS SERIES

* * * * * * * * * *

About the Author

David J. Perry received a Bachelor of Arts with Honors in Classics from Williams College and a Master of Arts in Teaching Latin and Classical Humanities from the University of Massachusetts at Amherst, with additional graduate study at Fordham University. He has taught at all levels from from 6th grade to undergraduate and adults. From 1980 to 2016, he taught Latin in the Rye City School District, Rye, New York where he served as chair of the Foreign Language Department from 1992 to 2003. Active in professional organizations, he has presented many workshops at regional and national conferences, served as Vice President of the Classical Association of the Empire State, as Secretary-Treasurer of the New York State Council on Languages, and as a consultant to the National Latin Examination and the New York State Education Department. In 2014 the American Classical League awarded him its Meritus award for service to the profession. Mr. Perry is co-author of *Fabulae Romanae* and of Book III of *Ecce Romani*. He also has a longstanding interest in using computers to support the work of scholars and teachers in less commonly taught languages, which led to writing the book *Document Preparation for Classical Languages* (2nd ed., 2010) and to creating the Cardo computer typeface for scholars.

A Call to Conquest

Readings from Caesar's *Gallic Wars*

David J. Perry

A Prentice Hall Latin Reader

PEARSON

Boston, Massachusetts
Chandler, Arizona
Glenview, Illinois
Upper Saddle River, New Jersey

Cover photo: bronze statue of Julius Caesar at the Porta Palatina, Turin, Italy.

Typeset in Minion® Pro and Myriad® Pro.
Page composition by David J. Perry.

Acknowledgments appear on page 310, which constitutes an extension of this copyright page.

13-digit ISBN: 978-0-13-320521-3
10-digit ISBN: 0-13-320521-5

11 19

Contents

✷ ✷ ✷ ✷ ✷ ✷ ✷ ✷ ✷

List of Illustrations, Diagrams, and Maps

✷ ✷ ✷ ✷ ✷ ✷ ✷ ✷ ✷

Preface

THE REVISION of the Advanced Placement[1] Latin syllabus, with the addition of Caesar as a required prose author for the first time, provided the immediate impetus for the creation of this book. It includes the required readings from *De bello Gallico* in both Latin and English and so provides all the material needed by students who are preparing for the Caesar portion of the AP[1] Latin examination.[2] It will also serve the needs of teachers and students, both at the high school and college levels, who want to read Caesar in a non-AP course.

The addition of Caesar as a required AP author will, we expect, lead to a revival of interest in this important author. A staple in American classrooms from colonial times onward, Caesar was dethroned from his position in the late 1960s. After colleges dropped Latin as an entrance requirement, enrollment in high school Latin dropped severely. Teachers scrambled to revise their curricula to attract students and often eliminated Caesar, who came to be seen as old fashioned, as uninteresting to many students (especially to girls) and—in the era of the Vietnam war and its concomitant social upheavals—as militaristic and imperialistic. Of course, some teachers have continued to use Caesar. But in general he has been "off the radar" for the past forty-plus years, as far as most high school teachers and classical scholars are concerned, although historians have continued to take an interest in Caesar. This hiatus now makes it possible for teachers and scholars to return to Caesar without much of the baggage of past and to take advantage of the many things that he has to offer our students.

Caesar was added to the AP curriculum partly because many college Classics departments felt that incoming students needed more experience reading Latin prose before undertaking advanced work. This book is different from most Latin readers, whether specifically designed for AP Latin or not, in that it explicitly attempts to help students become more proficient at reading Latin prose. This is done through the "Reading Caesar's Latin" section in the Introduction, through the Reading Strategy notes found throughout the book, through the comments about word order and expectations in the Summary of Grammar, and through additional suggestions and activities given in the accompanying Teacher's Guide. My own practices in this regard have been strongly influenced by Dexter Hoyos of the

---

[1] **Advanced Placement** and **AP** are registered trademarks of the College Board, which was not involved in the production of, and does not endorse, this book.

[2] For the Vergil portion of the AP Latin course, Pearson publishes a companion textbook, *A Song of War: Readings from Vergil's Aeneid* by Richard A. LaFleur and Alexander G. McKay.

University of Sydney, Australia. His book *Latin: How to Read It Fluently* (Classical Association of New England Press, 1998) should be read by anyone who wants to help his or her students be better readers. For more about this topic, see the Teacher's Guide.

The Teacher's Guide for *A Call to Conquest* provides translations of the Latin readings, answer keys for the comprehension and discussion questions, additional background information for the Latin readings, teaching suggestions, and a vocabulary frequency list. Bibliography and additional resources, enlarged versions of the Latin readings for projection, a master vocabulary list, sample questions in AP Latin format, and various other materials are located in the online course on Realize.

The author and the publisher would like to thank Penguin Books for permission to use the translation of *De bello Gallico* by S. A. Handford (1951) as revised for the Penguin Classics series by Jane F. Gardner and published under the title *Caesar: The Conquest of Gaul* (1982). The English portions of Books I and VI plus the complete Book VII that are found in this text appear in Handford's translation. Questions to accompany these sections in English were written for this edition. A few additional footnotes are also included to supplement those found in the Penguin translation; they are marked with the symbol ❧ at the end of the note.[3] Translations in the Student Edition other than those of Books I, VI, and VII, and all translations in the accompanying Teacher's Guide, are my own.

I am grateful to numerous people at Pearson, particularly Cathy Wilson and Jennifer Creane. Gilbert Lawall and the fine readers he has produced taught me a great deal about how to write a good Latin textbook. Richard A. LaFleur helped make this book consistent with Pearson's AP Vergil reader, *A Song of War*. Dexter Hoyos suggested some useful inscriptions. Caroline Kelly supplied the photograph of the bust of Plancus and Nichole Chiffriller provided technical help with the illustrations. I am particularly indebted to the reviewers who read the manuscript and offered valuable suggestions: Robert Brown of Vassar College, Poughkeepsie, New York; Ronald B. Palma of Tulsa, Oklahoma; and Lynne West of Bellarmine College Preparatory School, San Jose, California. I am of course responsible for any remaining errors.

David J. Perry
Poughkeepsie, New York

---

[3] This symbol, a traditional printer's ornament now found in several computerized typefaces, derives ultimately from the ivy leaves (**hederae**) often found in ancient Roman inscriptions.

A Call to Conquest

Readings from Caesar's *Gallic Wars*

Time Line

All dates are BCE.

102	Marius defeats the Teutones, and the Cimbri the following year
100	Caesar born
86	Marius dies; Cinna, a **populāris**, is dictator
83	Caesar marries Cornelia, daughter of Cinna
82	Caesar proscribed, then pardoned, by Sulla; leaves Rome for the East
81	Caesar is ambassador to King Nicomedes of Bithynia
81–78	Caesar serves on staff of provincial governors in Asia and Cilicia
78	Sulla dies; Caesar returns to Rome
77	Caesar held for ransom by pirates while returning from Rhodes
73	Caesar chosen for membership in the college of priests
68	Caesar serves in Spain as quaestor
65	Caesar holds office of curule aedile
63	Caesar becomes **pontifex maximus**, head of the college of priests; consulship of Cicero; conspiracy of Catiline exposed
62	Caesar serves as praetor
61	Caesar is propraetor (governor) of Further Spain Pompey returns from the East
60	Pompey, Crassus, and Caesar form the First Triumvirate; Caesar and Crassus elected consuls for the following year
59	Caesar holds consulship
58–49	Caesar serves as governor of Transalpine Gaul, Cisalpine Gaul, and Illyricum
56	First Triumvirate renewed at conference in Luca, northern Italy
55	Pompey and Crassus are consuls
54	Crassus killed fighting the Parthians; Julia, daughter of Caesar and wife of Pompey, dies
50	Caesar quarrels with the Senate as his term in Gaul comes to an end
49	Civil war begins; Caesar becomes dictator and is confirmed again in this office every year
48	Caesar defeats Pompey and senatorial forces at battle of Pharsalus; Pompey killed in Egypt
46	Caesar defeats Republican army at Thapsus; celebrates quadruple triumph
45	Final defeat of senatorial opposition at the battle of Munda, in Spain
44	Caesar receives office of **dictātor perpetuus**; assassinated 15 March

Introduction

THIS BOOK PROVIDES a selection of passages, some in Latin and others in English, from Caesar's own account of his conquest of Gaul, with vocabulary, notes, maps, and other features to help you read and understand the text. The selections are those required for the Advanced Placement® Examination in Latin offered by the College Board and can also be used by those who wish to read Caesar even if they are not preparing for the AP Latin examination.

Why Read Caesar?

Gaius Julius Caesar is one of the iconic figures of Western civilization. In his own time he was recognized as an outstanding politician, general, and man of letters. We still hear echos of him in the plays of Shakespeare, in the titles *kaiser* and *czar*, and in phrases such as *Alea iacta est* and *Veni, vidi, vici* that are familiar even to those who know hardly any Latin. Reading Caesar's own account of his conquests gives insight into the personality of this man who still figures so prominently in our culture.

Caesar's Latin has long been recognized as appropriate reading for students at the intermediate level. His sentences, although not always simple, are usually less complex than those of Cicero and other authors. He uses certain vocabulary and constructions over and over, which helps you become accustomed to his style and read more easily. He narrates events in a relatively straightforward way. In short, if you wish to become more adept at reading Latin prose, Caesar's writings provide an excellent means of building up your skills before taking on more difficult authors.

But reading Caesar is not just an exercise in Latin prose. There are many things going on underneath Caesar's seemingly straightforward narrative of the conquest of Gaul. You will want to consider carefully why Caesar wrote the way he did and how he may have wanted to use his book for political ends. Reading *De bello Gallico* also provides an opportunity to consider how the Romans regarded the peoples whom they conquered and ultimately absorbed into their empire and what kind of leadership Caesar provided that enabled him to be so successful.

Caesar's Life

Caesar was born in 100 BCE on the 12th of Quinctilis (the month later renamed in his honor) to an ancient patrician family who claimed descent from Iulus, also known as Ascanius, the son of Aeneas and grandson of the goddess Venus. Although belonging to the senatorial class, the family was not particularly influential; none of its members had been elected consul in a long time. Caesar's aunt Julia had married Gaius Marius, the famous general, military dictator, and leader of the **populārēs**, the political faction that claimed to favor the interests of the common people. Caesar himself grew up during a period of turmoil in Rome as the **populārēs** and the conservative faction, the **optimātēs**, vied for supremacy. After his father's death in 85, Caesar married Cornelia, daughter of Lucius Cornelius Cinna, an ally of Marius. In 82 Lucius Cornelius Sulla, leader of the **optimātēs**, returned to Rome after defeating King Mithridates of Pontus. Backed by his legions, he became dictator and began a ruthless campaign against the supporters of Marius. Caesar was targeted, particularly after he refused to divorce Cornelia, and was saved only by the intervention of his mother's family, some of whom supported Sulla. Sulla grudgingly agreed to spare the young man, saying that he saw many Mariuses in Caesar; and, in fact, Caesar remained a **populāris** throughout his career.

Caesar decided that it would be safer for him to leave Rome, so he joined the army in the East. He won a **corōna cīvica**, an honor given to soldiers who saved the lives of their comrades in battle, and served on a diplomatic mission to the court of King Nicomedes of Bithynia. After Sulla's death in 78, Caesar returned to Rome and entered public life by prosecuting two former governors for extortion. In 77, however, he went to Rhodes to study oratory with the famous teacher Molo. On his way back, he was captured by pirates and held for ransom. According to his biographer Plutarch, Caesar jokingly told the pirates that he would return and take revenge on them; after being ransomed, he organized a fleet, defeated the pirates, and crucified them.

Upon his return to Rome in 73, Caesar was elected **pontifex**, one of a group of priests who oversaw many aspects of Roman religion. He embarked on a political career, serving as quaestor in Spain in 68 and as aedile in 65. In 63 he was elected **pontifex maximus**, high priest of the state religion, a political coup in which he defeated several older, more influential men—a clear demonstration of his skills as a politician (and of the effectiveness of bribery). He was accused of supporting the conspiracy of Catiline, but Cicero dismissed this accusation. Caesar did argue, however, against putting the conspirators to death. He held the praetorship in 62 and was sent as propraetor (governor) to Further Spain in 61.

His term as propraetor was an important time for Caesar. He had become a prominent man in Rome, clearly an astute politician, but had only limited military experience as a young man. If he was to compete at the very highest levels of Roman politics against men such as Pompey, the famous general who had recently returned triumphant from the East, Caesar needed both additional military experience and a reputation as a general. He got some of both during his time in Spain, where he fought successfully against the native Iberian tribes. While these victories were not important in the larger history of Rome, they gave Caesar additional experience and perhaps a sense that he could be a truly successful general. In Spain he also obtained enough money to pay off the enormous debts he had incurred to finance the lavish entertainments he gave during his year as aedile.

Upon returning to Rome, Caesar hoped to become consul but realized that he did not have the necessary political strength. He therefore formed a private alliance with Pompey and Marcus Crassus, the richest man in Rome, which historians call the First Triumvirate although, unlike the Second Triumvirate of Octavian, Antony, and Lepidus, it had no legal status. Together, the three men were strong enough to make permanent the arrangements that Pompey had made for the government of the East, to provide land for his veteran soldiers, and to elect Caesar as consul for the year 59.

It was customary for praetors and consuls to serve as provincial governors, called propraetors and proconsuls, after their terms were over. This system provided experienced administrators for the provinces; it also gave the Roman officials an opportunity to enrich themselves through bribes and (in the case of frontier provinces) through the sale of slaves and loot captured in war. Caesar needed both a greater military reputation and a lot of money, since he had borrowed heavily and used the money to finance his campaign for consul, including considerable bribery of voters. Caesar's opponents, wishing to deprive him of this opportunity, had passed a law stating that the consuls of 59 would be assigned as proconsuls to supervise agriculture and forests in Italy. With Pompey's help, Caesar was given instead a five-year term as governor of Cisalpine Gaul (northern Italy) and Illyricum (on the Adriatic coast, now Croatia, Bosnia, and neighboring countries). After the governor of Transalpine Gaul died, Pompey arranged for that assignment to go to Caesar also. See the map on page 21 for the location of Caesar's provinces.

It is difficult to know exactly what Caesar looked like. Most of the statues we have that claim to represent Caesar were made after his death and show an idealized portrait. The best evidence comes from the coins that were minted during his dictatorship, such as the denarius shown here. The inscription **CAESAR DICT QVART** shows that it was minted in 44 BCE, when Caesar received the office of dictator for the fourth time. Caesar's biographers tell us that he was going bald and enjoyed the privilege, granted to him by the Senate, of wearing a laurel wreath whenever he wished. Caesar is shown with a **lituus**, a sacred staff symbolizing his position as **pontifex maximus**.

While preparing to go north, Caesar received word that the Helvetians, a Gallic tribe, were planning to pass through Roman territory while searching for a new homeland. You will read in Book I of Caesar's commentaries how he dealt with this situation. During the next five years he conquered all of Gaul, but the conquest was not complete because some of the Gauls still hoped to throw off Roman rule.

While Caesar was in Gaul, Pompey and Crassus looked after his interests in Rome. In 56, Pompey, Crassus and Caesar met and renewed their association for another five years; Caesar needed the time to finish what he had started in Gaul, and by staying there for ten years he would be eligible to run again for consul upon his return to Rome. Pompey and Crassus would be consuls in 55 and each would receive a five-year military command such as Caesar had: Pompey in Spain and Crassus in the East. Gradually, however, the triumvirate fell apart. Crassus was killed fighting the Parthians on Rome's eastern borders. Julia, Caesar's daughter, had married Pompey and was instrumental in maintaining the relationship between the two ambitious men, but she also died. Pompey became increasingly jealous and suspicious of Caesar and gradually moved to ally himself with the conservative senators, who had always disliked Caesar.

As the end of Caesar's governorship approached, the Senate passed a law that required Caesar to return to Rome as a private citizen, without his army. This would have been political suicide. Caesar instead responded by crossing the Rubicon River, the southern boundary of Gallia Cisalpina, and marching on Rome. It was on this occasion that he uttered the famous phrase **Ālea iacta est**, *The die is cast*, because there was no turning back once he had brought his army out of his own province. Within four years (48–45 BCE) Caesar had defeated all the senatorial forces. Early in 44, the Senate, now packed with Caesar's appointees, granted him the office of **dictātor perpetuus**. Soon thereafter, he was assassinated by a clique of senators on 15 March 44, the famous Ides of March.

The Gauls

The Celtic peoples had their origin in central Europe along the upper reaches of the Danube River. Beginning in the seventh century BCE, groups of Celts began to move west and south; eventually they occupied all of what is now Britain, Ireland, Belgium, France, and northern Italy, displacing the earlier inhabitants. They also moved into north central Spain, although here the native Iberian culture remained more significant. Rome itself was sacked in 390 BCE by a group of Celts, although they returned north rather than settling in central Italy. Caesar says that there were three main groups of Celts in Gaul at the time he arrived: the Belgae in the northeast, the Galli in the center and the southeast, and the Aquitani in the southwest. Despite being widely dispersed, the Celtic peoples shared common cultural and artistic traditions. At the same time they were influenced by the other peoples with whom they interacted. The Belgae were a mixture of Celtic and Germanic tribes while the Aquitani were strongly affected by the language and culture of the earlier Iberian inhabitants.

By Caesar's time, Gaul was a prosperous and relatively wealthy region. The Gauls practiced agriculture, built roads, and established fortified towns; they were skilled metal workers and issued coinage. They wrote using the Greek script, although only very small amounts of their language have been preserved in inscriptions. (By contrast, the Germans, whose territory was across the Rhine from Gaul, lived mainly by hunting and foraging and did not have permanent cities.) Archaeologists have found many statues, ceramics, and metal objects that testify to the sophistication of Gallic life. Some elements of Greek culture were introduced into Gaul by merchants based in Massilia, a Greek colony founded near the mouth of the Rhône River about 600 BCE, who traded up the rivers into the interior of Gaul.

At the same time, Celtic society continued to be a warrior culture; the bravery and skill of Celtic fighters was well known to the Greeks and Romans. Much of our knowledge about Celtic culture comes from various Greek and Roman authors, including Caesar, who describes some customs of the Gauls in Book VI of *De bello Gallico* (included in this reader).

Celtic society was made up of tribes, each independent of the others. Some historians have compared the tribes of Gaul to the native American peoples. There are parallels in that neither the Gauls nor the native Americans had any central authority. The various tribes fought with each other or made alliances, both with other tribes and with foreign powers (the Romans or the French and British in North America). At the time of Caesar's arrival, there were two factions among the tribes in central Gaul. One, headed by the Aedui, generally favored the Romans, while the other, led by the Sequani and the Arverni, generally opposed them. In both Gaul and the Americas a lack of polical unity and infighting between tribes made it more difficult for the native peoples to resist the invaders who possessed superior weapons (although the native Americans, who did not manufacture firearms, were at a much greater disadvantage in this respect than the Gauls were).

Roman Involvement in Gaul

Groups of Celts had settled in the valley of the Po River in northern Italy during the 7th–6th centuries BCE. These Celts, along with other inhabitants of northern Italy such as the Etruscans, gradually came under Roman control; by 191 BCE all the Celtic areas had been conquered. During the late Republic, northern Italy was organized as the province of **Gallia Cisalpīna**, *Gaul on this side of the Alps*, with its southern boundary at the Rubicon River. The area became Romanized quite soon, a fact reflected in the term **Gallia togāta**, *toga-wearing Gaul*, that was sometimes applied to it in contrast to **Gallia comāta**, *long-haired Gaul*, on the other side of the Alps. After 90 BCE, Roman settlers in northern Italy possessed full rights as citizens, which meant that Caesar could enlist men from the area as legionary soldiers. The province was prosperous and stable. Several famous Romans were born there, including the poets Catullus and Vergil and the historian Livy. Eventually the province of **Gallia Cisalpīna** was dissolved and the area made officially a part of Italy by Octavian about 42 BCE.

In contrast, the Romans had little to do with **Gallia Trānsalpīna**, *Gaul across the Alps*, until 121 BCE. In this year, Rome intervened to protect her ally Massilia (now Marseille in southern France), which was threatened by a coalition of Gallic tribes, and annexed a strip of territory along the Mediterranean coast. This area was referred to by Caesar and other Romans simply as **prōvincia**, *the (Roman) Province*; this usage is preserved in the French name for the area, Provence. Its official name was Gallia Narbonensis, after its capital, the Roman colony of Narbo. Because it had been controlled by the Romans for less than a hundred years when Caesar became governor of Gaul, it was not very thoroughly Romanized.

Caesar became well known among later generations for his conquest of the remainder of Gaul. It does not appear, however, that he originally planned such a conquest. Caesar arranged to become governor of the provinces of Gallia Cisalpina and Illyricum after his term as consul in 59 BCE. As mentioned above, Caesar was very heavily in debt after his campaign for consul and wanted to build up his reputation as a military commander in order to compete with Pompey. Therefore he must have intended some military campaigns during his term as governor; probably he believed that Illyricum would offer him this opportunity. Some scholars have suggested that he planned to attack the Dacians, to the east of Illyricum, but there is no clear proof of this.

When the governor of Gallia Transalpina died unexpectedly, this province was given to Caesar as well. In 58 BCE, while he was preparing to go north to assume his command, Caesar received word of a threat to the Roman Province from the Helvetians, a Gallic tribe. You will read about this campaign and the subsequent war with Ariovistus, a German king who had settled in Gaul, in Book I of *De bello Gallico*. At some point Caesar must have decided that Gaul offered him the opportunities that he was seeking. In the fall of 58 he set up winter quarters for his army in northeastern Gaul rather than bringing them back south into the Province, which clearly signaled his intention to bring all of Gaul under Roman control. The outline on page 249 lists Caesar's campaigns in the order they appear in *De bello Gallico*.

Caesar's Writings

Caesar was a highly accomplished public speaker and writer. He wrote a number of books on various topics, but only his accounts of the campaigns in Gaul and during the civil war that followed have survived.

The full title of Caesar's account of his Gallic campaigns is *Commentarii de bello Gallico*, often shortened to *De bello Gallico*. The word **commentāriī** means *diaries* or *notebooks*. Caesar chose this title to suggest a simple, staightforward account of his conquests, in contrast to **historia**, which would have indicated a more elaborate, "literary" treatment. And, indeed, Caesar's work lacks the rhetorical flourishes and elaborate speeches that are often found in Greek and Roman historians. Cicero described Caesar's commentaries as follows:

> Valde quidem probandos; nudi enim sunt, recti et venusti, omni ornatu orationis tamquam veste detracta. Sed dum voluit alios habere parata, unde sumerent qui vellent scribere historiam, ineptis gratum fortasse fecit, qui volent illa calamistris inurere: sanos quidem homines a scribendo deterruit; nihil est enim in historia pura et inlustri brevitate dulcius.

> Indeed they are very much to be approved; for they are unadorned, direct, and attractive, with all oratorical ornament, like clothing, removed. But while he wanted others to have material ready from which those who wanted to write history could work, he has perhaps done a favor for the foolish, who will be willing to curl them with hot irons [i.e., to make them artificially attractive while trying to improve them]: in fact he has frightened sane men away from writing [about his Gallic campaigns]; for there is nothing in history sweeter than a pure and clear brevity.
>
> (Brutus 261–262)

Caesar organized his work chronologically, with a separate book devoted to each year of his time in Gaul. Caesar himself completed only the first seven books, covering 58–52 BCE. His lieutenant Aulus Hirtius wrote an eighth book, for 51–50, to complete the record of Caesar's time in Gaul. Some scholars believe that Caesar wrote one book per year, possibly sending each one back to Rome so that word of his conquests could spread. It seems more likely, though, that all seven books were written (or finalized from notes made each year) toward the end of his term as governor. There is no question that *De bello Gallico* was intended at least partly for political purposes, to promote a favorable image of Caesar or to justify his conduct; and this raises another question.

Are Caesar's accounts accurate? In general, yes, as far as we can tell, given that we have no other source for much of the material. Caesar does admit some of his own mistakes. Furthermore, many members of the Roman upper classes had served with Caesar during his nine years in Gaul; his work would have developed a reputation for inaccuracy if he had deviated very far from the truth. Certainly Caesar wanted to convey the impression of truthfulness—he clearly avoids exaggerated accounts of his own accomplishments. But the fact that the work does not contain factual errors does not mean it is unbiased. Indeed, the fact that it appears so simple and straightforward may lull the reader into forgetting who wrote it and why. To give just one example: in Book V Caesar tells the story of two rival centurions who fought against a group of Gauls. This story adds nothing to the main narrative, so why did Caesar include it? It may be meant to suggest to the reader that if men like these two—so brave and so skillful at fighting—are typical of those in Caesar's army, then he must be a great leader.

In addition to helping his reputation and political career, Caesar may have just wanted to tell his story in his own words. Adding such a large amount of territory to the empire in the face of formidable Gallic resistance was a major accomplishment, and Caesar had the literary skills to tell the tale. Cicero, in another passage from the *Brutus*, compares reading Caesar's speeches to looking at paintings in a good light. The same clarity of narrative is evident throughout *De bello Gallico*. Caesar also knew how to tell a dramatic story, as you will see in the selections from Book V, in which a large part of Caesar's army is almost wiped out. So we should be glad that Caesar took the time to write about his accomplishments.

The Roman Army

Historical Background

During most of the Republic, the Roman army was a citizen militia. Soldiers were drafted from citizens who possessed a certain amount of property and served for short terms (often one campaigning season). Soldiers were organized in legions under the command of a consul or military tribunes. This traditional system was modified by the general and politician Gaius Marius (157–86 BCE) in several important ways.

First, in 107 BCE Marius opened military service to all citizens, regardless of wealth, and volunteers who enlisted for longer terms replaced the former draftees. Second, Marius improved the organization, training, and equipment of the armies; the description of life in the Roman army given below reflects many practices introduced by Marius. After the Social War (91–88 BCE), citizenship was granted to all inhabitants of Italy south of the Po River. From this point forward the army was made up of legions raised in Italy and auxiliary troops (**auxilia**), consisting of lightly armed infantry, cavalry, slingers, and archers, recruited from the provinces. Armies were stationed permanently in some of the provinces; in addition, generals with long-term commands such as Caesar had the power to recruit additional legions if necessary. Soldiers in such legions gave their loyalty more to their own general than to the state as a whole. They often joined because of the reputation of a particular commander, and he in turn looked after their welfare while they served and provided land or other arrangements for their support when the time came to disband the legion. Former soldiers would support their general politically, while those still on active service would fight for him even if the usual tumultuous maneuvering of Roman politics disintegrated into a civil war, as happened several times during the last century of the Republic.

Organization of the Legion

The diagram on page 10 shows the organization of a legion at the time of Caesar. Each legion nominally contained 6000 men, but usually had fewer, often in the range of 5000–3500. It was divided into ten cohorts, each of which was subdivided into maniples and centuries. A legion was identified by a number and often by a phrase that indicated its origin and/or its qualities. For example, Legio IX Hispana was raised by Pompey in Spain in 65 BCE. Caesar commanded it as propraetor in Spain and then brought it over to Gaul in 59, where it served throughout his Gallic campaigns and also fought for him in the civil wars that followed. Caesar disbanded it in 45 and settled its veterans in Picenum on the east coast of Italy. Octavian recalled the veterans of this legion in 43 to fight against Sextus Pompeius (son of Pompey the Great) and used it at the battle of Actium in 31. Legio IX remained in service, stationed in several different parts of the empire, until it was apparently destroyed in the early 2nd century CE.

Each century was commanded by a centurion, roughly equivalent to a captain in a modern army. Centurions were the backbone of the Roman army: they trained the soldiers, disciplined their men, and provided an example of courage in battle. They were normally promoted from within the ranks, although sometimes a wealthy family would obtain a commission as centurion for a young man. Above the centurions were the **tribūnī mīlitum**, military tribunes, young men from aristocratic families who traditionally served in the army before beginning a political and legal career.[1] Each provincial governor also had several high-ranking assistants called **lēgātī**, to whom he could assign whatever job needed doing at a particular time. These men belonged to the senatorial class and were nominated by the governor and confirmed by the Senate or the popular assembly. Each governor also had a **quaestor** who was in charge of the legions' finances, including soldiers' pay. Caesar, the overall commander (**dux** or **imperātor**) of the army, utilized a flexible system of command assignments. He would assign, e.g., an inexperienced **tribūnus mīlitum** to command part of a legion while on the march or in camp, but he gave command during a battle to one of his **lēgātī** or even to the **quaestor**, if the latter was an experienced officer.

On the March

A Roman army on the move had a lot of things to carry: tools, tents, blankets, food, **tormenta** (*artillery*), and much else. It took on the order of 500 animals per legion to carry all of this. In addition, each soldier carried a pack with his food and other items that weighed about 60 pounds. Hence the term **impedīmenta**, *baggage*—literally, that which prevents one from moving quickly. A large number of non-combatants—drivers, officers' servants, traders—also went with the army.

---

[1] Military tribunes are not the same as tribunes of the people, **tribūnī plēbis**, elected officials who were charged with protecting the common people against exploitation by the senators,

Organization of a Roman Legion

◇◇◇◇◇◇◇◇◇◇◇◇◇◇◇◇◇◇◇◇◇ LEGION ◇◇◇◇◇◇◇◇◇◇◇◇◇◇◇◇◇◇◇◇◇◇◇◇◇									
Cohort I	Cohort II	Cohort III	Cohort IV	Cohort V	Cohort VI	Cohort VII	Cohort VIII	Cohort IX	Cohort X

Maniple		Maniple		Maniple	
CENTURY	CENTURY	CENTURY	CENTURY	CENTURY	CENTURY
Prīmus Pīlus	Pīlus Posterior	Prīnceps Prior	Prīnceps Posterior	Hastātus Prior	Hastātus Posterior

Maniple		Maniple		Maniple	
CENTURY	CENTURY	CENTURY	CENTURY	CENTURY	CENTURY
Pīlus Prior	Pīlus Posterior	Prīnceps Prior	Prīnceps Posterior	Hastātus Prior	Hastātus Posterior

Cohort = ¹⁄₁₀ of a legion (600 men)
Maniple = ⅓ of a cohort (200 men)
Century = ½ of a maniple (100 men)

Each century was commanded by a centurion.

- There were six grades of centurions. The title of each is shown directly below the word CENTURY in each box.
- The titles of the centurions in the 2nd–10th cohorts were the same, as shown in the bottom row of the chart.
- The 1st cohort, shown in gray, was special; its senior centurion was called **prīmus pīlus** and was the senior centurion of the entire legion. The six centurions of this cohort were called **centuriōnēs prīmōrum ōrdinum**, *centurions of the first rank*.
- Centurions could be promoted both within a cohort (until they reached the rank of **pīlus prior**) and from one cohort to another. The 10th cohort was the least prestigious, and so was given to centurions newly promoted from the ranks, while the 1st cohort was the most prestigious.

Life in Camp

The construction of fortified camps was one one of the essential elements of Roman warfare. When on the march, a Roman army would travel from early morning until early afternoon and then stop to construct a camp. This was done every single day, despite the amount of work involved. The work went faster than might be imagined (three to four hours) because the Romans systematized the whole process. Among his baggage, each soldier carried some stakes and a shovel, which he used to help dig a trench (**fossa**). The earth from the trench was piled up to create a rampart or wall (**vāllum**), on top of which a palisade was constructed from the wooden stakes. (See the diagram on page 146.) The layout of the camp was standardized: there were two main streets which intersected in front of the general's headquarters (**praetōrium**), four gates, locations reserved for cooking and storage of the baggage, etc. Such standardization not only made construction of temporary camps efficient, it also made it easier for soldiers to do their jobs: no one wasted time wondering where anything was located. The soldiers were housed in tents while on the march. The camp provided a defensible place where the legion could spend the night or to which it could retreat if a battle went badly. Wooden towers (**turrēs**) could also be built at intervals along the rampart, from which spears and other missiles could be hurled at an attacking enemy with greater effectiveness.

If an army planned to remain somewhere for a longer period, such as during the winter, a more permanent camp was constructed along the same lines: the fortifications were made more substantial and the soldiers had small barracks buildings or cabins instead of tents. See the plan on page 12. Many of these permanent camps evolved into cities as the Empire grew. English place names such as Lancaster, Colchester and Rochester are derived from the Latin **castra**.

Fighting a Battle

Roman generals usually arranged their troops for battle in long lines (**aciēs**); one formation favored by Caesar was the triple line, but there were any number of variations possible. This was in fact the great strength of the Roman legion: it could be subdivided into cohorts or even into maniples and the various units deployed as needed. This was a much more flexible arrangement than the phalanx formation developed by the Macedonians and used by many other ancient peoples, including the Gauls and the Romans themselves early in their history. A phalanx was essentially one large mass of soldiers, which could be very effective in certain situations, such as when trying to break through an enemy's line, but which lacked the flexibility to regroup or move around to meet unforeseen developments—which, as Caesar remarks, happen all the time in war. The Romans used military standards (**signa**), symbols mounted on poles, to direct the movements of the cohorts. The standard-bearer (**signifer**) took his orders from the officers and men of his unit would follow the standard. There were other standards that belonged to the legion as a whole, such as the eagle (**aquila**), a symbol of Jupiter and the Roman state. To allow the standards to be captured by an enemy was a source of great shame. See pages 78 and 81 for pictures of the **aquila** and other standards.

Besieging a Town

The Gauls had large number of fortified towns (**oppida**) and the Romans employed specialized techniques for capturing them. The Gauls were not familiar with most of these methods when Caesar became governor, but they learned quickly and used many of the Roman techniques against Caesar's own troops when they attacked Roman camps.

If the walls of a town were low or poorly built, the Romans would try to force an opening by pulling stones out of the walls at ground level, by yanking stones from the top of the walls with hooks on long poles, or by undermining the walls from beneath. If the fortifications were more substantial, they constructed siege towers (**turrēs ambulātōriae**) which they could wheel up to the walls and let down a drawbridge over which the legionaries could gain access to the town. Another technique was to build an earthen ramp (**agger**) up to the height of the walls, over which the soldiers could enter. Soldiers doing such work were protected from enemy fire with moveable screens and sheds.

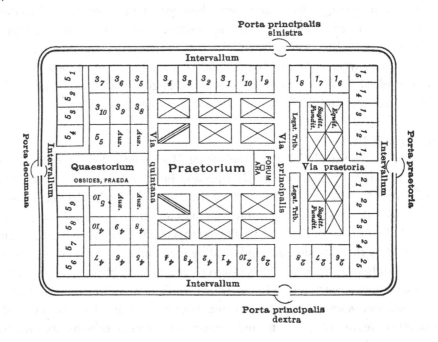

This diagram shown the layout of a typical Roman camp. This is a large camp designed for five legions plus auxiliary troops, but smaller camps used the same layout. The **Praetorium** is the headquarters of the commanding general. Note the open space with an altar (**forum**, **āra**) used for ceremonies. 1_2 = First Legion, Second Cohort, etc.

Reading Caesar's Latin

Caesar's Style

As mentioned above, Caesar's prose has been admired since his own time for its clarity and its ability to draw the reader into the action. It is written in the third person; always keep in mind that Caesar is describing himself and his own actions even though he uses the first person only three times. He uses the same vocabulary over and over, avoiding synonyms or words found mainly in poetry (a river, e.g., is always a **flūmen**, never a **fluvius** or an **amnis**). He is particularly fond of the ablative absolute and indirect statement. His sentences, although not always simple for non-native speakers of Latin, are not usually as complex as those found in Cicero and other writers. Caesar's relatively straightforward style is, to some extent at least, inherited from the **commentāriī** written by earlier generations of Romans.

The Reading Process

You cannot translate a Latin sentence until you understand it. We therefore suggest the following process for reading Latin:

- Read a sentence through, more than once if needed.
- As you meet each word, note the ending and think about what information this gives you and what expectations it raises about what may appear later in the sentence.
- Focus on the structure of the sentence, i.e., where phrases and clauses begin and end.
- Reading this way will give you a general idea of what the sentence is about, although you will not understand everything at this point.
- Only after doing this should you look at the facing vocabulary and notes, and look up other words in the end vocabulary as needed.
- Read the sentence again, as often as needed.
- By this point you should be able to answer the comprehension question(s) that relate to the sentence you are reading .
- Finally, translate the sentence, if desired.

We cannot stress enough how important it is to pay attention to sentence structure. Some students begin by looking up unfamiliar words; there is nothing wrong with wanting to know what the words mean, but thinking about meaning of words before sentence structure will often lead to misunderstandings. By "sentence structure" we mean, at the most basic level, noun endings: is a word the direct object, subject, etc.? At a higher level, we mean how the word fits into a larger sentence: is it a main verb or a subordinate element such as a participle, ablative absolute, or subordinate verb? Does it begin or end a clause, or is it in the middle of an incomplete expression?

As an example of this approach, on the opposite page is a sentence from §5 of Book I. It is printed at the left, broken up into logical sections—called <u>sense units</u>—with suggestions at the right about things you should notice as you read through the sentence. Some background: the Helvetians, a Gallic tribe, have decided to leave their homes and find new lands. They have burned their towns so that they will not be able to return to their original home if they have trouble finding a new one.

Now read the chart. ⟶

Some things that are mentioned on the opposite page, such as the fact that **ūtor** takes an object in the ablative, may be new to you; they are explained in the facing notes in this book. The fact that you will meet some such items that are new to you is one of the reasons we suggest multiple readings for all but the simplest sentences. On a first reading you might realize that 'they' persuaded three groups of people to do something, and did something else to the Boii. A second and third reading, in conjunction with the notes on the facing page, will make things clearer: but even without knowing what some of the words mean you should, with practice, be able to observe the structure markers and see how the sentence works as whole. Structure, not vocabulary, is always the place to begin. If you are curious, after all this discussion, about the final meaning of the sentence, it is:

> They (the Helvetians) persuade the Raurici and the Tulingi and the Latovici, their neighbors, after adopting the same plan, when their towns and villages had been burned out, to set out together with them, and they join to themselves as allies the Boii, who had lived across the Rhine and had crossed into the territory of Noricum and had attacked Noreia, who had (already) been accepted among them.

Nested Clauses

In the chart opposite, each clause or participial phrase has been indented; only main clauses are placed at the left margin. You will notice that the participial phrase **eōdem ūsī cōnsiliō** and the ablative absolute **oppidīs suīs vīcīsque exustīs** are sandwiched inside the indirect command **ut . . . proficīscantur**. Such phrases or clauses are said to be <u>nested</u> or <u>embedded</u> inside a larger unit. Such nesting of phrases and clauses is extremely common in literary Latin. You must watch carefully for boundary markers, such as a participle or verb coming at the end, so that you can see where such items begin and end. If you do not, you may translate a word that belongs in one clause as part of another, leading to significant misunderstandings. The notes in this book provide help in situations where it is difficult to sort out such nested elements.

Persuādent Rauricīs et Tulingīs et Latovīcīs fīnitimīs	**persuādeō** takes the dative, so these four nouns are probably objects of **Persuādent**
ut	**ut** begins a new clause and must be completed by a conjugated verb (not by an infinitive or a participle)
eōdem ūsī cōnsiliō,	**ūsī** is the perfect participle of the verb **ūtor**; it takes the ablative, so **eōdem cōnsiliō** is its object; **ūsī** is probably nom. pl., so it may refer to "they" understood with **Persuādent**
oppidīs suīs vīcīsque exustīs,	here are two nouns and a perfect participle, both in the ablative, so we are dealing with an ablative absolute
ūnā cum eīs proficīscantur,	**proficīscantur** is present subjunctive, so this is the completion of the clause begun by **ut**; the meaning of **Persuādent** shows that this is an indirect command with the subjunctive
Boiōsque,	**Boiōs** is accusative plural; **-que** introduces another main clause, since the first main clause introduced by **Persuādent** was completed by **proficīscantur**
quī trāns Rhēnum incoluerant	**quī** introduces a relative clause, which at first might seem to be completed by **incoluerant**
et in agrum Nōricum trānsierant	but the relative clause is not complete; **et** begins another part of this relative clause
Nōreiamque oppugnārant,	**-que** begins a third section of the relative clause (the fact that **incoluerant**, **trānsierant**, and **oppugnārant** are all pluperfect helps you to see that they make up one long relative clause)
receptōs ad sē	**receptōs** is the perfect participle of **recipiō**; it probably modifies **Boiōs**, making a participial phrase
sociōs sibi ascīscunt.	**ascīscunt** is a conjugated verb, completing the clause begun with **Boiōsque**

Note how the main clauses in this chart are placed at the left
margin, with subordinate units indented.

Here is a very important rule about nested clauses: <u>a nested clause must be completed before the main clause can resume</u>. In visual terms, you have this:

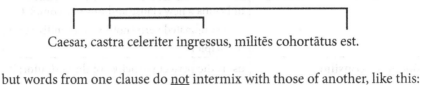

Caesar, castra celeriter ingressus, mīlitēs cohortātus est.

but words from one clause do <u>not</u> intermix with those of another, like this:

More about Expectations
Here is a list of some common expectations:

- An adjective raises the expectation of a noun that it will modify; if there is no noun for an adjective to modify, then it probably is taking the place of a noun in the clause (called a substantive).
- A preposition raises the expectation of an object (either in the acc. or the abl.).
- A relative pronoun begins a clause and is completed by a conjugated verb.
- A subordinating conjunction (**cum, dum, postquam**, etc.) raises the expectation of a conjugated verb to complete it.
- An infinitive suggests that it will complete the meaning of a verb such as **posse, velle, cupere**, etc. or that it will be found with an accusative and a verb of saying, thinking, etc. as part of indirect statement.

Conclusion
This may seem like a very complex and artificial way to read. Perhaps so in the beginning, but keep the following in mind:

- If you focus on the meanings of words and pay little attention to structure, misunderstandings will certainly result (you might look at **Boiōs** in the example on the previous page and think that the Boii did something, i. e.., were a subject rather than a direct object).
- As you get better at reading Latin, noticing certain things will become almost automatic; some of the things mentioned above may already be automatic for you, depending on your previous experience in reading Latin and on your general aptitude for language study. Because Caesar's style is so consistent you will get more adept at reading his Latin, perhaps fairly quickly.

Using This Book

The text of Caesar's *De bello Gallico* is printed on right-hand pages. On the left-hand pages appear running vocabulary lists and explanatory notes. Observe the following:

- Words that you may not have learned from your basic Latin textbook are glossed. Depending on how much Latin reading you have done, and from which authors, before beginning this book, you may already know some of the glossed words. If so, that's great; since students will come to this book with a variety of backgrounds, we have chosen to gloss generously.

- If a word appears more than once in the readings in the book, it is marked with an asterisk (*) and is not repeated in the running vocabularies; so be sure to learn the words with asterisks.

- A word may be repeated in the facing vocabulary lists if it occurs with a different meaning than it had when you first met it; such cases are marked "additional meaning."

- Some words that you can easily deduce from your knowledge of basic Latin vocabulary and/or from English derivatives are not glossed. Such words do appear in the vocabulary at the end of the book if you need them, and sometimes we give hints to help you deduce their meanings.

- Note carefully the following rules about vocabulary entries:

  - If a word is used more than once on a single page, it is glossed only once the first time it appears.
  - Definitions and translations are always *printed in italics*; items in the notes that appear in regular type are explanations, not translations; observe this distinction carefully.
  - Literal or basic definitions of a word appear first, followed by other meaning(s) that may be appropriate to a particular context.
  - Additional, non-literal translations are sometimes given and are marked "less literal." These translations can help you understand what Caesar means by a certain phrase, but may not be appropriate in situations where a literal translation is expected (as on the AP Latin examination).

In addition to the running vocabularies and notes, you will find additional material presented under the following heads:

- Reading Strategies: suggestions for how to read Latin prose effectively.
- Vocabulary: ways to increase your Latin vocabulary effectively.
- Text: notes about the Latin text, in cases where the correct reading is doubtful.
- Forms: information about the forms of the words you meet in Caesar's text.
- Structure: help with advanced sentence structures.
- Cultural Context: cultural information related to the Latin readings.

Each reading is followed by a set of questions called "Initial Explorations" that will help you get the basic meaning of the text; we suggest answering them before translating. Additional questions headed "Discussion" offer some things you will want to consider after reading and understanding the text.

Forms charts appear at the end of the book, as does a summary of Latin grammar. The facing notes sometimes refer you to this syntax section, but you should use it whenever necessary to review the grammar you learned in your previous study of Latin.

Cross-references are given in the following formats:

4.28:10 = Book 4, chapter 28, line 10

The line numbers are specific to this book, while book and chapter numbers are the same as in any standard text of *De bello Gallico*.

Expanding Your Vocabulary

In order to read more easily, you want to build up your vocabulary as fast as possible. Here are some suggestions:

- Memorize the words with asterisks. Pay attention to the basic meanings that are listed first as well as to any other meaning required for the context.
- Use the lists of asterisked words that are provided for review. These are printed at the end of each book. However, you should not wait until you reach the end of a book to use them, since they are broken down into smaller sections, each of which covers a few chapters.
- Take advantage of the information about etymology (formation or origin of a word) that is presented inside square brackets with some words; learning related words is one of the very best ways to build your vocabulary.
- Make flash cards for yourself and/or make personal vocabulary lists (i.e., add or remove words from the lists printed in the books to reflect those that you already know or still need to learn).
- Study the information in the "Vocabulary" notes found at intervals in this book.
- Review as often as possible!

Rhetorical Devices and Figures of Speech

Caesar's style is relatively straightforward and generally lacks the rhetorical flourishes that the Romans often used in their writing. Therefore you will not find many instances of the figures of speech that you may have learned while reading other Roman authors; nonetheless, there are a few. The ones that occur in this book are defined on the opposite page and are identified in the facing notes by being PRINTED IN SMALL CAPITALS. As you read, refer back to the list on the opposite page for any whose meaning you do not know.

ALLITERATION: repetition of the same sound at the beginning of successive words.

ASYNDETON: Gr. "without connectives," omission of connecting words such as **et** or **sed** where they would normally be expected in a series of words.

CHIASMUS: words appearing in a crisscross pattern A-B-B-A. Chiasmus can be created with different parts of speech (e.g., noun-verb-verb-noun) or with different case forms (e.g., dative-accusative-accusative-dative). It can emphasize an opposition or can draw the elements of the chiasmus closer together. The name, Gr. for "crossing," is derived from the Gr. letter chi, which has the same shape as a Latin 'X.'

ELLIPSIS: omission of a word or words that are required to make a clause grammatically complete. This is particularly common with forms of **esse**.

HENDIADYS: Gr. "one through two," an idea expressed through two nouns connected by a conjunction rather than through a noun modified by an adjective; e.g., "a difficulty and a situation" rather than "a difficult situation." Hendiadys gives more prominence or emphasis to an image than it would otherwise have.

HISTORIC INFINITIVE: an infinitive used in place of a past tense main verb. This usage is found most often in works of history. It conveys a sense of haste or urgency. Translate such infinitives as past tense verbs.

HISTORIC PRESENT: use of a verb in the present to describe actions that took place in the past, in order to make the events more vivid for the reader or listener. The author may switch back and forth between historic present and past tenses in the course of a single narrative. This figure of speech is very common in Caesar. You may translate historic presents either as present tense or past tense in English; just be consistent. Example: **profectiōnem lēge cōnfirmant**, *they establish their depature by law* (1.3; note that verbs in this chapter prior to cōnfirmant are in the perfect.)

HYPERBATON: Gr., "stepping across," a figure in which words that logically belong together are widely separated, which emphasizes the words involved.

INTERLOCKING WORD ORDER or **SYNCHYSIS**: words that are arranged in the order A-B-A-B, often emphasizing the connection between two ideas or images.

LITOTES: Gr. "plainness," a kind of understatement that also emphasizes what is said; this is done by negating the opposite of what is meant, e.g., **nōn longiōre ōrātiōne**, *with a not very long (= short) speech* (2.21).

METONYMY: use of one word, generally a noun, to suggest another with which it is closely related. E.g., **ferrum**, *iron*, may represent an item made of iron, such as a *sword*.

PARALLEL STRUCTURE: use of similar grammatical forms for elements that are of the same level of importance in a sentence. The use of similar forms makes it easier for the reader to recognize that the elements function the same way in the sentence. E.g., "For years he ran marathons, now he enjoys long hikes" consists of two clauses, each with a time expression followed by a subject, a verb, and a direct object.

POLYSYNDETON: Gr. "many connectives," presence of an extra connecting word such as **et** or **que** that is not logically required in a series.

TMESIS: Gr. "cutting," separation of a compound word into its component parts.

Symbols and Abbreviations

§ = section or chapter

† = reading of Latin text is uncertain

✦ = footnote added for this edition
(not in Handford's translation)

* * * * * * * * *

abl. = ablative case

abs. = absolute

acc. = accusative case

act. = active voice

adj(s). = adjective(s), adjectival

adv(s). = adverb(s), adverbial

BCE = before Christian era

ca. = about (Lat. **circā**)

CE = Christian era

cf. = compare (Lat. **cōnfer**)

cl(s). = clause(s)

conj. = conjunction

dat. = dative case

decl. = declension

e.g. = for the sake of example
(Lat. **exemplī grātiā**)

Eng. = English

esp. = especially

etc. = and others (Lat. **et cētera**)

f., fem. = feminine gender

ff. = and following

f.p. = future perfect tense

Fr. = French

fut. = future tense

gen. = genitive case

Gr. = Greek

i.e. = that is (Lat. **id est**)

imper. = impersonal

impf. = imperfect tense

indecl. = indeclinable

indef. = indefinite

ind. = indirect

indic. = indicative mood

infin. = infinitive

interrog. = interrogative

intrans. = intransitive

irreg. = irregular

Lat. = Latin

lit. = literal, literally

m., masc. = masculine gender

n. = neuter gender

nom. = nominative case

obj(s). = object(s)

p., pp. = page, pages

part. = participle, participial

pass. = passive voice

perf. = perfect tense

pers. = person, personal

pl. = plural

plpf. = pluperfect tense

prep(s). = preposition(s), prepositional

pres. = present tense

pron. = pronoun

rel. = relative

sc. = supply, namely (Lat. **scīlicet**)

SG = Summary of Grammar

sing. = singular

state. = statement(s)

subjunct. = subjunctive mood

superl. = superlative

trans. = transitive

vs. = as opposed to, in comparison with
(Lat. **versus**)

Italy and Neighboring Provinces, 59 BCE

- Roman territory in 59 BCE
- Caesar's conquests
- —— Boundary of Roman territory
- —— Roman provincial boundary
- --- Boundary between the three parts of Gallia
- *Aeduī* Gallic tribe

BRITANNIA

Belgae

GERMĀNIA

Ubiī

Suēbī

Rhēnus F.

Mātrōna F.

Sēquana F.

Liger F.

Sēquanī

Celtae

Aeduī

Iūra mōns

Helvētiī

NORICUM

Lacus Lemannus

Genāva

Noreia

Allobrogēs

Alpēs Montēs

Aquileia

Ōceanus

Garumna F.

Rhodanus F.

Padus F.

Gallia
Cisalpīna

Rubicō F.

Illyricum

Aquitānī

Gallia Trānsalpīna

Arīminum

Massilia

Narbō

Pȳrēnaeī Montēs

Italia

•Rōma

Mare Hadriāticum

Corsica
et
Sardinia

•Neāpolis

Hispānia

Mare Internum

Sicilia

•Carthāgō

Āfrica

| 0 | 100 | 200 English mi. |
| 0 | 100 | 200 Roman mi. |

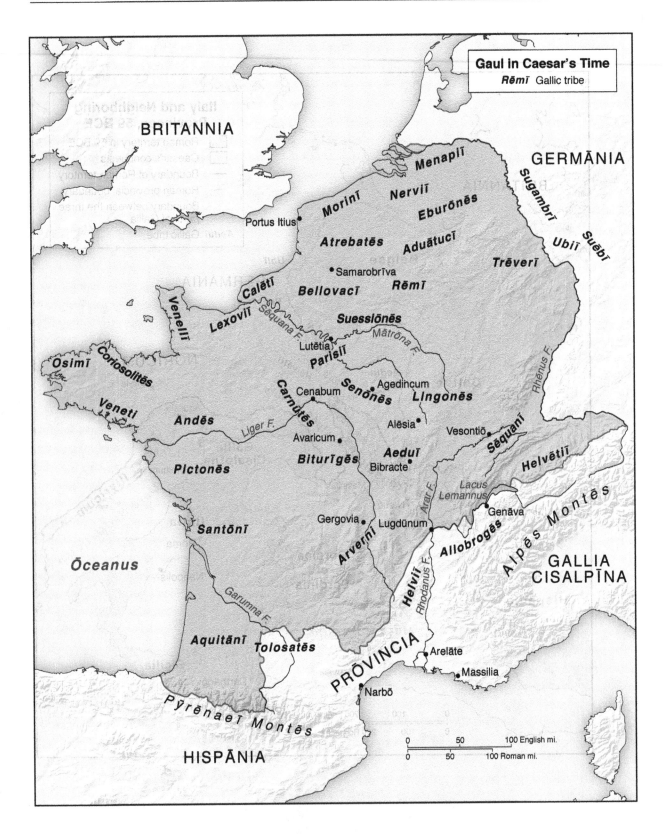

Gaul in Caesar's Time

Rēmī Gallic tribe

BRITANNIA

GERMĀNIA

Portus Itius

Menapiī

Morinī

Nerviī

Eburōnēs

Atrebatēs

Aduātucī

Sugambrī

Ubiī

Suēbī

Trēverī

Calētī

Samarobrīva

Bellovacī

Rēmī

Venelli

Lexoviī

Sēquana F.

Suessiōnēs

Mātrōna F.

Lutētia

Parisiī

Osimī

Coriosolitēs

Veneti

Carnutēs

Cenabum

Senōnēs

Agedincum

Lingonēs

Rhēnus F.

Andēs

Liger F.

Avaricum

Biturīgēs

Aeduī

Bibracte

Alēsia

Vesontiō

Sēquanī

Helvētiī

Pictonēs

Lacus Lemannus

Genāva

Santōnī

Gergovia

Arar F.

Lugdūnum

Arvernī

Allobrogēs

Alpēs Montēs

GALLIA CISALPĪNA

Ōceanus

Helviī

Rhodanus F.

Garumna F.

Aquitānī

Tolosatēs

PRŌVINCIA

Arelāte

Massilia

Narbō

Pȳrēnaeī Montēs

HISPĀNIA

| 0 | 50 | 100 English mi. |
| 0 | 50 | 100 Roman mi. |

Book I

58 BCE

CAESAR OPENS HIS COMMENTARIES with a brief description of the peoples and geography of Gaul. The first sentence informs the reader that Gaul is divided into three parts, a description that has become familiar to many generations of Latin students and has passed into popular culture.

We then learn that the Helvetii, a Gallic tribe who made their home in what is now Switzerland, had decided to migrate west in search of better land and wished to travel through the Roman Province (the portion of Gaul controlled by Rome, located along the Mediterranean coast). Word of the Helvetians' planned migration arrived very soon after Caesar began his term as governor of Gaul and Illyricum. In fact, he was still outside Rome, making preparations to take up his new post, when he heard what the Helvetians were planning. Upon receiving the news, Caesar hurried north. He had not anticipated trouble in this part of the territory he governed, and three of his four legions were at Aquileia, on the border between Cisalpine Gaul and Illyricum, with only one in Transalpine Gaul. (See the map on page 21.)

The Helvetians' request to move through the Province presented three concerns to Caesar. First, would the Helvetians keep their word not to cause any problems as they passed? Second, where would they settle; how would this affect Roman interests? Third, what would happen to the land the Helvetians had left—would it be occupied by hostile Germans? Uneasy on all these counts, Caesar decided to prevent the Helvetians from seeking a new home. You will read in the first half of Book I how he dealt with the Helvetian challenge; chapters 1–7 in Latin are included here, with the rest in English.

Caesar then relates that his success against the Helvetians had earned him respect from the other tribes of Gaul. Some of them asked his help in dealing with Ariovistus, a German king from across the Rhine who had settled with his followers in the territory of the Gallic Sequani. Caesar agreed to help them since he wanted to discourage any more Germans from moving into Gaul. Caesar's campaign against Ariovistus occupies the second half of Book I, which is presented here in English translation.

1 *Gallia, -ae, f., *Gaul.*

    omnis: *as a whole.*

    *incolō, incolere, incoluī, *to live in, inhabit.*

    *Belgae, -ārum, m. pl., *the Belgae,* a large group of tribes in northeastern Gaul.

2   Aquitānī, -ōrum, m. pl., *the Aquitani,* a people in what is now southwestern France.

    *tertius, -a, -um [< trēs, three], *third.*

    tertiam: the ASYNDETON emphasizes that Celtic Gaul was the largest and most important of the areas included in **Gallia**. (Remember that you can check definitions of figures of speech whose names are printed IN SMALL CAPITALS using the list on page 19.)

    quī: = eī quī, *those who*; see the first Reading Strategy on page 27.

    lingua, -ae, f., *tongue; language.*

    ipsōrum linguā: *in the language of (the people) themselves,* less lit., *in their own language.*

    Celtae, -ārum, m. pl., *Celts* (see pages 4–5 for background about these people).

    nostrā: **lingua** is understood with **nostrā**; see the Reading Strategy opposite.

    *Gallī, -ōrum, m. pl., *Gauls,* the Roman name for the Celts.

3 *īnstitūtum, -ī, n., *custom.*

    *lēx, lēgis, f., *law.*

    inter sē: *between themselves,* less lit., *from each other.*

    Garumna, -ae, f., *the Garonne River* in southwestern France.

4 *flūmen, flūminis, n., *river.*

    Mātrōna, -ae, f., *the Marne River* in northern France.

    Sēquana, -ae, f., *the Seine River* in northern France.

The geography and peoples of Gaul.

1 [1] Gallia est omnis dīvīsa in partēs trēs, quārum ūnam incolunt Belgae, ali-
2 am Aquitānī, tertiam quī ipsōrum linguā Celtae, nostrā Gallī appellantur. Hī
3 omnēs linguā, īnstitūtīs, lēgibus inter sē differunt. Gallōs ab Aquitānīs Ga-
4 rumna flūmen, ā Belgīs Mātrōna et Sēquana dīvidit.   (continued)

Initial Explorations

1. What are the three main groups of tribes in Gaul? (1–2)
2. In what respects do these groups differ from one another? (3)
3. What geographical features form the boundaries between these groups?
   (3–4)

Reading Strategy: Gapping

• Instead of repeating a word, an author may omit it and rely on the reader to supply it mentally. This happens with the words **linguā** and **appellantur** (2) above. Linguists use the term 'gapping' to describe this phenomenon. The key to identifying a gapped word is to notice PARALLEL STRUCTURE. In this passage, the phrase **ipsōrum linguā Celtae** consists of a possessive word, an ablative noun, and a nominative plural noun; it is followed by **nostrā Gallī**, a possessive and a nominative plural. This parallelism shows that **linguā** is gapped, i.e., is equivalent to **nostrā (linguā) Gallī**. The parallel structure of these two phrases then shows that the verb **appellantur** is to be supplied in the first instance also.

• We sometimes use gapping in English, but usually in the opposite direction from what happens in Latin: "Mary reported on water pollution and John on renewable energy" would be expressed in Latin as "Mary on water pollution and John on renewable energy reported."

• Locate another instance of gapping in the Latin text on this page.

5 *propterea, adv., *for this reason, therefore*; when used together with **quod** = an emphatic way of saying *because*.

   *cultus, -ūs, m., *care; culture, civilization*.

   hūmānitās, hūmānitātis, f., *human nature; kindness; refinement*.

6 *prōvinciae: *the (Roman) province*, Gallia Narbonensis, a strip of land on the Mediterranean controlled by the Romans before Caesar's arrival. See page 6 for more information and also the map on page 21.

   *longissimē: longē, the adverb from **longus, -a, -um**, means *by far* or *far off, far away*.

   minimē: connected with **saepe**, *least often*.

7 commeō, -āre, *to come and go, go back and forth, go to visit*.

   effēminō, -āre, -āvī, -ātus [< fēmina, woman], *to make effeminate; to weaken*.

   ad animās effēminandās: a gerundive phrase expressing purpose, *to weaken their spirits*. For this construction, see **H5b** in the Summary of Grammar, page 280.

   *animus, -ī, m., *soul, spirit*.

   *pertineō, pertinēre, pertinuī, [per + teneō], *to reach to, extend; to pertain, refer; to tend*.

   ea quae . . . pertinent: among other things, Caesar is probably thinking of wine, which the Gauls greatly enjoyed and which was not yet produced in Gaul.

8 *Germānī, -ōrum, m. pl., *the Germans*.

   *Rhēnus, -ī, m., *the Rhine River*, the border between Gaul and Germany.

   continenter, adv., *continuously*.

9 *Helvētiī, -ōrum, m. pl., *the Helvetians*, a Gallic tribe living in what is now Switzerland. Caesar mentions them in particular because they unexpectedly became his first challenge as governor.

   *reliquus, -a, -um [< relinquō, leave behind], *the rest, the remaining, other*.

   *virtūs, virtūtis [< vir, man], f., *courage*.

10 praecēdō, praecēdere, praecessī, praecessūrus, *to go in front, surpass*.

   *ferē, adv., *almost, approximately*; note that this common adverb is not a form of the verb **ferō, ferre**.

   *cotīdiānus, -a, -um [< quot + diēs], *daily*.

   *proelium, -ī, n., *battle*.

   *contendō, contendere, contendī, contentus, *to stretch, strain; to strive, struggle*.

11 *fīnis, fīnis, m., *end, boundary*; in plural, *territory*.

   *prohibeō, prohibēre, prohibuī, prohibitus [prō + habeō], *to keep someone* (acc.) *away from something* (abl.).

Vocabulary

♦ Information about the etymology (origin or formation) of some words is given inside square brackets; the symbol < means that the word comes from or is related to the word that follows the <. Paying attention to such etymologies will help you remember the meanings and build up your Latin vocabulary efficiently.

5 Hōrum omnium fortissimī sunt Belgae, proptereā quod ā cultū atque hū-
6 mānitāte prōvinciae longissimē absunt, minimēque ad eōs mercātōrēs sae-
7 pe commeant atque ea quae ad effēminandōs animōs pertinent important,
8 proximīque sunt Germānīs, quī trāns Rhēnum incolunt, quibuscum conti-
9 nenter bellum gerunt. Quā dē causā Helvētiī quoque reliquōs Gallōs virtūte
10 praecēdunt, quod ferē cotīdiānīs proeliīs cum Germānīs contendunt, cum
11 aut suīs fīnibus eōs prohibent aut ipsī in eōrum fīnibus bellum gerunt.

(continued)

4. What does Caesar say about the Belgae? (5)
5. What three reasons does Caesar give to explain this fact? What grammatical form does he use to explain each reason? (5–9)
6. Locate all the places and peoples mentioned so far on the map on page 21.
7. What tribe among the Celtic Gauls is the bravest? Why? (9–10)
8. For what two reasons do the Helvetians fight with the Germans? (11)

Reading Strategies

◆ It is very common in Latin to find a form of the pronoun is, ea, id followed by the relative pronoun quī, quae, quod. Such combinations may be translated *the one who, the person who* or, if neuter, *the thing which, that which*. You met ea quae, *the things which*, in line 7 above. Sometimes the form of is is omitted and must be supplied, as with (eī) quī, *those who*, in line 2 on page 25.

◆ When you meet the conjunction cum, always note whether it is completed by a verb in the indicative or subjunctive. If the verb is indicative (cum . . . prohibent aut . . . gerunt, above: 11), then the cum clause expresses time and must be translated *when*. If the verb is subjunctive, then cum can express cause (*since, because*), circumstances (*when, after*), or concession (*although*).

Cultural Context

◆ The word virtūs is an important one in Caesar. Literally *manliness* or *manhood*, it can mean *strength, vigor, courage, ability, worth, excellence*, or *virtue*. In Caesar's battle narratives *courage* is usually the appropriate translation, but be alert for other senses of the word. As you read think about some larger questions that lurk in the background: who has virtūs? how does one get it? how does one display it? what happens when it is missing?

12 **eōrum:** this refers back to the territory (**fīnēs,** m. pl.) of the Gauls as a whole, not just the Helvetians.

    Gallōs: here Caesar means specifically the Celts, as opposed to the Belgae or the Aquitani.

    obtinēre: this word = *to control* (lit., ob + teneō, *to hold against*), not *obtain*.

    dictum est: this verb governs an indirect statement whose subject is **Gallōs obtinēre** and whose object is **quam.** A non-literal translation might be *which, as has been mentioned, the Celts control.* (What is the literal translat)

    *****initium, -ī,** n., *beginning.*

    initium capit: throughout the remainder of this passage, Caesar is writing from the perspective of someone located in the Roman Province, looking north. If you locate the Rhône river on the map on page 21 and move clockwise, you will be able to follow Caesar's description easily.

13 *****Rhodanus, -ī,** m., *the Rhône River;* it begins in the Swiss Alps, flows west through Lake Geneva, then joins with the Saône and flows south to the Mediterranean.

    *****contineō, continēre, continuī, contentus** [con + teneō], *to hold together, contain, enclose, border.*

    *****Ōceanus, -ī,** m., *the Ocean.* The Greeks and Romans believed that the land mass with which they were familiar (including Europe, Africa, Asia Minor, and India) was surrounded on all sides by the Ocean. In this sentence, **Ōceanus** includes both the Atlantic and the English Channel.

    attingō, attingere, attigī, attāctus [ad + tangō], *to touch, reach, extend up to.*

14 *****Sēquanī, -ōrum,** m. pl., *the Sequani,* a tribe on the eastern edge of Celtic Gaul.

    ab Sēquanīs et Helvētiīs: *from the (territory of) the Sequani and the Helvetii.* Caesar often uses the names of Gallic tribes as a shorthand way of referring to the lands in which they lived; the lands may have had no other names.

    vergō, vergere, *to turn, incline; to lie, be situated, face.*

    septentriōnēs, septentriōnum, m., *the seven oxen; the north.* This is the Roman name for the group of stars called the Big Dipper. The two outer stars of the dipper's bowl point to the north star, Polaris, so it also means *north.*

15 *****extrēmus, -a, -um,** *outermost, farthest.*

    Galliae: here referring specifically to Celtic Gaul.

    *****orior, orīrī, ortus sum,** *to rise, arise, begin.*

    *****īnferior, īnferiōris,** *lower.* Caesar refers to the area near the coast, where the Rhine flows into the North Sea. (Cf. the English phrases 'downstream' and 'upstream.')

16 **spectant:** in this context = *are oriented toward, face.*

    in septentriōnēs et orientem sōlem: *toward the north and the rising sun,* i.e., to the northeast.

    Aquitānia, -ae, f., *Aquitania,* the southwestern part of Gaul.

17 **Pȳrēnaeī, -ōrum,** m. pl., *the Pyrenees Mountains,* between France and Spain.

    eam partem Ōceanī quae est ad Hispāniam: the Bay of Biscay, north of Spain and west of France.

18 **inter occāsum sōlis et septentriōnēs:** *between the setting of the sun and the north,* i.e., to the northwest.

12 Eōrum ūna pars, quam Gallōs obtinēre dictum est, initium capit ā flūmine
13 Rhodanō; continētur Garumnā flūmine, Ōceanō, finibus Belgārum; attin-
14 git etiam ab Sēquanīs et Helvētiīs flūmen Rhēnum; vergit ad septentriōnēs.
15 Belgae ab extrēmīs Galliae finibus oriuntur; pertinent ad īnferiōrem partem
16 flūminis Rhēnī; spectant in septentriōnēs et orientem sōlem. Aquitānia ā
17 Garumnā flūmine ad Pȳrēnaeōs montēs et eam partem Ōceanī quae est ad
18 Hispāniam pertinet; spectat inter occāsum sōlis et septentriōnēs.

9. What are the boundaries of Celtic Gaul? (12–14)
10. What three things does Caesar say about the territory of the Belgae? (15–16)
11. What are the boundaries of Aquitania? (16–18)

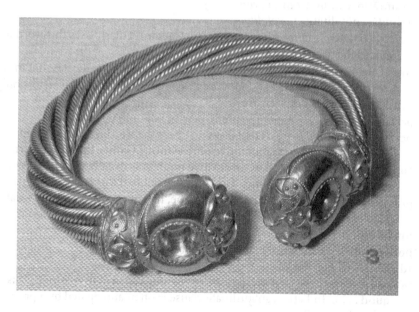

The Gauls were skilled metalworkers and created beautiful jewelry, such as this gold torque from the first century BCE. Torques were ornaments designed to be worn around the neck and were a sign of nobility or prestige among the Gauls; Greek and Roman statues and coins show Gauls wearing them. The word 'torque' derives from the Latin verb **torquēre**, *to twist*, since torques were often made by combining and twisting a number of small rods, as is clearly shown in this example. The ends were covered with decorative caps.

The Roman consul Titus Manlius in 361 BCE challenged a Gaul to single combat, killed him, and thereafter wore the torque he took from the slain enemy. In honor of this exploit he received the **cognōmen** Torquatus, and the Romans adopted the torque as a military decoration.

1   ***apud**, prep. + acc., *at the house of, near, with, among.*
    dītissimus: superlative of **dīves, dīvitis**, *rich.*
    Orgetorīx, Orgetorīgis, m., *Orgetorix, a Helvetian noble.*
    M. Messalā et M. Pūpiō Pīsōne cōnsulibus: since consuls were elected annu-
      ally for a one-year term, the Romans very often identified the year with an
      ablative absolute consisting of the two consuls' names plus **cōnsulibus**: *when*
      Marcus Messala and Marcus Pupius Piso were consuls, less lit., *during the con-*
      sulship of . . .   Messala and Piso were consuls in 61 BCE. When you read the
      Latin text aloud, always say the **praenōmina** using the correct case endings.

2   ***rēgnum, -ī**, n., *royal power, rule; kingdom*; in this context = *supreme power.*
    cupiditās, cupiditātis, f., *desire.*
    indūcō, indūcere, indūxī, inductus, *to lead on, influence.*
    rēgnī cupiditāte inductus: the tribes of Gaul had traditionally been ruled by
      kings. By Caesar's time, only the northern tribes were still governed this
      way; the central and southern ones had developed into oligarchies, where
      the noble families ran the affairs of the tribe, with magistrates elected every
      year. However, ambitious nobles still sometimes attempted to seize power for
      themselves, as in the case of Orgetorix.
    *coniūrātiō, coniūrātiōnis, f., *conspiracy.*

3   **nōbilitās, nōbilitātis**, f., *nobility.*
    *cīvitās, cīvitātis, f., *citizenship; state, tribe.* Caesar regularly uses this word to
      refer to the tribes of Gaul.

4   ***cōpia, -ae**, f., *supply, abundance*; pl., *resources, forces.* This indicates that the en-
      tire tribe would migrate, as oppposed to a raid conducted by warriors only.
    exīrent: deduce from **ex + eō, īre.**
    *perfacilis, -is, -e, *very easy.* The prefix **per-** in adjs. often means *very.*
    perfacile esse: *(and he said) that it was . . .* ; see the Reading Strategy opposite.
      This is completed by the infinitive phrase **tōtīus Galliae imperiō potīrī.**
    cum: when **cum** is followed by an ablative noun, it is usually the preposition; but
      here **cum** is the conjunction. How can you tell that this is the case?
    *praestō, praestāre, praestitī, praestitus [prae, in front, + stō, to stand] + dat., *to*
      stand out, surpass.

5   ***imperium, -ī**, n., *power, rule.*
    *potior, potīrī, potītus sum + abl. or gen., *to get possession of, get control of.*
    Id: the idea of migrating.
    hōc: ablative (note the long 'ō'), *because of this*, introducing the following clause
      (**quod . . .**). In Latin a subordinate clause is often anticipated by a pronoun
      such as **hoc** or **illud.**
    persuāsit: the root meaning of **persuādēre**, *to make something* (acc.) *agreeable to*
      someone (dat.), is more appropriate here than the secondary meaning *persuade.*
    *undique, adv., *from all sides, in all directions.*
    locī: *the place*, less lit., *the geography, the terrain.*

6   **continentur**: this word is gapped (see the Reading Strategy on page 25) and must be
      supplied three times in the remainder of this sentence, which appears on page 33.

Orgetorix persuades the Helvetians to migrate.

1 [2] Apud Helvētiōs longē nōbilissimus fuit et dītissimus Orgetorīx. Is, M.
2 Messalā et M. Pūpiō Pīsōne cōnsulibus, rēgnī cupiditāte inductus coniūrā-
3 tiōnem nōbilitātis fēcit et cīvitātī persuāsit ut dē fīnibus suīs cum omnibus
4 cōpiīs exīrent: perfacile esse, cum virtūte omnibus praestārent, tōtīus Gal-
5 liae imperiō potīrī. Id hōc facilius eīs persuāsit, quod undique locī nātūrā
6 Helvētiī continentur: (continued)

Initial Explorations

1. How is Orgetorix described? (1)
2. What did he do in the year 61 BCE? Why? (1–3)
3. What did he persuade the Helvetians to do? (3–4)
4. What did he say would be easy, and why? (4–5)
5. What fact made it easier for Orgetorix to win the Helvetians to his point of
   view? (5–6)

Forms

♦ You probably already know **cuius, eius, huius,** and **illīus,** genitive singulars of **quī, is,
hic,** and **ille** respectively. There are several other adjectives and pronouns that have a
genitive ending in -**īus**; **tōtus** (**tōtīus,** above: 4) is one such. These adjectives have first
and second declension endings, like **magnus, -a, -um,** except that they use -**īus** in the
genitive singular and -**ī** in the dative singular (like **illī** and **eī,** datives of **ille** and **is**).
Alter, *another,* **ūllus,** *any,* **nūllus,** *no,* **ūnus,** *one,* **uter,** *which (of two),* and **uterque,**
both, also belong to this group and are found in the selections in this book.

Reading Strategies

♦ Indirect statement is one of the most common constructions in Caesar's Latin; you
will meet it constantly in the selections in this book. If you are not comfortable with
this type of sentence, see **Q4**, page 290, or seek help from your teacher.

♦ It is very common in Caesar to find indirect statements where the context shows that
someone is speaking, even if a verb such as **dīxit** is not expressed. You met **persuāsit**
(above: 3) which shows that Orgetorix was addressing the nobles; this context and
the fact that **esse** is an infinitive show that Caesar has moved into indirect statement
beginning with **perfacile esse.** You may put an expression in parentheses to clarify
the structure of the sentence, as suggested in the note for line 4 opposite.

♦ The word order adjective – preposition – noun is very common with prepositional
phrases that contain an adjective: e.g., **quā dē causā,** *for this reason,* or **hīs dē rēbus,**
concerning these things. Recognizing this pattern helps you see that the words **ūnā ex
parte** (2:7, page 33) make a phrase and are not connected with the noun **flūmine** and
the following adjectives, even though they are also in the ablative.

7 *lātus, -a, -um, *broad, wide.*
   *altus, -a, -um, *tall, high; deep.*
8 *Iūra, -ae, m., *the Jura mountains.*
9 tertiā: this cannot agree with lacū, which is masc. (like all fourth decl. nouns
      except manus). What fem. noun, used previously in the sentence, is gapped?
   lacus Lemannus, lacūs Lemannī, m., *Lake Geneva.*
10 Hīs rēbus: *Because of these factors.*
   fiēbat: the verb fierī = *to happen* when completed by an ut clause (see the Sum-
      mary of Grammar, O3c).
   vagor, vagārī, vagātus sum, *to wander.*
11 *fīnitimus, -a, -um [< fīnis, boundary], *neighboring;* as substantive, *neighbor.*
   *īnferō, īnferre, intulī, illātus, irreg., *to bring, carry on, inflict on.*
      *bellum īnferre, *to make war upon someone* (dat.)
   parte: in this context = *reason,* not the geographical sense (*direction, side*) seen
      earlier in this chapter.
   bellō, -āre, -āvī, -ātus, *to make war.*
12 *cupidus, -a, -um [< cupiō, to desire], *desirous of* (+ gen.), *eager to.*
   *dolor, dolōris [< doleō, to feel pain, grieve], m., *pain, distress; anger, resentment.*
   *adficiō, adficere, adfēcī, adfectus [ad + faciō], *to do, treat, affect.*
   prō: *in proportion to, relative to.*
   *multitūdō, multitūdinis, f., *large number, large amount.*
13 fortitūdō, fortitūdinis, f., *bravery.*
   *angustus, -a, -um, *compressed, narrow.*
   angustōs: modifies fīnēs, even though the pronoun sē is nested in between.
   *arbitror, -ārī, -ātus sum, *to think.*
14 *longitūdō, longitūdinis, f., *length.*
   *mīlle passūs, plural, mīlia passuum, n., *mile* (literally, *a thousand paces*). Mīlle
      is indeclinable in the singular, but in the plural it is a neuter noun followed
      by a partitive genitive. The Roman mile was slightly shorter than the English
      mile, about 4800 feet.
   CCXL: = ducenta quadrāgintā. Numbers higher than ten will be given in the facing
      vocabulary so that you can say them when you read out loud. For one to ten, see
      chart V, page 253.
   lātitūdō, lātitūdinis, f., *width.*
   CLXXX: = centum octōgintā.
   *pateō, patēre, patuī, *to lie open, be accessible; to stretch out, extend.*

Forms

- All third declension nouns that end in the suffix -tūdō, gen. -tūdinis, are feminine:
  e.g., on the opposite page you met multitūdō (12), fortitūdō (13), and longitūdō (14).
  Learning such patterns can help you read more easily without constantly checking
  gender in the back of the book.

- Keep in mind that -ō can be a nominative singular ending in the third declension,
  in addition to its use in the very common dative and ablative singular forms in the
  second declension.

7 ūnā ex parte flūmine Rhēnō lātissimō atque altissimō, quī agrum Helvētium
8 ā Germānīs dīvidit; alterā ex parte monte Iūrā altissimō, quī est inter Sēquanōs
9 et Helvētiōs; tertiā lacū Lemannō et flūmine Rhodānō, quī prōvinciam nos-
10 tram ab Helvētiīs dīvidit. Hīs rēbus fīēbat ut et minus lātē vagārentur et mi-
11 nus facile fīnitimīs bellum īnferre possent: quā ex parte hominēs bellandī
12 cupidī magnō dolōre adficiēbantur. Prō multitūdine autem hominum et prō
13 glōriā bellī atque fortitūdinis angustōs sē fīnēs habēre arbitrābantur, quī in
14 longitūdinem mīlia passuum CCXL, in lātitūdinem CLXXX patēbant.

6. List the three boundaries of the Helvetian territory. From what people did
   each boundary separate the Helvetians? (7–10)
7. What was the result of the situation described in the previous sentence?
   (10–11)
8. How did this make the Helvetians feel? Why? (11–12)
9. What did the Helvetians believe and why? (12–13)
10. How big was the land of the Helvetians? (13–14)

> You may wish to use the Vocabulary Review for Book I (pages 48–49) to
> make sure you remember the asterisked words introduced in §§1–2.

Reading Strategies

◆ In indirect statement, the verb of saying or thinking may be placed either before or
  after the accusative and infinitive. In line 13 above, **arbitrābantur** comes after sē . . .
  habēre. In such situations the structure will not be clear until you reach the end of
  the clause or sentence, so remember to read and notice structure before translating.

◆ It is not difficult to understand a noun or phrase in the ablative when it is introduced
  by a preposition. You know, however, that the ablative is often used without a preposition, and it may not be immediately clear what the meaning is in such situations.
  The ablative case most often makes a noun act like an adverb; therefore, you may be
  able to understand the meaning of ablative nouns or phrases—including the ablative
  absolute, so common in Caesar—if you ask yourself the following questions:

  how? by what means?
  when?
  why?

◆ See the Summary of Grammar **A5** (page 269) for more about the ablative. From now
  on, references to the Summary of Grammar at the back of the book will be given
  simply as boldfaced, sans-serif letter and number combinations such as **G4b**.

1 *addūcō, addūcere, addūxī, adductus, *to lead forward, lead on, influence.*
   *auctōritās, auctōritātis, f., *prestige.*
   *permoveō, permovēre, permōvī, permōtus, *to move thoroughly; to influence, prevail upon, persuade.*

2 iumentum, -ī, n., *draft animal.*
   *carrus, -ī, m., *wagon, cart.*

3 *quam maximum: remember the special meaning of quam plus a superlative, *as . . . as possible.*
   coëmō, coëmere [con- + emō], *to buy*; the dieresis over the 'e' shows that the two vowels are pronounced separately.
   sēmentis, sēmentis, f., *planting, sowing* (in this context, of grain).

4 *frūmentum, -ī, n., *grain.*
   suppetō, suppetere, suppetīvī, suppetītūrus, *to be at hand, be available.*
   *pāx, pācis, f., *peace.*
   *amīcitia, -ae [< amīcus, friend], f., *friendship.*

5 *cōnfirmō, -āre, -āvī, -ātus, *to strengthen, establish.*
   Ad eās rēs cōnficiendās: a gerundive expressing purpose; see H5b.
   biennium, -ī [< bis + annus], n., *(period of) two years.*
   *dūxērunt: the verb dūcere can have a mental sense, *to think about, consider*, and this meaning is common in Caesar. When dūcere has this meaning, it can introduce an indirect statement, as it does here (biennium . . . esse).

6 *profectiō, profectiōnis [< proficīscor, to set out], f., *departure.*
   cōnfirmant: this and the following main verbs are in the HISTORIC PRESENT.

7 dēligō, dēligere, dēlēxī, dēlēctus, *to choose.*
   lēgātiō, lēgātiōnis [< lēgātus, ambassador], f., *diplomatic mission, embassy.*
   suscipiō, suscipere, suscēpī, susceptus, *to undertake, take on.*
   sibi lēgātiōnem suscēpit: Orgetorix apparently believed that by becoming the leader of this migration and making arrangements with the neighboring tribes that worked to his advantage, he would have enough power to fulfill his ambition of becoming sole ruler.

8 Casticus, -ī, m., *Casticus*, a Sequanian noble.
   Catamantaloedis, -is, m., *Catamantaloedis*, former king of the Sequani.

9 populī Rōmānī amīcus: an honorary title given to foreign leaders who supported Roman interests.

10 *occupō, -āre, -āvī, -ātus, *to seize.*

Reading Strategy

♦ The first sentence in §3 (opposite: 1–5) shows the importance of reading the whole sentence and observing its structure before translating. If you do this, you will spot four infinitives and know that the Helvetians decided to do four things, even though all the details may not be immediately clear.

Preparations for the migration.

1 [3] Hīs rēbus adductī et auctōritāte Orgetorīgis permōtī cōnstituērunt ea
2 quae ad proficīscendum pertinērent comparāre, iūmentōrum et carrōrum
3 quam maximum numerum coëmere, sēmentēs quam maximās facere, ut in
4 itinere cōpia frūmentī suppeteret, cum proximīs cīvitātibus pācem et amīci-
5 tiam cōnfirmāre. Ad eās rēs cōnficiendās biennium sibi satis esse dūxērunt;
6 in tertium annum profectiōnem lēge cōnfirmant. Ad eās rēs cōnficiendās
7 Orgetorīx dēligitur. Is sibi lēgātiōnem ad cīvitātēs suscēpit. In eō itinere per-
8 suādet Casticō, Catamantaloedis fīliō, Sēquanō, cuius pater rēgnum in Sē-
9 quanīs multōs annōs obtinuerat et ā senātū populī Rōmānī amīcus appel-
10 lātus erat, ut rēgnum in cīvitāte suā occupāret, quod pater ante habuerat;

(continued)

Initial Explorations

1. Why did the Helvetians agree to make preparations for departure? (1)
2. What three things did they do to prepare? (2–5)
3. When did the Helvetians plan to depart and why? (5–6)
4. What was Orgetorix chosen to do? What additional job did he take on him-self? (6–7)
5. Who was Casticus? What does Caesar tell us about his father? (8–10)
6. What did Orgetorix persuade Casticus to do? (10)

Text

• Prose texts of ancient Greek and Roman authors are divided into chapters (also called sections) in modern printed editions. In this book these divisions are marked by square brackets. Such divisions do not come from the ancient authors, but are added by modern editors. Usually the numbering system follows that used in one of the early printed editions. Because the development of printing in Europe coincided with the Renaissance, when scholars were eager to read books from antiquity, most classical texts were first printed during the 15th and 16th centuries. The *editio princeps* (first printed edition) of *De bello Gallico* was published in Rome in 1469.

• Be aware that all punctuation, capitalization, etc., is added by modern editors and varies from one edition to another, depending on how the editor interprets the text.

• Ancient writers knew that their books would be copied and sold on rolls of papyrus, which were prepared in standardized lengths—a roll (**volūmen**, from **volvere**, *to roll*) could hold about 1000 lines of poetry. Authors therefore created their works with such divisions in mind; each of the twelve books of Vergil's *Aeneid*, for instance, forms an artistic whole on its own, in addition to being part of the larger epic poem. Caesar organized *De bello Gallico* by the simple method of making one book for each year of his governorship.

11 *item, adv., *likewise.*

  Dumnorīx, Dumnorīgis, m., *Dumnorix,* an Aeduan nobleman.

  Aeduus, -a, -um, *of the Aedui, Aeduan.*

  Dīviciācus, -ī, m., *Diviciacus,* a chieftain of the Aedui who supported Roman inter-
    ests, elder brother of Dumnorix.

  quī: the antecedent is Dumnorix, not Diviciacus.

  *prīncipātus, -ūs [< prīnceps, leader], m., *leadership.*

12 acceptus: *accepted = acceptable to, pleasing to, popular with.* The Aeduan leader-
    ship generally supported the Romans, but a faction headed by Dumnorix op-
    posed them. See the Cultural Context note opposite.

  idem: neuter, *the same thing,* i.e., to seize power.

13 Perfacile factū: *(a) very easy (thing) to do.* Factū is a supine; see §I if you are not
    familiar with this form.

  *probō, -āre, -āvī, -ātus, *to approve; to prove, demonstrate, show.*

  probat: governs an indirect statement whose subject is the infinitive phrase
    cōnāta perficere; *he shows that to complete their undertakings . . .*

14 *perficiō, perficere, perfēcī, perfectus, *to complete.*

  esset: a subordinate clause with its verb in the indicative becomes subjunctive
    when it appears inside indirect statement; see Q4e.

15 nōn esse: the indirect statement introduced by probat (13) continues.

  *quīn, conj. + subj., *but that, that;* see O3f.

  plūrimum posse, idiom, *to be the most powerful.*

16 rēgna: plural because Orgetorix was going to help two men become rulers.

  conciliō, -āre, -āvī, -ātus, *to win over, reconcile; to gain, secure.*

    conciliātūrum: esse is understood, making a future infin. whose subject is sē.

    cōnfirmat: *to declare, assert,* a different meaning of this verb than the one found
      previously in this passage. This verb governs the last section of indirect state-
      ment, sē . . . conciliātūrum.

  *ōrātiō, ōrātiōnis, f., *oration, speech.*

17 *fidēs, fideī, f., *faith, good faith; pledge.*

  *iūs, iūris, n., *rightness, justice; legal power, authority.*

    *iūs iūrandum, iūris iūrandī, n., *oath.*

  *potēns, potentis, *powerful.*

  trēs . . . populōs: i.e., the Helvetii, the Sequani, and the Aedui.

18 tōtīus Galliae . . . spērant: a simpler word order would be spērant sēsē posse
    potīrī tōtīus Galliae.

  sēsē: *they;* see the Forms note below and the second Reading Strategy opposite.

  *spērō, -āre, -āvī, -ātus [< spēs, hope], *to hope.*

Forms

- sēsē (18) is an alternative form of sē, the accusative and ablative of the reflexive pronoun (*himself, herself, itself, themselves*). There is no difference in meaning; either
  form can be singular or plural, and Caesar makes frequent use of both forms.

- conciliātūrum: Caesar almost always omits esse in future infinitives (ELLIPSIS).

11 itemque Dumnorīgī Aeduō, frātrī Dīviciācī, quī eō tempore prīncipātum in
12 cīvitāte obtinēbat ac maximē plebī acceptus erat, ut idem cōnārētur persuā-
13 det, eīque fīliam suam in mātrimōnium dat. Perfacile factū esse illīs pro-
14 bat cōnāta perficere, proptereā quod ipse suae cīvitātis imperium obtentū-
15 rus esset: nōn esse dubium quīn tōtīus Galliae plūrimum Helvētiī possent; sē
16 suīs cōpiīs suōque exercitū illīs rēgna conciliātūrum cōnfirmat. Hāc ōrātiōne
17 adductī inter sē fidem et iūs iūrandum dant et rēgnō occupātō per trēs
18 potentissimōs ac firmissimōs populōs tōtīus Galliae sēsē potīrī posse spērant.

7. Who was Dumnorix? Who was Diviciacus and how was he related to Dumnorix? (11–12)
8. What did Orgetorix persuade Dumnorix to do? (12)
9. How did Orgetorix strengthen the ties between himself and Dumnorix? (13)
10. For what three reasons did Orgetorix say it would be very easy to do what
    they had undertaken? (13–16)
11. What did Casticus and Dumnorix do after being persuaded by Orgetorix?
    (16–17)
12. What did they hope they could do? How? (17–18)

Reading Strategies

◆ **Dumnorīgī Aeduō** (above: 11) is clearly dative case, but its function in the sentence
  is not immediately apparent. As you continue reading, you see the description of
  Dumnorix, then the clause **ut idem cōnārētur**, and finally the verb **persuādet**. At
  this point you understand the reason for the dative **Dumnorīgī Aeduō** (object of
  the intransitive verb **persuādet**) and also that **ut idem cōnārētur** is an indirect command. Once again you see the importance of reading and observing sentence structure before translating.

◆ In indirect statement, the pronoun **sē** (or its alternate form **sēsē**) always refers back
  to the subject of the verb of saying, thinking, etc., that governs the indirect statement.
  So in line 15 **sē** = *he* (the subject of **cōnfirmat**), while in line 18 **sēsē** = *they* (subject
  of **spērant**).

Cultural Context

◆ The Aedui led a pro-Roman faction among the Gallic tribes, while the Arverni and
  Sequani headed an anti-Roman coalition. But even within most tribes there were
  pro- and anti-Roman elements, as is shown by the split between Diviciacus and his
  brother Dumnorix. Caesar skillfully exploited these factional divisions. Watch for
  more instances of such factionalism as you read further in *De bello Gallico*.

1   **indicium, -ī,** n., *information, disclosure*, i.e., through an informant.
    ēnūntiō, -āre, -āvī, -ātus, *to announce, report.*
    est . . . ēnūntiāta: perfect passive. The helping verb usually comes after the per-
        fect participle (**ēnūntiāta est**), but Caesar frequently reverses the usual order
        and sometimes splits up the two parts of the verb form, as here.
    *****mōs, mōris,** m., *habit, custom.*
    mōribus suīs: *in accordance with their customs.*
2   *****vinculum** or **vinclum, -ī,** n., *chain.*
        ex vinclīs: Latin says *from chains* but English says *in chains.*
    causam dīcere, *to plead a case* (legal term).
    *****cōgō, cōgere, coēgī, coāctus,** *to gather, collect; to force, compel.* The second mean-
        ing applies in line 2, but the first in line 4 below.
    Damnātum: the participle here has a conditional sense, *If he were condemned.*
    poenam sequī, *that the punishment follow (him)*, less lit., *be applied (to him), be
        imposed (on him);* **eum** is omitted since the participle **Damnātum** (a substan-
        tive) clearly shows that the dir. obj. is masc. sing.
    *****oportet, oportēre, oportuit,** *it is fitting, it is proper, ought.*
    ut ignī cremārētur: many of the Gallic tribes had only recently ceased being
        ruled by kings (see the note for **rēgnī** in line 2 on page 30). Perhaps the
        Helvetians had established such a severe penalty for those who tried to seize
        royal power in order to dissuade ambitious nobles—a deterrent that obvi-
        ously did not stop Orgetorix.
3   **ignī:** Caesar uses this abl. form in preference to **igne.**
    diē cōnstitūtā: diēs, usually masc., may be fem. when it refers to a specific day.
    dictiō, dictiōnis, f., *pleading* (a case).
    *****iūdicium, -ī,** n., *judgment; trial, court.*
4   **familiam:** remember that this normally means *household*, including servants
        and retainers as well as blood relatives, not "family" in the American sense;
        in this context = *retinue* or *followers.*
    *****ad:** with numbers = *about, approximately.* Recall that in §2 Caesar described
        Orgetorix as **apud Helvētiōs longē nōbilissimus et dītissimus,** so it is not
        surprising that he was able to bring so many supporters to his trial.
5   *****cliēns, clientis,** m., *client, dependent.* In Roman society poor people often re-
        ceived assistance and protection from a wealthy man and were called **clientēs**
        (not the same as the modern English "client"). Caesar describes in Book VI
        how ordinary people in Gaul often entered into a kind of servitude to a pow-
        erful man in return for protection. Such people are probably what Caesar
        means by **clientēs** here.
    obaerātus, -ī [< aes, aeris, bronze, money], m., *debtor.*
    *****eōdem** [< īdem, the same], adv., *to the same place.*
6   *****condūcō, condūcere, condūxī, conductus,** *to lead together, gather.*

(Vocabulary and notes continued on opposite page.)

Orgetorix's plan is discovered and he is put on trial.

1 **[4]** Ea rēs est Helvētiīs per indicium ēnūntiāta. Mōribus suīs Orgetorīgem
2 ex vinclīs causam dīcere coēgērunt. Damnātum poenam sequī oportēbat ut
3 ignī cremārētur. Diē cōnstitūtā causae dictiōnis Orgetorīx ad iūdicium om-
4 nem suam familiam, ad hominum mīlia decem, undique coēgit, et omnēs
5 clientēs obaerātōsque suōs, quōrum magnum numerum habēbat, eōdem
6 condūxit; per eōs nē causam dīceret sē ēripuit. Cum cīvitās ob eam rem in-
7 citāta armīs iūs suum exsequī cōnārētur, multitūdinemque hominum ex
8 agrīs magistrātūs cōgerent, Orgetorīx mortuus est; neque abest suspiciō, ut
9 Helvētiī arbitrantur, quīn ipse sibi mortem cōnscīverit.

Initial Explorations

1. How did the Helvetians learn about Oregetorix's plans? (1)
2. How would Orgetorix have to respond to the charges? (1–2)
3. What would happen if he were found guilty? (2–3)
4. Whom did Oregetorix bring to court with him? (3–6)
5. What happened with the help of these people? (6)
6. How did the Helvetians respond to this development? (6–8)
7. What happened in the meantime? (8)
8. What do the Helvetians think really happened? (8–9)

nē causam dīceret: *so that he would not (have to) plead his case*, less lit., *from
pleading his case.* This is a purpose clause depending upon **ēripuit**, which
comes after it.
ēripiō, ēripere, ēripuī, ēreptus [ē + rapiō], *to snatch out; to rescue, save.*
*ob, prep. + acc., *because of.*
*incitō, -āre, -āvī, -ātus, *to set in motion; to spur on, stir up.*
7 *arma, -ōrum, n. pl., *weapons, arms; force of arms.*
   exsequor, exsequī, execūtus sum, *to follow through, carry out.*
8 *magistrātus, -ūs, m., *official, magistrate.*
   multitūdinem . . . cōgerent: the Helvetians had no standing army or police force
to arrest Orgetorix and compel him to stand trial, and many of his retainers
would have fought to protect him. So the Helvetian leaders had to collect an
army from the population before they could go after him.
   neque abest suspiciō: LITOTES.
9 **cōnscīscō, cōnscīscere, cōnscīvī, cōnscītus**, *to approve, decide upon.*
   sibi mortem cōnscīverit: *decided upon death for himself*, i.e., *committed suicide.*

1 **nihilō minus**, adv., often written as one word, *nevertheless.*
   id quod: another example of the **is quī** construction (see the first Reading
       Strategy on page 27).

3 *__oppidum__, -ī, n., *town.* This word indicates a fortified town or stronghold,
       in contrast to unfortified villages (**vīcī**).
   numerō: *in number,* an ablative of specification (**A5e**).
   duodecim: deduce from **duo** + **decem**.
   vīcus, -ī, m., *village.*
   *__quadringentī__, -ae, -a, *four hundred.*

4 *__incendō, incendere, incendī, incēnsus__, *to burn, set fire to.*
   praeterquam, adv., *beyond, besides, except.*

5 **combūrō, combūrere, combussī, combustus**, *to burn up.*
   reditiō, reditiōnis [< **redeō, redīre**, to return], f., *return.*
  *__spēs, speī__, f., *hope.*
  *__tollō, tollere, sustulī, sublātus__, *to lift, raise; to pick up, take away.*

6 **subeō, subīre, subiī** or **subīvī, subitūrus** [**sub** + **eō, -īre**], irreg., *to undergo.*
   trium: genitive of **trēs**.
  *__mēnsis, mēnsis__, m., *month.*
    trium mēnsum: *of three months,* less lit., *(enough) for three months.*
   molita cibāria: *ground grain.*
  *__quisque, quidque__, indef. pron., *each person, each one, every one.*

7 **efferre**: deduce from **ex** + **ferō**.
   Rauricī, -ōrum, m. pl., *the Raurici.*
   Tulingī, -ōrum, m. pl., *the Tulingi.*
   Latovīcī, Latovīcōrum, m. pl., *the Latovici.* These were three tribes living near
      the Rhine.
  *__fīnitimus, -a, -um__ [< **fīnēs**, territory], *neighboring*; as substantive, *neighbor.*
  *__utī__: an older form of the conjunction **ut**, very common in Caesar.

8 *__ūtor, ūtī, ūsus sum__ + abl., *to use, make use of.* See **A5o** for the other deponent
      verbs that take the ablative.
   ūsī: *having made use of,* less lit., *having adopted, after adopting.*
   exūrō, exūrere, exussī, exustus, *to burn up, burn out.*
  *__ūnā__, adv., *together.*

9 **Boiī, -ōrum**, m. pl., *the Boii,* a small Celtic tribe with no permanent home that
      had been living on the eastern side of the Rhine. Under pressure from other
      tribes, they moved westward and allied themselves with the Helvetians.
   Nōricus, -a, -um, *of Noricum,* a territory between the Danube and the Alps.
   trānsierant: deduce form **trāns** + **eō**.

10 **Nōreia, -ae**, f., *Noreia,* a city in Noricum.
  *__oppugnō, -āre, -āvī, -ātus__ [**ob** + **pugnō**], *to attack.*
    oppugnārant: = **oppugnāverant**; see **F2h** for such contracted forms.
  *__socius, -ī__, m., *ally.*
   ascīscō, ascīscere, ascīvī, ascītus, *to take, receive, join* (as allies).
   Boiōs . . . ascīscunt: lit., *they join to themselves* (**sibi**) *as allies the Boii who had
      been received among them* (**ad sē**), less lit., *they received among their own
      people and joined to themselves as allies the Boii.*

The Helvetians continue preparations for departure.

1 [5] Post eius mortem nihilō minus Helvētiī id quod cōnstituerant facere
2 cōnantur, ut ē fīnibus suīs exeant. Ubi iam sē ad eam rem parātōs esse arbitrātī
3 sunt, oppida sua omnia, numerō ad duodecim, vīcōs ad quadrīngentōs, reli-
4 qua prīvāta aedificia incendunt; frūmentum omne, praeterquam quod sēcum
5 portātūrī erant, comburunt, ut, domum reditiōnis spē sublātā, parātiōrēs ad
6 omnia perīcula subeunda essent; trium mēnsum molita cibāria sibi quemque
7 domō efferre iubent. Persuādent Rauricīs et Tulingīs et Latovīcīs fīnitimīs utī
8 eōdem ūsī cōnsiliō, oppidīs suīs vīcīsque exustīs, ūnā cum eīs prōficiscantur,
9 Boiōsque, quī trāns Rhēnum incoluerant et in agrum Nōricum trānsierant
10 Nōreiamque oppugnārant, receptōs ad sē sociōs sibi ascīscunt.

Initial Explorations
1. What happened after Orgetorix' death? (1–2)
2. What happened to the Helvetians' towns and villages? How many were involved? (3–4)
3. What grain did they burn? Why? (4–6)
4. What did the officials order each person to bring with him? (6–7)
5. Who were the Raurici, the Tulingi, and the Latovici? How did they figure in the Helvetians' plans? (7–8)
6. Where had the Boii lived previously? (9–10)
7. What had been the relationship between the Boii and the Helvetians? How did this now change? (10)

Reading Strategies
- The sentence that begins in line 2 (**Ubi . . .**) is long, but is split into three segments with semicolons in this edition. Each segment describes one thing that the Helvetians did as they prepared for departure.

- The second segment is **frūmentum omne comburunt** (4–5), with the **praeterquam** clause nested inside it. See page 14 if you are not familiar with the concept of nested clauses.

- This segment is followed by **ut** (5). You anticipate a conjugated verb to complete **ut**, and this verb, **essent**, appears in line 6. Nested inside the **ut** clause is an ablative absolute, **domum . . . sublātā** (5).

- The ablative absolute is one of the most common constructions in Caesar's Latin. See **A5i** to review it. Ablative absolutes often come at the beginning of a sentence; they may, however, be nested inside clauses, as in lines 5 and 8 above.

- Note the phrase **eōdem ūsī cōnsiliō** (8). It is common in Caesar to find a noun-adjective phrase split up by an intervening word (**ūsī**); cf. **angustōs sē fīnēs** (2.13).

1 *omnīnō [< omnis, all], adv., *altogether, in all.*

    quibus itineribus: Caesar sometimes repeats the antecedent of a relative pronoun inside the relative clause. In such cases the repeated noun can be put in parentheses or omitted. This is true also of **quā diē** in line 11 below.

3 *vix, adv., *with difficulty, scarcely.*

    *quā, adv., *where, by what route, along which.*

    singulī, -ae, -a, *one at a time.*

    impendeō, impendēre, impendī, impēnsus, *to hang over.*

4 perpaucī, -ae, -a, *very few*; **perpaucī** is a substantive, *very few (men).*

    prohibēre: an object such as **eōs** (= **Helvētiōs**) is understood. This refers to the Pas de l'Écluse, a spot where the mountains come very close to both sides of the Rhône River.

5 *expedītus, -a, -um, *unimpeded, without baggage; available, convenient.*

    *Allobrogēs, Allobrogum, m. pl., *the Allobroges,* a tribe in the Roman Province.

6 nūper, adv., *recently.*

    pācō, -āre, -āvī, -ātus [< pāx, pācis, peace], *to pacify.*

    nūper pācātī erant: the Allobroges had revolted and been brought back under Roman rule in 61 BCE; **pācātī erant** is a euphemism.

    fluō, fluere, flūxī, flūctus, *to flow.*

    *nōn nūllus, -a, -um, often written as one word **nōnnūllus**, *some, several.*

    nōn nūllīs locīs: = **in nōn nūllīs locīs**, abl. of place where with the prep. omitted (**B4b**).

7 *vādum, -ī, n., *shallow place, ford* (a place where a river is shallow enough to be crossed by wading).

    trānsitur: deduce from **trāns + eō, īre**. The Rhône at this point formed the boundary of the Roman province. The Helvetii could stay on the north bank and take the narrow road, which would require the permission of the Sequani, or cross to the south bank and go about 50 miles through the Province.

8 *Genāva, -ae, f., *Genava,* on the site of the modern city of Geneva, Switzerland.

    *pōns, pontis, m., *bridge.*

9 persuāsūrōs: supply **esse** to make a future infinitive, used with **sēsē** in indirect statement depending on **exīstimābant** at the end of the clause; again, reading the entire sentence through and noticing such structural elements is essential prior to translating.

    *nōndum, adv., *not yet.*

    bonō animō: abl. of description, *of good mind,* less lit., *favorable, well disposed.*

    in: *toward.*

10 *exīstimō, -āre, -āvī, -ātus [ex + aestimō, to think], *to evaluate, judge, consider, think.*

    *vīs, acc., **vim**, abl., **vī**, pl., **vīrēs**, f., *violence, force.*

    coāctūrōs: parallel to **persuāsūrōs**; so what two words must be supplied here?

11 *diem dīcere, idiom, *to fix a day, name a day.*

12 rīpa, -ae, f., *bank* (of a river).

    a.d. V Kal. Aprīl.: = **ante diem quīntum Kalendās Aprīlēs**, March 28.

    L. Pīsōne: Lucius Calpurnius Piso, Caesar's father in law, was consul with Aulus Gabinius in 58 BCE. For this type of abl. abs., see the note for line 1, page 30.

The Helvetians have two routes available to them.

1   [6] Erant omnīnō itinera duo, quibus itineribus domō exīre possent: ūnum
2   per Sēquanōs, angustum et difficile, inter montem Iūram et flūmen Rhoda-
3   num, vix quā singulī carrī dūcerentur; mōns autem altissimus impendēbat,
4   ut facile perpaucī prohibēre possent; alterum per prōvinciam nostram, mul-
5   tō facilius atque expedītius, proptereā quod inter fīnēs Helvētiōrum et Al-
6   lobrogum, quī nūper pācātī erant, Rhodanus fluit, isque nōn nūllīs locīs
7   vādō trānsitur. Extrēmum oppidum Allobrogum est proximumque Helvē-
8   tiōrum fīnibus Genāva. Ex eō oppidō pōns ad Helvētiōs pertinet. Allobrogi-
9   bus sēsē vel persuāsūrōs, quod nōndum bonō animō in populum Rōmānum
10 vidērentur, exīstimābant vel vī coāctūrōs ut per suōs fīnēs eōs īre pateren-
11 tur. Omnibus rēbus ad profectiōnem comparātīs, diem dīcunt, quā diē ad
12 rīpam Rhodanī omnēs conveniant. Is diēs erat a. d. v Kal. Aprīl., L. Pīsōne,
13 A. Gabīniō cōnsulibus.

Initial Explorations

1. Give three facts about the first route that was available for the Helvetians to leave their home. (1–3)
2   What additional fact made this route less desirable? (3–4)
3. Where was the second route? How does Caesar describe it? (4–5)
4. What body of water lies along this route? How would the Helvetians cross it? (5–7)
5. Give three facts about the town of Genava. (7–8)
6. Why did the Helvetians think they could persuade the Allobroges to let them pass through their territory? (8–10)
7. What would they do if persuasion failed? (10–11)
8. At what point did the Helvetians announce a date for their migration? (11)
9. What date was this? (12–13)
10. Locate the places mentioned in this reading on the map on page 45.

Cultural Context

♦ The Helvetii lost their identity as a tribe during the Roman empire. Beginning in the 17th century, however, the name was revived and used to refer to the Swiss people.

♦ Confoederatio Helvetica, the Latin form of the official name Swiss Confederation, appears on postage stamps, coins, and in the state seal of Switzerland. From this Latin form comes the abbreviation CH used on international automobile license plates and in Internet domain names.

♦ The typeface Helvetica, now often used on computers, was created in the 1950s by two Swiss designers.

1 **Caesarī**: here and throughout *De bello Gallico*, Caesar consistently writes about his own activities in the third person. Note the emphatic position of **Caesarī**, placed first in the sentence and to the left of the clause marker **cum**, at the point when the general himself appears in the narrative for the first time.

   id: the indirect statement **eōs . . . cōnārī** explains what the pronoun means.

2 **mātūrō, -āre, -āvī, -ātus**, *to hurry.*

   mātūrat: HISTORIC PRESENT.

   urbe: here, as normally, when a Roman author says "the city" without any other identification, he means Rome. Caesar was outside Rome, because someone holding a high-level military command (**imperium**) was not allowed inside the city, and was preparing to go north when he heard what the Helvetians were planning.

   quam . . . itineribus: since **quam** with a superlative regularly means *as . . . as possible*, Caesar's inclusion of **potest** here and in line 4 below seems unnecessary. Perhaps he wanted to stress that he travelled as fast as humanly possible in order to get to Gaul to deal with the developing situation there; **iter** refers to the amount travelled in one day. Two of Caesar's notable traits as a leader were his **celeritās**, his ability to move swiftly, and his willingness to push himself and his men as hard as necessary in emergencies.

3 **ulterior, ulterior, ulterius**, *further, farther.*

   in Galliam ulteriōrem: Gallia ulterior was another name for the Roman territory north of the Alps, also called **Gallia Trānsalpīna**, in contrast to **Gallia Cisalpīna**, *Gaul on this side of the Alps.*

   ad Genāvam: **ad** = *in the vicinity of, near.*

   ***perveniō, pervenīre, pervēnī, perventūrus** [per + veniō], *to arrive.*

   Prōvinciae tōtī . . . imperat: when **imperō** is found with a direct object (acc. case) and a dative, it means *give orders for, requisition, demand something* (acc.) *from someone* (dat.).

5 **legiō ūna**: the 10th legion, which Caesar frequently mentions in *De bello Gallico*; he often personally commanded this legion and it became his favorite.

   rescindō, rescindere, rescīdī, rescissus, *to cut down.*

Caesar reacts to the Helvetians' plan.

1 [7] Caesarī cum id nūntiātum esset, eōs per prōvinciam nostram iter fa-
2 cere cōnārī, mātūrat ab urbe proficīscī et quam maximīs potest itineribus
3 in Galliam ulteriōrem contendit et ad Genāvam pervenit. Prōvinciae tōtī
4 quam maximum potest mīlitum numerum imperat (erat omnīnō in Galliā
5 ulteriōre legiō ūna); pontem quī erat ad Genāvam iubet rescindī.

(continued)

Initial Explorations

1. What news was delivered to Caesar? (1–2)
2. How did he react to this? (2–3)
3. What two steps did he take after arriving in the vicinity of Geneva? (3–5)

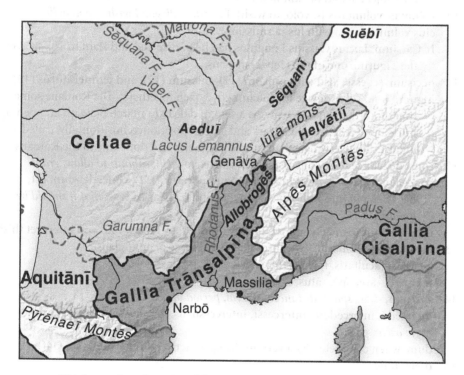

This is an enlarged portion of the map on page 21. The Rhône River (**Rho-danus F.**) flows to the west out of Lake Geneva (**Lacus Lemannus**) then turns south after merging with the Saône. For most of the distance between Geneva and the junction with the Saône, the Rhône formed the boundary between the Province and independent Gaul; this boundary is marked by a dark line. You can see how the Jura Mts. blocked the Helvetii from moving north and how the mountains come down very close to the Rhône, making the route through territory controlled by the Sequani less attractive.

6 *adventus, -ūs [< adveniō, to arrive], m., *arrival*.
  *certior fierī, idiom, *to be made more certain, to be informed*.
  *lēgātus, -ī, m., *legate, deputy, assistant; envoy, ambassador*; see page 9.
7 lēgātiō, lēgātiōnis, f., *diplomatic mission, embassy*.
  Nammeius, Verucloetius: Helvetian representatives.
  *prīnceps, prīncipis, *leading, chief*; as substantive, *important man, leader*. You
    may have learned this word as *emperor*, but that meaning derives from Au-
    gustus' use of this title to describe his position after he became sole ruler
    of Rome. In all Latin written before the time of Augustus, and sometimes
    thereafter, it is simply identifies an important person.
8 quī dīcerent: a rel. cl. with its verb in the subjunct. may express purpose, *to say*.
  sibi: to whom does this refer? See the second Reading Strategy on page 37.
  sibi in animō esse: *that they had in mind*, a dative of possession (see **A3f**).
  *ūllus, -a, -um, *any*.
  maleficiō: deduce from **male** + **faciō**.
9 rogāre: the indirect statement begun with **dīcerent** (8) continues; supply sē as
    the subject, based on **sibi** in line 8.
10 *voluntās, voluntātis [< volō, to wish], f., *wish, will; good wishes, goodwill*.
   eius voluntāte: i.e., with his permission.
   L. Cassium: Lucius Cassius Longinus had been defeated and slain in 107 BCE by
     the Tigurini, one of the Helvetian clans.
11 occīsum: sc. **esse**; also with **pulsum** (11), **missum** (12), and **temperātūrōs** (13).
   *iugum, -ī, n., *yoke* (device for hitching two oxen together). The Romans some-
     times forced an enemy army, as a sign of defeat, to march beneath an opening
     made up of two upright spears and a third positioned horitiontally, called a
     iugum. The Helvetians had turned the tables and done this to the Romans.
12 *concēdō, concēdere, concessī, concessūrus, *to yield, submit; to allow, grant*.
   concēdendum: an impersonal passive periphrastic (**H2**), **concēdendum est**,
     has been put into indirect statement with ELLIPSIS of **esse**: *that it should be
     granted*.
   inimīcō animō: in §6 you met **bonō animō** (9); so how would you interpret this?
13 data facultāte: this ablative absolute has the force of an *if*-clause.
   *facultās, facultātis, f, *opportunity*.
   temperō, -āre, -āvī, -ātus, *to refrain*.
14 *spatium, -ī, n., *space, distance; interval, period of time*.
   intercēdō, intercēdere, intercessī, intercessūrus, *to come in between*; of time,
     to occur, pass.
   dum: when completed by a verb in the subjunctive, **dum** = *until* (see **O4f**).
15 diem: *time*.
16 sūmō, sūmere, sūmpsī, sūmptus, *to take*.
   *quid: see the Reading Strategy on the opposite page.
   sī quid vellent: i.e., to continue the conversation, to find out Caesar's decision.
   ad: *about*.
   reverterentur: Caesar would have used the imperative (**revertiminī**) when
     speaking directly to the Helvetian ambassadors. When a command such as
     this is put into indirect statement, the imperative becomes subjunctive.

6 Ubi dē eius adventū Helvētiī certiōrēs factī sunt, lēgātōs ad eum mittunt
7 nōbilissimōs cīvitātis, cuius lēgātiōnis Nammeius et Verucloetius prīncipem
8 locum obtinēbant, quī dīcerent sibi esse in animō sine ūllō maleficiō iter
9 per prōvinciam facere, proptereā quod aliud iter habērent nūllum: rogāre
10 ut eius voluntāte id sibi facere liceat. Caesar, quod memoriā tenēbat L. Cas-
11 sium cōnsulem occīsum exercitumque eius ab Helvētiīs pulsum et sub iu-
12 gum missum, concēdendum nōn putābat; neque hominēs inimīcō animō,
13 datā facultāte per prōvinciam itineris faciendī, temperātūrōs ab iniūriā et
14 maleficiō exīstimābat. Tamen, ut spatium intercēdere posset dum mīlitēs
15 quōs imperāverat convenīrent, lēgātīs respondit diem sē ad dēlīberandum
16 sūmptūrum: sī quid vellent, ad Īd. Aprīl. reverterentur.

4. How did the Helvetians react when they heard about Caesar's arrival? (6–8)
5. What message did the Helvetians give to Caesar? (8–10)
6. What was Caesar's reaction to the message? (10–12)
7. For what two reasons did Caesar react this way? (10–14)
8. Why did he not give the Helvetians an immediate decision? (14–15)
9. What was Caesar's reponse to the Helvetians? (15–16)

Discussion
1. Why do you think Caesar writes about himself in the third person?
2. Summarize the reasons that Caesar gives for refusing to let the Helvetians cross the Province. Do these seem reasonable? Could anything else be going on that Caesar does not say?
3. Caesar could have omitted the story of Orgetorix and begun Book I simply by stating that the Helvetians had decided to migrate. Why did he include this story?

Reading Strategy

♦ After the words **sī**, **nisi**, **num**, and **nē**, **quis** = *someone, anyone* and **quid** = *something, anything*; i.e., they are equivalent to **aliquis** and **aliquid**. There may be words intervening between the conjunction and the form of **quis**, or there may be two forms of **quis** involved: e.g., **sī hīc quis quid discat**, *if someone were to learn anything here*.

✳ ✳ ✳ ✳ ✳ ✳ ✳ ✳ ✳

The rest of Book I is presented in English, beginning
on page 50, after the vocabulary review.

Vocabulary Review: Book I

The following asterisked words were introduced in §§1–2:

adficiō	imperium	proptereā
altus	incolō	prōvincia
angustus	īnferior	rēgnum
animus	īnferō	reliquus
apud	initium	tertius
arbitror	īnstitūtum	undique
cīvitās	lātus, -a, -um	virtūs
coniūrātiō	lēx	
contendō	longē	**Proper nouns**
contineō	longitūdō	Belgae
cōpia	mīlle passūs	Gallī
cotīdiānus	multitūdō	Gallia
cultus, -ūs	orior	Germānī
cupidus	pateō	Helvētiī
dolor	perfacilis	Iūra
extrēmus	pertineō	Ōceanus
ferē	potior	Rhēnus
fīnis	praestō, -āre	Rhodanus
fīnitimus	proelium	Sēquanī
flūmen	prohibeō	

The following asterisked words were introduced in §§3–5:

ad + numbers	incitō	potēns
addūcō	item	prīncipātus
amīcitia	iūdicium	probō
arma	iūs	profectiō
auctōritās	magistrātus	quadringentī
carrus	mēnsis	quam + superl.
cliēns	mōs	quīn
cōgō	ob	quisque
condūcō	occupō	socius
cōnfirmō	oportet	spērō
dūcō = consider	oppidum	spēs
eōdem, adv.	oppugnō	tollō
fidēs	ōrātiō	ūnā
fīnitimus	pāx	utī
frūmentum	perficiō	ūtor
incendō	permoveō	vinculum

The following asterisked words were introduced in §§6–7:

adventus, -ūs	nōndum	ūllus
certior fierī	nōnnūllus	vādum
concēdō	omnīnō	vīs
diem dīcere	perveniō	vix
exīstimō	pōns	voluntās
expedītus	prīnceps	
facultās	quā	**Proper nouns**
iugum	quid after sī	Genāva
lēgātus	spatium	Allobrogēs

INTRODUCTORY NOTE: Book I and the other portions of *De bello Gallico* included in this book in English were translated by S. A. Handford. Originally published in Britain, this translation contains some instances of spelling and word usage that differ from American practice. You may notice these differences but they should not cause any problems in comprehending the text. Some additional footnotes were added for this edition; such notes are marked with the symbol ⟡.

* * * * * * * * *

[8] In the meantime he employed the legion he had with him, and the troops that had been raised in the Province, to fortify the bank of the Rhône for a distance of eighteen miles[1] between the Lake of Geneva and the Jura, the frontier between the Helvetii and the Sequani. This was effected by means of a rampart sixteen feet high with a trench running parallel. He then placed redoubts[2] at intervals along the fortification and garrisoned them with pickets,[3] so that he could stop the Helvetii more easily, should they attempt to force a passage. When on the appointed day the envoys returned, he told them that it would be contrary to precedent and the traditions of the Roman state to allow anyone to march through the Province, and that if they tried to use force he would stop them. Disappointed of this hope, some of the Helvetii endeavoured—generally, though not always, by night—to get across by lashing boats together and making a number of rafts, others by wading through the shallowest places. But the Roman troops always hastened up to the danger-points, and aided by the fortifications drove them back with volleys of missiles and forced them to abandon their attempts.

[9] There remained only the route through the land of the Sequani, which was so narrow that it could not be used without their consent. Being unable to obtain permission by their own efforts, the Helvetii sent an embassy to Dumnorix the Aeduan, hoping by his intercession to gain what they desired. Dumnorix's popularity and open-handedness had won him great influence among the Sequani, and he was well-disposed towards the Helvetii because he had married a woman of their country; a daughter of Orgetorix. His ambition for kingly power made him favour political change, and he wanted to lay as many tribes as possible under obligations to himself. Accordingly he undertook the commission, induced the Sequani to let the Helvetii go through, and arranged an exchange of hostages between them. The Helvetii undertook to pass through without harming anyone or doing any damage; the Sequani, to let them travel without interference.

[10] Caesar was informed that the Helvetii intended to cross the territories of the Sequani and the Aedui and to enter the country of the Santoni, which is not

---

[1] There were several locations where the Rhône could be forded; Caesar had to fortify only these spots, not the entire eighteen miles. ⟡

[2] A small defensive enclosure, usually outside a larger fortification. ⟡

[3] Soldiers placed to give advance warning of an enemy approach. ⟡

far from that of the Tolosates, a tribe living in the Roman Province.[4] He saw that it would be very dangerous to the Province to have a warlike people, hostile to Rome, established close to its rich cornlands,[5] which were without any natural defences. Accordingly, leaving Titus Labienus, one of his generals, in charge of the fortifications he had constructed, he marched at top speed into northern Italy, enrolled two new legions there, sent for the three which were in winter quarters near Aquileia, and hastened back with all five by the shortest route over the Alps into Gaul. An attempt was made to hinder his march by the Ceutrones, Graioceli, and Caturiges, who seized some commanding heights. Beating them off in several engagements, Caesar marched in six days from Ocelum, the westernmost town in the Alpine district of Italy, into the territory of the Vocontii in the Province, and then continued through the country of the Allobroges into that of the Segusiavi, the first people on the west bank of the Rhône who live beyond the Provincial frontier.

[11] By this time the Helvetii had marched through the pass and across the country of the Sequani, and had reached that of the Aedui, whose land they were pillaging. Unable to protect themselves or their property, the Aedui sent to ask Caesar for help, pleading that they had always been loyal to Rome, and that it was not right to allow their land to be ravaged almost under the eyes of his army, their children carried off into slavery, and their towns taken by storm. At the same time the Ambarri, who had ties of friendship and kindred with the Aedui, informed Caesar that their fields too had been pillaged, and that it was almost more than they could do to repel the Helvetii's assaults upon their towns. The Allobroges also, who had villages and estates beyond the Rhône, came fleeing for refuge and said that they had been robbed of everything but the bare soil of their country. These complaints convinced Caesar that he must act immediately: if he delayed, his allies would have all their property destroyed and the Helvetii get clear away to the country of the Santoni.

[12] There is a river called the Saône, which flows through the territories of the Aedui and the Sequani into the Rhône with an extremely sluggish current, so that the eye cannot tell in which direction it is going. The Helvetii were crossing this river on rafts and small boats tied together. On learning from his patrols that they had got three quarters of their forces across, but that the remaining quarter was still on the east bank, Caesar left camp with three legions some time after midnight and came into contact with the division that had not yet crossed. Attacking them unexpectedly when they were hampered by baggage, he destroyed a large number, and the rest took to flight and hid in the neighbouring woods. The troops in this division formed one of the four clans into which the Helvetian people was divided,

---

[4] Since the route through the territory of the Sequani lay outside the Roman Province, Caesar had, strictly speaking, no right to interfere further. But the danger of which he speaks may have been a real one (although the territory of the Santoni was some 130 miles from the frontier of the Province), and there was precedent for such preventive action on the part of provincial governors.

[5] Wheat-growing regions; 'corn' in British English = 'wheat' in American usage. ▨

known as the Tigurini. Fifty years earlier, the men of this clan had left home independently of the others, and after the battle in which the consul Cassius was killed had sent his army under the yoke. Thus, whether by accident or by divine providence, the section of the Helvetii that had inflicted a signal defeat upon Rome was the first to suffer for it. In thus punishing the Tigurini Caesar avenged a private injury as well as that done to his country; for a general named Lucius Piso, grandfather of the Lucius Piso who was Caesar's father-in-law, had been killed in the same battle as Cassius.

[13] After this success Caesar wanted to pursue the remaining forces of the Helvetii. He therefore built a bridge over the Saône and led his army across. Alarmed by his unexpected arrival and seeing that he had effected in one day the crossing which they had the greatest difficulty in accomplishing in twenty days, they sent an embassy to him headed by Divico, who had been their commander in the campaign against Cassius. He told Caesar that if Rome made peace with the Helvetii they would go and remain wherever Caesar chose to settle them. If, however, he persisted in making war upon them, he would do well to remember the Romans' previous reverse and the traditional bravery of the Helvetii. He had made a surprise attack on one clan at a moment when their comrades who had crossed the river could not come to their help; but he should not on that account exaggerate his own prowess or despise them. They had learned from their fathers and ancestors to fight like brave men, and not to rely on trickery or stratagem. So let him beware; or it might be that the place where they stood would become famous in future ages as the scene of a Roman disaster and the destruction of a Roman army.

[14] Caesar replied that he had no hesitation about the action he should take, especially as he had not forgotten the Roman reverse to which the envoys referred, a misfortune that he resented all the more because it was undeserved. If the Romans at that time had been conscious of any act of oppression, it would have been easy to take precautions; they were caught off their guard because they knew they had done nothing to justify apprehension and thought it undignified to fear without cause. Even if he were willing to forget this old affront, could he banish the recollection of their fresh insults—their attempt to force a passage through the Province in defiance of his prohibition, and their attacks upon the Aedui, the Ambarri, and the Allobroges? 'The victory of which you boast so arrogantly,' he said, 'and the surprisingly long time during which you have escaped punishment, are both due to the same cause. When the gods intend to make a man pay for his crimes, they generally allow him to enjoy moments of success and a long period of impunity, so that he may feel his reverse of fortune, when it eventually comes, all the more keenly. However, if you will give hostages as a guarantee that you mean to carry out your undertakings, and will recompense the Aedui and the Allobroges for the injury you have done to them and their allies, I am willing to make peace with you.' Divico replied that it was the traditional custom of the Helvetii to demand hostages

of others, but never to give them—as the Romans had good cause to know. With this rejoinder he departed.

[15] The next day the Helvetii quitted their encampment. Caesar did the same, sending ahead, to discover in what direction they were marching, his entire force of four thousand cavalry, raised from various parts of the Province and from the Aedui and their allies. These pursued the Helvetian rearguard too eagerly, and engaging their cavalry on unfavourable ground suffered a few casualties. The Helvetii were elated at repulsing such a large force with only five hundred horsemen, and with increased boldness halted several times and challenged the Romans with their rearguard. Caesar would not allow his men to fight them, and contented himself for the moment with preventing them from foraging, looting, and ravaging the country. So the two armies marched for about a fortnight, the enemy's rear and the Roman vanguard being never more than five or six miles apart.

[16] Meanwhile Caesar was daily demanding from the Aedui the grain which, as he reminded them, their government had promised. For on account of the cold climate the standing corn was still unripe, and there was not even a sufficient supply of hay. Some grain that Caesar had brought up the Saône was of little use at the moment because the Helvetii had diverged from the river, and he did not want to lose contact with them. The Aedui kept putting him off from day to day, saying that the grain was being collected, was in transit, was on the point of arriving, and so forth. When he saw that there was going to be no end to this procrastination, and the day on which the soldiers' rations were due was approaching, he summoned the numerous Aeduan chiefs who were in the camp, including Diviciacus and Liscus, their chief magistrate—the Vergobret, as the Aedui call him—an annually elected officer holding power of life and death over his countrymen. Caesar reprimanded them severely for failing to help him at such a critical moment, when the enemy was at hand and it was impossible either to buy corn or to get it from the fields. He pointed out that it was largely in response to their entreaties that he had undertaken the campaign, and in still stronger terms than he had yet used accused them of betraying him by this neglect.

[17] His remarks at last induced Liscus to drop concealment and speak out. 'There are a number of private individuals in our state,' he said, 'who have great influence over the masses, and are more powerful than the magistrates themselves. It is these who, by criminal and seditious talk, work on the fears of the people to prevent them from bringing in the grain that is due. They argue that if the Aedui are no longer able to maintain their supremacy in Gaul, it is better to have Gauls as masters than Romans, and say they are certain that, if you defeat the Helvetii, you mean to rob the Aedui of their liberty along with all the rest of the Gauls. These men also keep the enemy informed of your plans and of all that goes on in the camp, and I have no power to control them. Indeed—in case you wonder why I have waited to

be compelled before revealing these facts—I realize I am running a very grave risk in doing so. That is why I held my tongue as long as I could.'

[18] Caesar perceived that Liscus' remarks alluded to Diviciacus' brother Dumnorix, and as he did not want the matter discussed with a number of others present, he promptly dismissed the assembly, telling Liscus to stay behind. When they were alone he questioned him about what he had said in the meeting, and Liscus now spoke with greater freedom and confidence. On putting the same questions to others in private, Caesar found that his report was true. It was indeed Dumnorix that he had referred to, a man of boundless daring, extremely popular with the masses on account of his liberality, and an ardent revolutionary. For many years he had bought at a cheap price the right of collecting the river-tolls and other taxes of the Aedui, because when he made a bid at the auction not a soul dared bid against him. In this way he had made a fortune and amassed large resources to expend in bribery. He maintained at his own expense a considerable force of cavalry, which he kept in attendance upon him, and his power was not confined to his own country, but extended over the neighbouring tribes. To increase it he had arranged a marriage for his mother with a nobleman of very great influence among the Bituriges; his own wife was a Helvetian and he had married his half-sister and other female relations to members of other tribes. On account of his matrimonial connection he was a keen partisan of the Helvetii, and he had his own reasons for hating Caesar and the Romans because their arrival in Gaul had decreased his power and restored his brother Diviciacus to his former position of honour and influence. If disaster should befall the Romans, he felt sure that with the aid of the Helvetii the throne was within his grasp, whereas a Roman conquest of Gaul would mean that he could not hope even to retain his present standing, much less make himself king.[6] Caesar also learnt in the course of his enquiries that, in the cavalry reverse a few days before, it was Dumnorix and the Aeduan horsemen under his command—sent to Caesar's aid by the tribal authorities—who had been the first to turn tail, and so made the rest of the cavalry lose their nerve.

[19] The suspicions aroused by these revelations were confirmed by certain indubitable facts. Dumnorix had secured a passage for the Helvetii through the territory of the Sequani, and arranged an exchange of hostages between them. He had done this not merely without the authority of Caesar or the Aeduan government, but actually without their knowledge; and he was denounced by the chief magistrate of his tribe. Caesar therefore decided that he had good grounds for either punishing him himself or calling on his fellow tribesmen to do so. The one objection to this course was that he knew Dumnorix's brother Diviciacus to be an enthusiastic supporter of Roman interests, a very good friend to him personally, and a man

---

[6] It suits Caesar's purpose to represent Dumnorix as merely an ambitious adventurer; but the facts suggest that he was really the leader of a popular party which opposed, in the national interest, the pro-Roman policy of the Aeduan nobles.

of exceptional loyalty, fair-mindedness, and moderation; and there was reason to fear that he would be much displeased if his brother were executed. Accordingly, before taking any action he sent for Diviciacus, and dismissing the ordinary interpreters talked to him with the assistance of Gaius Valerius Procillus,[7] a prominent man in the Province of Gaul and an intimate friend of his own, in whom he had entire confidence. He reminded Diviciacus of what he himself had heard said about Dumnorix in the meeting, informed him of what had been stated in his private interviews with various persons, and earnestly begged him not to take offence, but to consent to his either hearing the case himself and passing judgement on Dumnorix, or else instructing the Aeduan state to do so.

[20] Bursting into tears, Diviciacus embraced Caesar and besought him not to deal too severely with his brother. 'I know,' he said, 'that the allegations against him are true, and no one regrets it more than I do. For when I had great power at home and in the rest of Gaul, while he was too young to have much influence it was I that raised him to greatness; and the resources and strength that he thus acquired he is now using, not only to weaken my position, but to bring me near to ruin. Nevertheless, he is my brother; and apart from my own feelings, I cannot afford to be indifferent to public opinion. If you take severe measures against him, everyone will think—in view of my friendly relations with you—that I desired it, and I shall become very unpopular throughout Gaul.' He was continuing to plead at some length, with tears in his eyes, when Caesar grasped his hand, reassured him, and bade him say no more. 'So high is my regard for you,' he said, 'that, since you wish it and beg me so earnestly, I will both overlook the injury to Roman interests and swallow my own indignation.' He then summoned Dumnorix and in his brother's presence stated his reasons for complaint about his conduct, mentioning the information he had received and the charges made against him by his own government. He warned him to avoid henceforth giving any cause for suspicion; what was past, he would overlook for his brother's sake. However, he placed Dumnorix under surveillance in order to ascertain what he was doing and whom he talked with.

[21] That same day the patrols brought word that the Helvetii had stopped at the foot of a hill eight miles from Caesar's camp, whereupon he sent a party to reconnoitre the hill and find out what the ascent was like on the farther side. They reported that it was quite easy. Shortly after midnight be explained his plans to Labienus, his second-in-command, and detailed him to climb to the summit with two legions, taking as guides the men who had reconnoitred the ground. In the early hours of the morning Caesar himself marched towards the enemy, following the route by which they had proceeded, and sending all the cavalry in front. They

---

[7] The name shows that this man was a Gaul who had received Roman citizenship, as frequently was done for local leaders who supported Roman interests. In such cases a man took the **praenōmen** and **nōmen** of his Roman patron and kept his original name as **cognōmen**. The patron in this case was Gaius Valerius Flaccus, governor of Transalpine Gaul in the 80s BCE, who had given citizenship to Troucillus' father. ❧

were preceded by a patrol under command of Publius Considius, who was reputed a first-class soldier, and had served under Sulla and later under Crassus.

[22] At daybreak Labienus was actually in possession of the summit, while Caesar was not more than a mile and a half from the enemy's camp; and he learned afterwards from prisoners that neither his own approach nor that of Labienus had been observed. But suddenly Considius galloped up and said that the hill Labienus had been sent to occupy was held by the enemy; he knew this, he said, because he had recognized their Gallic arms and the crests of their helmets. Accordingly Caesar withdrew to a hill close by and formed his line of battle. Labienus had been instructed not to engage until Caesar's force was seen close to the enemy's camp, so that they might be attacked on all sides at once. After occupying the hill, therefore, he was waiting for Caesar to appear, without offering battle. It was only quite late in the day that Caesar learned the truth from his patrols—that it was the Romans who were in possession of the hill, that the Helvetii had moved camp, and that Considius had lost his head and reported that he had seen what was not there to be seen. During that day Caesar followed the enemy at the usual interval and pitched his camp three miles from theirs.

[23] Next day, as the distribution of rations was due in two days' time and he was only seventeen miles from Bibracte, by far the largest and richest town of the Aedui, he thought it advisable to secure his food supply, and therefore diverged from the route that the Helvetii were following and marched towards the town. His movements were reported to the enemy by some runaway slaves of Lucius Aemilius, the commander of Caesar's Gallic cavalry. The Helvetii perhaps thought that we were breaking contact with them out of fear, especially as we had declined an engagement the day before, although we had the advantage of position; or it may be they were confident of being able to cut us off from access to supplies. In any case they changed their plan, altered the direction of their march, and began to hang upon our rear and harass it.

[24] Observing this, Caesar withdrew to a hill close at hand and sent out his cavalry to meet the enemy's attack. In the meantime he formed up his four veteran legions in three lines half-way up the hill, and posted the two recently levied in Italy on the summit with all the auxiliaries, so that the whole of the hillside above him was occupied with troops. The baggage and packs he ordered to be collected in one place, and defence works to be dug round them by the veterans posted in the top line. The Helvetii, who were following us with the whole of their transport, now parked it all together, and, after repulsing our cavalry with a battle line drawn up in very close order, formed a phalanx[8] and climbed towards our first line.

---

[8] A phalanx was a closely packed mass of troops, formed up in considerable depth and—at any rate in the original form used by the Macedonians—armed with very long pikes, so as to present to an enemy an impenetrable thicket of spearpoints. When this formation was adopted by the Gauls and Germans, the men in the front rank held their shields overlapping one another in front of their bodies.

[25] Caesar had all the horses—starting with his own—sent away out of sight, so that everyone might stand in equal danger and no one have any chance of flight. Then he addressed the men and joined battle. By throwing down spears from their commanding position the troops easily broke the enemy's phalanx, and then drew their swords and charged. The Gauls were much hampered in action because a single spear often pierced more than one of their overlapping shields and pinned them together; and, as the iron bent, they could not pull them out. With their left arms thus encumbered it was impossible for them to fight properly, and many, after repeated attempts to jerk their arms free, preferred to drop the shields and fight unprotected. At length, exhausted by wounds, they began to fall back towards a hill about a mile away. They had gained the hill, and our men were approaching to dislodge them, when the fifteen thousand Boii and Tulingi who protected the rear of their column suddenly marched up, attacked us on the right flank,[9] and surrounded us. Thereupon the Helvetii who had retreated to the hill began to press forward again and renew the battle. We changed front and advanced in two divisions—the first and second lines to oppose the Helvetii whom we had already once defeated and driven back, the third to withstand the newly arrived troops.

[26] This double battle was long and fiercely fought. When they could no longer sustain the Roman charges, the Helvetii resumed their retreat up the hill, while the Boii and Tulingi retired to the laager[10] where the baggage was stacked, to continue the struggle—for throughout this battle, which lasted from midday till evening, not a single man of them was seen in flight. At the laager fighting actually continued until late at night, for the enemy had made a barricade of the wagons, and rained down missiles on all who approached; some also wounded our men with spears and javelins discharged low down between the wagons and between the wheels. After a long struggle we captured the laager and the baggage it contained, and also Orgetorix's daughter and one of his sons. About a hundred and thirty thousand Helvetii who survived the battle marched without halting all that night, and arrived after three days in the country of the Lingones. We had not been able to pursue immediately because we spent these days in attending to the wounded and burying the dead. But Caesar sent a letter and a message to the Lingones warning them not to supply the Helvetii with grain or aid them in any way, on pain of being treated as enemies, and three days later he started in pursuit with the whole army.

[27] The Helvetii were compelled by want of all kinds of supplies to send envoys offering surrender. These met Caesar on the march, prostrated themselves before him, and with tears of supplication besought him to grant them peace. Caesar commanded that the Helvetii should stay where they were until he arrived. They obeyed, and on reaching the place he required them to give hostages and to sur-

---

[9] It was the custom in ancient warfare to attack, if possible, the right flank of enemy troops, because on that side they could not easily protect themselves with their shields.

[10] An encampment surrounded by a protective circle of wagons.

render their arms and the slaves who had deserted to them. While these were being searched for and collected, six thousand men of the clan known as the Verbigeni quitted the encampment in the early hours of the night and set out for the German frontier on the Rhine. Either they were afraid that they would be massacred when once they had given up their arms, or they hoped to escape punishment altogether, thinking that they could get away unobserved in such a large crowd of prisoners, and that the Romans might never learn of their departure.

[28] But Caesar heard of it, and sent word to the tribes through whose territory the fugitives were passing that they were to hunt them down and bring them back, or he would hold them responsible. When they were brought back he put them to death; but all the rest were allowed to surrender after handing over the hostages, deserters, and arms. The Helvetii, together with the Tulingi, Latovici and Rauraci, were bidden to return to their own country; and as all their produce was gone, so that they had nothing at home to live on, Caesar directed the Allobroges to supply them with grain, and ordered the Helvetii themselves to rebuild the towns and villages they had burnt. His chief reason for doing this was that he did not want the country they had abandoned to remain uninhabited, lest the Germans across the Rhine might be induced by its fertility to migrate into Switzerland, and so become near neighbours of the Roman Province, and especially of the Allobroges. The Boii were given a home in the country of the Aedui, who asked Caesar to consent to this arrangement because the Boii were known as a people of exceptional bravery. The Aedui assigned them land, and later admitted them to equality of rights and liberties with themselves.

[29] Some documents found in the Helvetian camp were brought to Caesar. They were written in Greek characters, and contained a register of the names of all the emigrants capable of bearing arms, and also, under separate heads, the numbers of old men, women, and children. The grand total was 368,000, comprising 263,000 Helvetii, 36,000 Tulingi, 14,000 Latovici, 23,000 Rauraci, and 32,000 Boii; and the list of men fit for military service contained 92,000 names. By Caesar's orders a census was taken of those who returned home, and the number was found to be 110,000.

Questions

1. Do the reasons Caesar gives for fighting the Helvetians in §10 seem realistic? Be sure to look at the map on page 22 before answering this question.
2. Caesar is known for his willingness to move swiftly in an emergency. What examples of this do you find in §§10–13?
3. In §§17–19, how does Caesar characterize Dumnorix? Cite specific examples from the text. Compare this with Caesar's description of Dumnorix's brother Diviciacus; why the difference? Read between the lines!

4. What themes reappear in the story of Dumnorix that first appeared in Caesar's account of Orgetorix (§§2–4)?
5. Why did Caesar arrange his troops as he did when preparing to fight the Helvetians (§24)?
6. Caesar never denies that the Gauls were courageous fighters. What evidence does he give of the Helvetians' courage in §§25–26?

Expulsion of Ariovistus from Gaul

[30] On the conclusion of the Helvetian campaign the leading men of tribes in almost every part of Gaul came to offer Caesar congratulations. They realized, they said, that although his motive in fighting the Helvetii was to punish them for their past injuries to Rome, what had happened was just as much to the advantage of Gaul as of the Romans; for the intention of the Helvetii, in abandoning their home at a time when they enjoyed great prosperity, was to make war on all Gaul and become masters of it, and so to have the whole country from which to select the district they thought most fertile and convenient for settlement, and to compel the other tribes to pay tribute. The deputies asked Caesar to let them fix a day for convening a pan-Gallic assembly, saying that there were certain requests they would like to submit to him when they were all agreed about them. With Caesar's consent they appointed a date for this assembly, and swore to one another not to disclose its proceedings without its express authority.

[31] When the assembly had met and concluded its business, the same chieftains who had been with Caesar before returned and asked leave to interview him privately in a place secluded from observation, in order to discuss a matter that concerned not only their own interest, but that of the whole country. When the interview was granted they all prostrated themselves before him with tears in their eyes. They explained that they were very anxious to prevent what they said from being disclosed; this was just as important to them as obtaining the request they had come to make, because its disclosure would bring the most cruel punishment upon them. Their spokesman was the Aeduan Diviciacus.

The Gauls, he said, were divided into two parties, one dominated by the Aedui, the other by the Arverni. After a fierce struggle for supremacy, lasting many years, the Arverni and Sequani hired some German mercenaries to help them [70–65 BCE]. A first contingent of about fifteen thousand had crossed the Rhine; but when the uncivilized barbarians had acquired a taste for residence in Gaul, with its good land and high standard of life, more were brought over, and there were at present about a hundred and twenty thousand of them in the country. The Aedui and their satellite tribes had fought the Germans more than once, and had suffered disastrous defeats, by which they lost all their noblest citizens, councillors, and knighthood.[11] These calamities had broken the supremacy which they formerly maintained in Gaul by their own prowess and by the ties of hospitality and friendship that united them with the Romans; and they had been forced to surrender their most distinguished citizens as hostages to the Sequani, and to bind themselves by oath not to attempt to recover them and not to solicit the aid of Rome, but to submit for ever without demur to the sovereign power of their conquerors.

'I myself,' he said, 'am the only man of the whole Aeduan nation who could not be prevailed upon to swear this oath or to give my children as hostages. That was why I fled from my country and went to Rome to claim assistance from the Senate—because I alone was not restrained either by an oath or by the surrender of hostages.'

But a worse fate, he went on to say, had befallen the victorious Sequani than the conquered Aedui. For the German king Ariovistus had settled in their territory and seized a third of their land—the best in all Gaul. And now he was bidding them evacuate another third, because a few months previously he had been joined by twenty-four thousand men of the Harudes, and must find them a home to settle in. In a few years' time the whole population of Gaul would be expatriated and all the Germans would migrate across the Rhine; for there was no comparison between the soil of Germany and that of Gaul, or between their respective standards of living. After a single victory over the united Gallic forces at Admagetobriga [61 BCE], Ariovistus had shown himself an arrogant and cruel tyrant, demanding the children of every man of rank as hostages, and making an example of them by the infliction of all manner of torture, if the least indication of his will and pleasure was not instantly complied with. The man was an ill-tempered, headstrong savage and it was impossible to endure his tyranny any longer. Unless Caesar and the Romans would help them, the Gauls must all do as the Helvetii had done—leave their homes, seek other dwelling-places out of reach of the Germans, and take their chance of whatever fortune might befall them.

'If my words come to the ears of Ariovistus,' he concluded, 'I do not doubt that he will inflict the most inhuman punishment on all the hostages he has in his power. But your great prestige, the recent victory of your army, and the terror of the Roman name, could deter him from bringing fresh German hordes across and protect all Gaul from his depredations.'

[32] When Diviciacus had finished his speech, the whole deputation began with many tears to implore Caesar's aid. He noticed, however, that the Sequanian representatives did not follow the example of all the rest, but hung their heads in dejection with their eyes fixed on the ground. In astonishment he asked them the reason for this behaviour, but without making any reply they maintained their attitude of silent dejection. After he had questioned them repeatedly without being

---

[11] The cavalry of the Gallic tribes was made up of nobles, but do not imagine them in full suits of armor like the knights of the Middle Ages. ⚓

able to get a word out of them, Diviciacus spoke again. The lot of the Sequani, he explained, was even more grievous and miserable than that of the rest, because they alone dared not, even in secret, complain or beg for relief. They stood in terror of Ariovistus' cruelty, even when he was far away, just as much as if they were in his presence; for while the others could at any rate flee away out of his reach, the Sequani, having admitted him into their midst and allowed all their towns to fall into his power, must submit to any atrocities he chose to commit against them.

[33] On receiving this information Caesar reassured the Gauls and promised to attend to the matter, adding that he had great hopes that the privilege he had secured for Ariovistus, as well as the weight of his authority, would induce him to cease his oppression. He then dismissed the meeting. In addition to what he had been told, many other considerations convinced him that this problem must be faced and some action taken. The most important was the fact that the Aedui, who had frequently been styled by the Senate 'Brothers and Kinsmen of the Roman People', were enslaved and held subject by the Germans, and that Aeduan hostages were in the hands of Ariovistus and the Sequani, which, considering the mighty power of Rome, Caesar regarded as a disgrace to himself and his country. Furthermore, if the Germans gradually formed a habit of crossing the Rhine and entering Gaul in large numbers, he saw how dangerous it would be for the Romans. If these fierce barbarians occupied the whole of Gaul, the temptation would be too strong for them: they would cross the frontier into the Province, as the Cimbri and Teutoni had done before them [109–101 BCE], and march on Italy, for the Roman Province lay just across the Rhône from the territory of the Sequani. This danger, he considered, must be provided against immediately. Moreover, Ariovistus personally had behaved with quite intolerable arrogance and pride.

[34] Accordingly Caesar decided to send envoys requiring him to select for a conference some place lying between their present positions, as he wished to discuss business of state of the highest importance to them both. To this delegation Ariovistus replied: 'If I wanted anything from Caesar, I should go to him; so if he wants anything of me, he must come to me.' He added that he dared not come without the protection of his army into the part of Gaul occupied by Caesar, and that to concentrate his forces would mean making elaborate and troublesome arrangements for provisioning them. He could not imagine what business Caesar, or the Romans at all for that matter, had in the part of Gaul which was his by right of conquest.

[35] At this Caesar sent a second embassy to remind Ariovistus of the important privilege conferred upon him by himself and the Roman government, when during Caesar's consulship [59 BCE] he received from the Senate the titles of 'King' and 'Friend'. Since his way of showing his gratitude was to refuse an invitation to a conference for the discussion of matters affecting their common interest, the envoys were instructed to deliver him an ultimatum: first, he was not to bring any more large bodies of men across the Rhine into Gaul; secondly, he was to restore

the Aeduan hostages he held, and to authorize the Sequani to restore those whom they held; finally, he was not to oppress the Aedui or to make war on them or their allies. On these conditions Caesar and the Roman government would maintain cordial and friendly relations with him. If these demands were refused, then, in accordance with a decree of the Senate passed in the consulship of Marcus Messala and Marcus Piso [61 BCE], directing all governors of the Province of Gaul to do everything consistent with the public interest to protect the Aedui and other Roman allies, Caesar would not fail to punish his ill-treatment of them.

[36] In reply Ariovistus said that it was the recognized custom of war for victors to rule the vanquished in any way they pleased, and that the Romans acted on this principle by governing their conquered subjects, not according to the dictates of any third party, but at their own discretion. Since he did not dictate to them how they were to exercise their rights, he ought not to be interfered with in the exercise of his. It was because the Aedui had tried the fortune of war, and were the losers in the fight, that they had to pay him tribute; and Caesar was doing him a serious wrong in coming to Gaul and causing him a loss of revenue. He would not return the hostages to the Aedui, but would refrain from making any wanton attack upon them or their allies, if they kept their agreement and paid the tributes regularly every year; if they did not, the title of 'Brothers of the Roman People' would not save them from the consequences. 'I am not impressed,' he concluded, 'by Caesar's threat to punish my "oppression" of these people. No one has ever fought me without bringing destruction upon himself. Let him attack whenever he pleases. He will discover what German valour is capable of. We have never known defeat, we have had superb training in arms, and for fourteen years have never sheltered beneath a roof.'

[37] At the very moment when this message was being reported to Caesar, delegations arrived from the Aedui and the Treveri. The Aedui came to complain that the Harudes, who had lately crossed into Gaul, were ravaging their territory, and that even the surrender of hostages had failed to induce Ariovistus to leave them in peace. The Treveri stated that a hundred clans of the Suebi had encamped on the bank of the Rhine and were trying to cross under the command of Nasua and his brother Cimberius. Caesar was much perturbed by this news, and decided that he must act immediately, lest, if this fresh horde of Suebi joined forces with Ariovistus' veteran troops, it might become more difficult to resist them. Accordingly, he arranged for a supply of grain as quickly as he could, and advanced at top speed towards Ariovistus.

[38] After three days' march it was reported that the German was hastening with all his forces to occupy Besançon, the largest town of the Sequani, and had already advanced three days' journey beyond his own frontier. Caesar felt that he must take energetic measures to prevent the fall of this town, for it contained an abundance of military stores of every kind, and its natural defences were so strong that it offered every facility for protracting hostilities. The river Doubs forms an

almost complete and perfect circle round it; the gap left unprotected is little more than five hundred yards wide, and is blocked by a high hill so completely that the spurs at its base run right down to the river bank on either side. This hill was girt by a wall which gave it the strength of a citadel and joined it with the town. Caesar hastened there by forced marches continued day and night, occupied the town, and placed a garrison in it.

[39] During the few days that they spent near Besançon to lay in a stock of corn and other provisions, the soldiers began to question the Gauls and merchants there, who talked about the enormous stature, incredible courage, and splendid military training of the Germans. Some affirmed that on many occasions when they had met them in battle, the very expression on their faces and the fierce glance of their eyes were more than they could endure. This gossip threw all ranks into a sudden panic that completely unnerved them. It began with the military tribunes, the prefects[12] of the auxiliary troops, and the men with little experience of war who had followed Caesar from Rome in order to cultivate his friendship. Most of these alleged some urgent reason or other for leaving camp, and asked Caesar's permission to go. Some stayed out of shame and a desire to avoid the suspicion of cowardice. But they were unable to hide their feelings, and at times could not help shedding tears; skulking in their tents, they bemoaned their fate or joined their friends in lamenting the peril that threatened them all alike. All over the camp men were signing and sealing their wills. The talk of these frightened people gradually affected even seasoned campaigners, including some centurions and cavalry officers. Those who wished to be thought less timid than the rest said that it was not the enemy they feared, but the narrow defiles through which they had to pass and the great forests that lay between them and Ariovistus, or pretended to be afraid that it would prove impossible to maintain an adequate supply of corn. Some even went so far as to tell Caesar that when he gave the command to strike camp and advance, the soldiers would be too panic-stricken to obey.

[40] Observing this state of affairs, Caesar summoned the centurions of every grade[13] to a council, and began by severely reprimanding them for presuming to inquire or conjecture where he was leading them, or with what object. At the time of his consulship, he said, Ariovistus had sought the friendship of Rome with great eagerness; and what reason was there for thinking that he would so light-heartedly refuse to carry out his obligations? For his own part, he was convinced that when the king was acquainted with his demands and saw the fairness of the terms proposed, he would not reject the friendship offered by the Roman government and by himself. If, however, a mad impulse should lead him to make war, what reason had

---

[12] Prefect (Lat. **praefectus**, *placed in charge*) was a title given to commanders of cavalry and other auxiliary troops. 🔊

[13] Usually only the **centuriōnēs prīmōrum ōrdinum** (see chart on page 10) attended such councils. 🔊

they after all for being afraid? Both their own courage and his careful attention to his duties gave good grounds for confidence.

'Our countrymen faced this enemy,' he continued, 'in our fathers' time, when Gaius Marius won a victory over the Cimbri and Teutoni by which, as all agreed, the whole army earned as much glory as its commander. They faced them again more recently in Italy, when they defeated the rebellious slaves,[14] aided though these were to some extent by the military training and discipline that they had acquired from their Roman masters. This shows what a great advantage resolute courage is: for a long time the Romans had an unreasoning fear of the slaves while they were still unarmed, yet afterwards defeated them when they were not only armed but flushed with victory. Moreover these Germans are the same men whom the Helvetii have often met in battle, not only in Switzerland but also in Germany, and have generally beaten; yet the Helvetii were not a match for our army.

'If anyone is alarmed by the fact that the Germans have defeated the Gauls and put them to flight, he should inquire into the circumstances of that defeat. He will find that it happened at a time when the Gauls were exhausted by a long war. Ariovistus had remained for many months under cover of his camp and the surrounding marshes, so that they had no chance of fighting him; and then he attacked suddenly, when in despair of bringing him to battle they had broken up into scattered groups. Thus his victory resulted from his cunning strategy rather than the bravery of his troops. The employment of such strategy was possible against inexperienced natives, but even Ariovistus can have no hope of being able to trick our armies by such means.' He went on to say that those who tried to disguise their cowardice by pretending to be anxious about the corn supply or the difficulties of the route were acting presumptuously: it was plain that they either lacked confidence in their general's sense of duty or else meant to dictate to him. He was attending to these matters. Corn was being supplied by the Sequani, Leuci, and Lingones, and the harvest was already ripe in the fields; and as to the route, they would soon be in a position to judge for themselves. The suggestion that the men would not obey orders to advance did not trouble him at all; for he knew that in all cases in which an army had refused obedience, it was either because their generals had been unsuccessful and were regarded as unlucky, or because they were proved dishonest by the discovery of some misconduct. His own integrity was attested by his whole life; his power of commanding success, by the campaign against the Helvetii. Therefore he was going to do that very night what he had at first intended to defer till later; he would move camp in the early hours of the morning, so as to find out with the least possible delay whether their sense of honour and duty or their fear was the stronger. If no one else would follow him, he would go all the same, accompanied only by the

---

[14] The slave war referred to was fought in 73–71 BCE. A Thracian gladiator named Spartacus raised a large force and defeated several Roman armies. He was eventually crushed by Crassus, the future triumvir.

10th legion; of its loyalty he had no doubt, and it should serve as his bodyguard. (Caesar placed the highest confidence in this legion for its bravery and had shown it particular favour.)

[41] This address had a dramatic effect on all ranks, and inspired them with the utmost enthusiasm and eagerness for action. First of all, the men of the 10th commissioned their military tribunes to thank Caesar for his high opinion of them and to assure him that they were ready to take the field at any moment. Then the other legions prevailed on their tribunes and first grade centurions to make their peace with him, professing that they had never entertained doubts or fears, and had never imagined that it was for them to direct the campaign, which they realized was their Commander's business. Accepting their excuses, Caesar told Diviciacus to study the available routes, because he trusted him more than any of the other Gauls, and was advised by him to make a detour of some fifty miles, which would enable them to march through open country, Starting in the small hours, as he had said he would, he marched without interruption for six days, and was then informed by his patrols that Ariovistus' forces were twenty-three miles[15] away.

[42] Hearing that Caesar had moved nearer, Ariovistus sent a message saying that he had no objection to arranging the interview previously requested, as he thought he could now do so without risk. Caesar did not reject his offer, thinking that Ariovistus was now coming to his senses again, since he undertook of his own accord to do what he had refused before when asked. He hoped too that the recollection of the great favours the king had received from himself and the Roman government would make him abandon his stubborn attitude, when he heard what was required of him. The interview was arranged for the fifth day following, and in the meantime messengers kept going to and fro between them. Ariovistus insisted that Caesar should not bring any infantry to the conference; he was afraid, he said, of being caught in a trap. Each of them must come with a mounted escort only; otherwise he would not come at all. As Caesar did not want to give him an excuse for cancelling the meeting, yet dared not entrust his safety to the Gallic cavalry, he decided that his best course would be to take away all their horses and mount upon them the infantrymen of the 10th legion, in whom he had such complete confidence, and thus have an escort on whose devotion he could rely absolutely in case of need. While this was being done one of the legionaries made quite a witty remark. 'Caesar's being better than his word,' he said. 'He promised to make the 10th his bodyguard, and now he's knighting us.' [16]

[43] In an extensive plain[17] there stood a fairly high mound of earth, about equidistant from the camps of Caesar and Ariovistus. Here they came, as agreed,

---

[15] Twenty-eight Roman miles. All distances in the translated portions are given in English miles. 🔖

[16] The soldier is punning on the two meanings of **equitēs**; literally *cavalry*, but also applied to the class of rich businessmen. 🔖

[17] The plain in which Caesar and Ariovistus were encamped was the plain of Alsace.

to hold their conference. The mounted legion that Caesar had brought was posted some three hundred yards away from the mound, and Ariovistus' horsemen took up their position at an equal distance. The king stipulated that they should confer on horseback, each accompanied by ten men. On reaching the place Caesar began by recalling the favours that he himself and the Senate had conferred on Ariovistus—how he had been honoured with the titles of 'King' and 'Friend', and had received handsome presents—pointing out that very few princes had been granted such distinctions, which were usually reserved for those who had rendered important services to Rome. 'You would have had no right,' he said, 'to apply to the Senate for any such favours; you owe them entirely to my kindness and my generosity and that of the Senate. The friendship between my country and the Aedui is of long standing and founded on solid grounds. Resolutions of the Senate, expressed in most complimentary terms, have repeatedly been passed in their honour. They held a position of supremacy in Gaul all along, even before they sought our friendship; and since it has always been our policy to see that our allies and friends, far from losing anything they had already, should have their credit, honour and importance increased, how can we allow them to be robbed of what they already had when they became our friends?' He then repeated the demands which he had instructed his envoys to present—that Ariovistus should not make war on the Aedui or their allies; that he should restore their hostages; and even if he could not send any of the Germans back home, he should at least not let any more cross the Rhine.

[44] Ariovistus had little to say in reply to these demands, but spoke at length about his own merits. He had crossed the Rhine, he said, not of his own accord but in response to the invitation of the Gauls, and it had needed the prospect of a rich reward to induce him to leave his home and his relatives. The possessions he had in Gaul had been ceded to him by the Gauls themselves, and the hostages had been given voluntarily. As for the tribute he exacted, this was customarily regarded as the right of a victorious belligerent. He had not been the aggressor: the Gauls had attacked him, all their tribes having marched out and taken the field against him. He had completely routed their entire force in a single battle. If they wanted to try their luck again, he was quite ready for another fight; if they wanted peace, it was unfair for them to object to the tribute that they had hitherto paid without demur. The friendship of the Roman people ought to be a distinction and a protection to him, not an occasion of loss, and it was with this expectation that he had sought it. If through Roman interference his subjects were absolved from payment and withdrawn from his control, he would be just as ready to discard that friendship as he had been to seek it. The large numbers of Germans he was bringing into Gaul were brought to secure his safety, not for aggression; the proof of that was that he had not come till he was asked, and had fought only in self-defence. However, he had come there before the Romans, whose armies had never before marched beyond the frontier of the Province. What did Caesar mean by invading his dominions?

'This part of the country,' he said, 'is my province, just as the other part is yours. I could not expect you to let me make raids into your territory with impunity, and it is a gross injustice for you to interfere with me in the exercise of my lawful rights. You say that the Aedui have been called "Brothers" by the Roman Senate. Well, I may be a "Barbarian"; but I am not such a barbarian, and not so ignorant, as not to know that in the recent revolt of the Allobroges [61 BCE] you got no help from the Aedui, and that they had to do without the benefit of your assistance in the war they have just fought with me and the Sequani. I suspect that this talk of friendship is just so much pretence, and that your object in keeping an army in Gaul is to crush me. Unless you take yourself off from this country, and your army with you, it won't be as a "Friend" that I shall treat you. In fact, if I killed you, there are plenty of nobles and politicians in Rome who would thank me for it; I know this, because they themselves commissioned their agents to tell me so. I could make them all my grateful friends by putting an end to you. But if you will go away and leave me in undisturbed possession of Gaul I will reward you handsomely, and whenever you want a war fought, I will see the job through for you, without your lifting a finger or running any risk!'

[45] Caesar explained at some length why he could not think of abandoning his intention. It was contrary to his principles and to those of the Roman government to desert a loyal ally; and he could not admit that Gaul belonged to Ariovistus any more than to Rome. The Arverni and the Ruteni had been conquered by Quintus Fabius Maximus [121 BCE], although the Roman people afterwards pardoned their hostility and refrained from annexing their land or exacting tribute from them. If priority of arrival was to be the criterion, the Romans' title to rule Gaul was unimpeachable. If they were to abide by the decision of the Senate, Gaul ought to be independent, since the Senate had determined that, although conquered, it should be allowed self-government.

[46] While these questions were being argued, word was brought to Caesar that Ariovistus' horsemen were approaching nearer the mound, riding towards our soldiers, and throwing stones and javelins at them. Caesar broke off the conversation, went to his men, and forbade them to throw a single missile in retaliation. For although he knew that a legion of picked troops could engage cavalry without the slightest risk, he did not choose to give anyone the chance of saying, if the enemy were driven off, that he had broken his word by treacherously attacking them during a parley. When the news spread through the ranks of the army that Ariovistus had arrogantly warned the Romans off the whole of Gaul, and that his cavalry had interrupted the conference by attacking our troops, the men's enthusiasm and eagerness for battle knew no bounds.

[47] The next day Ariovistus sent envoys to Caesar to say that he wished to resume their interrupted discussion, and to ask him either to appoint a day for another personal interview, or, if he did not want to do that, to send an officer to repre-

sent him. Caesar did not see that anything was to be gained by a further interview, especially as on the previous day Ariovistus had been unable to restrain his men from attacking the Roman troops, and he thought it would be running a great risk to send a Roman officer and place him at the mercy of such savages. He decided that his best plan was to send Gaius Valerius Procillus, a young man of high character and liberal education, whose father Gaius Valerius Caburus had been granted Roman citizenship by Gaius Valerius Flaccus. Procillus was a man who could be trusted. His knowledge of the Gallic language would be useful, since by long practice Ariovistus had learnt to speak it fluently; and in his case the Germans would have no motive for foul play. With him he sent Marcus Metius, who was bound to Ariovistus by ties of hospitality, and their orders were to hear what the king had to say, and report to Caesar. But as soon as Ariovistus saw them at his camp headquarters, he shouted out in front of his whole army: 'What are you coming here for? To play the spy, I suppose?' And when they attempted to speak, he stopped them and had them put in chains.

[48] On the same day he advanced and took up a position at the foot of a mountain six miles from Caesar's camp. The next day he marched his army past the camp and himself encamped two miles farther on, with the object of intercepting the convoys of grain and other supplies that were being sent up from the Sequani and the Aedui. On each of the five days following, Caesar led his troops out in front of his camp and kept them for some time in line of battle, so as to give Ariovistus the opportunity of fighting if he wanted to; but each day the king kept his main forces in camp, merely engaging in cavalry skirmishes. The Germans were trained in the use of a special battle technique. They had a force of six thousand cavalry, each of whom had selected from the whole army, for his personal protection, one infantryman of outstanding courage and speed of foot. These accompanied the cavalry in battle and acted as support for them to fall back upon. In a critical situation they ran to the rescue and surrounded any cavalryman who had been unhorsed by a severe wound. They acquired such agility by practice, that in a long advance or a quick retreat they could hang on to the horses' manes and keep pace with them.

[49] Caesar saw that the Germans were not going to come out of their camp, and since he could not afford to be cut off from supplies any longer, he chose a suitable site for a camp about a thousand yards beyond the enemy's position, and marched there in battle formation of three lines. The first and second lines were ordered to stand by under arms; the third, to make fortifications for the camp. The place being less than a mile away, Ariovistus sent some sixteen thousand light infantry and all his cavalry to overawe our soldiers and prevent them from continuing the work. Caesar, however, did not vary his original plan; the first two lines were told to drive off the enemy, while the third finished their task. When the entrenchments of the camp were completed, he left two legions and a detachment of auxiliaries to occupy it, and led the other four legions back to the large camp.

[50] The next day he followed his usual routine by bringing the troops out of both camps, deploying them for action a short distance from the large camp, and offering battle. Finding that even then the enemy would not come out, he returned to camp about midday, whereupon Ariovistus at last sent a detachment to attack the small camp, and a hotly contested battle was kept up until evening. At sunset, after severe casualties had been sustained by both sides, Ariovistus retired. On inquiring from prisoners why he would not fight a general engagement, Caesar was told that the German matrons, who used to draw lots and employ other methods of divination to decide whether it was advisable to join battle, had pronounced that the Germans were not destined to win if they fought before the new moon.

[51] Next day, leaving adequate garrisons in the two camps, Caesar posted all his auxiliaries in front of the small camp, where they would be visible to the enemy and give an impression of strength—since his regular infantry was numerically weak in comparison with the Germans. He then drew up the legions for action in three lines and advanced right up to Ariovistus' camp. The enemy was now compelled to lead his forces out, and drew up the various tribal contingents at equal intervals—Harudes, Marcomanni, Triboci, Vangiones, Nemetes, Eudusii, and Suebi. So that there might be no hope of escaping by flight, they formed a barrier of carriages and wagons along the rear of their whole line, and in them placed their women, who as the men marched to battle stretched out their hands and implored them with tears not to let them be enslaved by the Romans.

[52] Caesar placed each of his five generals ahead of a legion and detailed his quaestor to command the remaining legion, so that every soldier might know that there was a high officer in a position to observe the courage with which he conducted himself, and then led the right wing first into action, because he had noticed that the enemy's line was weakest on that side. Our troops attacked with such vigour when the signal was given, and the enemy also dashed forward so suddenly and swiftly, that there was no time to throw spears at them. So the men dropped their spears and fought hand to hand with their swords. By quickly adopting their usual phalanx formation the Germans were able to withstand the sword thrusts, but many of our soldiers actually threw themselves on the wall of shields confronting them, wrenched the shields out of the enemy's hands, and stabbed them from above. The Germans' left was thus routed, but their right began to press our troops hard by weight of numbers. Their perilous position attracted the attention of young Publius Crassus, who was in charge of the cavalry and better able to move about and see what was happening than those in the fighting line. He therefore sent up the third line to their relief.

[53] This move turned the battle once more in our favour, and the enemy's whole army broke and fled without stopping until they came to the Rhine, some

fifteen miles away.[18] A very few of the strongest tried to swim the river, and a few others saved themselves by finding boats—including Ariovistus, who had the luck to come across a small craft moored to the bank. All the rest were hunted down and killed by our cavalry. Ariovistus' two wives both perished in the flight—one a Suebic woman whom he had brought from Germany, the other a Norican whom his brother King Voccio sent to him while he was in Gaul; and of his two daughters, one was killed and the other captured. Valerius Procillus was being dragged along by his guards among the German fugitives, fettered with three chains, when Caesar himself, who was with the pursuing cavalry, came up with him. This fortunate chance pleased Caesar as much as the actual victory, for the man whom it rescued from the enemy's clutches and restored to him was the worthiest in the whole Province, besides being his own friend and host; and his death, which Providence thus averted, would have marred the pleasure and rejoicing that attended so splendid a triumph. Procillus recounted how, before his very eyes, the German had three times cast lots to decide whether he should be burnt to death at once or reserved for execution later, and how he owed his life to the way the lots had fallen. Metius also was found and brought back to Caesar.

[54] When the news of the battle reached the other side of the Rhine, the Suebi, who had advanced as far as the river bank, turned back homewards, and the Rhineland tribes, seeing what a panic they were in, pursued and killed a large number of them. Caesar had completed two important campaigns in a single summer. He now took the army into winter quarters in the country of the Sequani[19] somewhat earlier than the usual time of year, and leaving Labienus in command started for northern Italy to hold the assizes.[20]

---

[18] According to the manuscripts of Caesar's text the Rhine was 'some five miles' away from the battlefield. But although the site of the battle cannot be certainly identified, none of the possible sites is less than twelve miles from the Rhine. Perhaps the numeral should be xv instead of v.

[19] The winter quarters of the legions in the country of the Sequani were presumably at Besançon. The fact that Caesar did not withdraw them to the Province for the winter made it clear for the first time that he intended to attempt the conquest of Gaul. Apart from his personal ambition, it might be urged that the only way of preventing renewed German invasions was to hold the Rhine frontier..

[20] An assize (lit., *a sitting*, < Fr. **assise** < Lat. **assessus**, perf. part. of **ad** + **sedeō**) is a court session held periodically in a particular location by a travelling judge. As governor of Cisalpine Gaul and Illyricum, Caesar had to visit cities in these provinces and hear cases that required a decision from him; he normally did this during the winter. ✍

Questions

1. What had the political situation in Gaul been? How was it changed by the arrival of the Germans?

2. Caesar was governor of Transalpine Gaul but had not been authorized to conduct military operations beyond its borders. With this in mind, evaluate the reasons Caesar gives for undertaking a war against Ariovistus. What motive does he not mention which may have played a part in his decision?

3. How does Caesar portray Ariovistus? Cite specific examples from the text. Why might Caesar have characterized Ariovistus this way? How was Caesar's own behavior different?

4. How does Ariovistus compare with Gallic leaders like Dumnorix?

5. Why would it not be surprising that the military tribunes and prefects of cavalry were the first to panic (§39)? What factors in addition to those Caesar mentions might have contributed to the fear his men felt?

6. Caesar says that his intervention (§§40–41) successfully dealt with the potential mutiny by his troops. Why were his actions effective?

7. Do you find the arguments that Ariovistus makes (§§36 and 44) against Roman interventions reasonable? Why or why not? How does Caesar respond to them? Do you find it surprising that Caesar included them in his account?

8. Why might some Gallic tribes have been willing to accept Roman rule while others did not? What were the advantages and disadvantages of Roman imperialism for conquered peoples and for the Romans themselves?

This engraving shows Caesar's fleet arriving in Britain. Cliffs of white chalk line this part of the British coast, which is closest to Gaul. There is a natural break in the cliffs at what is now the town of Dover, in the center of the picture, with a good natural harbor. Caesar had probably learned of this harbor from his officer Volusenus, whom he had sent in a galley to scout the coast. However, Caesar was forced by the Britons to land further east, as he describes in the passage below.

* * * * * * * * *

Caesar reached Britain about the fourth hour of the day with the first of his ships and there he caught sight of the armed enemy troops drawn up on all the hills. The nature of this place was such and the sea was so closely bordered by hills that from these heights a spear could be thrown onto the beach. Thinking that this was in no way a suitable place for disembarking, he waited at anchor into the ninth hour, until the other ships could assemble. . . . Having caught both a favorable wind and the tide at the same time, after giving the signal and weighing anchor, he advanced about seven miles from this place and grounded his ships on an open and flat beach. (*De bello Gallico* 4.23)

Book IV

55 BCE

THE FOURTH YEAR of Caesar's governorship of Gaul included two important events: a campaign against the Germans and an expedition to Britain. Although neither was intended to bring additional territory under Roman control, these events are notable because for the first time Roman troops crossed the Rhine and the English Channel.

Once Caesar had decided to bring all of Gaul into the Roman empire, he wanted to establish the Rhine as a clear boundary. Two German tribes, the Usipetes and the Tencteri, had crossed into Gaul to raid and withdrew after suffering severe losses. To discourage any further incursions, Caesar built a wooden bridge over the Rhine, a remarkable feat of engineering. He punished the Sugambri, who had aided the Usipetes and Tencteri, took steps to protect the Ubii (the only Germans to ally themselves with Rome) from the large tribe of the Suebi, and returned to Gaul after eighteen days.

The Romans had very little information about Britain, although they knew that the Britons had been aiding tribes in Gaul that were unwilling to accept Roman rule. After his campaign against the Germans, Caesar realized that there was not enough time left before winter for a full-scale assault on Britain, but he decided to take two legions and go to see what he could learn about the island, as well as to make it clear that the Romans would not tolerate the tribes there helping those in Gaul who wanted to keep up the fight against Rome.

Meanwhile a delegation from several British tribes came to Caesar and promised to give him hostages and to accept Roman rule. Caesar encouraged them in this decision and sent Commius, king of the Gallic Atrebates, back to Britain with them to persuade additional tribes to accept the Roman presence. Caesar sailed about 26 August with 80 transport ships carrying the Seventh and Tenth Legions. Eighteen additional ships carrying cavalry were to leave as soon as they were ready.

Caesar made landfall near what is now the town of Dover. He was not able to disembark his men there because the Britons had taken up positions on the adjacent hills, as he describes in the passage from *De bello Gallico* printed on the opposite page. Caesar eventually landed on a flat shoreline, probably near the modern town of Walder. The Britons had followed his movements and were ready to oppose the Romans' landing, as you will read in the selection from Book IV presented in Latin on the following pages.

1 **barbarī**: what effect was Caesar's use of this word to describe the Britons meant to have on the reader?

  praemittō, praemittere, praemīsī, praemissus, *to send ahead.*

  *equitātus, -ūs, m., *cavalry.*

  essedārius, -ī [< essedum, a type of chariot used by the Britons], m., *warrior who fights from a chariot.* Caesar gives more details about the **essedāriī** in §33.

2 *plērumque*, adv., *generally, mostly.*

  genus, generis, n., *type, class.*

  quō . . . genere: the relative pronoun **quō** appears to the left of its antecedent **genere**: *a type (of fighting) which,* referring both to cavalry and to chariot fighters. For this use of the ablative, see **A5o**.

  cōnsuēscō, cōnsuēscere, cōnsuēvī, cōnsuētus, *to become accustomed*; in perfect, *to be accustomed, to be in the habit.*

  subsequor, subsequī, subsecūtus sum, *to follow closely, follow.*

3 **nostrōs**: Caesar often uses the possessive adjectives **nostrī** and **suī** as substantives (**C2**), meaning *our (men)* and *their (men)* respectively.

  ēgredī prohibēbāt: **prohibeō** completed by an infin. = *prevent* (someone) *from.*

4 *propter*, prep. + acc., *because of, on account of.*

  magnitūdō, magnitūdinis, f., *large size, size.*

  altum, -ī [substantive < altus, -a, -um], n., *the deep, the sea.*

  nisi in altō: *except in deep (water).* **Nisi** here = *except*; it does not start a new clause (*unless . . .*).

  cōnstituī: you may know this verb = *decide*; its more basic meaning is *to establish, set up, arrange*; in military language it often means *to station, position* (troops, etc.). The transport ships were brought in as close to shore as possible, but the soldiers had to jump into perhaps four to five feet of water. Caesar describes this as "deep water" because the warships, which had shallower drafts, could get in closer, with their bows run onto the beach.

5 **mīlitibus**: dative of agent, connected with the three gerundive phrases found later in the sentence. See the Reading Strategy opposite for some help with this part of the sentence.

  ignōtus, -a, -um, *unknown.*

  ignōtīs locīs: this could be an abl. abs., parallel to the following phrase **impedītīs manibus**, = *the places (being) unknown, since the places were unknown*; it could also be an abl. of place where with **in** omitted = *in unknown places*, as often happens with the word **locus** (**B4b**).

  impedītus, -a, -um [in- + pēs, pedis; cf. expedītus, 1.6], *obstructed, impeded, hindered, burdened.*

  onus, oneris, n., *burden, load.*

6 *dēsiliō, dēsilīre, dēsiluī, dēsultūrus*, *to leap down, jump down.*

  dēsiliendum: **erat** (7) is gapped. This and the other two gerundives to make a phrase expressing obligation, *the soldiers had to . . .*

  flūctus, -ūs, m., *wave.*

  cōnsistō, cōnsistere, cōnstitī, *to halt, stand, take a stand*; of soldiers, *to take a position*, i.e., get their footing.

The Britons oppose Caesar's landing.

1 [24] At barbarī, cōnsiliō Rōmānōrum cognitō, praemissō equitātū et esse-
2 dāriīs, quō plērumque genere in proeliīs ūtī cōnsuērunt, reliquīs cōpiīs sub-
3 secūtī nostrōs nāvibus ēgredī prohibēbant. Erat ob hās causās summa diffi-
4 cultās, quod nāvēs propter magnitūdinem nisi in altō cōnstituī nōn pote-
5 rant, mīlitibus autem, ignōtīs locīs, impedītīs manibus, magnō et gravī onere
6 armōrum oppressīs simul et dē nāvibus dēsiliendum et in flūctibus cōn-
7 sistendum et cum hostibus erat pugnandum;   (continued)

Initial Explorations

1. What did the Britons do first after realizing the Romans' intentions? (1–2)
2. What does Caesar tell us about this tactic? (2)
3. What did the Britons do next? How did this affect the Romans? (2–3)
4. What was the source of Caesar's difficulty? (4–5)
5. What three things did the Roman soldiers have to do? (5–7)
6. Give three reasons why it was difficult for them to do this. (5–6)

Reading Strategies

◆ **mīlitibus autem . . . pugnandum** (above: 5–7) is complex. On a first reading you might notice a bunch of ablatives and then three gerundives. After a second reading, you might realize that Caesar is telling three things that the soldiers had to do, with the help of the notes about **erat** being gapped and connecting the dative **mīlitibus** with the gerundives. The three phrases between **mīlitibus autem** and the gerundives describe the situation in which the soldiers found themselves. The first two are ablative absolutes; then Caesar switches to a participial phrase (**oppressīs** modifies the dative **mīlitibus**) for the third. **Autem** marks the transition from the first source of difficulty, the ships' inability to be run onto the shore, to the second, the difficulties the soldiers encountered while going ashore.

◆ You might find it useful to break down long sentences, such as the second sentence in this chapter, into sense units. See page 15 for a model.

◆ This sentence continues on page 77. The **cum** clause (lines 8–9) that describes the Britons is not as complex as the preceding portions of the sentence, but notice that Caesar again uses a participial phrase and two ablative absolutes, parallel to those used in the preceding description of the Romans, to describe the circumstances of the British fighters. The similar language reinforces the contrast between the situation in which the Romans found themselves, as compared with the Britons; study it carefully.

8   **illī**: = *they,* the Britons; as often, **ille** marks a change of subject.
   *āridum, -ī, n., *dry land, land.*
   *paulum, -ī, n., *a little.*
   *membrum, -ī, n., *limb.*
9 *nōtus, -a, -um, *well known, familiar.*
   *tēlum, -ī, n., *spear.*
   *coiciō, coicere, coiēcī, coiectus [con + iaciō], *to throw.* You would expect this
      word to be spelled **coiiciō**, but the Romans wrote it with only one 'i.' How-
      ever, the 'y' sound is still pronounced: co-yicio. Recall that a short 'a' or 'e' in
      a verb stem becomes a short 'i' in compounds: e.g., **reficiō** from **faciō**.
   īnsuēfactus, -a, -um, *accustomed; trained, well trained.*
10 *pugna, -ae, f., *fight*
   *imperītus, -a, -um, *inexperienced, unskilled.*
11 **alacritās, alacritātis, f.,** *speed, quickness.*
   *studium, -ī, n., *enthusiasm, zeal*
   pedester, pedestris, pedestre, *on foot,* i.e., on land.
   quō . . . cōnsuerant: this rel. clause is nested inside the clause **nōn eādem . . .
      ūtēbantur.** Remember that **ūtor** takes the abl.; **quō** is the object of **ūtī,** while
      eādem alacritāte ac studiō are the objects of **ūtēbantur** (12).

1 *animadvertō, animadvertere, animadvertī, animadversus [< animus + vertō],
      to observe, notice, perceive.
   nāvēs longās: *galleys, warships,* so called because they were designed for speed
      and hence narrow relative to their length, compared to transport ships (**nāvēs
      onerāriae**), which were wider and deeper in order to have room for cargo.
   speciēs, speciēī, f., *appearance.*
2 **inūsitātus, -a, -um,** *unfamiliar.*
   *mōtus, mōtūs [< mōtus, -a, -um, past part. of moveō], m., *movement.*
   *ūsus, ūsūs [< ūsus, -a, -um, past part. of ūtor], m., *use.*
   *onerārius, -a, -um [< onus, oneris, load], *designed for cargo.*
3 **rēmus, -ī, m.,** *oar.*
   *latus, lateris, n., *side.*
   *apertus, -a, -um [perf. part. of aperiō, to open], *open; unprotected.*
   latus apertum: soldiers carried their shields on their left arms and therefore were
      more vulnerable to attack from the right side.
4 *inde, adv., *from there.*
   *funda, -ae, f., *slingshot.*
   sagitta, -ae, f., *arrow.*
   **tormentum, -ī [< torqueō, to twist, because twisted ropes provided the power],
      n., *catapult.*
   *prōpellō, prōpellere, prōpulī, prōpulsus, *to drive forward; to drive away.*
   submoveō, submovēre, submōvī, submōtus, *to move away.*
   quae rēs: a linking **quī,** *(and) this action . . . .*
5 **magnō ūsuī nostrīs**: a double dative (**A3i**).
   figūra, -ae, f., *appearance.*
   pedem referre, idiom, *to bring one's foot back, withdraw, retreat.*

8   cum illī aut ex āridō aut paulum in aquam prōgressī, omnibus membris expe-
9   dītīs, nōtissimīs locīs, audācter tēla coicerent et equōs īnsuefactōs incitārent.
10 Quibus rēbus nostrī perterritī atque huius omnīnō generis pugnae imperītī, nōn
11 eādem alacritāte ac studiō quō in pedestribus ūtī proeliīs cōnsuerant ūtēbantur.

> 7. How was the situation different for the Britons? (8–9)
> 8. What were the Britons doing? (9)
> 9. In what two ways does Caesar describe his troops at this point? (10)
> 10. How did they behave as a result? (10–11)

Caesar sends help; one soldier's courage inspires the others.

1 [25] Quod ubi Caesar animadvertit, nāvēs longās, quārum et speciēs erat
2 barbarīs inūsitātior et mōtus ad ūsum expedītior, paulum removērī ab one-
3 rāriīs nāvibus et rēmīs incitārī et ad latus apertum hostium cōnstituī atque
4 inde fundīs, sagittīs, tormentīs hostēs prōpellī ac summovērī iussit; quae rēs
5 magnō ūsuī nostrīs fuit. Nam et nāvium figūrā et rēmōrum mōtū et inūsitātō
6 genere tormentōrum permōtī barbarī cōnstitērunt ac paulum modo pedem
7 rettulērunt.   (continued)

Initial Explorations
1. In what two ways does Caesar describe the warships? (1–2)
2. What orders did he give for the movement of the warships? (2–3)
3. What were the warships to do once in position? (4)
4. How does Caesar describe this maneuver (4–5)
5. By what things were the Britons distressed? (5–6)
6. What did they do in response? (6–7)

Reading Strategies

- nāvēs (25:1) clearly begins a clause, and longās suggests that it is acc. not nom. pl. Then a relative clause begun by quārum interrupts it and turns out to be a two-part clause completed at expedītior. The nāvēs-clause resumes with paulum removērī, but the reason for the infinitive is not immediately clear. As you continue reading you see four more passive infinitives (incitārī, cōnstituī, prōpellī, summovērī); the infinitive phrases are connected by et and ac. Finally the structure becomes clear when you reach iussit at the end of the sentence.

- Noticing parallelism is key to understanding this sentence. The PARALLEL STRUC-TURE in the relative clause (quārum . . .) helps you realize that erat (1) must be supplied in the second half. The multiple infinitive phrases raise the expectation that a verb will govern them all, an expectation fullfilled by iussit (4).

8 **cūnctor, -ārī, -ātus sum**, to *delay, hesitate.*

*****altitūdō, altitūdinis** [< altus, tall, deep], f., *height; depth.*

9 **quī: = is quī.** The sentence provides a strong indication that an antecedent must be supplied; can you figure out what that indication is? (Hint: think about the rules that govern relative pronouns.)

decimus, -a, -um, *tenth.* Each legion had a number to identify it.

*****aquila, -ae,** f., *eagle.* The eagle, the bird of Jupiter, was used as a symbol of the Roman state, and each legion carried an eagle among its standards. See the coin on page 81, which depicts an **aquila,** as well as the drawing below.

contestor, -ārī, -ātus sum [< testis, witness], *to call to witness, call upon, appeal to.* The **aquilifer** (*eagle-bearer*) prays to the gods before starting for shore.

10 **fēliciter,** *fortunately, successfully.*

ēveniō, ēvenīre, ēvēnī, ēventūrus [ē + veniō], *to come out, turn out.* For the use of **ut** + subjunct. with this verb and others like it, see **N3c.**

*****prōdō, prōdere, prōdidī, prōditus** [prō + dō, dare], *to hand over, hand down; to betray.*

11 *****imperātor, imperātōris,** m., *commander, general.*

*****officium, -ī,** n., *duty, service.*

praestiterō: in this context **praestō** = *to provide, offer.*

12 **nāvī:** Caesar often uses **nāvī** rather than **nāve** for the abl. sing. of this noun.

13 *****coepī, coepisse, coeptus,** *to begin.* This verb is used only in the perfect, pluperfect, and future perfect tenses.

*****cohortor, -ārī, -ātus sum,** *to encourage.*

dēdecus, dēdecoris, n., *shame, disgrace.*

admittō, admittere, admīsī, admissus, *to let in; to become guilty, commit* (crime).

14 *****ūniversus, -a, -um** [ūnus + vertō, lit., turned into one], *all together.*

†proximīs prīmīs†: see the Text note opposite.

15 **appropinquārunt:** for the form, see **F2h.**

Signa mīlitāria.

8 Atque nostrīs mīlitibus cūnctantibus, maximē propter altitūdinem maris,
9 quī decimae legiōnis aquilam ferēbat, contestātus deōs, ut ea rēs legiōnī
10 fēlīciter ēvenīret, 'Dēsilīte,' inquit, 'mīlitēs, nisi vultis aquilam hostibus prō-
11 dere: ego certē meum reī pūblicae atque imperātōrī officium praestiterō.'
12 Hoc cum vōce magnā dīxisset, sē ex nāvī prōiēcit atque in hostēs aquilam
13 ferre coepit. Tum nostrī cohortātī inter sē, nē tantum dēdecus admitterētur,
14 ūniversī ex nāvī dēsiluērunt. Hōs item ex †proximīs prīmīs† nāvibus cum
15 cōnspexissent, subsecūtī hostibus appropinquārunt.

7. Why were the soldiers not eager to jump down? (8)
8. Who spoke to the soldiers? (9)
9. What did he do first? (9–10)
10. What did he say? (10–11)
11. Describe two things that this man did after finishing his speech. (12–13)
12. How did the soldiers on his ship react? (13–14)
13. What did the soldiers on nearby ships do? (15)

Discussion

1. At several points in *De bello Gallico*, Caesar describes the bravery of individual soldiers—usually centurions, but sometimes others such as the **aquilifer** in this passage. What did Caesar hope to gain by relating this anecdote?

Text

♦ Because all books in Antiquity and the Middle Ages were copied by hand, it was easy for errors to be introduced. Sometimes scribes were just careless; they also made other sorts of mistakes, such as substituting a familiar word for an unfamiliar one that looks like it. Scholars compare the readings from a number of manuscripts to establish the most reliable text. Usually the oldest manuscripts have the fewest errors.

♦ All the manuscripts of Caesar read **ex proximīs prīmīs nāvibus** (above: 14), which would mean *from the first closest ships*. This is not impossible but seems strange. The editor of the Oxford Classical Text placed two words between daggers (†). This convention indicates a problem with the text for which the editor is not confident of the correct reading.

♦ A 19th century scholar named Madvig suggested reading **prīmī** instead of **prīmīs**, where **prīmī** = *leaders*. Others have suggested that since the two words **prīmīs** and **proximīs** are almost synonyms, one of them crept in by accident and should be deleted. Which of these suggestions makes more sense to you?

1 **Pugnātum est ācriter:** *It was fought fiercely,* less lit., *There was fierce fighting, The fighting was fierce.* This is an impersonal passive; see **F3d**.

   *ācriter, adv., *fiercely.*

   *uterque, utraque, utrumque, *each* (of two), *both.*

   ab utrīsque: *by both sides,* less lit., *on both sides.*

   *ōrdō, ōrdinis, m., *order;* (military) *formation, rank.*

2 *servō, -āre, -āvī, -ātus, *to save, preserve.*

   ōrdinēs servāre: Roman troops were carefully trained to move and fight as part of a unit. This level of discipline was an important element in the Romans' military success and distinguished them from many of the peoples against whom they fought, including the Gauls. In this situation, the Romans are experiencing so much difficulty in getting ashore that they cannot easily form up into their cohorts, which made them less effective and also demoralized them, since they were not accustomed to fighting this way.

   firmiter [adv. from firmus, -a, -um], *firmly, steadily.*

   *īnsistō, īnsistere, īnstitī, *to stand on; to push forward, advance.*

   *signum, -ī, n., *sign, signal; standard.* Each unit in a Roman legion had its own **signum,** a symbol mounted on a pole; soldiers knew how to move in battle by following the **signum** of their unit. See the coin opposite.

   alius aliā ex nāvī: *one from one ship, (another from another),* less lit., *men from different ships.* This is a kind of gapping and is common in Latin.

3 *quīcumque, quaecumque, quodcumque, *whichever, whatever.*

   *occurrō, occurrere, occurrī, occursūrus + dat., *to meet.*

   aggregō, -āre, -āvī, -ātus [ad + grex, gregis, flock, herd], *to join.*

   magnopere, adv. from **magnus, -a, -um,** *greatly.*

   *perturbō, -āre, -āvī, -ātus, *to disturb, confuse.*

4 *vērō [adv. from vērus, -a, -um, true], *in truth, truly, indeed; however.*

   lītus, lītoris, n., *shore.*

   *aliquī, aliquae, aliquod, *some.*

   *singulāris, -is, -e, *single, one at a time, individual.*

5 cōnspexerant: *when(ever) they caught sight of . . . they attacked;* see the Structure note on pages 82–83.

   incitātīs equīs: the verb **incitō, -āre** is often translated *to urge on, spur on.* But a non-literal English equivalent *such as with their horses at full speed* conveys better what was happening.

   *adorior, adorīrī, adortus sum [ad + orior] *to rise up against, attack.*

6 *paucī, -ae, -a, *a few.*

   plūrēs paucōs: note the juxtaposition of these two words which, along with the ASYNDETON, emphasize the Romans' situation.

   *circumsistō, circumsistere, circumstetī, *to take a stand around; to surround.*

The Romans struggle to get ashore.

1 [26] Pugnātum est ab utrīsque ācriter. Nostrī tamen, quod neque ōrdinēs
2 servāre neque firmiter īnsistere neque signa subsequī poterant atque alius
3 aliā ex nāvī quibuscumque signīs occurrerat sē aggregābat, magnopere per-
4 turbābantur; hostēs vērō, nōtīs omnibus vādīs, ubi ex lītore aliquōs singulā-
5 rēs ex nāvī ēgredientēs cōnspexerant, incitātīs equīs impedītōs adoriēban-
6 tur, plūrēs paucōs circumsistēbant; aliī ab latere apertō in ūniversōs tēla
7 coiciēbant.   (continued)

Initial Explorations

1. How does Caesar describe the fighting? (1)
2. What were three things that the Roman soldiers could not do? (1–2)
3. For what other reason were they disorganized? (2–3)
4. Why did the Britons have an advantage? (4)
5. How did the Britons deal with small groups of soldiers as they came ashore? (4–6)
6. What were other Britons doing that affected Caesar's forces as a whole? (6–7)

Structure: Prepositions with Compound Verbs

♦ To complete the meaning of a compound verb such as **ēgredior**, the Romans sometimes used a preposition (**ex nāvī ēgredientēs**, above: 5) and sometimes omitted the
preposition since it was already present in the verb (**nāvibus ēgredī**, 24:3). The two
usages are about equally common.

This silver denarius was minted by Mark Antony to pay his troops before the battle
of Actium (31 BCE). It shows a typical Roman warship (**nāvis longa**) with Antony's
name, abbreviated **ANT·AVG** = **Antōnius Augur**, and the letters **III·VIR·R·P·C** =
triumvir reī pūblicae cōnstituendae, *triumvir for the organization of the state*, the
legal title that was given to the members of the Second Triumvirate, on the obverse.
On the reverse are legionary standards, including the **aquila**, along with the legion's
identifying number, LEG XV.

8   **Quod:** i.e., the Britons attacking the Romans as the latter tried to land. A connecting relative (**N7**) that is neuter sing. refers to the general idea of the preceding sentence, unless there is a specific neuter noun to which it can refer.

scapha, -ae, f., *boat.*

speculātōrius, -a, -um, *designed for spying or scouting.*

9   **nāvigium, -ī,** n., *vessel, boat.*

speculātōria nāvigia: *scouting vessels.* Both the ships' boats from the galleys and the scouting vessels were small and could land troops in places where the large ships could not.

* **compleō, complēre, complēvī, complētus,** *to fill.*

labōrantēs: this verb can mean *to suffer, struggle, be in difficulty* as well as *to work.*

10   ***subsidium, -ī,** n., *assistance, aid.*

simul: = **simul atque,** *as soon as.*

cōnstitērunt: *got a firm footing* (lit., *took a stand*).

11   **cōnsequor, cōnsequī, cōnsecūtus sum,** *to catch up.*

***impetus, -ūs,** m., *attack.*

***fuga, -ae,** f., *flight.*

in fugam dare, *to give into flight, put to flight,* i.e., *cause to flee.*

12   **longius:** *too far.*

prōsequī: deduce from **prō + sequor.**

equitēs: Caesar had ordered the cavalry he planned to take to Britain to sail in eighteen ships separate from his main fleet. The departure of these ships was delayed because the cavalry took too long to board and the ships missed the tide. In this sentence **equitēs** refers to the ships carrying the cavalry.

***cursus, -ūs,** m., *course.*

capere: in this context = *to reach* (not *to capture*). Caesar could not pursue the Britons once they fled from the shore since he had no cavalry.

13   **ad:** *in reference to, in comparison to, relative to.*

***prīstinus, -a, -um,** *former, original; previous.*

ad prīstinam fortūnam: this is ironic since in §28 Caesar will describe some serious setbacks the Romans experienced.

***dēsum, dēesse, dēfuī, dēfutūrus** + dat., *to be missing, be lacking.* The Romans said "Something is lacking to me" whereas we say "I lack something;" i.e., the thing lacked is the subject of **dēesse** and the person goes in the dative. Note that this is the same structural arrangement as with a dative of possession (e.g., **Caesarī sunt nāvēs,** *ships are to Caesar = Caesar has ships*); see **A3f.**

Structure: Tenses in General Statements

♦ In sentences that express generalizations or repeated actions, the perfect and pluperfect are used in subordinate clauses where English would use the present and the simple past. E.g., **quōs labōrantēs cōnspexerat, hīs subsidia submittēbat** (opposite: 9–10) is literally translated *(Those) whom he had caught sight of in difficulty, to these he sent help(s).* A non-literal translation that better conveys Caesar's meaning would be *Whenever he caught sight of any in difficulty, he sent them help.*

8   Quod cum animadvertisset Caesar, scaphās longārum nāvium, item specu-
9   lātōria nāvigia mīlitibus complērī iussit, et, quōs labōrantēs cōnspexerat,
10 hīs subsidia submittēbat. Nostrī, simul in āridō cōnstitērunt, suīs omnibus
11 cōnsecūtīs, in hostēs impetum fēcērunt atque eōs in fugam dedērunt; neque
12 longius prōsequī potuērunt, quod equitēs cursum tenēre atque īnsulam ca-
13 pere nōn potuerant. Hoc ūnum ad prīstinam fortūnam Caesarī dēfuit.

　　7. What orders did Caesar give? (8–9)
　　8. What did he do then? (9–10)
　　9. When did the Roman soldiers attack the enemy? (10–11)
　 10. What was the result? (11)
　 11. Why could the Romans not pursue the Britons? (11–13)
　 12. What comment does Caesar make about his inability to pursue them? (13)

Reading Strategy

♦ You know that Latin has many compound verbs and that in most cases the meaning of the compound is clear from the meaning of the prefix and the root verb. E.g.,
saliō = *to leap* and **dēsiliō** = *to leap down*; **orior** = *to rise up* and **adorior** = *to rise up
against, attack*. You can enlarge your vocabulary easily by paying attention to such
compound verbs.

♦ In some cases the meaning of a compound is clear but is difficult to bring out in
English translation. For instance, **prōsequī** (above: 12) clearly expresses the idea of
following the Britons further as they retreated (**prō** in compounds often has this idea;
cf. **prōpellī**, 25:4). In line 11, **cōnsecūtīs** gives a clear picture of the soldiers leaving
the ships, following the men who had gone before, and gradually coming together
(**con-**) into formation in their units; *catch up* is an acceptable translation but does not
convey the whole picture.

♦ In other cases it is not clear to us, who are not native speakers of Latin, why a Roman author chose a compound over the simple verb. He probably had a reason but
the subtle distinction is lost on us. Caesar, for instance, usually uses the compound
coicere rather than the plain verb **iacere**, usually with no difference in meaning that
we can perceive.

(Structure note continued from opposite page)

♦ In such general statements, the pluperfect is used in general statements that refer to
the past (above: 9–10 and 4–6, page 81), while the perfect is used in those that refer
to the present. Here is an example with the perfect: **Sī quī Gallī Rōmānīs fāvērunt,
Caesar eīs praemia dat**, *If any Gauls support the Romans, Caesar gives them rewards.*

1 *superō, -āre, -āvī, -ātus, *to overcome, defeat.*
    simul atque, *as soon as.*
    sē recēpērunt: *recovered (themselves)*; not the idiom = *to withdraw.*

2 *obses, obsidis, m., *hostage.*
    obsidēs . . . pollicitī sunt: if you read the whole clause, you see that it is an indirect statement with the verb of saying at the end; **sēsē** is the subject accusative that works with both **datūrōs** and **factūrōs** (supply **esse** with both to make a future infinitive).
    quaeque: neuter plural relative pronoun with -**que** tacked onto the end (not a form of the word **quisque** = *each*).
    imperāsset: see **F2h** for the form. The pluperfect subjunctive inside indirect statement here replaces a perfect subjunctive; the direct statement would be **Pollicēmur nōs quae imperāveris factūrōs esse.**

3 *polliceor, pollicērī, pollicitus sum, *to promise.*
    Commius: see the Introduction to Book IV on page 73.
    *Atrebās, Atrebatis, m., *Atrebatian, member of the tribe of the Atrebates.*
    *suprā, adv., *above; previously.*
    *dēmōnstrō, -āre, -āvī, -ātus, *to point out, show, mention.*

4 **praemissum:** sc. **esse;** deduce the meaning from **prae** + **mittō.**
    Hunc: this sentence begins with a direct object, modified by **ē nāvī ēgressum;** the clause **cum . . . dēferret** is embedded inside the main clause **Hunc . . . comprehenderant.**
    illī: = **Britannī.**

5 **ōrātōris modo:** *in the manner of an orator,* i.e., as a spokesman or ambassador.
    **mandātum, -ī, n., *command, order.*
    *dēferō, dēferre, dētulī, dēlātus, irreg., *to carry down; to report, deliver.*

6 *comprehendō, comprehendere, comprehendī, comprehēnsus, *to seize.*

7 **culpa, -ae, f., *fault, blame.*
    multitūdinem: i.e., the common people; the British representatives claimed that the people of their tribes had been so hostile toward the Romans that they were forced to imprison Caesar's representative Commius.

8 **ignōscō, ignōscere, ignōvī, ignōtus** + dat., *to forgive, pardon.*
    ut ignōscerētur: the head verb **petīvērunt** is placed after the indirect command.
    **queror, querī, questus sum, *to complain.*
    questus: *although he complained. Although* is one possible translation for a participle, less frequently encounted than other meanings such as *because.*
    quod: after a verb expressing emotion, **quod** = *that.*

9 *ultrō, adv., *beyond, furthermore; voluntarily, without being asked.*
    *continēns, continentis [noun < contineō], f., *continent, mainland* (of Europe).
    sē: *him* (= Caesar); an INDIRECT REFLEXIVE (**E2b**).

10 **ignōscere . . . dīxit:** sc. **sē.**
    **imprūdentia, -ae, f., *lack of wisdom, poor judgment.*

11 *longinquus, -a, -um, *far away, distant.*
    **accersō, accersere, accersīvī, accersītus, *to call, summon.*

12 **remigrō, -āre, -āvī, -ātus [re- + migrō], *to move back, go back.*

13 **commendō, āre, -āvī, -ātus, *to commit for protection, entrust.*

The Britons sue for peace; Caesar tells the story of Commius.

1 [27] Hostēs proeliō superātī, simul atque sē ex fugā recēpērunt, statim ad
2 Caesarem lēgātōs dē pāce mīsērunt; obsidēs datūrōs quaeque imperāsset
3 sēsē factūrōs pollicitī sunt. Ūnā cum hīs lēgātīs Commius Atrebās vēnit,
4 quem suprā dēmōnstrāveram ā Caesare in Britanniam praemissum. Hunc
5 illī ē nāvī ēgressum, cum ad eōs ōrātōris modo Caesaris mandāta dēferret,
6 comprehenderant atque in vincula coiēcerant; tum proeliō factō remīsē-
7 runt. In petendā pāce eius reī culpam in multitūdinem coiēcērunt et prop-
8 ter imprūdentiam ut ignōscerētur petīvērunt. Caesar questus quod, cum
9 ultrō in continentem lēgātīs missīs pācem ab sē petīssent, bellum sine causā
10 intulissent, ignōscere imprūdentiae dīxit obsidēsque imperāvit; quōrum illī
11 partem statim dedērunt, partem ex longinquiōribus locīs accersītam paucīs
12 diēbus sēsē datūrōs dīxērunt. Intereā suōs remigrāre in agrōs iussērunt,
13 prīncipēsque undique convenīre et sē cīvitātēsque suās Caesarī commen-
14 dāre coepērunt.

Initial Explorations
1. What did the Britons do after they recovered from their defeat? (1–2)
2. What promises did they make? (2–3)
3. Who was Commius and what was his connection to Caesar? (3–4)
4. What was Commius doing? (4–5)
5. What had the Britons done to him? (4–6)
6. Whom did the ambassadors blame for the treatment of Commius? (7)
7. What request did they make? (7–8)
8. What complaint did Caesar make first? (8–10)
9. What was his actual response to the Britons (two items)? (10)
10. What happened regarding the hostages (two items)? (10–12)
11. What did the Britons order their men to do? (12)
12. What action did the British chieftains take? (13–14)

1 **post diem quārtam quam:** *on the fourth day after.* The Romans counted inclusively; we would say on the third day. The date was about 30 August.

 est . . . ventum: *it was arrived,* less literal, *they arrived, the arrival took place.* This is an impersonal passive (see **F3d**).

2 **dē quibus . . . dēmōnstrātum est:** Caesar first mentions this in §4.22 (not included in this book) and alludes to it in 4.26, page 82.

3 ***superior, superiōris,** higher.* Caesar's main fleet sailed from a harbor he calls Portus Itius, which may be the modern city of Boulogne. The transport ships had been prevented by unfavorable winds from joining the main fleet, and Caesar had ordered them to assemble at what he calls the "upper port," probably Ambleteuse, slightly north of Boulogne.

 portus, -ūs, m., *harbor.*

 lēnis, -is, -e, *soft, gentle.*

 solvō, solvere, solvī, solūtus, *to set free, release, untie; to set sail* (referring to untying the ropes that held a ship to the dock).

4 ***tempestās, tempestātis,** f., *weather; storm.* The storm probably came from the northeast.

 ***coorior, coorīrī, coortus sum,** *to arise.*

5 ***unde,** adv., *from where.*

6 **ad īnferiōrem partem īnsulae:** as before, Caesar uses *lower* to mean further from his own position; i.e., the ships were driven further along the coast.

 ***propius,** adv., *nearer.* This adverb is derived from the preposition **prope** and, like **prope,** is followed by an accusative noun.

 sōlis occāsum: *the setting of the sun,* i.e., the west.

7 **suī:** genitive of the pronoun **sē**; it modifies **perīculō,** *danger of themselves,* less lit., *to themselves.*

 ***dēiciō, dēicere, dēiēcī, dēiectus,** *to throw down;* (of a ship) *to drive off course.* For the pronunciation of compounds of **iaciō**, see note for 24:9, page 76.

 ***ancora, -ae,** f., *anchor.*

8 **cum:** the subjunctive verb **complērentur** shows that this is the conjunction, not the preposition (**flūctibus** is an abl. of means); the impf. subj. = *were beginning to fill* (lit., *to be filled*). Apparently the sailors' attempts to keep the ships in position with anchors made things worse since they took on more water.

 necessāriō, adv., *necessarily, of necessity.*

 adversus, -a, -um [past part. of advertō, to turn toward], *turned towards, facing; standing opposite.*

 adversā nocte: *when night was facing,* less lit., *when night was approaching, as night was falling.*

 prōvehō, prōvehere, prōvexī, prōvectus, *to carry forwards, carry along;* in pass., *move, advance, sail, put out to sea.*

9 **continentem petiērunt:** even if they had been able to remain on the coast of Britain, the cavalry transports were far from Caesar's camp and would have been attacked by the Britons if they had landed.

The cavalry fails to arrive.

1 [28] Hīs rēbus pāce cōnfirmātā, post diem quārtum quam est in Britanni-
2 am ventum nāvēs xviii, dē quibus suprā dēmōnstrātum est, quae equitēs
3 sustulerant, ex superiōre portū lēnī ventō solvērunt. Quae cum appropin-
4 quārent Britanniae et ex castrīs vidērentur, tanta tempestās subitō coorta
5 est ut nūlla eārum cursum tenēre posset, sed aliae eōdem unde erant pro-
6 fectae referrentur, aliae ad īnferiōrem partem īnsulae, quae est propius sōlis
7 occāsum, magnō suī cum perīculō dēicerentur; quae tamen, ancorīs iactīs,
8 cum flūctibus complērentur, necessāriō adversā nocte in altum prōvectae
9 continentem petiērunt.

Initial Explorations

1. On what day did these events occur? (1–2)
2. How many ships were involved? What were they carrying? (2–3)
3. Under what circumstances did they set sail? (3)
4. Where were the ships when the storm arose? (3–4)
5. What was the general result of the storm? (5)
6. What happened to some of the ships? (5–6)
7. What happened to the others? (6–7)
8. Why were the ships in danger? (8)
9. What did the ships do in the end? (8–9)

Reading Strategy

♦ tanta . . . ut (above: 4–5): these words clearly introduce a result clause. Read carefully and you will find three subjunctive verbs that complete the result clause, with two other clauses nested inside.

This gold Gallic coin was found near Dover, England. Its presence there is an indication of the trade between Britain and the mainland Celts. The stylized horse is a motif often seen in Celtic art.

1 *accidit, accidere, accidit [ad + cadit], *it happens.*
    accidit: perfect tense.
  ut esset: see **O3c** for this type of clause.
  quī diēs: the antecedent appears inside the relative clause.
  maritimus, -a, -um [< mare, sea], *of the sea, maritime.*
  aestus, -ūs, m., *heat; agitation, surge, ebb and flow.*
    maritimōs aestūs: *tides.*
  Ita ūnō tempore: see the Reading Strategy opposite for help with this sentence.

2 maximōs: during a full moon or a new moon, the sun and moon are aligned, causing unusually strong tides; the sea comes up further on the beach than normal at high tide, and goes further out at low tide.
  *efficiō, efficere, effēcī, effectus [ex + faciō], *to bring about, cause.*
  incognitus, -a, -um [negative prefix in- + cognōscō], *unknown.*
  incognitum: the Romans were accustomed to sailing in the Mediterranean, where the tides rise and fall only a few inches. Two years previously, Caesar had fought a campaign against the Veneti, a coastal tribe of northwestern Gaul, and had built a fleet (some ships of which were used in his expedition to Britain). Apparently, however, the Romans had not learned that the highest tides come at the full moon.

4 cūrō, -āre, -āvī, -ātus, *to take care of, arrange for.*
  exercitum trānsportandum cūrāverat: *had arranged for the army to be transported*: see Structure note below.
  *subdūcō, subdūcere, subdūxī, subductus, *to draw up from below, raise, haul up.* Ancient ships were commonly pulled up onto the beach when not needed for immediate use, as Caesar did with his warships. He did not do so with the transport ships, probably because their larger size made this difficult, or perhaps because he saw no need to do so.

5 *dēligō, -āre, -āvī, -ātus, *to bind, tie up.*
  *adflictō, -āre, -āvī, -ātus, *to shatter, damage severely.*
  neque ūlla . . . facultās: *and no opportunity.*
  nostrīs: referring to the Romans on shore.

6 *administrō, -āre, -āvī, -ātus, *to administer, manage* (the ships).
  auxilior, -ārī, -ātus sum, *to help.*

Structure: Gerundive with the Verb Cūrāre

♦ The future passive participle (gerundive) is used with the verb **cūrāre** to express the idea of getting something done. On tombstones, for instance, we often find statements such as **Hērēs monumentum pōnendum cūrāvit,** *The heir had the stone put up.* Another example: **Dominus servōs līberandōs cūrat,** *The master is arranging for the slaves to be freed.* In such sentences the future pass. part. modifies the direct object of **cūrāre.**

The forces of nature cause more problems.

1 [29] Eādem nocte accidit ut esset lūna plēna, quī diēs maritimōs aestūs
2 maximōs in Ōceanō efficere cōnsuēvit, nostrīsque id erat incognitum. Ita
3 ūnō tempore et longās nāvēs, quibus Caesar exercitum trānsportandum
4 cūrāverat, quāsque in āridum subdūxerat, aestus complēverat, et onerāriās,
5 quae ad ancorās erant dēligātae, tempestās adflictābat, neque ūlla nostrīs
6 facultās aut administrandī aut auxiliandī dabātur.   (continued)

Initial Explorations

   1. What happened on the same day as the storm? (1)
   2. According to Caesar, what does this cause? (1–2)
   3. Where were the warships? How were they affected? (3–4)
   4. Where were the transport ships? What happened to them? (4–5)
   5. What were the Romans on shore not able to do? (5–6)

Reading Strategies

- You should be able to deal with the sentence that begins **Ita ūnō tempore** . . . (above: 2–6) if you take advantage of the strategies discussed so far in this book.

- Read the entire sentence through. After the introductory phrase **Ita ūnō tempore**, how many main clauses are there? What coordinating conjunctions mark the beginnings of these main clauses?

- What case is **longās nāvēs** (3)? What is its likely function in the sentence? (This is probably the single most important thing to notice in order to understand the sentence correctly.)

- What subordinate clauses are nested inside the main clauses?

- What word is gapped with **onerāriās** (4)? Note the gender to help with this.

- How does Caesar employ PARALLEL STRUCTURE to organize the thought?

7 *complūrēs, -ēs, -a, *several.*
 frangō, frangere, frēgī, frāctus, *to break*; of ships, *to wreck.*
 fūnis, fūnis, f., *rope.*
8 armāmenta, -ōrum, n. pl., *tackle* (equipment on a ship).
 *āmittō, āmittere, āmīsī, āmissus, *to lose.* In early Latin this verb is found = *to send away*, but it evolved into the meaning that we find in Caesar and Cicero. This is one of the very few compound verbs whose etymology might easily lead to a misunderstanding.
 inūtilis, -is, -e [negative prefix in- + ūtor, to use], *useless.*
9 perturbātiō, perturbātiōnis [per + turbō], f., *disturbance.* All such -tiō nouns are feminine; knowing this helps you realize that **magna** modifies **perturbātiō** despite the intervening **id quod** clause and the genitive **tōtīus exercitūs** (which also modifies **perturbātiō**).
10 quibus . . . possent: a relative clause of result (**O2i**).
 *reficiō reficere, refēcī, refectus [re- + faciō], *to make again, restore, repair.*
11 erant ūsuī: a dative of purpose (**A3g**), *were of use.*
 *cōnstō, cōnstāre, cōnstitī, cōnstatūrus, *to stand together, stand firm, agree*; impersonal, *it is agreed.*
 *hiemō, -āre [< hiems, winter], *to spend the winter.*
 cōnstābat . . . oportēre: *it was agreed by everyone that it was proper.* **Omnibus** is a dative of reference (**A3h**), which in this context is best translated *by* . . .
12 hīs in locīs: *in these places*, less lit., *in this region*, a common sense of **locus** in the plural.
 *hiems, hiemis, f., *winter.*
 *prōvideō, prōvidēre, prōvīdī, prōvīsus, *to forsee; to provide against, provide for.*

Reading Strategy: Enclosing Word Order

• You will often meet phrases of the pattern **magna in Italiā vīlla**, *a large villa in Italy*, or **cum frātris amīcō**, *with his brother's friend*. The first word begins the phrase, is followed by another word or words that clearly cannot complete the phrase, and finally is completed by the required form. English speakers often ask, "Why didn't the Romans just say **cum amīcō frātris?**"

• To a Roman, who responded subconsciously and automatically to the information provided by the endings of words, such phrases were often clearer than if they had been written in English word order. Recall the principle of expectation (see **M1a–M1e**, and esp. **M1f**). The order used in the examples above shows that the words **in Italiā** and **frātris** belong to the phrase under discussion and not to some other, coming later in the sentence. We use the term ENCLOSING WORD ORDER for such phrases.

• In lines 8–9 opposite we have **magna . . . perturbātiō**. The statement in the previous bullet point applies here, although an unusually large number of words is contained within the enclosing adj./noun pair. In addition, placing words that logically belong together very far apart (HYPERBATON) creates strong emphasis; Caesar wants the reader to understand that his soldiers were really upset by what had happened.

7   Complūribus nāvibus frāctīs, reliquae cum essent fūnibus, ancorīs reliquīs-
8   que armāmentīs āmissīs ad nāvigandum inūtilēs, magna, id quod necesse
9   erat accidere, tōtīus exercitūs perturbātiō facta est. Neque enim nāvēs erant
10 aliae quibus reportārī possent, et omnia dēerant quae ad reficiendās nāvēs
11 erant ūsuī, et, quod omnibus cōnstābat hiemāre in Galliā oportēre, frūmen-
12 tum hīs in locīs in hiemem prōvīsum nōn erat.

    6. What happened to several of the warships? (7)
    7. In what condition were the others? (7–8)
    8. What was the result? (8–9)
    9. What three difficulties for the Romans does Caesar mention? (9–12)

Discussion
    1. Why do you think Caesar includes the clause **id quod necesse erat accidere**
       (8–9)?

Reading Strategy

- The function of **reliquae** (above: 7) is not immediately clear. The context suggests
  that it might be nom. pl. fem., referring to **nāvēs**, but that is not certain at first, nor is
  how it relates to the clause that begins **cum** . . . .

- **ancorīs . . . āmissīs** is clearly an ablative phrase nested inside the **cum** clause, but its
  function is not yet clear.

- After you read **ad nāvigandum inūtilēs**, the structure becomes clear: **reliquae** agrees
  with **inūtilēs** (it does indeed refer to ships) and belongs inside the **cum** clause. The
  abl. abs. **ancorīs . . . āmissīs** explains why the ships were useless.

- Caesar placed **reliquae** to the left of its clause marker **cum** in order to provide a
  clearer transition from mentioning the ships that had been wrecked (**Complūribus
  nāvibus frāctīs**) to discussing those that survived the storm.

3   **dēesse**: for the construction used with this word, see the note for 26:13, page 82.
   *__intellego, intellegere, intellēxī, intellēctus__, *to understand.*
   *__paucitās, paucitātis__ [< paucī, a few], f., *small number.*
   __exiguitās, exiguitātis__, f., *scantiness, scarcity, smallness.*
4   **angustiōra**: sc. than usual, than normal.
   __hōc__: *because of this,* less lit., *for this reason.*
   *__impedīmenta, -ōrum__, n. pl., *baggage.* Caesar's army had of course brought some
      equipment with it, but only the minimum needed for a short stay.
5   **factū**: a supine in the abl.; see **I2**.
   __dūxērunt__: *thought,* as often in Caesar.
6   __commeātus, -ūs__, m., *going to and fro; convoy; provisions, supplies.*
   __frūmentō commeātūque__: abl. of separation, **A5a**.
   __prōdūcō, prōdūcere, prōdūxī, prōductus__, *to lead forward; to prolong, extend.*
7   **eīs . . . interclūsīs**: the ablative absolute has a conditional sense, *if they were . . . .*
   __reditus, -ūs__, m., *return.*
   __reditū__: another abl. of separation.
   __interclūdō, interclūdere, interclūsī, interclūsus__ [inter + claudō, to close], *to shut
      out, shut off, cut off.*
   *__posteā__, adv., *later on, afterwards.*
8   **trānsitūrum**: a future infinitive; supply **esse**.
   *__cōnfīdō, cōnfīdere, cōnfīsus sum__, *to trust confidently, be assured, believe.*
   *__rūrsus__, adv., *again.*
   __rūrsus coniūrātiōne factā__: coniūrātiō here = something like *mutual loyalty* (not
      conspiracy); a non-literal trans. might be *after renewing their mutual loyalty.*
9   *__paulātim__, adv., *little by little, gradually;* i.e., the Britons left a few at a time so as
      not to arouse the Romans' suspicions.
   *__discēdō, discēdere, discessī, discessūrus__, *to go away, depart, leave.*
   __clam__, adv., *secretly.*

Reading Strategies

♦ The first sentence in this chapter (opposite: 1–8) is long and very complex. It begins
   in a straightforward way, up through the participial phrase **inter sē collocūtī**. Then
   comes a **cum** causal clause, in two parts, with each section closed by a subjunctive
   verb (**intellegerent**, 3, and **cognōscerent**, 4) Both these verbs govern indirect statements in which the acc. and infin. appear in front of the head word. **Quae** (4) introduces a clause that describes the camp, followed by a causal clause (**quod . . .**) that
   explains the statement about the size of the camp.

♦ The main verb, **dūxērunt** (5), also governs an indirect statement that appears in front
   of it, **optimum factū esse**, *that the best thing to do was . . . ;* this ind. state. is completed
   by two infinitive phrases **frūmentō . . . prohibēre** and **rem in hiemem prōdūcere**
   (6–7). The final structure in the sentence is a causal clause (**quod . . .** , 7–8) which
   is interrupted by an abl. abs. **eīs . . . interclūsīs** immediately after it begins. The
   verb **cōnfīdēbant** also governs an indirect statement **nēminem . . . trānsitūrum** that
   comes before it.

The Britons take advantage of Caesar's troubles.

1 [30] Quibus rēbus cognitīs, prīncipēs Britanniae, quī post proelium ad Cae-
2 sarem convēnerant, inter sē collocūtī, cum equitēs et nāvēs et frūmentum
3 Rōmānīs dēesse intellegerent et paucitātem mīlitum ex castrōrum exiguitāte
4 cognōscerent, quae hōc erant etiam angustiōra quod sine impedīmentīs Cae-
5 sar legiōnēs trānsportāverat, optimum factū esse dūxērunt, rebelliōne factā,
6 frūmentō commeātūque nostrōs prohibēre et rem in hiemem prōdūcere,
7 quod eīs superātīs aut reditū interclūsīs nēminem posteā bellī īnferendī causā
8 in Britanniam trānsitūrum cōnfīdēbant. Itaque, rūrsus coniūrātiōne factā,
9 paulātim ex castrīs discēdere ac suōs clam ex agrīs dēdūcere coepērunt.

Initial Explorations

1. Who held a conference? (1–2)
2. Of what Roman difficulty were they aware? (2–3)
3. What impression did they get from the small size of the Roman camp? Why was this misleading? (3–5)
4. What did they believe was the best thing to do (two parts)? (5–6)
5. Why did they decide to do this? (7–8)
6. What two things did they begin to do? (8–9)

(Continued from opposite page.)

◆ This sentence reinforces the point you that you need to get comfortable with indirect statements that appear in front of their head verbs (there are four of them in one sentence). You will spot these only if you read the sentence through—often multiple times—before translating.

◆ One way to approach a complicated sentence such as this one is to focus initially on the verb forms. You can, as a temporary measure, ignore subordinate items such as relative clauses and ablative absolutes. By doing so, you would learn that the British chiefs conferred, understood and learned some things, decided that it was best to do two things, because . . . . This is not a complete understanding of the sentence, but it is a place to begin. This sentence is very complicated, so don't feel bad if it doesn't come easily!

1 **At Caesar:** note the strong transition from the previous two chapters, which
    dealt with the storm and the Britons' reaction, to Caesar's own response.
  *****etsī,** conj., *even if, although.*
  *****ēventus, -ūs** [< ēveniō, to turn out], *occurrence, event; consequence, result*; i.e., as
    the result of what had happened to the ships.
2 **ex eō quod:** Latin often uses a neuter pronoun as antecedent for a clause. This is
    not required in English, and **eō** can be omitted in translation.
  quod: *the fact that.*
  *****intermittō, intermittere, intermīsī, intermissus,** *to leave off, neglect; to pause,*
    cease.
  *****fore:** an alternate form of **futūrus esse,** the future infinitive of **sum.**
  fore id quod accidit: indirect statement introduced by **suspicābātur,** with **id** as
    subject of the infinitive **fore;** *that the thing which (already) happened would be*
    (the case), i.e., that the Britons would revolt.
3 *****suspicor, -ārī, -ātus,** *to suspect.*
  suspicābātur: *began to suspect.*
  *****cāsus, cāsūs,** m., *accident, misfortune, emergency.*
  subsidia: in this context = *safeguards.*
4 **cotīdiē,** adv., *daily.*
5 *****māteria, -ae,** f., *matter, material;* in this context = *timber.*
  quae . . . nāvēs: the rel. cl. comes in front of its antecedent: *the ships which . . . .*
  *****aes, aeris,** n., *bronze.* Bronze does not rust and so was used on ships instead of iron.
  quae . . . nāvēs, eārum māteriā . . . ūtēbātur: *the ships which . . . he used their*
    timber and bronze = *he used the timber and bronze of the ships which . . .*
  quae: not feminine as in the previous clause, but neuter plural with **ea** under-
    stood as antecedent, *those things which.*
6 **comportārī:** deduce from **con- + portō, -āre.**
  cum: how can you tell that this is the conjunction, not the preposition?
  summō studiō: since the soldiers had been upset by the damage to the ships, it
    is not surprising that they worked eagerly to repair those that could be made
    seaworthy.
7 **administrārētur:** an impersonal passive (**F3d**). Look for a translation that gives
    an idea of an ongoing process.
  xii: = **duodecim.**
  xii nāvibus āmissīs: the ablative absolute has a concessive force, *although . . . .*
    Recall that Caesar had brought about 80 warships to Britain.
  reliquīs: this word appears to the left of its clause marker **ut** to mark the transi-
    tion from talking about the ships that were destroyed to those that could be
    salvaged. It is ablative of means with **nāvigārī** (8) which is an impersonal
    passive: *he brought it about that to be sailed was possible in the others,* less lit.,
    that the others could be sailed.
8 *****commodē,** *suitably, properly, appropriately, well.*
  effēcit: as often, this verb is completed by an **ut** clause with the subjunctive
    (**O3c**); here the **ut** clause precedes **effēcit.**

Caesar takes steps to deal with the situation.

1 [31] At Caesar, etsī nōndum eōrum cōnsilia cognōverat, tamen et ex ēventū
2 nāvium suārum et ex eō quod obsidēs dare intermīserant fore id quod ac-
3 cidit suspicābātur. Itaque ad omnēs cāsūs subsidia comparābat. Nam et frū-
4 mentum ex agrīs cotīdiē in castra cōnferēbat et, quae gravissimē adflictae er-
5 ant nāvēs, eārum māteriā atque aere ad reliquās reficiendās ūtēbātur et quae
6 ad eās rēs erant ūsuī ex continentī comportārī iubēbat. Itaque, cum summō
7 studiō ā mīlitibus administrārētur, XII nāvibus āmissīs, reliquīs ut nāvigārī
8 commodē posset effēcit.

Initial Explorations

1. What two factors led Caesar to be concerned? (1–2)
2. What suspicions did Caesar have? (2–3)
3. What was Caesar's overall response to this? (3)
4. What did he gather and from where? (3–4)
5. What did Caesar do with the most badly damaged ships? (4–5)
6. From where did he get other things needed to repair the ships? (6)
7. What was the soldiers' attitude as they worked on the ships? (6–7)
8. How many ships had been lost? (7)
9. In what condition were the remaining ships? (7–8)

Discussion

1. What impression do you get of Caesar as a leader from this chapter? Support
your answer from the text.

A Roman
galley (nā-
vis longa).

1 *cōnsuētūdō, cōnsuētūdinis [< cōnsuēscō, to accustom], f., *custom, habit.*
    ex cōnsuētūdine: *from custom, according to custom,* less lit., *as usual.*
  ūnā: agrees with legiōne (not cōnsuētūdine) to form an abl. abs. with missā.
  frūmentor, -ārī, -ātus sum [< frūmentum, grain], *to find food, forage.* Grain was
    the staple of the legionary soldier's diet; it was boiled with water and eaten
    like modern hot cereal. It was supplemented with whatever food could be
    obtained locally. Soldiers were given a ration of grain twice a month that
    they had to carry with them as they marched. So it is not surprising that the
    military term *to forage* is based on the word for *grain.*
  frūmentātum: a supine expressing purpose (**I3a**), *to forage.*
2 ūllā . . . suspiciōne: another example of enclosing word order (cf. the Reading
    Strategy on page 90).
  *interpōnō, interpōnere, interposuī, interpositus, *to put between, insert,*
    introduce.
3 pars hominum: referring to the Britons, not the Roman soldiers.
  remanēret: deduce from re- + maneō.
  *ventitō, -āre, -āvī, -ātūrus, *to come often, keep coming, go back and forth.* The
    presence of the British in the fields and near the camp suggested that no
    attack was imminent.
4 porta, -ae, f., *gate.*
  statiō, statiōnis [< stō, to stand], f., *standing still; position, post, guard duty.*
  pulvis, pulveris, f., *dust, cloud of dust.*
5 quam cōnsuētūdō ferret: lit., *than custom brought,* less lit., *than usual.*
  quam in partem: another instance where Caesar repeats the antecedent of a
    relative pronoun inside the relative clause.
6 id quod erat: *that which was,* i.e., the truth, the actual situation.
7 *ineō, inīre, inīvī or iniī, initus [in + eō], *to go into, enter; to enter upon, begin,*
    undertake.
  initum: sc. esse; suspicātus (6) introduces an indirect statement.
  cōnsiliī: a partitive genitive, modified by novī and depending on aliquid, *some-*
    thing of a new plan, some new plan.
  *cohors, cohortis, f., *cohort,* one-tenth of a legion.
8 *succēdō, succēdere, successī, successūrus, *to go under, enter; to follow, take the*
    place of.
  *armō, armāre, armāvī, armātus, *to arm.*
  armārī: the passive infinitive here has a reflexive sense, *to arm themselves.*
9 *cōnfestim [< festīnō, to hurry], adv., *immediately, without delay.*
  *paulō, adv., *by a little, a little.*
  *prōcēdō, prōcēdere, prōcessī, prōcessūrus, *to go forward, advance.*
10 *premō, premere, pressī, pressus, *to press, press upon, press hard.*
  *aegrē [< aeger, aegra, aegrum, sick, troubled], *uncomfortably, with dislike, with*
    difficulty.
  *sustineō, sustinēre, sustinuī, sustentus [sub + teneō], *to sustain, endure, with-*
    stand, hold out.
  *cōnfertus, -a, -um, *pressed together, dense, closely packed.*

The Britons attack one legion while it searches for food.

1 [32] Dum ea geruntur, legiōne ex cōnsuētūdine ūnā frūmentātum missā
2 quae appellābātur septima, neque ūllā ad id tempus bellī suspiciōne inter-
3 positā, cum pars hominum in agrīs remanēret, pars etiam in castra venti-
4 tāret, eī quī prō portīs castrōrum in statiōne erant Caesarī nūntiāvērunt pul-
5 verem maiōrem quam cōnsuētūdō ferret in eā parte vidērī quam in partem
6 legiō iter fēcisset. Caesar id quod erat suspicātus, aliquid novī ā barbarīs
7 initum cōnsiliī, cohortēs quae in statiōnibus erant sēcum in eam partem
8 proficīscī, ex reliquīs duās in statiōnem cohortēs succēdere, reliquās armārī
9 et cōnfestim sēsē subsequī iussit. Cum paulō longius ā castrīs prōcessisset,
10 suōs ab hostibus premī atque aegrē sustinēre et cōnfertā legiōne ex omnibus
11 partibus tēla coicī animadvertit.   (continued)

Initial Explorations

1. What does Caesar tell us about the Seventh Legion? (1–2)
2. Why did the Romans not think that hostilities would resume? (2–4)
3. What did the guards at the gate report to Caesar? (4–6)
4. What did Caesar suspect? (6–7)
5. What three orders did Caesar give? (7–9)
6. What did Caesar observe was the situation with the Seventh Legion? (10–11)

Vocabulary: Frequentative Verbs

♦ **ventitāret** (above: 3) belongs to a class of verbs called FREQUENTATIVES, which indicate a repeated or habitual action. They are normally formed from the supine
   or fourth principal part of a root verb and belong to the first conjugation, as with
   ventitāre from **ventum**, supine of **veniō**.

12 **omnī**: modifies **frūmentō**, enclosing the entire abl. abs.

    dēmetō, dēmetere, dēmessuī, dēmessus, *to mow, reap, harvest.*

13 *****hūc** [> hic, this], adv., *to this place, here.*

    *****noctū**, adv., *at night.*

    dēlitēscō, dēlitēscere, dēlituī, *to conceal oneself, hide.*

14 **dispergō, dispergere, dispersī, dispersus**, *to disperse, scatter.*

    dēpositīs: deduce from **dē** + **pōnō**.

    metō, metere, messuī, messus, *to mow, reap.*

15 *****incertus, -a, -um**, *uncertain; disorganized.*

    incertīs ōrdinibus: you will recall from §26 (page 80) that the effectiveness of a Roman legion depended in large part on the soldiers' fighting in formation. Here the Romans were surprised while harvesting grain and had difficulty in forming up. **Incertīs ōrdinibus** is an ablative absolute, *since/while (their) ranks were disorganized.*

16 *****essedum, -ī**, n., *chariot* of a type used by the Britons and formerly by the mainland Celts. See the coin on page 101.

    circumdō, circumdare, circumdedī, circumdatus, *to surround.*

The emperor Trajan (reigned 98–117 CE) built a new forum in Rome. In addition to a basilica, a library, and a market, it contains a column celebrating Trajan's two victorious campaigns against the Dacians. The column is decorated with carvings that depict many aspects of life in the Roman army. This scene shows soldiers foraging for grain, just as Caesar describes.

12 Nam quod omnī ex reliquīs partibus dēmessō frūmentō pars ūna erat reli-
13 qua, suspicātī hostēs hūc nostrōs esse ventūrōs noctū in silvīs dēlituerant;
14 tum dispersōs, dēpositīs armīs in metendō occupātōs, subitō adortī, paucīs
15 interfectīs reliquōs incertīs ordinibus perturbāverant, simul equitātū atque
16 essedīs circumdederant.

7. What did the enemy suspect that the Roman soldiers would do? Why?
   (12–13)
8. How had they acted on their suspicions? (13)
9. Describe the beginning of the attack on the Romans. (14–15)
10. How did the encounter continue? (15–16)

Reading Strategies

♦ In line 14 you meet **dispersōs**, which is certainly acc. pl. but whose function is not yet clear—it might refer to **nostrōs** (13) or to **hostēs** (13) or perhaps to some word yet to come. It is followed by an ablative absolute, which should not be difficult to recognize as such since it is a very typical one, and then by another masc. acc. pl. word **occupātōs**.

♦ The participle **adortī** (14) brings the phrase to an end. You can now see that **dispersōs** and **occupātōs** must be the direct objs. of **adortī**, since there is no other object. Since there is no masc. pl. noun in the clause, these words must be substantives: *(the men) who had scattered.*

♦ The presence of an obvious direct object in the acc. case also shows that **adortī** must be a deponent, since true passive verbs do not take a direct object. This rule can be useful if you do not have access to a dictionary and are unsure about whether a verb is deponent.

♦ Authors of narrative prose in Latin usually present events in the order that they occur. The main verb shows the most important action, while other actions are included as subordinate clauses, participial phrases, ablative absolutes, etc.; regardless of the structures used, the events are given in order. To help understand a difficult sentence, it is an excellent practice to list the events in order in one column and opposite each event place the structure that is used to present it. Here is the beginning of such a list for this sentence; complete it, and use this technique on other sentences.

grain harvested from most areas	ablative absolute, **omnī . . . frūmentō**
one area left	causal clause, **quod . . . pars ūna erat reliqua**
Britons get an idea	participial phrase, **suspicātī . . . ventūrōs**
Britons hide	main clause, **in silvīs dēlituerant**
Romans scatter	perfect passive participle, **dispersōs**

1 **perequitō, -āre** [per + equus], *to ride through.*
2 **ipsō terrōre equōrum:** i.e., the terror caused by the horses.
  strepitus, -ūs, m., *noise.*
  rota, -ae, f., *wheel.*
3 **turma, -ae,** f., *squadron.* In the Roman army such squadrons consisted of about
    30 horsemen; exactly how the British organized their formations is unknown.
  inter equitum turmās: among their own cavalry (not the enemy's). After the
    chariot fighters had dismounted, the British battle formation consisted of al-
    ternating groups of cavalry and foot soldiers.
  īnsinuō, -āre, -āvī, *to wind one's way among, bring in*; see **F2k** for the tense.
4 **proelior, -ārī, -ātus sum** [< proelium, battle], *to fight (a battle).*
  aurīga, -ae, m., *charioteer.* The historian Tacitus mentions that the charioteers
    were of noble birth while retainers did the fighting—the opposite of what we
    might assume.
  *****interim,** adv., *meanwhile.*
5 *****excēdō, excēdere, excessī, excessūrus** [ex + cēdō], *to go out.*
  currus, -ūs, m., *chariot.* **Currus** is the general Latin word for *chariot*; **essedum**
    refers specifically to the type of chariot used by the Britons.
  *****collocō, -āre, -āvī, -ātus** [< locus, place], *to locate, place.*
6 **receptus, -ūs,** m., *a drawing back, withdrawal, retreat.*
7 **pedes, peditis** [< pēs, pedis, foot], m., *foot soldier.*
  praestant: *offer, provide* (additional meaning)
  *****exercitātiō, exercitātiōnis** [< exerceō, to train], f., *training, practice.*
8 **utī:** this clause is completed by **cōnsuerint** (10); nested in between are five infini-
    tives, all complementary infins. depending on **cōnsuerint**.
  dēclīvis, -is, -e [< clīvus, slope], *sloping, downhill.*
  praeceps, praecipitis [prae + caput, capitis], *headfirst; steep.*
  locō: *ground, terrain.*
  equōs incitātōs: see the note for §26:5, page 80.
  sustinēre: here = *to control, keep in check.*
9 **brevī:** *quickly*; a noun such as **tempore** or **spatiō** is understood.
  moderor, -ārī, -ātus sum, *to control.*
  flectō, flectere, flexī, flexus, *to bend; to turn.*
  tēmō, tēmōnis, m., *pole, tongue* (pole that fits between two horses that are
    pulling a chariot, wagon, etc.).
  *****sē recipere,** idiom, *to take oneself back, retreat.*
10 **cito,** adv., *swiftly, quickly.*

Forms

♦ The Latin noun suffix -**tās**, -**tātis** is the origin of English nouns that end in -*ty*; e.g.,
  lībertās, *liberty*. Knowing this, you can easily deduce the meanings of **mōbilitātem**
  and **stabilitātem** (opposite: 6 and 7). All such nouns are feminine, like those that
  end in -**tūdō**; there is a strong tendency in Latin for abstract nouns to be feminine.
  (Abstract nouns are concepts, ideas, and other things that do not physically exist.)

Caesar describes the British chariot fighters.

1 [33] Genus hoc est ex essedīs pugnae. Prīmō per omnēs partēs perequi-
2 tant et tēla coiciunt atque ipsō terrōre equōrum et strepitū rotārum ōrdinēs
3 plērumque perturbant, et, cum sē inter equitum turmās īnsinuāvērunt, ex
4 essedīs dēsiliunt et pedibus proeliantur. Aurīgae interim paulātim ex proe-
5 liō excēdunt atque ita currūs collocant ut, sī illī ā multitūdine hostium pre-
6 mantur, expedītum ad suōs receptum habeant. Ita mōbilitātem equitum, sta-
7 bilitātem peditum in proeliīs praestant, ac tantum ūsū cotīdiānō et exer-
8 citātiōne efficiunt utī in dēclīvī ac praecipitī locō incitātōs equōs sustinēre et
9 brevī moderārī ac flectere et per tēmōnem percurrere et in iugō īnsistere et
10 sē inde in currūs citissimē recipere cōnsuerint.

Initial Explorations

1. How do the chariot fighters begin a battle? (1–2)
2. What effect does this have on the enemy? Why (2–3)
3. What do they do after returning among their own forces? (3–4)
4. Where do the drivers station the chariots? Why? (4–6)
5. What two advantages does this style of fighting offer? (6–7)
6. Give two examples of the Britons' exceptional ability to control their horses. (8–9)
7. How have they acquired the ability to do this? (7–8)
8. What other impressive feat can some warriors do in their chariots? (9–10)

This Roman coin, minted in 48 BCE, shows a Gallic man with a shield behind his head on the obverse. On the reverse is an **essedum**, with the warrior clearly visible standing and the driver seated at the front. The sides are low and the front seems open, which would allow the warrior to run out onto the pole as Caesar describes. The name on the coin, L. Hostilius Saserna, is that of the moneyer (the official responsible for minting the coin).

1 **nostrīs**: dative of indirect object with **auxilium tulit**, modified by **perturbātīs**;
      Quibus rēbus is an ablative of means or cause.
   novitās, novitātis [> novus, new], f., *newness, novelty.*
   novitāte pugnae: ablative of cause, *owing to the novelty of the fighting*; the
      Romans had never encountered such chariot fighters before.
   *****opportūnus, -a, -um**, *convenient, suitable, advantageous, helpful.*
2 **namque** [stronger form of nam], conj., *for indeed.*
3 **sē recēpērunt**: *recovered*; **recipiō** is a transitive verb in Latin and so must have a
      direct object (**sē**). (This is not the idiom *to retreat* introduced in §33.)
   lacessō, lacessere, lacessīvī, lacessītus, *to provoke, challenge.*
   *****committo, committere, commīsī, commissus** [con- + mittō], *to bring together,*
      join; to enter into, engage in, begin.
4 **proelium**: supply this word with **ad lacessendum**; it is gapped.
   *****aliēnus, -a, -um**, *belonging to another, foreign; inappropriate, unfavorable.*
   aliēnum: modifies **tempus** (not **proelium**).
   suō . . . locō: = **in suō locō** (**B4b**).
5 **intermissō**: with time expressions **intermittō** = *to go by, pass.*
6 **reliquī**: this is the antecedent of **quī**; the rel. cl. appears in front of its antecedent.
8 *****nūntius, -ī**, m., *messenger; message.*
9 *****dīmittō, dīmittere, dīmīsī, dīmissus** [dis- + mittō], *to send away.*
   *****praedicō, -āre, -āvī, -ātus**, *to declare publicly, report, announce.*
10 *****quantus, -a, -um**, *how much, how great, what a great.*
   *****praeda, -ae**, f., *loot.*
   praedae faciendae: this genitive phrase modifies **facultās**, lit., *opportunity of mak-*
      ing loot, less lit., *opportunity to seize loot.* This claim was exaggerated, since
      Caesar, planning only a short stay in Britain, had left most of the the army's
      baggage behind when he crossed the Channel (30:4).
   *****perpetuus, -a, -um**, *perpetual, everlasting*; **in perpetuum**: *forever.*
   suī: genitive of the reflexive pronoun **sē**, modified by the gerundive **līberandī**, *of*
      freeing themselves; like **praedae faciendae**, it modifies **facultās**.
11 **Hīs rēbus**: *By these means.*
12 *****peditātus, -ūs** [< pēs, pedis, foot], m., *infantry, foot soldiers.*
   coācta: from **cōgō**.

Reading Strategies

◆ The next to last sentence in this chapter (**Interim . . .** ; opposite: 8) is complex. It
   begins with a straightforward clause that ends at **dīmīsērunt** (9); the verb marks the
   end of this clause.

◆ **-que** (9) like **et**, can connect two items within a clause or mark the beginning of a new
   clause; here it does the latter, and the verb **praedicāvērunt** marks the end.

◆ **et** (9) begins a third clause. On a first reading, you might not grasp much except that
   dēmōnstrāvērunt (11) is parallel to **dīmīsērunt** and **praedicāvērunt**, so you are dealing with a sentence of three clauses, the last one longer and more complex than the
   others. Remember: think structure before you try to translate!

Caesar rescues the foragers; bad weather prevents fighting.

1   **[34]** Quibus rēbus perturbātīs nostrīs novitāte pugnae tempore opportū-
2   nissimō Caesar auxilium tulit: namque eius adventū hostēs cōnstitērunt,
3   nostrī sē ex timōre recēpērunt. Quō factō, ad lacessendum et ad commit-
4   tendum proelium aliēnum esse tempus arbitrātus, suō sē locō continuit et,
5   brevī tempore intermissō, in castra legiōnēs redūxit. Dum haec geruntur,
6   nostrīs omnibus occupātīs, quī erant in agrīs reliquī discessērunt. Secūtae
7   sunt continuōs complūrēs diēs tempestātēs, quae et nostrōs in castrīs con-
8   tinērent et hostem ā pugnā prohibērent. Interim barbarī nūntiōs in omnēs
9   partēs dīmīsērunt paucitātemque nostrōrum mīlitum suīs praedicāvērunt et
10   quanta praedae faciendae atque in perpetuum suī līberandī facultās darētur,
11   sī Rōmānōs castrīs expulissent, dēmōnstrāvērunt. Hīs rēbus celeriter magnā
12   multitūdine peditātūs equitātūsque coāctā ad castra vēnērunt.

Initial Explorations

1. Why were the Roman soldiers uneasy? (1)
2. What did Caesar do? (2)
3. What two things resulted from Caesar's action? (2–3)
4. What did Caesar think? (3–4)
5. What two actions did he therefore take? (4–5)
6. How did the Gauls react to this? (5–6)
7. What two things resulted from the several days of bad weather? (7–8)
8. What did the Britons do during this time? (8–9)
9. What fact did they announce? (9–10)
10. What opportunities did they see in this situation? (10–11)
11. What was the result? (11–12)

- Rereading the third clause, you note that **quanta** (10) could be fem. sing. or neuter pl. There are no neuter pl. words in the clause, but **facultās** (10) is fem. sing. nom. (recall the Vocabulary note about -tās nouns on page 100). The separation of **quanta** and **facultās** shows that the items contained between the two words all belong to this phrase; **atque** connects two items in the phrase rather than beginning a new one. The note for line 10 opposite helps you see that the two genitive phrases **praedae facien-dae** and **suī līberandī** modify **facultās**.

- The third clause, introduced by **et**, is completed by **dēmōnstrāvērunt** (11). Inside this clause you see the question word **quanta** and the subjunctive **darētur** (10); these, together with the verb **dēmōnstrāvērunt**, help you understand that you are dealing with an indirect question. The head word of an indirect question often comes first, as in English, but may come after the subjunctive clause, as it does here; you need to get used to this pattern, which is less obvious to English speakers.

1 **idem**: *the same thing* (where does "thing" come from?)

  idem . . . fore vidēbat: an indirect statement with the relative clause **quod . . . acciderat** nested inside.

  superiōribus diēbus: when used in reference to time, **superior** = *previous*.

2 *__celeritās, celeritātis__ [< celer, quick], f., *quickness, speed.*

  ut . . . celeritāte perīculum effugerent: this is a kind of result clause explaining what Caesar means by **idem** (1).

  tamen: the point here is that even though Caesar had gotten a few cavalry, they were not enough to do any serious damage to the fleeing enemy; but he decided to engage anyway. Several hundred or a thousand cavalry was a more typical number in a major battle. Cavalry were used at the beginning of a battle, if possible, to surround the enemy's line and break it up from the rear, and at the end to pursue a defeated enemy and inflict more casualties as they retreated (or fled, in the case of a total rout).

  nancīscor, nancīscī, nactus sum, *to get, obtain.*

3 *__circiter__, adv., *about, approximately.*

  XXX: = **trīgintā**.

  Commius Atrebās: on Commius, see the introduction to Book IV, page 73, and §27:3–8, page 85.

4 *__aciēs, aciēī__, f., *line of battle.*

  diūtius: *for too long*, comparative of **diū**, *for a long time.*

5 **ferre**: *to endure, withstand*, a less common meaning of this verb (just as in English 'to bear' can mean either 'to carry' or 'to endure').

  terga vertere, idiom, *to turn the backs*, less lit., *to turn and flee.*

6 **tantō spatiō**: *over as much distance*, an ablative of route rather than the accusative of extent of space that we might expect; **tantō** correlates with **quantum** in the next clause, *as much . . . as.*

  cursū et vīribus: *with (their) running and strength*, less lit., *with their strength at running/to run* (HENDIADYS). Remember that **vīrēs** is the pl. of **vīs** = *power, strength*; the third decl. endings show it cannot be a form of **vir**, which belongs to the second decl.

  potuērunt: the unexpressed subject of this and the following verbs is *they* = the Romans; only the overall context shows that the subject has changed from *they* = the Britons in the previous sentence.

7 **longē lātēque**: *far and wide.*

Caesar offers battle and defeats the Britons.

1 [35] Caesar, etsī idem quod superiōribus diēbus acciderat fore vidēbat, ut,
2 sī essent hostēs pulsī, celeritāte perīculum effugerent, tamen nactus equitēs
3 circiter xxx, quōs Commius Atrebās, dē quō ante dictum est, sēcum trāns-
4 portāverat, legiōnēs in aciē prō castrīs cōnstituit. Commissō proeliō, diū-
5 tius nostrōrum mīlitum impetum hostēs ferre nōn potuērunt ac terga ver-
6 tērunt. Quōs tantō spatiō secūtī quantum cursū et vīribus efficere potu-
7 ērunt, complūrēs ex eīs occīdērunt, deinde omnibus longē lātēque aedificiīs
8 incēnsīs sē in castra recēpērunt.

1 [36] Eōdem diē lēgātī ab hostibus missī ad Caesarem dē pāce vēnērunt.

Initial Explorations

1. What did Caesar realize? (1–2)
2. How many cavalry did Caesar locate? From where had they come? (2–4)
3. What did Caesar do after locating the cavalry? (4)
4. How did the enemy behave after the battle began? Why? (4–6)
5. How did the Romans react? What was the result? (6–7)
6. What final action did the Romans taken before returning to camp? (7–8)

7. What happened later the same day? (1)

* * * * * * * * *

As soon as he had negotiated peace terms with the Britons, Caesar took his army back to Gaul. It was already the middle of September and the fall equinox was reputed to be a stormy season, so Caesar was anxious to cross back to the mainland. Two ships got separated from the others and landed in the territory of the Morini, who attacked the men from these ships as they made their way back to the main army. Caesar heard what was happening and sent cavalry to rescue the trapped soldiers; then Caesar's **lēgātus** Titus Labienus took a legion and laid waste the country of the Morini to punish them. Finally Caesar sent his army into winter quarters, stationing them among the Belgae because he considered these tribes the most likely to revolt against the Roman occupation. Only two British tribes sent the promised hostages. When word of Caesar's victory over the British was received in Rome, the Senate decreed twenty days of public thanksgiving.

Vocabulary Review: Book IV

The following asterisked words were introduced in §§24–25:

altitūdō	flūctus	onerārius
altum (n. subs.)	funda	paulum
animadvertō	genus	plērumque
apertus	impedītus	prōdō
aquila	imperātor	prōpellō
āridum	imperītus	propter
coepī	inde	pugna
cohortor	latus, lateris	studium
coiciō	magnitūdō	subsequor
cōnsistō	membrum	tēlum
cōnsuēscō	mōtus, -ūs	ūniversus
dēsiliō	nōtus	ūsus, -ūs
equitātus	officium	

The following asterisked words were introduced in §§26–28:

ācriter	dēsum	quīcumque
adorior	fuga	servō, -āre
aliquī	impetus	signum
ancora	īnsistō	singulāris
circumsistō	longinquus	subsidium
compleō	obses	superior
comprehendō	occurrō	superō
continēns	ōrdō	suprā
coorior	paucī	tempestās
cursus	perturbō	ultrō
dēferō	polliceor	unde
dēiciō	prīstinus	uterque
dēmōnstrō	propius	vērō, adv.

The following asterisked words were introduced in §§29–31:

accidit	dēligō, -āre	māteria
adflictō	discēdō	paucitās
administrō	efficiō	paulātim
aes	etsī	posteā
āmittō	ēventus	prōvideō
cāsus	fore	reficiō
clam	hiemō	rūrsus
commodē	hiems	subdūcō
complūrēs	impedīmenta	suspicor
cōnfīdō	intellegō	
cōnstō	intermittō	

The following asterisked words were introduced in §§32–35:

aciēs	dīmittō	paulō
aegrē	essedum	peditātus
aliēnus	excēdō	perpetuus
armō	exercitātiō	praeda
celeritās	hūc	praedicō
circiter	incertus	premō
cohors	ineō	prōcēdō
collocō	interim	quantus
committō	interpōnō	sē recipere
cōnfertus	noctū	succēdō
cōnfestim	nūntius	sustineō
cōnsuētūdō	opportūnus	ventitō

Diodorus Siculus on the Gauls

Diodorus of Sicily wrote a *Universal History* during the second half of the first century BCE. Here is some of what he has to say about the Gauls (5.29–30).

* * * * * * * * *

On their travels and when they go into battle they use teams of two horses, with a chariot holding a driver and a warrior. When they meet cavalry in the fighting they throw javelins at the enemy and, after stepping down from their chariots, they begin to fight with swords. Some of them despise death to such an extent that they enter the perils of battle naked, wearing only a loincloth. They also bring their free men as servants, choosing them from among the poor, and they use these men in battle as charioteers and shield-bearers. After the battle lines are drawn up, they often go forward from the lines and challenge the bravest of their opponents to single combat, brandishing their weapons to frighten the enemy. When anyone accepts the challenge to battle, then they start singing about the brave deeds of their ancestors and boasting about their own accomplishments, and they disparage and tear down their opponent and with such words take away all the courage of his spirit. They cut off the heads of their fallen enemies and tie them around the necks of their horses; and handing over to their servants the bloody weapons they carry them off as prizes, singing a paean[1] and bursting into a song of victory. They nail these special objects to their houses, just as men do sometimes with animal heads after they have subdued wild beasts in hunting. They embalm the heads of their most renowned enemies in cedar oil and carefully preserve them in a box, and they show the heads to visitors, solemnly claiming that in exchange for this head one of their ancestors, or their father, or even the host himself, was offered but did not accept a large amount of money.

They make use of remarkable clothing: shirts dyed and decorated in many different shades, and trousers, which they call bracae. They wear cloaks with buckles on the shoulder, made heavy for winter but light for summer, woven with closely set checks of various colors.[2] For armor they use shields as tall as a man, made in a style not found elsewhere: some of the shields have bronze figures of animals applied to them, carefully designed not only for appearance but also for protection. They wear bronze helmets that have large pieces projecting from them and that give the effect of great size to the wearers. On some of them are placed horns made as a single piece with the helmet, on others are made the front parts of birds or four-footed animals.

---

[1] A song of thanksgiving or exultation.

[2] Similar to the tartans of the Scottish highlands.

Book V

54 BCE

THE FIFTH YEAR of Caesar's governorship is notable for two things: a second expedition to Britain and the revolts by several Gallic tribes during the winter. After his first visit to Britain, Caesar decided to go back to the island and ordered a large number of ships constructed during the winter of 55–54. As he usually did, Caesar spent the winter in Cisalpine Gaul and Illyricum, dealing with administrative matters. Upon his return in the spring, he began organizing his invasion force. Just before leaving for Britain Caesar had to deal with a situation among the Treveri, an important tribe. One of its leaders, Cingetorix, was a supporter of Rome whom Caesar had rewarded while the other, Indutiomarus, was anti-Roman. Caesar compelled Indutiomarus to give him a large number of hostages to insure his good behavior. Leaving Titus Labienus, one of his lēgātī, with a sizeable army to keep an eye on things in Gaul, Caesar sailed for Britain.

The Romans landed and made their way inland. Several British tribes united under a king named Cassivellaunus to oppose the Romans. Caesar joined forces with the Trinobantes, longtime enemies of Cassivellaunus, and with their help won several victories. A number of tribes then gave hostages and promised to pay tribute. It was now the middle of September and Caesar needed to go back to Gaul for the winter. Caesar may have hoped for profit and glory by bringing a new, unknown territory into the Roman empire, but he did not achieve this goal. He was occupied for the next three years putting down revolts in Gaul; then the political situation in Rome demanded his attention. No Roman army came back to Britain for over a hundred years, until the island was added to the empire during the reign of Claudius (beginning in 43 CE). The historian Tacitus wrote a biography of his father in law Agricola, who served as governor of Britain. Tacitus remarks:

> Therefore the deified Julius (Caesar) was the first of all Romans to enter Britain with an army. Although he terrified the inhabitants with successful battles and got control of the coast, he can be seen to have shown (Britain) to posterity, not to have handed it over to them. (*Agricola* 13)

The rest of Book V, most of which you will read on the following pages, is one of the most compelling parts of *De bello Gallico*. As one Roman army is wiped out and another almost destroyed in its winter quarters, we can see clearly the character of Caesar and his officers as well as the determination of the Gauls to free themselves from Roman domination before it is too late.

1 **subductīs nāvibus**: after returning from the second expedition to Britain. Ancient Roman ships were normally hauled up (**subdūcere**) onto the beach when not in use.

   ***concilium, -ī**, n., *council*. (Do not confuse with **cōnsilium**, *plan*.) Caesar was in the habit of holding conferences with Gallic leaders at least once a year.

   ***Samarobrīva, ae.**, f., *Samarobriva*, capital city of the Ambiani, now Amiens in northern France.

   Samarobrīvae: locative case (**B4**).

   peragō, peragere, perēgī, perāctus, *to carry though, accomplish, complete*.

2 **siccitās, siccitātis** [< siccus, -a, -um, dry], f., *drought*.

   angustius: *rather scantily*, less literal, *in rather small quantity*.

   prōvēnerat: *had come forth*, i.e., had come out of the ground, had grown.

   coāctus est: the subject is *he* = Caesar.

3 ***aliter**, adv., *in another way, differently*.

   ac: after words that suggest a comparison, ac = *than* or *as* (not *and*); cf. **īdem ac**, *the same as*.

   aliter ac superiōribus annīs: in previous years Caesar had assigned his legions to winter among the tribes he thought mostly likely to revolt, but this year he had to put them where food was available.

   Morinī, -ōrum, m. pl., *the Morini*, a Gallic tribe living near the English Channel.

   in Morinōs: *into the Morini* = *into (the territory of) the Morini*; Caesar often uses this phrasing to indicate the territory of Gallic tribes.

   dūcendam: a future passive participle, *to be led*; see **H1**.

   ***C. Fabiō**: Gaius Fabius was one of Caesar's legates (see page 9 for this term). A number of Caesar's other commanders are mentioned in this paragraph; not all are identified in these notes unless there is something special to know about them. We know from elsewhere that they were all legates, except Marcus Crassus and Lucius Roscius..

5 ***Nerviī, -ōrum**, m. pl., *the Nervii*, a Belgic tribe, opposed to Roman rule, who had suffered a severe defeat at Caesar's hands in 57 BCE.

   ***Q. Cicerōnī**: younger brother of the famous orator Marcus Cicero..

   Esubiī, -ōrum, m. pl., *the Esubii*, a tribe living west of the Sequana (Seine) River.

6 **Rēmī, -ōrum**, m. pl., *the Remi*, an important tribe living around what is now the city of Rheims.

   ***T. Labiēnō**: Titus Labienus was one of Caesar's most able legates, frequently mentioned in *De bello Gallico*; he later he split with Caesar and fought on the Republican side in the civil war.

   cōnfīnium, -ī, n., *common boundary, border*.

   ***Trēverī, -ōrum**, m. pl., *the Treveri*, a tribe in Gaul but originally from Germany.

7 ***M. Crassum**: elder son of Crassus, Caesar's partner in the First Triumvirate.

   ***quaestor, quaestōris**, m., *quaestor*, an official elected in Rome to manage finances and then assigned to a province. Caesar sometimes used his quaestor to command a legion, if he was an experienced military officer, as he did in the battle with Ariovistus (§1.52).

8 ***praeficiō, praeficere, praefēcī, praefectus**, *to put someone* (acc.) *in command of something* (dat.).

Caesar arranges winter quarters for his army.

1 [24] Subductīs nāvibus, conciliōque Gallōrum Samarobrīvae perāctō, quod
2 eō annō frūmentum in Galliā propter siccitātēs angustius prōvēnerat, coāctus
3 est aliter ac superiōribus annīs exercitum in hibernīs collocāre legiōnēsque
4 in plūrēs cīvitātēs distribuere. Ex quibus ūnam in Morinōs dūcendam C. Fa-
5 biō lēgātō dedit, alteram in Nerviōs Q. Cicerōnī, tertiam in Esubiōs L. Ros-
6 ciō; quārtam in Rēmīs cum T. Labiēnō in cōnfīniō Trēverōrum hiemāre
7 iussit. Trēs in Belgīs collocāvit: eīs M. Crassum quaestōrem et L. Munātium
8 Plancum et C. Trebonium lēgātōs praefēcit.   (continued)

Initial Explorations

1. What did Caesar do after returning from Britain? (1)
2. What had happened in Gaul this year and why? (2)
3. What was Caesar forced to do as a result? (2–4)
4. Give the location and the commanding officer that Caesar set up for his first four legions. (4–6)
5. Where did he send the next three? Who were their commanders? (7–8)

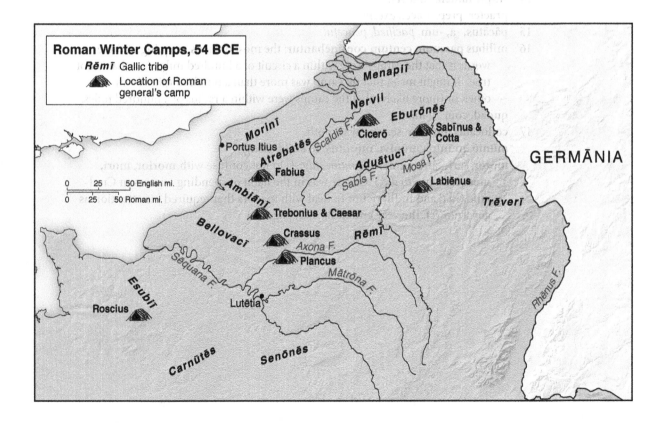

Roman Winter Camps, 54 BCE

Rēmī Gallic tribe
Location of Roman general's camp

9 **ūnam legiōnem . . . et cohortēs v:** this was the 14th legion, which had been recruited, along with the 13th, in 57 BCE. It is not known why Caesar had five
additional cohorts separated from a legion.

proximē: proximus means *closest* physically but *most recent* when referring to
time; cf. the two meanings of **superior**, *higher* and *previous*.

Padus, -ī, m., *the Po River* in northern Italy.

trāns Padum: as usual, Caesar writes from the perspective of someone in Rome,
so this = north of the Po.

ᶜōnscrībō, cōnscrībere, cōnscrīpsī cōnscrīptus, *to write down; to sign up, enlist.*

10 *Eburōnēs, Eburōnum,* m. pl., *the Eburones,* a small Belgic tribe.

Mosa, -ae, m., *the Mosa River,* now the Meuse.

11 *Ambiorīx, Ambiorīgis,* m., *Ambiorix,* a chieftain of the Eburones.

Catuvolcus, -ī, m., *Catuvolcus,* another leader of the Eburones.

Q. Titūrium Sabīnum: one of Caesar's legates.

12 *L. Aurunculeium Cottam:* another legate.

praesum, praeesse, praefuī, praefutūrus, irreg., + dat., *to be charge of, be in
command of.*

Ad hunc modum: *In this way.*

13 **inopia, -ae** [neg. prefix in- + ops, supply], *lack, shortage.*

frūmentārius, -a, -um [< frūmentum, grain], *having to do with grain, of grain.*

medeor, medērī + dat., *to heal, remedy, relieve.*

14 **Atque tamen:** *And yet.*

praeter, prep. + acc., *except.*

15 **pācātus, -a, -um,** *pacified, peaceful.*

16 **mīlibus passuum centum continēbantur:** the most obvious meaning of these
words is that the camps were within a circuit of a hundred miles, but that is not
true. It might mean that no camp was more than a hundred miles from another, or (more likely) that the camps were within a radius of a hundred miles.

quoad, conj., *until.*

17 **collocātās, mūnīta:** sc. **esse** with both.

mūniō, mūnīre, mūnīvī, mūnītus, *to build, fortify.*

moror, -ārī, -ātus sum, *to remain, stay.* (Do not confuse with **morior, morī,
mortuus sum,** *to die.*) Caesar was in the habit of spending winters in Cisalpine Gaul and in Illyricum to deal with matters that required his attention as
governor (cf. the very end of Book I, page 70).

9 Ūnam legiōnem, quam proximē trāns Padum cōnscrīpserat, et cohortēs v
10 in Eburōnēs, quōrum pars maxima est inter Mosam ac Rhēnum, quī sub
11 imperiō Ambiorīgis et Catuvolcī erant, mīsit. Eīs mīlitibus Q. Titūrium
12 Sabīnum et L. Aurunculeium Cottam lēgātōs praeesse iussit. Ad hunc mo-
13 dum distribūtīs legiōnibus facillimē inopiae frūmentariae sēsē medērī posse
14 exīstimāvit. Atque hārum tamen omnium legiōnum hiberna, praeter eam
15 quam L. Rosciō in pācātissimam et quiētissimam partem dūcendam dede-
16 rat, mīlibus passuum centum continēbantur. Ipse intereā, quoad legiōnēs
17 collocātās mūnītaque hiberna cognōvisset, in Galliā morārī cōnstituit.

6. What units did Caesar send into the territory of the Eburones? (9–10)
7. What does Caesar tell us about the Eburones? (10–11)
8. Whom did Caesar place in command of these units? (11–12)
9. What did Caesar believe would result from these arrangements? (12–14)
10. Where were the camps located, with the exception of that commanded by Lucius Roscius? (14–16)
11. Why was Roscius' command different? (15–16)
12. What decision did Caesar make? (16–17)

1 ***Carnūtēs, Carnūtum**, m. pl., *the Carnutes*, a tribe living in central Gaul on both
   sides of the River Liger (Loire).
   locō: *position, rank.*
   summō locō: the ablative is used with **nāscor** to indicate the social position;
   literally, one is *born from*, although in English we would say 'born into.'
   *nāscor, nāscī, nātus sum, *to be born.*
   *Tasgetius, -ī, m., *Tasgetius*, a prince of the Carnutes.
   maiōrēs: in the plural, this word = *ancestors* (i.e., those greater in age).
2 **Huic**: what case? Keep reading until the reason for this case becomes clear at the
   end of the sentence.
   prō: *in return for.*
   benevolentia, -ae [bene + volō], f., *good will.*
   prō eius virtūte atque in sē benevolentiā: another nice example of a prepositional phrase enclosing its modifiers (cf. the Reading Strategy on page 90).
3 ***singulārī**: in 4.26 you met this word = *one at a time*; it can also mean *unusual,*
   exceptional.
   *opera, -ae, f., *exertion, efforts, service.* **operā**: for the case, see **A5o**.
   fuerat . . . ūsus: = **ūsus erat**. Caesar sometimes uses this sort of double plpf.,
   with the helping verb plpf. (**fuerat**) even though it is normally impf. (**erat**).
   restituō, restituĕre, restituī, restitūtus, *to restore.*
   maiōrum locum restituerat: Caesar regularly played the various factions within
   a tribe against each other, supporting those who favored accommodation
   with Rome rather than resistance. (Recall the story of Dumnorix and Diviciacus from Book I.) But such support could backfire, since many Gauls
   resented being ruled by someone they saw as a Roman puppet.
4 **hunc tertium annum**: accusative (not ablative), suggesting perhaps that large
   portion of his third year as king has gone by when he was assassinated. Note
   that if **eum** is omitted (see the Text note opposite) then **hunc** refers to Tasgetius, rather than modifying **annum**.
   rēgnō, -āre, -āvī, -ātus [< rēgnum, royal power, kingdom], *to reign, rule.*
   †inimīcīs . . . eum†: see the Text note on the opposite page.
5 ***palam**, adv., *openly.*
   *auctor, auctōris [< auctus, perf. part. of augeō, to increase], m., *promoter,*
   advocate, creator, instigator.
6 ***vereor, verērī, veritus sum**, *to fear.*
   quod ad plūrēs pertinēbant: i.e., the murder was carried out, or approved, by a
   large number of people.
   nē . . . dēficeret: this clause is the object of **veritus**; how does the meaning of that
   verb affect the meaning of **nē**? (See **O3e** if necessary.)
   impulsus, -ūs [in + pellō], m., *pushing against, pressure; incitement, instigation.*
7 ***dēficiō, dēficere, dēfēcī, dēfectus** [dē + faciō], *to withdraw, desert, revolt.*
   Belgium, -ī, n., the southwestern part of **Gallia Belgica**, centered on the Somme
   River and including the Atrebates, Bellovaci, and Ambiani.
8 **quōrum**: the relative clause appears in front of its antecedent **hōs**.
10 ***trādō, trādere, trādidī, trāditus** [trāns + dō], *to hand over.*
   perventum: an impersonal passive (**E3d**) with **esse** understood.

The death of Tasgetius causes a change in plans.

1 [25] Erat in Carnūtibus summō locō nātus Tasgetius, cuius maiōrēs in suā
2 cīvitāte rēgnum obtinuerant. Huic Caesar prō eius virtūte atque in sē bene-
3 volentiā, quod in omnibus bellīs singulārī eius operā fuerat ūsus, maiōrum
4 locum restituerat. Tertium iam hunc annum rēgnantem †inimīcīs iam mul-
5 tīs palam ex cīvitāte et eīs auctōribus eum† interfēcērunt. Dēfertur ea rēs ad
6 Caesarem. Ille veritus, quod ad plūrēs pertinēbat, nē cīvitās eōrum impulsū
7 dēficeret, L. Plancum cum legiōne ex Belgiō celeriter in Carnūtēs proficīscī
8 iubet ibique hiemāre, quōrumque operā cognōverat Tasgetium interfectum,
9 hōs comprehēnsōs ad sē mittere. Interim ab omnibus lēgātīs quaestōribus-
10 que quibus legiōnēs trādiderat certior factus est in hiberna perventum lo-
11 cumque hibernīs esse mūnītum.

Initial Explorations

1. What three things does Caesar tell us about Tasgetius? (1–2)
2. What had Caesar done for him? Why? (2–4)
3. How did the people of Tasgetius' tribe feel about him? (4–5)
4. What happened to Tasgetius? (5)
5. Why was Caesar concerned when he heard this news? (6–7)
6. What three things did he order Lucius Plancus to do? (7–9)
7. What did Caesar learn in the meantime, and from whom? (9–11)

Discussion

1. Caesar starts this chapter using past tense verbs, switches to the HISTORIC
   PRESENT (**dēfertur**, 5, and **iubet**, 8) then returns to the past tense (**factus est**,
   10). Why did he use the tenses this way?

Text

- The text printed between daggers in lines 4–5 above is very awkward and many scholars believe it is corrupt. It may be interepreted as an ablative absolute in two parts,
  with a form of **esse** understood in the first: *since now many of his tribe were openly
  hostile and with them as instigators.* The word order, the transition to the second
  half, and the use of **eīs** are strange, and the subject of **interfēcērunt** is *they* referring
  vaguely to Tasgetius' tribe or some members of it.

- One group of manuscripts reads **inimīcī iam palam multīs ex cīvitāte auctōribus**
  (omitting **eum**). What would this mean? Does it make better sense?

- The plural **quaestōribus** (8) has also raised some questions, since there was normally
  one quaestor assigned to a province. Did Caesar really have more, or is the text corrupt here also? Or was Caesar just writing hastily?

1 **Diĕbus, quibus:** both abl. of time within which.

   *repentīnus, -a, -um** [< repente, suddenly], *sudden.*

2 **tumultus, -ūs,** m., *uproar.*

   dēfectiō, dēfectiōnis [< dēficiō, to rebel], f., *rebellion, revolt.*

3 **cum:** *although.*

   praestō esse, idiom + dat., *to be at hand, wait upon, attend upon* (as a sign of respect). Note that this adverb is not the same as the verb **praestō, -āre,** although it comes from the same roots.

4 **Indutiomārus, -ī,** m., *Indutiomarus,* a chief of the Treveri. Remember that he was anti-Roman and was particularly angry at Caesar for taking members of his family as hostages before leaving for Britain. At this point in time he felt free to oppose Caesar, so perhaps the hostages had been returned.

   *impellō, impellere, impulī, impulsus** [in + pellō] *to push against, strike; to set in motion, urge on, persuade.*

   *concitō, -āre, -āvī, -ātus,** *to put in motion, incite, stir up.*

5 **lignātor, lignātōris** [< lignum, wood], m., *one sent to gather wood, wood-cutter.*

   manū: remember the less common meaning of **manus,** *group, band.*

   oppugnātum: a supine in the accusative expressing purpose, 13a.

6 *vāllum, -ī,** n., *wall, rampart,* referring to the typical Roman wall around a camp, built of earth dug up while making the ditch (**fossa**) and topped with a wall of wooden stakes.

7 **Hispānus, -a, -um,** *from Spain, Spanish.* Caesar had been governor of Spain in 61 BCE, and elsewhere in *De bello Gallico* we hear that he got horses from there.

   equester, equestris, equestre [< equus, horse], *on horseback, with cavalry.*

   superiōrēs: in this context with a metaphorical meaning = *superior, victorious,* as opposed to the more common meaning *higher.*

8 *dēspērō, -āre, -āvī, -ātus** [dē + spēs, hope], *to give up hope.*

   *oppugnātiō, oppugnātiōnis,** f., *attack.*

   dēspērātā rē . . . redūxērunt: this whole attack was probably a ruse, designed to get the Romans to talk and set up what happens in the next few chapters.

9 **suō mōre:** *in accordance with their custom.* The Romans would have sent one or two men with such a request and probably found the Gallic custom strange.

   colloquium, -ī, n., *conversation, parley.*

   prōdeō, prōdīre, prōdiī or **prōdīvī, prōditūrus,** *to go forward, advance, come forth.* Note that this is a compound of **eō, īre** and is not the same as **prōdō, prōdere,** the compound of **dō, dare.**

10 **habēre sēsē:** what construction is this? Think about the context and about similar sentences you have seen.

   quae: *(some things) which.* (Where does *things* come from?)

   *commūnis, -is, -e,** *common.*

   *contrōversia, -ae,** f., *quarrel, dispute, disagreement.*

   rēbus: Caesar used the neuter plural **quae** (10) to express the idea of *things,* then he included the word **rēbus** with **quibus; rēbus** may be omitted or put in parentheses when translating.

11 *minuō, minuere, minuī, minūtus** [< minor, smaller], *to make smaller, lessen; to settle* (a dispute).

A revolt begins among the Eburones.

1   [26] Diēbus circiter quīndecim, quibus in hiberna ventum est, initium re-
2   pentīnī tumultūs ac dēfectiōnis ortum est ab Ambiorīge et Catuvolcō; quī,
3   cum ad fīnēs rēgnī suī Sabīnō Cottaeque praestō fuissent frūmentumque
4   in hiberna comportāvissent, Indutiomārī Trēverī nūntiīs impulsī suōs con-
5   citāvērunt subitōque oppressīs lignātōribus magnā manū ad castra oppug-
6   nātum vēnērunt. Cum celeriter nostrī arma cēpissent vāllumque ascendis-
7   sent atque ūnā ex parte Hispānīs equitibus ēmissīs equestrī proeliō superi-
8   ōrēs fuissent, dēspērātā rē hostēs suōs ab oppugnātiōne redūxērunt. Tum
9   suō mōre conclāmāvērunt, utī aliquī ex nostrīs ad colloquium prōdīret:
10   habēre sēsē quae dē rē commūnī dīcere vellent, quibus rēbus contrōversiās
11   minuī posse spērārent.

Initial Explorations

1. What happened within fifteen days of Sabinus' and Cotta's arrival at their winter camp? (1–2)
2. Why did the Romans believe that Ambiorix and Catuvolcus were not going to cause any problems? (3–4)
3. What caused Ambiorix and Catuvolcus to change their minds? (4)
4. What was the Eburones' first move against the Romans? Then what did they do? (4–6)
5. Describe how the Romans responded to the attack (four items). (6–8)
6. What did the Eburones do and why? (8)
7. What request did the Eburones make? How did they do this? (9)
8. What did the Eburones say that would have motivated the Romans to grant the request? (10–11)

Cultural Context

◆ The names of modern cities in what was ancient Gaul usually come from the tribe that lived there rather than from the actual ancient name of the city. Thus Autricum, the main town of the Carnutes, is now Chartres; Durocortorum, the capital of the Remi, is the modern Rheims; and Samarobriva became Amiens after its inhabitants the Ambiani. This phenomenon shows the continued importance of the tribes even after Gaul came under Roman control. The city known to the Romans as Lutetia was built by the Parisii on an island in the River Seine—so what is its modern name?

1 **eques**: here not *cavalryman* but *equestrian*, a member of the class of wealthy
businessmen.
familiāris, -is, m., *close friend.*
2 **Q. Titūrī**: Caesar sometimes refers to this legate by his **praenōmen** and **nōmen**
and sometimes by his **cognōmen**, Sabinus; likewise with his other legate, L.
Aurunculeius Cotta. You need to keep all parts of the names in mind.
iam: connect with **ventitāre cōnsuerat** (3).
ante: how can you tell that this is the adverb (= *previously*), not the preposition
(= *before*)?
missus, -ūs, m., almost always in abl., *a sending.*
  missū Caesaris: *by the sending of Caesar*, less lit., *sent by Caesar.*
4 **sēsē ... cōnfitērī**: indirect statement, introduced by **locūtus est**, begins here and
continues through the next to last sentence of this chapter; it is the longest
such piece of continuous indirect statement in this book. Remember that **sē**
and **sēsē** will usually mean *he*, Ambiorix, the subject of **locūtus est** (see **E2**).
prō ... beneficiīs: another example of ENCLOSING WORD ORDER (see the Reading Strategy on page 90).
beneficium, -ī [bene + faciō], n., *kindness, favor.*
cōnfiteor, cōnfitērī, cōnfessus sum, *to acknowledge, admit.*
5 **stīpendium, -ī**, n., *tribute.*
***Aduātucī, -ōrum**, m. pl., *the Aduatuci*, a tribe of Germanic origin in Gallia
Belgica (see the map on page 111).
6 ***pendō, pendere, pependī, pēnsus**, *to weigh; to pay.*
7 **apud sē**: *with them*; **sē** refers to the subject of the subjunctive clause, the Aduatuci.
***servitūs, servitūtis** [< servus, slave], f., *slavery.*
catēna, -ae, f., *chain.*
8 **neque**: negates **fēcisse** (9); the **quod**-clause is nested inside the ind. statement.
9 **fēcisse**: sc. **sē**.
coāctus, -ūs [< perf. part. of cōgō, to force], m., *forcing, compulsion.*
eiusmodī: written as one word, but simply = **eius modī**, *of this type.*
imperia: in this context = *government, rule* (translate as sing.).
10 **iūris**: partitive gen. with **nōn minus**.
11 **porrō**, adv., *onward, further on; next, in turn.*
cīvitātī: a dative of reference (**A3h**).
fuisse: the indirect statement continues throughout the rest of this chapter.
12 **potuerit**: the subject is *it* = the tribe of the Eburones.
humilitās, humilitātis, f., *lowness; low position, insignificance* (not 'humility' in
the English sense). Ambiorix is alluding to the fact that the Eburones were a
small tribe.
14 **omnibus ... oppugnandīs**: dative phrase with a gerundive, *for all the camps to
be attacked*, less lit., *for attacking all the camps.*
15 **nē qua legiō**: *so that no legion could*, lit., *so that any legion could not* (see **E1** for
the special meaning of **quis**); **nē** introduces a negative purpose clause.
16 **alterae legiōnī subsidiō**: a double dative (**A3i**).

Ambiorix addresses the Roman envoys.

1 [27] Mittitur ad eōs colloquendī causā C. Arpineius, eques Rōmānus, fami-
2 liāris Q. Titūrī, et Q. Iūnius ex Hispāniā quīdam, quī iam ante missū Caesaris
3 ad Ambiorīgem ventītāre cōnsuerat; apud quōs Ambiorīx ad hunc modum
4 locūtus est: sēsē prō Caesaris in sē beneficiīs plūrimum eī cōnfitērī dēbēre,
5 quod eius operā stīpendiō līberātus esset, quod Aduātucīs, finitimīs suīs,
6 pendere cōnsuēsset, quodque eī et filius et frātris filius ab Caesare remissī es-
7 sent, quōs Aduātucī obsidum numerō missōs apud sē in servitūte et catēnīs
8 tenuissent; neque id, quod fēcerit dē oppugnātiōne castrōrum, aut iūdiciō aut
9 voluntāte suā fēcisse, sed coāctū cīvitātis, suaque esse eiusmodī imperia ut
10 nōn minus habēret iūris in sē multitūdō quam ipse in multitūdinem. Cīvitātī
11 porrō hanc fuisse bellī causam, quod repentīnae Gallōrum coniūrātiōnī re-
12 sistere nōn potuerit. Id sē facile ex humilitāte suā probāre posse, quod nōn
13 adeō sit imperītus rērum ut suīs cōpiīs populum Rōmānum superārī posse
14 cōnfidat. Sed esse Galliae commūne cōnsilium: omnibus hibernīs Caesaris
15 oppugnandīs hunc esse dictum diem, nē qua legiō alterae legiōnī subsidiō
16 venīre posset.   (continued)

Initial Explorations

1. Who was sent to speak with the Gauls? What does Caesar tell us about these men? (1–3)
2. What did Ambiorix begin by acknowledging? (4–5)
3. What actions of Caesar caused Ambiorix to feel this way? (5–8)
4. What did Ambiorix claim about his attack on the Roman camp? (8–9)
5. Why had the attack taken place, despite Ambiorix's opposition? (9–10)
6. Why had his tribe been willing to make the attack? (10–12)
7. How does Ambiorix try to prove his claim? (12–14)
8. What was the Gauls' common plan? Why had they set this up? (14–16)

17 *negō, -āre, -āvī, -ātus, *to deny, say no.*
    *praesertim, adv., *especially, particularly.*
    reciperō, -āre, -āvī, -ātus, *to regain, recover.*
18 initum: sc. esse.
    Quibus: *For them,* i.e., his fellow Gauls.
    quoniam, conj., *because.*
    prō: *in regard to.*
    pietās, pietātis, f., *sense of duty, duty;* in this context = *patriotism.*
19 satisfaciō, satisfacere, satisfēcī, satisfactus, *to do enough.*
    Quibus . . . satisfēcerit: i.e., by attacking the Roman camp as he was asked to do
        by the other tribes.
    sē: again = Ambiorix, and understood with monēre and ōrāre in the next clause.
    *ratiō, ratiōnis, f., *reckoning, account; care, concern.*
20 *ōrō, -ōrāre, ōrāvī, ōrātus, *to beg.* monēre, ōrāre: note the ASYNDETON.
    hospitium, -ī, n., *hospitality, ties of hospitality.*
    *salūs, salūtis, f., *safety.*
    *cōnsulō, cōnsulere, cōnsuluī, cōnsultus, *to consider, reflect upon;* + dat., *to take
        care for, be mindful of.*
    Magnum . . . trānsīsse: a lie on Ambiorix's part.
21 manum: the less common meaning of manus, *band, group.*
    conductam: *hired* (additional meaning).
    *adsum, adesse, adfuī, adfutūrus, *to be present, be here.*
    adfore: remember that fore is an alternate form of futūrus esse.
    *biduum, -ī [bis + diēs], n., *space of two days, two days.*
22 Ipsōrum esse cōnsilium: *It was their own deliberation,* i.e., it was something that
        they needed to decide.
    velintne: -ne = *whether, if* when it introduces an indirect question.
    prius quam (often written as one word), conj., *before.*
    *sentiō, sentīre, sēnsī, sēnsus, *to perceive, notice, realize.*
    sentiant: when priusquam is completed by the subjunctive, it expresses anticipa-
        tion, *before they could realize.*
    ēductōs: sc. esse.
23 mīlitēs: forms an indirect statement with ēductōs (esse) and is also the direct
        object of dēdūcere; see the Reading Strategy opposite.
24 quīnquāgintā, *fifty.*
    amplius, adv., *more.*
    Illud: the pronoun anticipates the indirect statement tūtum iter per fīnēs
        datūrum; it may be omitted in translation or put between parentheses.
25 *tūtus, -a, -um, *safe.*
    datūrum: supply sē (from earlier in the sentence) and esse to form a fut. infin.
26 levō, -āre, -āvī, -ātus [< levis, light], *to lighten, relieve of something* (abl.).
    hibernīs levētur: i.e., relieved of the burden of supplying provisions to the
        Romans during the winter.
27 meritum, -ī, n., *kindness, favor.*
    *grātia, -ae, f., *favor, regard; thanks;* grātiam referre, *to make recompense.*
    ōrātiōnem habēre, idiom, *to deliver a speech.*

17 Nōn facile Gallōs Gallīs negāre potuisse, praesertim cum dē reciperandā
18 commūnī lībertāte cōnsilium initum vidērētur. Quibus quoniam prō pietāte
19 satisfēcerit, habēre nunc sē ratiōnem officī prō beneficiīs Caesaris: monēre,
20 ōrāre Titūrium prō hospitiō, ut suae ac mīlitum salūtī cōnsulat. Magnam
21 manum Germānōrum conductam Rhēnum trānsīsse; hanc adfore biduō.
22 Ipsōrum esse cōnsilium, velintne prius quam fīnitimī sentiant ēductōs ex
23 hibernīs mīlitēs aut ad Cicerōnem aut ad Labiēnum dēdūcere, quōrum alter
24 mīlia passuum circiter quīnquāgintā, alter paulo amplius ab eīs absit. Illud
25 sē pollicērī et iūre iūrandō cōnfirmāre tūtum iter per fīnēs datūrum. Quod
26 cum faciat, et cīvitātī sēsē cōnsulere, quod hibernīs levētur, et Caesarī prō
27 eius meritīs grātiam referre. Hāc ōrātiōne habitā discēdit Ambiorīx.

9. What did Ambiorix say was not possible and why? (17–18)
10. What did Ambiorix say that his participation in the attack on the camp enabled him to do, and why? (18–19)
11. What advice did Ambiorix give Titurius? (19–20)
12. What information did he pass on? (20–21)
13. What did the Romans need to decide, according to Ambiorix? (22–23)
14. How far away were the camps of Cicero and Labienus? (23–24)
15. What promise did Ambiorix make? How did he show his sincerity? (25)
16. By making this promise, what two different things could Ambiorix accomplish? (26–27)

Discussion

1. Outline the points that Ambiorix makes in his speech. Do you find his claims believable and his arguments persuasive? Why or why not?
2. What would you do if you were the Roman commander, and why? (Think about this before you read the next chapter!)

Reading Strategies

◆ In line 22 you meet **velint** and expect either an infinitive or a direct object to complete it. Then comes the clause **prius quam . . . sentiant**. Sentīre (= *to notice*) often introduces indirect statement, so you might expect that **dēductōs (esse)** would be part of an indirect statement whose subject would be masculine plural; then you see **mīlitēs**, which could be the subject accusative. Finally you encounter **dēdūcere**, which makes the structure clear: this infinitive completes **velint** (*they wish to escort . . .*) and requires a direct object, **mīlitēs**.

◆ Notice how **mīlitēs** acts like a hinge both to complete the indirect statement and to move the thought forward into the infinitive phrase **aut . . . dēdūcere**. Reread the sentence and this note until it all makes sense!

2 **rē**: *affair*; less lit., *development, turn of events.*

neglegenda: sc. **esse**, as also with **agendum** (7) and **discēdendum** (8).

3 **ignōbilis, -is, -e**, *unknown, undistinguished, obscure.*

4 **humilis, -is, -e**, *low, humble, insignificant.*

*sponte, *voluntarily, of one's own accord*; usually completed by an adj. such as **meā**.

*audeō, audēre, ausus sum, semi-deponent + infin., *to dare (to).*

ausam: sc. **esse** to make a perf. infin. in ind. statement with **cīvitātem** (3) as subj.

5 **cōnsilium**: Roman commanders sometimes called a council of war, which consisted of themselves, the military tribunes, and the senior centurions (**prīmōrum ōrdinum centuriōnēs**), who were probably the six centurions of the first cohort in a legion.

exsistō, exsistere, exstitī, exstitūrus [ex + stō], *to step forth, emerge, appear, arise.*

6 ***tribūnus, -ī**, m., *tribune*, a title given to several types of Roman officials. **Tribūnī mīlitum** were army officers, six to a legion, usually young men from aristocratic families sent to gain military experience. This title is more often encountered in reference to the **tribūnī plēbis**, *tribunes of the people*, who protected the common people from exploitation by the nobility.

7 ***centuriō, centuriōnis**, m., *centurion*, commander of (theoretically) a hundred men, roughly equivalent to a captain in a modern army.

temere, adv., *rashly, recklessly.*

agendum: sc. **esse**.

iniussus, -ūs [neg. prefix in- + perf. part. of iubeō], m., found only in the abl., *without an order.*

8 **quantusvīs, quantavīs, quantumvīs**, *as much as you wish, however great, however many.*

etiam: *even*; the Romans regarded the Germans as more serious opponents than the Gauls.

9 **mūnītīs hibernīs**: probably an ablative absolute, although it might be understood as an ablative of means or an ablative of place where, with **in** omitted.

*doceō, docēre, docuī, doctus, *to teach, inform, show.*

rem esse: why accusative and infinitive? **rem**, *(this) fact*, refers to the information given in the subsequent **quod** clause.

testimōnium, -ī, n., *proof*; **testimōniō** is a dative of purpose (**A3g**).

10 ***vulnus, vulneris**, n., *wound*. The point is that the Romans had not only repelled the attack but had in addition (**ultrō**) hurt the enemy.

11 **rēs frūmentāria, reī frūmentāriae**, f., *grain supply.*

premī: sc. **sē**.

12 ***postrēmō**, adv., *at last, in the end, finally.*

quid esset: an indirect question; a verb such as **rogāre** is implied, since it is clear from the context that Cotta and the other soldiers are continuing to present their arguments.

levis, -is, -e, *light; trivial, inconsistent, unreliable.*

13 ***turpis, -is, -e**, *disgraceful, shameful.*

auctōre hoste: a non-literal translation might be *on the advice of an enemy*; what would the literal meaning be?

A council of war debates what to do.

1 [28] Arpineius et Iūnius quae audiērunt ad lēgātōs dēferunt. Illī repentīnā
2 rē perturbātī, etsī ab hoste ea dīcēbantur, tamen nōn neglegenda exīsti-
3 mābant maximēque hāc rē permovēbantur, quod cīvitātem ignōbilem atque
4 humilem Eburōnum suā sponte populō Rōmānō bellum facere ausam vix
5 erat crēdendum. Itaque ad cōnsilium rem dēferunt magnaque inter eōs ex-
6 sistit contrōversia. L. Aurunculeius complūrēsque tribūnī mīlitum et prī-
7 mōrum ōrdinum centuriōnēs nihil temere agendum neque ex hibernīs in-
8 iussū Caesaris discēdendum exīstimābant: quantāsvīs etiam magnās cōpiās
9 Germānōrum sustinērī posse mūnitīs hibernīs docēbant: rem esse testi-
10 mōniō, quod prīmum hostium impetum multīs ultrō vulneribus inlātīs
11 fortissimē sustinuerint; rē frūmentāriā nōn premī; intereā et ex proximīs
12 hibernīs et ā Caesare conventūra subsidia; postrēmō quid esset levius aut
13 turpius, quam auctōre hoste dē summīs rēbus capere cōnsilium?

Initial Explorations

1. What was the reaction of the legates when they heard Ambiorix's message? (1–3)
2. What fact in particular concerned them? (3–5)
3. What happened at the council of war? (5–6)
4. Who sided with L. Aurunculeius Cotta? (6–7)
5. What did these men believe? (7–8)
6. What else did they point out? (8–9)
7. What proof did they offer for this statement? (9–11)
8. What two additional reasons did they give for staying put? (11–12)
9. What final argument did they make? (12–13)

Text

• There is a textual problem in line 8. The Oxford Classical Text, following all but one of the manuscripts, reads **quantāsvīs magnās etiam cōpiās**; but it makes little sense to have **quantāsvīs** and **magnās** together like this. One manuscript gives the reading adopted here, with **cōpiās** gapped: *however many (troops), even many troops of the Germans.* Another editor has suggested dropping **magnās** completely.

1   sērō, adv., *late*; in this context implies *(too) late*.
     factūrōs: sc. **sē** and **esse**. How do you know whether **sē** would mean *him* or *them*?
     clāmitō, -āre, -āvī, -ātus, *to shout repeatedly*, a FREQUENTATIVE verb (see p. 97).

2   **adiungō, adiungere, adiūnxī, adiūnctus**, *to join together, add*.
     calamitās, calamitātis, f., *disaster*. **calamitātis**: partitive genitive with **aliquid**.
     proximīs hibernīs: the camp of Sabinus and Cotta was the most northerly one; if the camps closest to theirs were captured, it would be even more difficult for them to reach safety.

3   *occāsiō, occāsiōnis, f., *opportunity*.

4   **arbitrārī**: sc. **sē**. The ind. state. begun by **clāmitābat** (1) continues.
     profectum: sc. **esse**.
     in Italiam: i.e., to Gallia Cisalpina; Caesar normally spent the winter there and in Illyricum dealing with administrative matters.

6   **nostrī**: genitive of the pronoun **nōs**; **contemptiōne nostrī** = *contempt for us*.
     Nōn hostem auctōrem: sc. **esse**; Sabinus is refuting the final point made by Cotta (28:12–13)

7   **spectāre**: sc. **sē**.
     subsum, subesse, *to be under; to be near, be close by*. The prep. **sub** sometimes means *at the edge of* rather than directly underneath (e.g., **sub monte** = *at the foot of the mountain*), and this sense is also found in compounds of **sub**.
     magnō esse Germānīs dolōrī: a double dative.
     Ariovistī: recall from Book I that Ariovistus fled to Germany after being defeated by Caesar. His death is not mentioned elsewhere in *De bello Gallico*.

8   **ardeō, ardēre, ārsī, ārsūrus**, *to be on fire, burn, be inflamed*; a word often used of passionate feelings as well as in the literal sense.
     *tot, adv., *so many*.
     contumēlia, -ae, f., *insult, affront, indignity*.

9   **redigō, redigere, redēgī, redāctus** [re- + agō], *to reduce, bring (into or under)*.
     rēs mīlitāris, reī mīlitāris, f., *art of war, warfare*.

11   *sententia, -ae, f., *feeling; opinion*.

12   **dūrus, -a, -um**, *hard, harsh, unfortunate*.
     dūrius: *too unfortunate*.

13   **cōnsentiō, cōnsentīre, cōnsēnsī, cōnsēnsus** [con + sentiō], *to be of the same opinion, agree, unite*.

14   **positam**: lit. = *placed*; in this context = *depending on*.
     Cottae . . . atque eōrum: the genitives modify **cōnsilium** (14).
     dissentīrent: deduce from **dis-** + **sentiō** (cf. **cōnsentīret** in line 13).

15   **exitus, -ūs** [< exeō, to go out], m., *result, outcome*.
     Cottae . . . cōnsilium quem habēre exitum: *(he asked) what outcome the plan of Cotta . . . would have*.
     praesēns, praesentis, *present, at the moment, at this time*.
     nōn: esset timenda (16) is gapped.
     longinquā: here = *prolonged* (additional meaning).

16   *obsidiō, obsidiōnis [< obsideō, to sit down in front, besiege], f., *siege*.
     *famēs, famis, f., *hunger, starvation*.

Sabinus offers a different opinion.

1 [29] Contrā ea Titūrius sērō factūrōs clāmitābat, cum maiōrēs manūs hos-
2 tium adiūnctīs Germānīs convēnissent aut cum aliquid calamitātis in prox-
3 imīs hibernīs esset acceptum. Brevem cōnsulendī esse occāsiōnem. Caesa-
4 rem arbitrārī profectum in Italiam; neque aliter Carnūtēs interficiendī Tas-
5 getī cōnsilium fuisse captūrōs, neque Eburōnēs, sī ille adesset, tantā con-
6 temptiōne nostrī ad castra ventūrōs esse. Nōn hostem auctōrem, sed rem
7 spectāre: subesse Rhēnum; magnō esse Germānīs dolōrī Ariovistī mortem
8 et superiōrēs nostrās victōriās; ardēre Galliam tot contumēliīs acceptīs sub
9 populī Rōmānī imperium redāctam, superiōre glōriā reī mīlitāris exstīnctā.
10 Postrēmō quis hoc sibi persuādēret, sine certā rē Ambiorīgem ad eiusmodī
11 cōnsilium dēscendisse? Suam sententiam in utramque partem esse tūtam:
12 sī nihil esset dūrius, nūllō cum perīculō ad proximam legiōnem perven-
13 tūrōs; sī Gallia omnis cum Germānīs cōnsentīret, ūnam esse in celeritāte
14 positam salūtem. Cottae quidem atque eōrum quī dissentīrent cōnsilium
15 quem habēre exitum, in quō sī praesēns perīculum nōn, at certē longinquā
16 obsidiōne famēs esset timenda?

Initial Explorations

1. According to Sabinus, under what two circumstances would it be too late to take action? (1–3)
2. For what two reasons did Sabinus believe that Caesar had already left Transalpine Gaul? (4–6)
3. What were the first two facts that Sabinus claims to be considering? (7–8)
4. What was the third fact? What was the reason for this? (8–9)
5. What rhetorical question did Sabinus ask? (10–11)
6. Sabinus mentions two possibilities and claims his proposal is safe either way. Explain the two possibilities and how Sabinus' idea works in each. (12–14)
7. What did Sabinus finally suggest would be the outcome of following Cotta's plan? (14–16)

Reading Strategy

♦ The final two sentences of this chapter provide a good example of how Roman authors could use the flexible word order of Latin to develop their ideas in logical order, even though the sentence structure can be very different from what we would normally use in English. We can imagine a modern politician saying something like the following: "My plan works this way . . . Now, my opponents—yes, they do have a plan. What would happen if we followed it? Even if it worked for the moment, . . ."

1 *disputātiō, disputātiōnis, f., *argument, debate.*
   prīmīs ōrdinibus: = centuriōnibus prīmōrum ōrdinum.
2 id: object of a verb such as dīxit understood.
3 clārus, -a, -um, *clear, loud.*
   exaudiō, exaudīre, exaudīvī, exaudītus, *to overhear.*
   ut. . . exaudīret: there would have been 15–20 men at the council, so it could
     have been held indoors; apparently the soldiers were crowding around out-
     side and listening.
   Neque is sum: *And I am not the one,* introducing a relative clause of characteristic.
4 hī: referring to the soldiers gathered outside; perhaps Sabinus gestured toward
     the door as he said this.
   sapiō, sapere, sapīvī or sapiī, *to be wise, be prudent, have good sense.*
   sī gravius quid: the meaning of quid depends on sī (E1), even though the two
     words are separated; for gravius, cf. dūrius, line 12 on the previous page.
     See also the Reading Strategy below.
5 abs: an alternative form of ab.
   tē: whom is Sabinus addressing here? Whom was he addressing at the begin-
     ning of the chapter (Vincitis, vultis, 2)?
   quī: the antecedent is *they,* understood subject of reposcent, not tē.
   reposcō, reposcere, *to demand back, claim, require.*
   perendinus, -a, -um, *after tomorrow.*
6 coniungō, coniungere, coniūnxī, coniūnctus, *to join together.*
7 reiciō, reicere, reiēcī, reiectus, *to throw back, cast off, cast out.*
   relegō, -āre, -āvī, -ātus, *to banish.*
   cēterī, -ae, -a, *the rest, the others.*
   ferrum, -ī, n., *iron;* by METONYMY, *sword.*
   *intereō, interīre, interīvī or interiī, interitūrus, *to perish, die.*

Reading Strategy: Conditional Sentences

◆ Lines 4–7 opposite contain two different types of conditional sentence (sī . . . repos-
  cent and sī . . . intereant). What tenses are used and what kind of a condition is each?
  This would be an good opportunity to review conditional sentences if necessary; see
  P2–P3 for help.

Sabinus continues to press for departure.

1 [30] Hāc in utramque partem disputātiōne habitā, cum ā Cottā prīmīsque
2 ōrdinibus ācriter resisterētur, "Vincite," inquit, "sī ita vultis," Sabīnus, et id
3 clāriōre vōce, ut magna pars mīlitum exaudīret: "Neque is sum," inquit, "quī
4 gravissimē ex vōbīs mortis perīculō terrear: hī sapient; sī gravius quid ac-
5 ciderit, abs tē ratiōnem reposcent quī, sī per tē liceat, perendīnō diē cum
6 proximīs hibernīs coniūnctī commūnem cum reliquīs bellī cāsum sustin-
7 eant, nōn reiectī et relegātī longē ab cēterīs aut ferrō aut famē intereant."

Initial Explorations

1. Describe the debate that took place in the council of war. (1–2)
2. Why did Sabinus raise his voice? (3)
3. How does Sabinus describe himself? (3–4)
4. How does he characterize the common soldiers? (4)
5. What will the soldiers do if things go badly? (4–5)
6. According to Sabinus, what will be the soldiers' situation if Cotta follows his advice? (5–6)
7. What does Sabinus suggest will happen if his advice is not followed? (7)

Discussion

1. Write a point-by-point comparison of the speeches of Cotta and Sabinus, and compare these points carefully with those made by Ambiorix in §27.
2. What does Sabinus mean by saying **Vincite, sī ita vultis** (2)? This can be interpreted in at least two different senses.
3. Sabinus implies, but does not explicitly state, several things.
   a) Why does he describe himself by saying **Neque is sum quī gravissimē ex vōbīs mortis perīculō terrear** (3–4)?
   b) What is the point of his rather pithy comment **Hī sapient**? (4)
4. What figure of speech does Caesar employ to emphasize the points Sabinus makes in lines 6–7?
5. Caesar very rarely uses direct speech in *De bello Gallico*. What is gained by giving Sabinus' words directly?

1 **cōnsurgitur**: an impersonal passive.
  comprehendunt: i.e., grasp their hands.
2 **dissensiō, dissensiōnis** [dis- + sentiō] f., *disagreement.*
  pertinācia, -ae, f., *obstinacy, stubbornness.*
3 **seu . . . seu**, *whether . . . or.*
  ūnum: *one (thing)*, a neuter substantive, i.e., one plan, one course of action.
4 **perspiciō, perspicere, perspexī, perspectus**, *to look into, examine; to observe,*
    perceive.
5 **dare manūs**, idiom, *to submit, yield.* The image is that of allowing one's hands to
    be bound, as when taken captive.
6 *****prōnūntiō, -āre, -āvī, -ātus**, *to proclaim, announce.*
  itūrōs: sc. **eōs** and **esse.**
  *****vigilia, -ae**, f., *wakefulness, sleeplessness. lack of sleep; watch* (one of four divisions
    of the nighttime in the Roman military). The general meaning applies here,
    the miliary meaning in line 10 below.
  vigiliīs: the plural may be translated by a singular in English; Caesar probably
    used the pl. to convey the image of all the soldiers not getting any sleep.
7 **sua**: a neuter plural substantive, *his own things*, less lit., *his possessions.*
  circumspiceret: deduce from **circum** and the other verbs from the same root
    that you know (e.g., **cōnspicere, respicere**).
  quid sēcum . . . . : a verb such as "thinking" or "wondering" is implied before this
    indirect question.
8 **īnstrumentum, -ī**, n., *implement, instrument, equipment.*
  *****relinquō, relinquere, relīquī, relictus**, *to leave behind, abandon.*
9 **excōgitō, -āre, -āvī, -ātus**, *to think up, contrive, devise, invent.*
  omnia excōgitantur: *all things are invented*, more freely, *they invent all sorts of*
    reasons; the soldiers were getting nervous about leaving.
  quārē, adv., *for what reason, why.*
  *****nec**: this word usually means *and . . . not* or *but . . . not*; sometimes, though, it is
    essentially = **nōn**, as in this sentence.
  maneātur: another impersonal passive.
  languor, languōris, m., *weariness.*
10 **augeō, augēre, auxī, auctus**, *to enlarge, increase.*
  languōre . . . augeātur: the soldiers imagine that if they stayed, they would
    be besieged and forced to remain constantly on guard and be worn down
    through fatigue. This was not a completely unreasonable fear, as shown by
    what happened when Cicero's camp was besieged, as you will read later.
  *****sīc**, adv., *thus, in this way, so.*
  ut: correlative with **sīc**, with the meaning *like* or *as.*
  quibus esset persuāsum: *to whom it had been persuaded*, less lit., *who had been*
    persuaded; see **F3e** for this use of the passive. **esset persuāsum** is subjunctive
    in a relative clause of characteristic (**O2f**).
12 **cōnsilium**: here = *advice, counsel.*
  datum: sc. **esse** in indirect statement depending on **esset persuāsum** (11).
  longissimō . . . impedīmentīs: this abl. phrase tells how the Romans set out.
  *****agmen, agminis**, n., *column, line of march.*

The debate is settled.

1 [31] Cōnsurgitur ex cōnsiliō; comprehendunt utrumque et ōrant, nē suā
2 dissēnsiōne et pertināciā rem in summum perīculum dēdūcant: facilem
3 esse rem, seu maneant, seu proficīscantur, sī modo ūnum omnēs sentiant
4 ac probent; contrā in dissēnsiōne nūllam sē salūtem perspicere. Rēs dispu-
5 tātiōne ad mediam noctem perdūcitur. Tandem dat Cotta permōtus manūs:
6 superat sententia Sabīnī. Prōnūntiātur prīmā lūce itūrōs. Cōnsūmitur vigi-
7 liīs reliqua pars noctis, cum sua quisque mīles circumspiceret, quid sēcum
8 portāre posset, quid ex īnstrūmentō hibernōrum relinquere cōgerētur. Om-
9 nia excōgitantur, quārē nec sine perīculō maneātur et languōre mīlitum et
10 vigiliīs perīculum augeātur. Prīmā lūce sīc ex castrīs proficīscuntur, ut qui-
11 bus esset persuāsum nōn ab hoste, sed ab homine amīcissimō Ambiorīge
12 cōnsilium datum, longissimō agmine maximīsque impedīmentīs.

Initial Explorations

1. What do the officers ask of Sabinus and Cotta during a break in the council? (1–2)
2. Under what circumstances could the situation be handled easily? (2–4)
3. What happens when the council resumes? (4–5)
4. What is the final result? (5–6)
5. What announcement is made to the soldiers? (6)
6. How do the soldiers spend the rest of the night? (6–8)
7. How do the soldiers try to convince themselves that leaving is the proper course of action? (8–10)
8. What was the attitude of the Romans as they left the camp? (10–12)
9. How did they march? (12)

Discussion

1. What do lines 6–10 (**Cōnsūmitur . . . augeātur.**) show about the soldiers' state of mind? Do you find this surprising? What factors might have contributed to this mindset?
2. Think carefully about the implications of the last sentence (**Prīmā lūce . . . impedīmentīs**, 10–12), particularly the final phrase. What does it suggest about the Romans' readiness to deal with any problems that may arise?

1   **posteā quam:** = postquam.

    *****nocturnus, -a, -um,** *during the night, at night.*

    fremitus, -ūs, m., *uproar.*

    vigiliīs: normally the camp would have become quiet as the soldiers went to
        sleep; the enemy could tell that tonight the Romans were staying awake.

2   **īnsidiae, -ārum,** f. pl., *ambush.*

    bipertītō, adv., *in two parts, in two divisions.*

    occultus, -a, -um, *hidden.*

3   **ā:** *at a distance of.*

4   **magnam:** in this context = *deep.*

    convāllis, -is, f., *narrow valley, enclosed valley, ravine.* The Roman camp was
        probably near the modern city of Tongeren in eastern Belgium. Other an-
        cient sources tell us that the hills to the south of Tongeren were thickly for-
        ested, which would have made it easy for the Gauls to conceal themselves.

    dēmīsisset: you can deduce the basic meaning from **dē** + **mittō**; with the reflex-
        ive **sē**, it means *to let oneself down, to descend.*

5   **parte:** *end* in this context. The Romans would have tried to get out of the ravine
        by going back the way they came, or perhaps by pushing ahead through the
        attacking Gauls.

    novissimōs: *the rear guard,* because the most recent recruits were placed at the
        back of the column.

6   **ascēnsus, -ūs,** m., *ascent, climbing.*

    inīquus, -ae, -um [neg. prefix in- + aequus, fair], *unfair, unfavorable.*

    prīmōs: the soldiers at the front of the Roman column.

    nostrīs: dative with the adj. **inīquissimō (A3j).**

Discussion

1. Look at the sculpture of Ambiorix shown on the opposite page. We have no
   information about what Ambiorix actually looked like. How did the sculptor
   want us to think of him, based on this statue?

2. Ambiorix's foot is placed on top of the **fascēs**, the bundle of sticks and an ax
   that symbolized a consul's power, and a laurel wreath. Why did the sculptor
   include these details?

The Gauls ambush the Romans.

1 [32] At hostēs, posteā quam ex nocturnō fremitū vigiliīsque dē profectiōne
2 eōrum sēnsērunt, collocātīs īnsidiīs bipertītō in silvīs opportūnō atque oc-
3 cultō locō ā mīlibus passuum circiter duōbus Rōmānōrum adventum ex-
4 spectābant, et, cum sē maior pars agminis in magnam convāllem dēmīsisset,
5 ex utrāque parte eius vāllis subitō sē ostendērunt, novissimōsque premere et
6 prīmōs prohibēre ascēnsū atque inīquissimō nostrīs locō proelium commit-
7 tere coepērunt.

Initial Explorations

1. What had the enemy realized, and how? (1–2)
2. What did the Gauls do to prepare to attack the Romans? (2)
3. Where did they do this? (2–3)
4. Where had the Romans gone? (4)
5. From where did the Gauls appear? (5)
6. Describe three things the enemy did. (5–7)

A 19th century statue of Ambiorix in the main square of Tongeren, Belgium.

1   **dēmum**, adv., *finally, at last.*

    quī . . . prōvīdisset: a relative clause with its verb in the subjunctive can indicate cause; translate *because he had provided.*

    trepidō, -āre, -āvī, *to be upset, be confused, panic.*

    concursō, -āre, -āvī, -ātus, *to run this way and that, run around.*

2   **dispōnō, dispōnere, disposuī dispositus** [dis + pōnō], *set out, arrange, deploy.*

    trepidāre, concursāre, dispōnere: see the Structure note on the opposite page.

    haec ipsa: a n. pl. substantive, *these very things*, referring to Sabinus' attempts to deal with the situation.

    haec . . . timidē: a verb such as **faciēbat** is understood.

    omnia: *everything*, less lit., *all his faculties.*

3   **dēficere**: here = *fail* (new meaning); Sabinus (**eum**) was so disoriented that he lost his ability to command effectively.

    *****negōtium, -ī**, n., *business; trouble, difficulty.*

4   **cōgitō, -āre, -āvī, -ātus**, *to think.*

    cōgitāsset: what would be the uncontracted form of this verb (see **E2g**)? The subjunctive indicates cause, as with **prōvīdisset** (1).

5   **nūllā in rē commūnī salūtī dēerat**: *in no regard was lacking for the common wel-fare*, i.e., he did everything he could for his fellow soldiers.

7   **officia**: this word is gapped, so needs to be translated with the previous phrase also. How could you spot the gapping for yourself, without this note?

    mīlitis officia: i.e., Cotta personally took part in the fighting.

    praestābat: *fulfill, discharge, perform* (additional and rather different meaning).

8   **per sē**: *personally.*

    obeō, obīre, obīvī or **obiī, obitūrus**, *to go towards; to perform, attend to.*

    quōque locō: = **in quōque locō.**

9   **prōnūntiāre**: supply **mīlitēs** or a similar acc. word.

10 *****orbis, orbis**, m., *circle.* This means a large hollow circle, with the high ranking officers, wounded soldiers, etc., in the center. As Caesar says, this arrange-ment made it easier to manage the situation, and also to protect the wounded and to provide a solid defense. But it was not a tactic that the Romans nor-mally used except when an army was afraid of being overwhelmed by the enemy, which explains the reaction on both sides (11–13).

    reprehendō, reprehendere, reprehendī, reprehēnsus, *to blame, find fault with, criticize.*

11 **incommodē**, adv., *inconveniently; unfortunately.*

12 **alacer, alacris, alacre**, *lively, eager.*

    nōn sine summō timōre et dēspērātiōne: LITOTES.

13 **factum**: sc. **esse.**

Sabinus and Cotta try to save the situation.

1   [33] Tum dēmum Titūrius, quī nihil ante prōvīdisset, trepidāre et concur-
2   sāre cohortēsque dispōnere, haec tamen ipsa timidē atque ut eum omnia
3   dēficere vidērentur; quod plērumque eīs accidere cōnsuēvit quī in ipsō ne-
4   gōtiō cōnsilium capere cōguntur. At Cotta, quī cōgitāsset haec posse in iti-
5   nere accidere atque ob eam causam profectiōnis auctor nōn fuisset, nūllā in
6   rē commūnī salūtī dēerat et in appellandīs cohortandīsque mīlitibus impe-
7   rātōris et in pugnā mīlitis officia praestābat. Cum propter longitūdinem ag-
8   minis minus facile omnia per sē obīre et quid quōque locō faciendum es-
9   set prōvidēre possent, iussērunt prōnūntiāre ut impedīmenta relinquerent
10   atque in orbem cōnsisterent. Quod cōnsilium etsī in eiusmodī cāsū repre-
11   hendendum nōn est, tamen incommodē accidit: nam et nostrīs mīlitibus
12   spem minuit et hostēs ad pugnam alacriōrēs effēcit, quod nōn sine summō
13   timōre et dēspērātiōne id factum vidēbātur.   (continued)

Initial Explorations

1. What did Titurius Sabinus do? (1–2)
2. Were his actions effective? Why or why not? (2–3)
3. What explanation does Caesar give for this? (3–4)
4. What had been Cotta's thinking? (4–5)
5. How does Caesar describe Cotta's actions in the battle? (6–7)
6. What general problem did Sabinus and Cotta have in trying to deal with the situation? (7–9)
7. What order did they give as a result? (9–10)
8. What does Caesar say in general about the tactic they used? How did it work in this particular situation? (10–11)
9. How did this tactic affect the Romans and the Gauls differently, and why? (11–13)

Structure: Historic Infinitive

◆ Roman authors sometimes used an infinitive in place of a conjugated verb in the imperfect or perfect. This conveys a sense of urgency or haste. It is most common in the writings of historians and so is called the HISTORIC INFINITIVE. You can identify an historic infinitive because it it has a nom. case subject (**Titūrius**, 1); in all other constructions the infinitive is used with an accusative subject. Translate an historic infinitive with a past tense verb in English.

14 ***praetereā**, adv., *in addition*.

    ut: introduces a result clause with three different subjects: **mīlitēs**, *he* (from **quisque**), and finally the plural **omnia**, with no connecting words to join the clauses (ASYNDETON).

  *vulgus, -ī, n., *crowd* (note the unusual gender).

    vulgō: abl. of **vulgus** used as an adv., *everywhere, generally, universally*.

  ab signīs discēderent: for the role of the **signa** in battle, see 4.25–26.

15 **quae**: What gender and number is this pronoun? What antecedent needs to be supplied? (Cf. the first Reading Strategy on page 27.)

  cārus, -a, -um, *precious, dear*.

  habēret: *held* (in mind), *considered*.

16 **arripiō, arripere, arripuī, arreptus** [ad + rapiō], *to seize*.

  properō, -āre, -āvī, -ātus, *to hurry*.

  flētus, -ūs [< fleō, to weep], m., *weeping*. Roman men—even tough legionaries— were much more open to expressing their feelings than are most American males. The soldiers were under no illusions about what was likely to happen to them, but this did not stop them from fighting bravely.

1 **dēfuit**: for the construction, see note for **dēsum**, 4.26:13, page 82.

  *dux, ducis, m., *leader*; *commander* (military term).

  prōnūntiāre: see note for 33:9, page 132.

3 **proinde** [prō- + inde, then], adv., *consequently*.

  omnia in victōriā posita (esse): i.e., that there would be no benefit for the ordinary Gauls from the battle unless the Romans were actually defeated.

4 ***pār, paris**, *equal*.

  Erant . . . parēs: There is a problem with the text here, since the larger context makes it clear that the Romans were outnumbered. Reading **studiō** for **numerō** has been suggested; this makes sense but is not certain to be correct.

  tametsī [contraction of tamen + etsī], conj., *even though, although*.

5 **dēserō, dēserere, dēseruī, dēsertus**, *to desert*.

6 **quotiēns**, adv., *as often as*.

  prōcurrerat: for the tense, see **F2j** or the Structure note on page 82.

7 **cadō, cadere, cecidī, cāsus**, *to fall; to die*. Do not confuse with **cēdō**, *to go, yield*, or with **caedō**, *to kill*.

  prōnūntiārī: imper. pass., *the word to be passed*, used as an infin. with **iubet**.

8 ***procul**, adv., *far off, in the distance, from a distance*.

  neu [shorter form of **nēve**], *and not*.

  accēdō, accēdere, accessī, accessūrus [ad + cēdō], *to come toward, approach*.

9 ***cēdō, cēdere, cēssī, cessūrus**, *to go, move; to give way, yield*. This is the root verb, many of whose compounds you have already learned. Note that the simple verb has the meaning *yield* which is not found in the compounds.

  levitās, levitātis, f., *lightness*.

  nihil: adverbial, as an emphatic way of saying **nōn**, = *not at all, in no way*.

10 **posse**: the impersonal **potest** = *it is possible* becomes an infin. in ind. statement.

  sē ad signa recipientēs: standards remained fixed while the cohorts advanced.

  īnsequor, īnsequī, īnsecūtus sum, *to follow after, pursue, press upon*.

14 Praetereā accidit, quod fierī necesse erat, ut vulgō mīlitēs ab signīs discē-
15 derent, quae quisque eōrum cārissima habēret ab impedīmentīs petere atque
16 arripere properāret, clāmōre et flētū omnia complērentur.

10. What other things happened as a result of the order to form a circle? (14–16)

Discussion
1. What do you make of the soldiers' behavior (14–16)? Why did they act as they did?
2. Caesar does not comment on this breach of military discipline. Why do you think he did not?

❊ ❊ ❊ ❊ ❊

The Gauls respond to the Roman tactics.

1 [34] At barbarīs cōnsilium nōn dēfuit. Nam ducēs eōrum tōtā aciē prōnūn-
2 tiāre iussērunt, nē quis ab locō discēderet, illōrum esse praedam atque illīs
3 reservārī quaecumque Rōmānī relīquissent: proinde omnia in victōriā po-
4 sita exīstimārent. Erant et virtūte et †numerō pugnandī† parēs. Nostrī, ta-
5 metsī ab duce et ā fortūnā dēserēbantur, tamen omnem spem salūtis in vir-
6 tūte pōnēbant, et quotiēns quaeque cohors prōcurrerat, ab eā parte magnus
7 numerus hostium cadēbat. Quā rē animadversā, Ambiorīx prōnūntiārī iubet
8 ut procul tēla coiciant neu propius accēdant et, quam in partem Rōmānī im-
9 petum fēcerint, cēdant: levitāte armōrum et cotīdiānā exercitātiōne nihil hīs
10 nocērī posse; rūrsus sē ad signa recipientēs īnsequantur.

Initial Explorations
1. What order did the Gallic leaders give? (1–2)
2. What did they say that would help keep the soldiers in line? (2–4)
3. What one hope did the Romans have of saving the situation? (4–6)
4. What tactic did the Romans employ? (6)
5. How successful was this tactic? (6–7)
6. What three orders did Ambiorix give after seeing what was going on? (7–9)
7. What statement did he make about the Gauls, if they followed this order? (9–10)
8. What final order did Ambiorix give? (10)

1   **praeceptum, -ī** [< **praecipiō**, to order], n., *command, order.*
   ***quispiam, quaepiam, quodpiam,** indef. adj., *any.*

2   **vēlōx, vēlōcis,** *swift, quick.*

3   **nūdō, -āre, -āvī, -ātus,** *to lay bare, expose.*
   ā latere apertō: see note for 4.25:3, page 76.

5   ***circumveniō, circumvenīre, circumvēnī, circumventus,** *to surround.*
   sīn [sī + -ne], conj., *but if.*

6   **nec virtūtī locus relinquēbātur:** i.e., no matter how brave the Romans were,
      staying in the circle offered them no chance to escape from the trap.

7   **vītō, -āre, -āvī, -ātus,** *to avoid.* (No connection to the noun **vīta, -ae,** f., *life.*)
   ***incommodum, -ī,** n., *inconvenience; trouble, misfortune.*
   cōnflīctō, -āre, -āvī, -ātus, *to strike; to harass, trouble, afflict.*

9   **ad hōram octāvam:** Romans divided daylight into twelve hours, so the eighth
      hour is 2/3 of the way from dawn to dusk; about 1–2 p.m. at this time of year.
   indignus, -a, -um + abl., *unworthy (of).*

10 **T. Balventiō:** a dative of reference (**A3h**); translate by an English possessive.
   prīmum pīlum dūxerat: *had led the **prīmus pīlus**;* i.e., had commanded the first
      century of the first cohort. After the military reforms of Marius (see page 8),
      the term **prīmus pīlus** came to refer to the first centurion of the first cohort,
      as well as to the century that he commanded. This was the most prestigious
      rank for centurions (note how Caesar describes Balventius in this sentence);
      the **prīmus pīlus** was considered the senior centurion of the entire legion.
      Apparently Balventius was no longer **prīmus pīlus;** Caesar does not tell us
      why, but he probably was an **ēvocātus,** a soldier whose enlistment was up but
      who remained in service at the request of his commander.

11 **femur, femoris,** n., *thigh.*
   ***trāgula, -ae,** f., *spear* of a type used by the Gauls.
   ***trāiciō, trāicere, trāiēcī, trāiectus** [trāns + iaciō], *to throw through, pierce.*

13 ***subveniō, subvenīre, subvēnī, subventūrus** + dat., *to come to the aid of.*
   adhortor, -ārī, -ātus sum, *to encourage.*

14 **in adversum ōs:** *into his turned-to face,* less lit., *directly in the face.*
   funda, -ae, f., *slingshot;* by METONYMY = a stone thrown from a slingshot.
   vulnerō, -āre, -āvī, -ātus, *to wound.*

Reading Strategy

♦ The first word in a Latin sentence often indicates the topic of discussion, whether or
not it is the grammatical subject. In the middle of this chapter Caesar describes the
general difficulties his men faced; then he wants to talk about some individuals. By
putting Balventius' name first, as a dative of reference, he clearly shows the transition. The reason for the dative (or possibly ablative) is not clear until the reader gets
to the end of the sentence, but the logic of the Latin word order is perfect. This can
be seen by comparing the Latin to an English transation: the only way to make sense
in English is to translate **Balventiō** as a possessive with **femur,** but that makes for a
very abrupt transition.

Things go badly for the Romans.

1 [35] Quō praeceptō ab eīs dīligentissimē observātō, cum quaepiam cohors
2 ex orbe excesserat atque impetum fēcerat, hostēs vēlōcissimē refugiēbant.
3 Interim eam partem nūdārī necesse erat et ab latere apertō tēla recipī. Rūr-
4 sus cum in eum locum unde erant ēgressī revertī coeperant, et ab eīs quī
5 cesserant et ab eīs quī proximī steterant circumveniēbantur. Sīn autem lo-
6 cum tenēre vellent, nec virtūtī locus relinquēbātur, neque ab tantā multi-
7 tūdine coiecta tēla cōnfertī vītāre poterant. Tamen tot incommodīs cōnflic-
8 tātī, multīs vulneribus acceptīs resistēbant et magnā parte diēī cōnsūmptā,
9 cum ā prīmā lūce ad hōram octāvam pugnārētur, nihil quod ipsīs esset in-
10 dignum committēbant. Tum T. Balventiō, quī superiōre annō prīmum pīlum
11 dūxerat, virō fortī et magnae auctōritātis, utrumque femur trāgulā trāicitur;
12 Q. Lūcānius eiusdem ōrdinis, fortissimē pugnāns, dum circumventō fīliō
13 subvenit, interficitur; L. Cotta lēgātus omnēs cohortēs ōrdinēsque adhortāns
14 in adversum ōs fundā vulnerātur.

Initial Explorations

1. What were some of the Roman cohorts doing? (1–2)
2. How did the Gauls react when this happened? (2)
3. In what difficulty did the Romans find themselves as a result? (3)
4. What happened when they began to retreat? (3–5)
5. What happened if they tried to stand their ground? (5–7)
6. How does Caesar describe the general condition of the troops? (7–8)
7. How long did the fighting go on? (8–9)
8. How did the Roman soldiers behave despite the difficulties? (9–10)
9. Who was Titus Balventius? How is he described? (10–11)
10. What happened to him? (11–12)
11. Under what circumstances was Quintus Lucanius killed? (12–13)
12. What was Cotta doing, and what happened to him? (13–14)

Discussion

1. What does Caesar mean by the phrase **nihil . . . indignum** (9–10)?
2. Why did Caesar include the details of what happened to the two senior
   centurions as well as to Cotta (10–14)?

2 **interpres, interpretis,** m., *interpreter.*

    Cn. Pompeium: this man was probably a Gallic client of Pompey the Great (**Cn. Pompeius Magnus**), since foreigners who were rewarded for their services with Roman citizenship took the **praenōmen** and **nōmen** of their patron.

    rogātum: a supine in the accusative, expressing purpose (**H3a**).

3 *****parcō, parcere, pepercī, parsūrus** + dat., to spare.

    Ille: this pronoun often marks a change in subject, here from Sabinus to Ambiorix. In line 6 below it marks the shift from Ambiorix back to Sabinus.

4 **spērāre:** sc. **sē.**

    ā multitūdine: notice that, as before (5.27:9–10), Ambiorix claims that he must have his people's assent for any deal.

    *****impetrō, -āre, -āvī, -ātus,** *to accomplish, bring to pass; to get, obtain, procure.* This verb usually suggests getting what you want by asking for it and it can also be translated *to obtain one's request.*

    quod . . . pertineat: this clause is the subject of the passive infinitive **impetrārī,** *that what concerned the safety of the soldiers could be obtained;* **pertineat** is subjunctive in a relative clause of characteristic.

5 **nocitūrum īrī:** the very rare future passive infinitive, used in an impersonal passive construction (**E3d–E3e**) with **ipsī** as its dat. object. Translate *that harm would not be done to him in any way,* less lit., *that he would not be harmed.*

    fidem interpōnere, idiom, *to pledge one's word.*

6 **saucius, -a, -um,** *wounded.*

    *****commūnicō, -āre, -āvī, -ātus,** *to communicate, share; to take counsel with, consult.*

    videātur: you know that **vidērī** = *to seem;* sometimes this passive also carries the notion *to seem good, seem best, seem advisable.*

    pugnā: this word comes to the left of its clause marker **ut;** for the use of the abl. with no prep., see the Structure note on page 81.

7 **spērāre:** sc. **sē** (= Sabinus); the indirect statement is introduced by the fact that Sabinus is speaking with Cotta in the previous clause.

    suā: *their own;* Sabinus is thinking about himself and Cotta, as shown by the plural verbs **excēdant** and **colloquantur.**

8 **in eō:** *in this,* i.e., his refusal to go.

9 **persevērō, -āre, -āvī, -ātus,** *to persist, persevere.*

Sabinus asks for a parley with Ambiorix.

1 [36] Hīs rēbus permōtus Q. Titūrius, cum procul Ambiorīgem suōs cohor-
2 tantem cōnspexisset, interpretem suum Cn. Pompeium ad eum mittit ro-
3 gātum ut sibi mīlitibusque parcat. Ille appellātus respondit: sī velit sēcum
4 colloquī, licēre; spērāre ā multitūdine impetrārī posse, quod ad mīlitum sa-
5 lūtem pertineat; ipsī vērō nihil nocitum īrī, inque eam rem sē suam fidem
6 interpōnere. Ille cum Cottā sauciō commūnicat, sī videātur, pugnā ut excē-
7 dant et cum Ambiorīge ūnā colloquantur: spērāre ab eō dē suā ac mīlitum
8 salūte impetrārī posse. Cotta sē ad armātum hostem itūrum negat atque in
9 eō persevērat.

Initial Explorations

1. Whom did Titurius send to Ambiorix? With what message? (2–3)
2. What was Ambiorix' general reply? (3–4)
3. What did Ambiorix hope might be possible? (4–5)
4. What particular message did Ambiorix address to Titurius? How did he reinforce this? (5–6)
5. What question does Titurius ask Cotta? (6–7)
6. What does he hope could happen? (7–8)
7. What was Cotta's response? (8–9)

Discussion

1. The words **spērāre ... interpōnere** (4–6) form an extended CHIASMUS. Explain what makes the chiasmus.
2. Chiasmus emphasizes or points out the words or phrases that make up the figure. Caesar probably did not know exactly what the translator said to the Roman officers; but, as a result of phrasing it this way, what seems foremost in Ambiorix's reply to Sabinus? Why might Sabinus have responded positively to an offer phrased this way?
3. When a word is seriously displaced from its normal position, it receives more stress than it otherwise would. Why did Caesar do this with **pugnā** (6)?
4. Sabinus repeats to Cotta (lines 7–8) what Ambiorix said almost word for word. What does this suggest about Sabinus?
5. How does Cotta's reply (8–9) increase the contrast between himself and Sabinus?

1 **quōs . . . tribūnōs mīlitum:** = **tribūnōs mīlitum quōs;** the antecedent is placed inside the relative clause.

*praesentia, -ae,** f., *presence.*

in praesentiā: *at that time, at the moment.*

3 **accessisset:** deduce from **ad + cēdō.**

abicere: deduce from **ab + iaciō** (review the note about **coiciō,** 24:9, page 76).

imperātum, -ī, [< **imperō,** to order], n., *an order.*

4 *condiciō, condiciōnis,** f., *condition* (here, of surrender).

inter sē agunt: *deal with each other.*

longior: modifies **sermō** (5); HYPERBATON.

cōnsultō, adv., *by design, deliberately.*

5 *īnstituō, īnstituere, īnstituī, īnstitūtus,** to put in place, establish; to fabricate, construct; to undertake, begin.

*sermō, sermōnis,** m., *speech, conversation.*

6 **ululātus, -ūs,** m., *howling.*

7 **nostrōs:** a substantive, *our men* (not an adjective agreeing with **ōrdinēs**).

ōrdinēs perturbant: this means the end for the Romans; once their lines are broken they have no hope of resisting the Gauls.

9 **aquilifer, aquiliferī,** m., *eagle-bearer,* the soldier who carried the standard of the eagle (cf. 4.25, where the **aquilifer** takes the lead in landing on the beach).

10 *intrā,** adv. and prep. + acc., *within.*

11 **ad ūnum:** *to a man.*

12 **sē ipsī interficiunt:** the Romans considered this an honorable way to die, in such a situation. The soldiers probably feared being captured and tortured to death by the Gauls, as Caesar describes happening in other situations.

ēlābor, ēlābī, ēlāpsus sum, *to slip out, escape.*

Dīligēbat quoque usque adeō, ut audītā clade Titūriānā barbam capillumque summīserit nec ante dēmpserit quam vindicāsset. *(Caesar) also loved (his soldiers) even to the extent that, after hearing about the disaster of Titurius, he allowed his beard and hair to grow long[1] and did not cut (them) until he had gotten revenge.*

(Suetonius, *Divus Iulius* 67)

---

[1] A sign of mourning among the Romans.

The battle ends in disaster for the Romans.

1   [37] Sabīnus quōs in praesentiā tribūnōs mīlitum circum sē habēbat et
2   prīmōrum ōrdinum centuriōnēs sē sequī iubet et, cum propius Ambiorī-
3   gem accessisset, iussus arma abicere imperātum facit suīsque ut idem faci-
4   ant imperat. Interim, dum dē condiciōnibus inter sē agunt longiorque cōn-
5   sultō ab Ambiorīge īnstituitur sermō, paulātim circumventus interficitur.
6   Tum vērō suō mōre victōriam conclāmant atque ululātum tollunt impetū-
7   que in nostrōs factō ōrdinēs perturbant. Ibi L. Cotta pugnāns interficitur
8   cum maximā parte mīlitum. Reliquī sē in castra recipiunt unde erant ēgres-
9   sī. Ex quibus L. Petrosidius aquilifer, cum magnā multitūdine hostium pre-
10 merētur, aquilam intrā vāllum prōiēcit; ipse prō castrīs fortissimē pugnāns
11 occīditur. Illī aegrē ad noctem oppugnātiōnem sustinent; noctū ad ūnum
12 omnēs dēspērātā salūte sē ipsī interficiunt. Paucī ex proeliō ēlāpsī incertīs
13 itineribus per silvās ad T. Labienum lēgātum in hiberna perveniunt atque
14 eum dē rēbus gestīs certiōrem faciunt.

Initial Explorations

1. Whom did Sabinus order to follow him? (1–2)
2. What is he ordered to do as he approaches Ambiorix? (2–3)
3. How does Sabinus respond to this order? (3–4)
4. How are the negotiations described? (4–5)
5. What happens to Sabinus as he is speaking with Ambiorix? (5)
6. How do the Gauls react to this? (6–7)
7. What happens to Cotta and most of the soldiers? (7–8)
8. What do the rest do? (8)
9. Who was Petrosidius and in what situation did he find himself? (9–10)
10. What action did Petrosidius take? What finally happened to him? (10–11)
11. What do the men in the camp do until nightfall? (11)
12. What do they do at night and why? (11–12)
13. What did the few soldiers who had escaped from the battle do? (12–14)

Discussion

1. In 35:12 Caesar switches to the historic present (**E2a**) and continues to use it through the end of §37. Why did Caesar use the historic present here?
2. Why did Caesar behave as though he were in mourning for a dead family member after the disaster, as described in the quotation from his biographer Suetonius printed on the opposite page?

✳ ✳ ✳ ✳ ✳ ✳ ✳ ✳ ✳

We do not know exactly how many Romans were killed. A legion theoretically contained 6,000 men but was usually smaller. The Romans often did not replace soldiers who were killed, preferring to put recruits into new legions. This meant that veteran legions sometimes were much under strength, even as low as 3,500 men. If we take a conservative figure of 2,000 men for the five cohorts and 4,500 for the legion, Caesar lost about 6,500 men, a very severe setback. You will read in Book VI how Caesar took vengeance on the Eburones for the destruction of Sabinus' and Cotta's command.

✳ ✳ ✳ ✳ ✳ ✳ ✳ ✳ ✳

Discussion

1. Review the passages from Book V so far and note all the places where Caesar mentions Sabinus. How does he talk about Sabinus and his actions? How do you react to this picture, given what happened in the end?

2. How are Sabinus' actions in §37 similar to his behavior earlier? Are you surprised that he acted as he did at this point? What do you make of the fact that he took the military tribunes and senior centurions with him, and that he readily surrendered his weapons and those of the men accompanying him?

3. What do you think about Sabinus' character? Why was he so insistent upon leaving? What were his strengths and weaknesses as a leader?

4. Cotta's opposition to leaving makes him a natural foil for Sabinus as Caesar writes a dramatic account of this disaster. Look carefully at the various times that Caesar talks about Cotta and explain how Caesar emphasizes the contrast between the two men.

5. For what reason(s) might Caesar have refrained from criticizing Sabinus more harshly than he did?

6. Why did Petrosidius behave as he did?

Vocabulary Review: Book V (First Part)

The following asterisked words were introduced in §§24–27:

adsum	nāscor	vāllum
aliter	negō	vereor
auctor	opera, -ae	
biduum	oppugnātiō	**Proper nouns**
commūnis	ōrō	Aduātucī
concilium	palam	Ambiorīx
concitō	pendō	Carnūtēs
cōnscrībō	praeficiō	Catuvolcus
cōnsulō	praesertim	Cicerō, Q.
contrōversia	praesum	Cotta, L. Aurunculeius
dēficiō	quaestor	Crassus, M.
dēspērō	ratiō	Eburōnēs
frūmentārius	repentīnus	Fabius, C.
grātia	salūs	Labiēnus, T.
impellō	sentiō	Nerviī
maiōrēs	servitūs	Sabīnus, Q. Titūrius
minuō	singulāris (new m.)	Samarobrīva
moror	trādō	Tasgetius
mūniō	tūtus	Trēverī

The following asterisked words were introduced in §§28–37:

agmen	intrā	relinquō
audeō	nec	sententia
cēdō	negōtium	sermō
centuriō	nocturnus	sīc
circumveniō	obsidiō	sponte
commūnis	occāsiō	subveniō
condiciō	orbis	tot
disputātiō	pār	trāgula
doceō	parcō	trāiciō
dux	postrēmō	tribūnus
famēs	praesentia	turpis
impetrō	praetereā	vigilia
incommodum	procul	vulgus
īnstituō	prōnūntiō	vulnus
intereō	quispiam	

1 **sublātus**: from **tollō**, *to lift, raise up*; here metaphorical, = *cheered up, excited, elated*.
2 **proficīscitur**: note Caesar's continued use of the historic present.
    neque noctem neque diem: i.e., he travels for about 24 hours without stopping.
4 *posterus, -a, -um*, *following, next*.
    hortāturque: see the Reading Strategy below.
    suī: genitive of the pronoun **sē**; here = *themselves*.
    in Nerviōs: the camp of Quintus Cicero was in the territory of the Nervii. Ambiorix had to get their support in order to besiege the camp successfully, so he carefully explains his reasoning, in contrast to his quick visit to the Aduatuci.
5 **ulcīscor, ulcīscī, ultus sum**, *to get revenge (on)*.
7 **nihil esse negōtī**: **negōtī** is a partitive genitive with **nihil**, *nothing of a task*, less lit., *no great task*; **esse** continues the indirect statement begun by **dēmōnstrat**.
    legiōnem . . . interficī: this acc. and infin. phrase completes the idea of **nihil esse negōtī**. **legiōnem** is modified by the participial phrase **subitō oppressam**.
8 **profiteor, profitērī, professus sum** [pro + fateor, to say], *to declare publicly, confess; to volunteer.*
    adiūtor, adiūtōris [< adiūtus, perf. part. of adiuvō, to help], m., *helper, assistant.*
    adiūtōrem: *as an assistant.*

Reading Strategy

- **hortātur** (4) begins a new clause, as you realize from the fact that that the previous clause is closed by **pervenit** and from the -que. The meaning of **hortātur** suggests that **nē** will introduce an indirect command; Ambiorix is encouraging someone (probably the Nervii) not to do something.

- **suī** is obviously genitive and **līberandī** (4) and **ulcīscendī** (5) seem to modify it, but how the genitive fits into the overall structure is not immediately clear; **Rōmānōs** makes sense as the direct object of **ulcīscendī**. Most likely there will be a noun on which the genitives depend; stay on the lookout for it.

- **prō eīs** (5) starts a prepositional phrase, which is immediately interrupted by the relative clause **quās accēperint**. **iniūriīs** clearly completes the prepositional phrase, and the fact that **iniūriīs** is feminine plural shows that it serves as the delayed antecedent of **quās**. But the function of the genitives is still not clear.

- **occāsiōnem** (5) is a noun and makes good sense if we connect the genitives with it; *an opportunity of . . .* ;

- finally we come to **dīmittant**. It is a transitive verb and so **occāsiōnem** is its direct object; it is also subjunctive and therefore completes the indirect command begun by **hortātur nē** back in line 4. Reread this part of the sentence until you follow the flow of ideas and the grammatical structure.

Ambiorix seeks allies to follow up on his victory.

1 [38] Hāc victōriā sublātus Ambiorīx statim cum equitātū in Aduātucōs, quī
2 erant eius rēgnō fīnitimī, proficīscitur; neque noctem neque diem intermit-
3 tit peditātumque subsequī iubet. Rē dēmōnstrātā Aduātucīsque concitātīs,
4 posterō diē in Nerviōs pervenit hortāturque nē suī in perpetuum līberandī
5 atque ulcīscendī Rōmānōs prō eīs quās accēperint iniūriīs occāsiōnem dī-
6 mittant; interfectōs esse lēgātōs duōs magnamque partem exercitūs inter-
7 īsse dēmōnstrat; nihil esse negōtī subitō oppressam legiōnem quae cum Ci-
8 cerōne hiemet interficī; sē ad eam rem profitētur adiutōrem. Facile hāc ōrā-
9 tiōne Nerviīs persuādet.

Initial Explorations

1. Describe Ambiorix's journey to the Aduatuci. (1–3)
2. What did he do there? (3)
3. What did Ambiorix encourage the Nervii to do? (4–6)
4. What information did he give the Nervii? (6–7)
5. What claim did Ambiorix make? (7–8)
6. How would Ambiorix be involved in this project? (8)
7. Was Ambiorix's appeal to the Nervii successful? (8–9)

Discussion

1. What language does Caesar use to show that Ambiorix made only a quick
   stop among the Aduatuci?

A catapult (**catapulta**), one of several types of artillery (**tormenta**). These were made in various sizes, with bundles of twisted rope (located vertically inside the casing at the front) providing the power. This machine was built to fire wooden stakes, while others could fire rocks. The carriage was pushed forward until the trigger (B) was over the bowstring. A block (C) was jammed under the trigger to hold it down. The carriage was pulled back and kept in place with a hook (D) while the arrow was loaded. Then the block was removed and the trigger fell of its own weight, releasing the string. The range could be controlled through a height adjustment (A).

1 **Ceutronēs ... Geidumnōs:** these were probably clans (**pāgī**) of the Nervii. They are not mentioned elsewhere by Caesar, who throws out the names here to suggest what a large force the Nervii could assemble.

3 **manūs:** *bands*, the second and less common meaning of this word.

dē imprōvīsō [< neg. prefix in- + prōvideō, to foresee], *unexpectedly*.

advolō, -āre, -āvī, -ātus, *to fly towards, rush to*.

4 *****fāma, -ae, f.,** *rumor; report*.

perlāta: deduce from **per** + **ferō**.

quod fuit necesse: i.e., it was inevitable that at some point men who had to go outside the camp for wood or other supplies would be attacked.

5 **nōn nūllī:** remember that this combination (often written as one word) = *some, several*.

lignātiō, lignātiōnis [< lignum, wood], f., *wood-gathering*.

*****mūnītiō, mūnītiōnis** [< mūniō, to fortify], f., *fortification*.

lignātiōnis mūnītiōnisque causā: this phrase forms a kind of HENDIADYS: *for the sake of gathering wood and the fortification(s) = for the sake of gathering wood for the fortifications*.

6 *****intercipiō, intercipere, intercēpī, interceptus,** *to intercept, cut off*.

Hīs circumventīs: the men presumably were killed, but the important point is that they were prevented from bringing Cicero news of the Gauls' arrival.

8 *****concurrō, concurrere, concurrī, concursūrus,** *to rush together, rush*.

9 **cōnscendō, cōnscendere, cōnscendī, cōnscēnsus,** *to climb*.

concurrunt ... cōnscendunt: note the ASYNDETON.

sustentō, -āre, -āvī, -ātus, *to keep up, preserve, hold out, endure*.

quod ... pōnēbant: i.e., the Gauls hoped to take the camp quickly and so attacked as forcefully as possible on the first day.

10 **adipīscor, adipīscī, adeptus sum,** *to reach, get, obtain*.

adeptī: this participle has a conditional sense, *if they obtained . . . .*

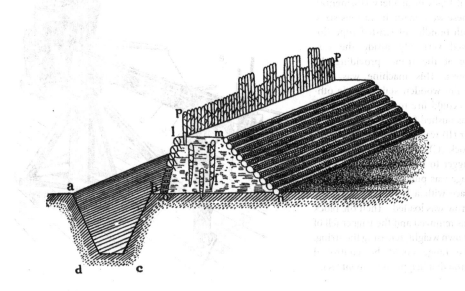

The Gauls attack the camp of Quintus Cicero.

1　[39] Itaque cōnfestim dīmissīs nūntiīs ad Ceutronēs, Grudiōs, Levācōs,
2　Pleumoxiōs, Geidumnōs, quī omnēs sub eōrum imperiō sunt, quam max-
3　imās manūs possunt cōgunt et dē imprōvīsō ad Cicerōnis hiberna advolant,
4　nōndum ad eum fāmā dē Titūrī morte perlātā. Huic quoque accidit, quod
5　fuit necesse, ut nōn nūllī mīlitēs, quī lignātiōnis mūnītiōnisque causā in sil-
6　vās discessissent, repentīnō equitum adventū interciperentur. Hīs circum-
7　ventīs, magnā manū Eburōnēs, Nerviī, Aduātucī atque hōrum omnium sociī
8　et clientēs legiōnem oppugnāre incipiunt. Nostrī celeriter ad arma concur-
9　runt, vāllum cōnscendunt. Aegrē is diēs sustentātur, quod omnem spem
10　hostēs in celeritāte pōnēbant atque hanc adeptī victōriam in perpetuum sē
11　fore victōrēs cōnfīdēbant.

Initial Explorations

1. How did the Nervii obtain additional troops? How many did they try to obtain? (1-3)
2. Why was the arrival of the Gauls at Cicero's camp unexpected? (4)
3. What Romans did the Gauls meet first? What happened to them? (5-6)
4. What Gauls took part in the attack on the camp? (7-8)
5. What did the Romans do in response? How did the battle go on the first day? (8-9)
6. Describe the strategy that the Gauls had adopted. (9-11)

Discussion

1. Was the Gauls' strategy a good one? Why or why not?

＊ ＊ ＊ ＊ ＊ ＊ ＊ ＊ ＊

The diagram on the opposite page shows the typical **vāllum** and **fossa** that the Romans used to fortify their camps. Earth removed while making the ditch (abcd) was used to create the rampart (lmno). **Fascinēs**, bundles of sticks or wickerwork, were inserted into the wall to stabilize the earth (f, f). In permanent camps logs or large branches were also used to strengthen the earthworks and (on the interior) to provide steps that made it easier for soldiers to climb to the top of the rampart. Wooden stakes or palisades (p, p) were used to make the wall or parapet, with merlons projecting upward to provide cover.

1 *littera, -ae, f., *letter* (of the alphabet); in pl., *letter* (written to someone).
   prōpōnō, prōpōnere, prōposuī, prōpositus, *to set forth, offer.*
2 *praemium, -ī, n., *reward.*
   sī pertulissent: note the abrupt shift from the letters and the rewards to the men
      who would carry the letters (= *they*).
   obsideō, obsidēre, obsēdī, obsessus [ob + sedeō], *to besiege; to watch closely* (less
      common meaning but applicable here).
3 *turris, turris, f., *tower.* See the Cultural Context note opposite.
   *admodum [ad + modus] adv., *to full measure, completely, absolutely.*
   turrēs admodum cxx: *a full 120 towers*; Caesar wants to emphasize that the Ro-
      mans really did build this many in one night, although they may have worked
      more on them subsequently (see note for contabulō, line 11 below).
4 *excitō, -āre, -āvī, -ātus, *to wake up, rouse up; to incite, inspire;* (of things) *to raise
      up, build, construct.*
   *opus, operis, n., *work,* here referring to the defenses of the camp, probably the
      ditch and earthen wall in particular.
6 *fossa, -ae, f., *ditch, trench* (around a camp; see the illustration on page 146).
   ratiōne: *way, method* (new meaning).
   prīdiē, adv., *on the day before.*
7 deinceps, adv., *one after the other, in succession.*
8 *vulnerō, -āre, -āvī, -ātus, *to wound.*
   quiēs, quiētis, f., *quiet, rest.*
9 opus sunt: opus, *work,* has an additional meaning = *need, necessity;* here it functions as an adjective, *whatever things are necessary.*
10 praeūrō, praeūrere, praeussī, praeustus, *to burn before, burn at the end.* The ends
   of the stakes were sharpened and then hardened by burning; such stakes were
   thrown by tormenta (catapults of various sizes, powered by twisted ropes).
   sudis, sudis, f., *stake.*
   *pīlum, -ī, n., *spear, javelin.*
   mūrālium pīlōrum: *wall javelins* were larger and heaver than the spears carried
   in battle, since they were intended to be thrown down onto the enemy.
11 contabulō, -āre, -āvī, -ātus, *to build up* (by adding another storey). The precise
   meaning of this word is unclear; it is connected to tabulātum, *floor* or *storey*
   of a building. Perhaps the towers had been built one level up on the first
   night and additional levels were added later, or the complete frameworks
   were built and the flooring and parapets added later.
   pinnae lōrīcaeque: lōrīca is a common word meaning *cuirass,* a type of leather
   armor, but can also mean any kind of defensive work; here it refers to *parapets,* protective walls for defenders; and pinnae are *merlons,* wall segments
   raised above the parapet. See the Cultural Context note opposite.
   crātis, crātis, f., *wicker.*
   attexō, attexere, attexuī, attextus, *to weave together.*
12 tenuis, -is, -e, *thin, fine; feeble, weak.*
   valētūdō, valētūdinis, f., *heath;* tenuissimā valētūdine: abl. of description (A5n).
   nē . . . quidem, adv., *not even.*
13 concursus, -ūs, m., *a running together, crowding around.*

The Romans strengthen their defenses.

1   [40] Mittuntur ad Caesarem cōnfestim ab Cicerōne litterae, magnīs prōpo-
2   sitīs praemiīs, sī pertulissent; obsessīs omnibus viīs missī intercipiuntur.
3   Noctū ex mātēriā, quam mūnītiōnis causā comportāverant, turrēs admo-
4   dum cxx excitantur incrēdibilī celeritāte; quae dēesse operī vidēbantur per-
5   ficiuntur. Hostēs posterō diē multō maiōribus coāctīs cōpiīs castra oppug-
6   nant, fossam complent. Eādem ratiōne, quā prīdiē, ab nostrīs resistitur. Hoc
7   idem reliquīs deinceps fit diēbus. Nūlla pars nocturnī temporis ad labōrem
8   intermittitur; nōn aegrīs, nōn vulnerātīs facultās quiētis datur. Quaecumque
9   ad proximī diēī oppugnātiōnem opus sunt noctū comparantur: multae
10   praeustae sudēs, magnus mūrālium pīlōrum numerus īnstituitur; turrēs
11   contabulantur, pinnae lōrīcaeque ex crātibus attexuntur. Ipse Cicerō, cum
12   tenuissimā valētūdine esset, nē nocturnum quidem sibi tempus ad quiētem
13   relinquēbat, ut ultrō mīlitum concursū ac vōcibus sibi parcere cōgerētur.

Initial Explorations

1. How did Cicero try to make sure that his letter to Caesar got through? (1–2)
2. What happened to the letter and why? (2)
3. In what two ways did the Romans strengthen the camp's defenses during the first night? (3–5)
4. What happened the next day? (5–6)
5. What two things does Caesar tell us that show how desperate the Romans were to maintain their defenses? (7–8)
6. Describe four things that were done during the night. (9–11)
7. How did Cicero himself behave? Why might this have been surprising? (11–13)
8. What forced Cicero to change his behavior? (13)

Discussion

1. Examine the Latin of this chapter carefully and show how Caesar communicates to the reader the haste and desperation of the defenders.

Cultural Context

◆ Look at the picture of the reconstructed fortifications at Alesia on page 242. You can see the wooden wall (parapet) above the ditch with the merlons projecting upwards from it. The reconstructed towers are probably somewhat larger and more substantial than those Cicero's men could construct while under attack, but they show the shape and how the towers fit into the system of fortifications. See also the diagram on page 146.

1 **tunc:** = **tum.**

　*aditus, -ūs [< aditus, supine of adeō, adīre to approach], m., *an approach.*

　aliquem sermōnis aditum: *some approach of speech,* i.e, the ability to speak to
Cicero, referring to leaders whom Cicero would permit to come in to speak
to him because he knew them.

2 **amīcitiae:** this word very often indicates an alliance of political or practical nature, not close personal friendship. Leaders of the Nervii with whom Cicero
had worked, e.g. to provide food for the camp, might call themselves **amīcī.**

3 ***potestās, potestātis,** f., *power; opportunity.*

　commemorō, -āre, -āvī, -ātus, *to recall, remind, mention.*

5 **addō, addere, addidī, additus,** *to add.*

6 **ostentō, -āre, -āvī, -ātus,** *to show, point out, call attention to.*

　fideī faciendae causā: i.e., the fact that Ambiorix is present in their camp shows
that they are telling the truth.

　errō, -āre, -āvī, -ātus, *to wander; to err, be mistaken.*

　*quisquam, quisquam, quicquam, *someone, something, anyone, anything.* This
pronoun is used in contexts with a negative word (**nōn, numquam,** etc.); here
errāre provides that context.

　hīs: antecedent of **quī** (7), *these who.*

7 ***praesidium, -ī,** n., *protection.*

　praesidī: partitive gen. with **quicquam,** *anything of protection = any protection.*

　diffīdō, diffīdere, diffīsus sum [dis- + fidēs], *to distrust, despair of.*

　hōc . . . animō: an ablative of description, *of this mind,* i.e., this was what they
wanted, this was their goal.

　in: *toward* (a common meaning of **in** when followed by a person's name).

8 **recūsō, -āre, -āvī, -ātus,** *to object, refuse, reject.*

　ut nihil nisi hiberna recūsent: i.e., they want to change only one thing in their
relationship with the Romans. This seems a reasonable request; Caesar
mentions elsewhere that the Gauls found it a burden to be forced to supply
provisions for the Roman winter camps. However, this would actually mean
giving up the idea of bringing Gaul under Roman control. Recall from Book
I that when Caesar announced in 58 BCE that his army would winter in the
north rather than returning south to the **prōvincia,** this was immediately understood as an indication of the Roman intention to conquer all of Gaul.

9 **inveterāscō, inveterāscere, inveterāvī,** *to grow old; to become established.*

　licēre: this infinitive continues the indirect statement begun with **dīcunt** (6);
discēdere and **proficīscī** are complementary infinitives with **licēre.**

　*incolumis, -is, -e, *unhurt, safe.*

　per sē: *as far as they are concerned.*

10 ***metus, -ūs** [< metuō, to be afraid], m., *fear.*

13 **ūtantur, mittant:** for the subjunctive use, see **P4d.**

(Vocabulary and notes continued on opposite page.)

The Nervii offer terms.

1 [41] Tunc ducēs prīncipēsque Nerviōrum quī aliquem sermōnis aditum
2 causamque amīcitiae cum Cicerōne habēbant colloquī sēsē velle dīcunt.
3 Factā potestāte eadem quae Ambiorīx cum Titūriō ēgerat commemorant:
4 omnem esse in armīs Galliam; Germānōs Rhēnum trānsīsse; Caesaris reli-
5 quōrumque hiberna oppugnārī. Addunt etiam dē Sabīnī morte; Ambiorī-
6 gem ostentant fideī faciendae causā. Errāre eōs dīcunt, sī quicquam ab hīs
7 praesidī spērent, quī suīs rēbus diffīdant; sēsē tamen hōc esse in Cicerōnem
8 populumque Rōmānum animō, ut nihil nisi hiberna recūsent atque hanc
9 inveterāscere cōnsuētūdinem nōlint: licēre illīs incolumibus per sē ex hi-
10 bernīs discēdere et quāscumque in partēs velint sine metū proficīscī. Cicerō
11 ad haec ūnum modo respondit: nōn esse cōnsuētūdinem populī Rōmānī
12 accipere ab hoste armātō condiciōnem; sī ab armīs discēdere velint, sē ad-
13 iūtōre ūtantur lēgātōsque ad Caesarem mittant; spērāre prō eius iūstitiā quae
14 petierint impetrātūrōs.

Initial Explorations

1. Who wanted to speak to Cicero? (1–2)
2. What were the first three things that they mentioned? (4–5)
3. How did they reinforce their arguments? (5–6)
4. What did they say about help coming from other Roman camps? (6–7)
5. What one thing did the Nervii say that they wanted? (8–9)
6. What would they allow the Romans to do if they gave up the camp? (9–10)
7. In what words did Cicero reject the Gauls' offer? (11–12)
8. What option did Cicero give the Gauls? (12–14)

Discussion

1. How do the actions of Quintus Cicero, in this chapter and the previous one,
   provide an additional contrast to the behavior of Sabinus?

lēgātōs: in this context = *ambassadors* (not military officers).
spērāre: sc. sē.
iūstitia, -ae, f., *justice, sense of justice, fairness.*
spērāre (eōs) prō eius iūstitiā quae petierint impetrātūrōs (esse): for reasons
   explained in the note for line 8 opposite, Cicero must have known that it was
   almost impossible that Caesar would agree to such a request; perhaps he was
   as willing to deceive the Gauls as they were to trick him!

1   **Ab hāc spē**: i.e., the hope of deceiving Cicero as they had Sabinus.
    repulsī: deduce from **re-** + **pellō**.
    fossā pedum xv: this refers to the width of the ditch. Caesar himself used this
        same proportion between the height of the wall and the width of the ditch, so
        the Gauls had indeed learned carefully from the Romans.
2   **cingō, cingere, cīnxī, cīnctus**, *to encircle, surround.*
    Haec et: *these things also.*
    cōnsuētūdine: in this context = *experience*, not *custom.*
3   **quōs . . . captīvōs**: the relative clause is placed before its antecedent, **eīs**.
    nūllā . . . cōpiā: an ablative absolute, *because there was . . .*
4   **ferrāmentum, -ī**, m., *tool.*
    idōneus, -a, -um + dat., *suitable (for).*
    caespes, caespitis, m., *turf. sod.*
5   **circumcīdō, circumcīdere, circumcīdī, circumcīsus**, *to cut around, cut.*
    sagulum, -ī, n., *cloak.*
    exhauriō, exhaurīre, exhausī, exhaustus, *to draw out, empty, remove.*
    vidēbantur: *were seen* (from the Roman camp); not the more common sense of
        seemed.
6   **tribus**: abl. of **trēs**.
7   **circuitus, -ūs**, m., *circuit, circumference.*
    III: say **trium** when you read aloud; it agrees with **mīlium**, which is gen. pl.
8   **turrēs**: here = *siege towers*; these were on wheels and would be moved forward
        when the time came for the assault on the camp. See the model shown on
        page 157.
    falx, falcis, f., *scythe, pruning hook; wall hook*, a hook on a long pole used as a
        siege weapon to pull down the wall when assaulting an enemy fort.
    *****testūdō, testūdinis**, f., *tortoise; mobile shelter* for attackers. Here this refers
        to wheeled sheds, called mantelets or mantlets, open at the front; see the
        illustration on page 155. These would be brought forward and soldiers inside
        would use hooks on poles to pull down part of the wall while protected to
        some extent from missiles thrown down by the defenders. The term **testūdō**
        is also used for a maneuver where a group of soldiers would approach a wall,
        with the men in the middle holding their shields over their heads to protect
        themselves.
    īdem: this word, literally *the same*, is frequently found = *likewise, also.*

The Nervii resume their attack.

1 **[42]** Ab hāc spē repulsī Nerviī vāllō pedum ix et fossā pedum xv hiberna
2 cingunt. Haec et superiōrum annōrum cōnsuētūdine ab nōbīs cognōverant
3 et, quōs clam dē exercitū habēbant captīvōs, ab eīs docēbantur; sed nūllā
4 ferrāmentōrum cōpiā quae esset ad hunc ūsum idōnea, gladiīs caespitēs
5 circumcīdere, manibus sagulīsque terram exhaurīre vidēbantur. Quā qui-
6 dem ex rē hominum multitūdō cognōscī potuit: nam minus hōrīs tribus
7 mīlium passuum in circuitū iii mūnītiōnem perfēcērunt; reliquīsque diēbus
8 turrēs ad altitūdinem vāllī, falcēs testūdinēsque, quās īdem captīvī docue-
9 rant, parāre ac facere coepērunt.

Initial Explorations

1. What did the Nervii do after realizing Cicero was not going to leave the camp? (1–2)
2. How had the Nervii learned these techniques of warfare? (2–3)
3. What problem did the Nervii have when doing this? (3–4)
4. How did they solve the problem? (4–5)
5. What did the Gauls do in less than three hours? (6–7)
6. What information could be deduced from this fact? (5–6)
7. What did the Gauls do on the following days? (7–9)

Text

• The best manuscripts read **mīlium p̃** (a scribal abbreviation for **passuum**) **xv in cir-cuitum mūnītiōnem** (line 7) But a circuit of 15 miles is clearly too large for a one-legion camp. Therefore the reading **circuitū iii** has been proposed; this makes more sense in terms of distance and the ablative is better than the accusative in this context.

• Among other things, editors of ancient texts consider how errors might have origi-nated and whether proposed corrections are plausible, given the possible origin. In some styles of medieval handwriting, three instances of the letter 'i' look very similar to an 'm,' which makes the proposed correction of **circuitum** to **circuitū iii** reason-able. To see why, look at the sample given below, which is a familiar Latin word; what word is it?

𝔪𝔦𝔫𝔦𝔪𝔲𝔪

1 **fervēns, ferventis**, *boiling, seething; burning, glowing, red-hot.*
   fūsilis, -is, -e, *softened.*
2 **argilla, -ae**, f., *potter's clay.* The exact construction of these red-hot bullets is
   not clear. The bullets may have been shaped and fired like pottery dishes to
   harden them, then reheated before use. Another suggestion is that the bullets
   were constructed of clay and another material such as peat or coal that was
   ignited before being thrown.
   glāns, glandis, m., *acorn; bullet*, i.e., an acorn-shaped projectile shot from a sling.
   fervefactus, -a, -um, *hot, heated*; cf. **ferventēs** (1).
   *****iaculum, -ī**, n., *javelin.*
   casās: in a permanent camp the soldiers were housed in cabins or simple barracks, whereas in the temporary camps built during the campaigning season
   they used tents.
   Gallicus, -a, -um, *Gallic.*
   mōre Gallicō: this ablative phrase tells how or why the cabins were thatched;
   what is the best English equivalent?
   strāmentum, -ī, n., *straw.*
3 **tegō, tegere, tēxī, tēctus**, *to cover.*
   coepērunt: the subject is *they* (the Nervii).
   ignem comprehendērunt: *caught fire.*
4 **magnitūdine**: *because of their force* (lit., *size*), an ablative of cause.
   distulērunt: *to carry in different directions, scatter, spread* (new meaning of
   differō). What gapped noun serves as object of **distulērunt**?
5 *****sīcutī**, adv., *as if, as, just as, just as if.*
   pariō, parere, peperī, partus, *to give birth to; acquire, gain.*
   explōrō, -āre, -āvī, -ātus, *to investigate; to assure, confirm.*
   sīcutī partā . . . victōriā: ablative absolute. We usually must supply conjunctions such as *since* or *although* when we translate an ablative absolute. On
   occasion, however, the Romans did include conjunctions as part of ablative
   absolutes, as Caesar does here with **sīcutī**. This ablative absolute indicates
   that the Nervii were overconfident because they believed victory was assured.
6 **scālae, -ārum**, f. pl., *ladder(s)* (plural noun with singular or plural meaning).

The Gauls try to storm the camp.

1 [43] Septimō oppugnātiōnis diē, maximō coortō ventō, ferventēs fūsilī ex
2 argillā glandēs fundīs et fervefacta iacula in casās, quae mōre Gallicō strā-
3 mentīs erant tēctae, iacere coepērunt. Hae celeriter ignem comprehendē-
4 runt et ventī magnitūdine in omnem locum castrōrum distulērunt. Hostēs
5 maximō clāmōre, sīcutī partā iam atque explōrātā victōriā, turrēs testūdi-
6 nēsque agere et scālīs vāllum ascendere coepērunt.   (continued)

Initial Explorations

1. When did the events described here take place and in what weather conditions? (1)
2. What detail does Caesar give about the cabins in the camp? (2–3)
3. In what unusual way did the Gauls attack the camp? (1–3)
4. What was the result? (2 parts) (3–4)
5. How did the Gauls react when they realized that their tactic had worked? (4–5)
6. What was the next phase of the assault? (5–6)

A **testūdō**, *mantlet*, a moveable shed designed to provide shelter for the besiegers as they attacked the walls. The roof was covered with animal skins soaked in water to resist attempts by the defenders to set the wooden structure on fire.

7 **At tanta**: see the Reading Strategy below for help with the first sentence.

   tanta: modifies both **virtūs** and **ea praesentia**.

   cum: *although*.

   ubīque, adv., *everywhere, on all sides, from all directions*.

8 **torreō, torrēre, torruī, tostus**, *to set on fire, scorch, burn*.

9 **cōnflāgrō, -āre, -āvī, -ātus**, *to burn up, be on fire*.

   nōn modo: *not only*; correlates with **sed** (10) and **ac tum** (11).

10 **dēmigrō, -āre, -āvī, -ātus**, *to move away, leave behind, abandon*.

   ***dēcēdō, dēcēdere, dēcessī, dēcessūrus**, *to go away, depart*.

   nēmō: note that the subject here is postponed until the end of its clause for dramatic effect.

   ***paene**, adv., *almost*.

   sed paene nē respiceret quidem quisquam: *but hardly anyone even looked back*.

Reading Strategy

• The sentence that begins **At tanta . . .** (7) is complex. The first clause clearly ends at **fuit**. This is followed by **ut**; given the presence of **tanta** in the previous clause, you would expect (correctly) that **ut** begins a result clause.

• Before the **ut** clause develops, however, you meet **cum**; this is clearly the conjunction, not the preposition (how do you know?) so you expect conjugated verb(s), probably in the subjunctive, to complete it. You meet **torrērentur** (8), but the **-que** on the next word (**maximaque**) suggests that the clause is not complete; then comes **premerentur**, another **-que**, and finally **intellegerent** (9), which concludes the **cum** clause. The last section of the **cum** clause includes **omnia impedīmenta . . . cōnflagrāre**; when you reach **intellegerent** you realize that this is an indirect statement with **intellegerent** as the verb of thinking, introduced by **suaque** (8).

• **nōn modo** (9) is very common as the first member of a pair, often completed by a phrase such as **sed etiam**. So you realize that a new clause begins and that there may be two parts to it. This clause ends with **dēcēderet nēmō**; the fact that **dēcēderet** is subjunctive suggests that it belongs to the result clause begun by **ut** in line 7. (Had you forgotten about that unfinished clause?) Finally you see **sed paene**, which correlates with **nōn modo** to introduce the second part of the clause. **nē** (10) might begin yet another clause, but reading two more words along shows you that it is the expression **nē . . . quidem**, not the conjunction. Finally the **ut** clause (and the sentence) ends with **pugnārent**.

• You will probably need to read this several times before it all makes sense. Writing this sentence out in a table of sense units (see page 15 for a model) would also be very helpful. You have a main clause, the beginning of a result clause, a long **cum** clause nested inside the result clause, and finally three parts to the result clause. Note that Caesar has helped guide you through this sentence by consistently using **-que** to keep the three parts of the **cum** clause connected and by structuring the result clause with the correlatives **nōn modo . . . sed paene**.

---

7 At tanta mīlitum virtūs atque ea praesentia animī fuit ut, cum ubīque flam-
8 mā torrērentur maximāque tēlōrum multitūdine premerentur suaque om-
9 nia impedīmenta atque omnēs fortūnās cōnflāgrāre intellegerent, nōn modo
10 dēmigrandī causā dē vāllō dēcēderet nēmō, sed paene nē respiceret quidem
11 quisquam, ac tum omnēs ācerrimē fortissimēque pugnārent.

(continued)

7. What three things does Caesar tell us about the situation in which the
   soldiers found themselves? (7–9)
8. How did the soldiers behave in this situation? (9–11)
9. What was the cause of this behavior? (7)

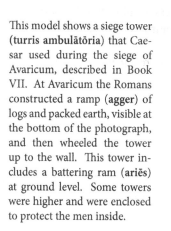

This model shows a siege tower (**turris ambulātōria**) that Caesar used during the siege of Avaricum, described in Book VII. At Avaricum the Romans constructed a ramp (**agger**) of logs and packed earth, visible at the bottom of the photograph, and then wheeled the tower up to the wall. This tower includes a battering ram (**ariēs**) at ground level. Some towers were higher and were enclosed to protect the men inside.

12 **ut**: *inasmuch as*; one of the less common uses of **ut** with the indicative is to introduce an explanation or reason for what has just been said.

14 **cōnstīpō, -āre, -āvī, -ātus**, *to crowd closely together, press together.*

   recessus, -ūs [< recessus, supine of recēdō], m., *a going back, departure, withdrawal*, less lit., *a way to withdraw.*

   ultimus, -a, -um, *last.*

   ultimī: a substantive, *the ones in back.*

   Paulum: take with **intermissā flammā.**

15 **quōdam locō**: = in **quōdam locō** (**B4b**).

   adigō, adigere, adēgī, adāctus, *to drive up , push forward.*

   contingō, contingere, contigī, contactus, *to touch, reach, make contact with.*

16 **ex eō**: eō . . . locō: note how the relative clause **quō stābant** is embedded within the prepositional phrase; another example of enclosing word order.

   recēdō, recēdere, recessī, recessūrus, *to move back, withdraw.*

17 **nūtus, -ūs**, m., *nod, gesture.*

   *__introeō, introīre, introīvī__ or **introiī, introitūrus**, irreg., *to go in, enter.*

   vocāre coepērunt: the centurions were trying to "psych out" the Gauls by reacting differently than they might have expected.

18 **nēmō**: note again how **nēmō** terminates its clause, for emphasis; cf. line 10 on the previous page.

   lapis, lapidis, m., *stone.*

   lapidibus coniectīs: i.e., by the Romans inside the camp.

19 **dēturbō, -āre, -āvī, -ātus**, *to force away, dislodge.*

   dēturbātī: = **dēturbātī sunt** (ELLIPSIS). The unexpressed subject of this verb is *they* (the Nervii), since the closest masculine plural reference is to *them* (**quōrum** in line 16).

   *__succendō, succendere, succendī, succēnsus__, *to set on fire, burn.*

12 Hic diēs nostrīs longē gravissimus fuit, sed tamen hunc habuit ēventum, ut
13 eō diē maximus numerus hostium vulnerārētur atque interficerētur, ut sē
14 sub ipsō vāllō constīpāverant recessumque prīmīs ultimī nōn dabant. Pau-
15 lum quidem intermissā flammā et quōdam locō turrī adāctā et contingente
16 vāllum, tertiae cohortis centuriōnēs ex eō quō stābant locō recessērunt su-
17 ōsque omnēs remōvērunt; nūtū vōcibusque hostēs, sī introīre vellent, vocāre
18 coepērunt; quōrum progredī ausus est nēmō. Tum ex omnī parte lapidibus
19 coiectīs dēturbātī, turrisque succēnsa est.

10. What was this day like, according to Caesar? (12)
11. What was the outcome of the day's action? (12–13)
12. What was one reason for this outcome? (13–14)
13. What was the Gauls' next move? (15–16)
14. How did the centurions react at first? (16–17)
15. What did they do after the Gauls gained access to the wall? (17–18)
16. How did the Gauls respond to this? (18)
17. In what ways did this part of the assault end? (18–19)

Discussion

1. How does the behavior the soldiers in lines 7–11 provide another contrast
   with the leadership of Sabinus?
2. If the Gauls had been able to enter the camp in large numbers through the
   siege tower, they would probably have overwhelmed the Romans. Yet the
   Romans seem to have had little difficulty avoiding this potential disaster.
   Why do you think this was?
3. Look closely at Caesar's language at the very end of the chapter and explain
   how he conveys the idea that the Romans made quick work of the Gauls on
   the siege tower.

1 **centuriōnēs**: this is one of several places in *De bello Gallico* where Caesar relates heroic deeds done by centurions. These officers were the backbone of the Roman army; in addition to training and disciplining the men under their command, they were expected to set an example in battle by their own fighting skill and bravery.

prīmīs ōrdinibus: *the first rank* (of centurions in a legion).

quī . . . appropinquārent: subjunctive in a relative clause of result. There is no easy way in English to bring out the force of this subjunctive, which depends on **fortissimī**—the two men were so brave that they were regularly promoted.

2 ***T. Pullō**, ***L. Vorēnus**: two centurions.

3 **quīnam, quaenam, quodnam**, *which*.

anteferō, anteferre, antetulī, antelātus, *to put in front, prefer*.

summīs: this could agree with **simultātibus** or with **locīs**. Most editors take it with **locīs**; *highest places* = *promotion*, with **simultātibus** as an abl. of respect.

simultās, simultātis, f., *animosity, rivalry*.

4 **contendēbant**: *competed*.

5 **Quid**: = **Cūr**.

dubitō, -āre, -āvī, -ātus, *to doubt, hesitate*.

locum: *opportunity* in this context.

***laus, laudis**, f., *praise*.

quem locum . . . virtūtis: *what opportunity for praise of your courage*. This is an awkward phrase and the reading **probandae** instead of **pro laude**, *of proving your courage*, has been adopted in some editions.

6 ***iūdicō, -āre, -āvī, -ātus**, *to judge, decide*.

7 **quaeque**: **quae** + **-que** (not a form of **quisque**, *each*). Note that the relative pronoun **quae** precedes its antecedent **pars**; logically the sentence should include a preposition—**in partem quae . . . irrumpit**.

irrumpō, irrumpere, irrūpī, irruptus, *to burst in*.

8 **Nē. . . quidem**, *Nor indeed*; you know that these two words are often paired = *not even*; here the pairing has a slightly different sense.

sēsē . . . vallō continet: *keeps himself within the stockade*, i.e., remains inside.

exīstimātiō, exīstimātiōnis [< **exīstimō**, to think, judge], f., *opinion, judgment*.

omnium veritus exīstimātiōnem: i.e., Vorenus was afraid of what his fellow soldiers would think if he did not emulate and try to surpass Pullo.

9 **mediocris, -is, -e**, *of medium size, fairly small*.

mediocrī spatiō relictō: i.e., the space left between Pullo and the group of Gauls; Pullo threw his spear at close range.

10 **immittit**: deduce from **in** + **mittō**.

percutiō, percutere, percussī, percussus, *to strike*.

11 ***exanimō, -āre, -āvī, -ātus**, *to knock unconscious*.

hunc: refers to the Gaul whom Pullo had wounded.

scūtum, -ī, n., *shield*.

prōtegō, prōtegere, prōtēxī, prōtēctus, *to protect, cover*.

prōtegunt: The understood subject of this verb and those that follow is *they* = the Nervii.

in hostem: = **in Pullōnem**.

Heroic deeds by two rival centurions.

1 [44] Erant in eā legiōne fortissimī virī, centuriōnēs, quī prīmīs ōrdinibus
2 appropinquārent, T. Pullō et L. Vorēnus. Hī perpetuās inter sē contrōversiās
3 habēbant, quīnam antēferrētur, omnibusque annīs dē locīs summīs simul-
4 tātibus contendēbant. Ex his Pullō, cum ācerrimē ad mūnītiōnēs pugnārē-
5 tur, "Quid dubitās," inquit, "Vorēne? aut quem locum tuae prō laude virtū-
6 tis spectās? Hic diēs dē nostrīs contrōversiīs iūdicābit." Haec cum dīxisset,
7 prōcēdit extrā mūnītiōnēs, quaeque pars hostium cōnfertissima est vīsa ir-
8 rumpit. Nē Vorēnus quidem sēsē vāllō continet, sed omnium veritus exīs-
9 timātiōnem subsequitur. Tum mediocrī spatiō relictō Pullō pīlum in hostēs
10 immittit atque ūnum ex multitūdine prōcurrentem trāicit; quō percussō et
11 exanimātō, hunc scūtīs prōtegunt, in hostem tēla ūniversī coiciunt neque
12 dant regrediendī facultātem. (continued)

Initial Explorations

1. What do we learn about Titus Pullo and Lucius Vorenus? (1–2)
2. Tell two facts about the relationship between these two men. (2–4)
3. How does Pullo taunt Vorenus when the fighting is at its peak? (5–6)
4. What does Pullo do after after saying this? (6–8)
5. How does Vorenus react and why? (8–9)
6. How does Pullo begin to engage the Gauls? (9–10)
7. In what two ways do the Gauls respond? (10–11)
8. What problem does Pullo have? (11–12)

13 **trānsfīgō, trānsfīgere, trānsfīxī, trānsfīxus**, *to pierce through.*
    Pullōnī: a dative of reference; may be translated by an English possessive, *Pullo's.*
    verūtum, -ī, n., *a javelin, short spear.*
    balteus, -ī, m., *sword belt.*
    dēfīgō, dēfīgere, dēfīxī, dēfīxus, *to stick firmly.* Cf. **trānsfīgō**, above.
    āvertō, āvertere, āvertī, āversus, *to turn aside, knock aside.*

14 **vāgīna, -ae**, f., *sheath, scabbard* of a sword.
    cōnantī: understand **eī**, *with reference to him (Pullo) trying, while he tries.*
    dexter, dextra, dextrum, *right.*
    morātur: This verb is often intransitive (= *to delay, remain*) but can be used
        transitively; with the dir. obj. **dextram manum**, it = *cause a delay, hinder.*
    impedītum: a substantive, *the hindered (man).*

15 **succurrō, succurrere, succurrī, succursūrus** + dat., *to give aid to, run to help.*
    inimīcus: *(his) rival.*
    labōrantī: a present participle used as a substantive, *the struggling (man).*

16 **hunc**: = **Vorēnum.**
    sē: referring to **omnis multitūdō.**
    convertō, convertere, convertī, conversus, *to turn.*

17 **illum**: = **Pullōnem.**
    occīsum: sc. **esse.**
    comminus [con- + manus], adv., *in close quarters, in hand to hand combat.*
    rem: based on this context, what translation for **rem** would you suggest?

18 **ūnō**: one of the Gauls.
    īnstō, instāre, institī [in + stō] + dat., to *pursue, press on.*
    locum . . . īnferiōrem: i.e., a dip or depression in the ground.

19 **dēiciō, dēicere, dēiēcī, dēiectus** [dē + iaciō], *to throw down*; in passive, *to fall.*
    concidō, concidere, concidī [con + cadō], *to fall down.*

20 **ambō, ambae, ambō**, *both.*

21 **sēsē**: = Pullo and Vorenus, the reflexive object of **recipiunt** (remember the idiom
        sē recipere, *to take oneself back, withdraw, retreat*).
    fortūna … utrumque versāvit: *each suffered a reversal of fortune*, lit., *fortune*
        turned each around.
    contentiō, contentiōnis, f., *struggle; rivalry.*
    certāmen, certāminis, n., *contest, competition.*

22 *****versō, -āre, -āvī, -ātus**, *to turn around, handle, deal with*; in passive, *to be in-*
        volved with, engaged with, move among. Do not confuse with **vertō, vertere**,
        the more general verb that = *to turn.*
    alter alterī: *one to/for the other.* **Alter** serves two functions: it goes with **alterī**
        inimīcus, *the one hostile to the other*; it also goes with **auxiliō salūtīque esset**,
        the one was a help and salvation for the other.
    dīiūdicō, -āre, -āvī, -ātus, *to judge, determine, decide.*

23 *****uter, utra, utrum**, *which one, which (of two)*; do not confuse with **uterque**, *each*
        (of two), *both.*
    anteferendus: a gerundive, lit. *to be preferred*, less lit., *preferable.*

13 Trānsfīgitur scūtum Pullōnī et verūtum in balteō dēfigitur. Āvertit hic
14 cāsus vāgīnam et gladium ēdūcere cōnantī dextram morātur manum, im-
15 pedītumque hostēs circumsistunt. Succurrit inimīcus illī Vorēnus et labō-
16 rantī subvenit. Ad hunc sē cōnfestim ā Pullōne omnis multitūdō conver-
17 tit; illum verūtō arbitrantur occīsum. Gladiō comminus rem gerit Vorēnus
18 atque ūnō interfectō reliquōs paulum prōpellit; dum cupidius īnstat, in lo-
19 cum dēiectus īnferiōrem concidit. Huic rursus circumventō fert subsidium
20 Pullō, atque ambō incolumēs complūribus interfectīs summā cum laude
21 sēsē intrā mūnītiōnēs recipiunt. Sīc fortūna in contentiōne et certāmine ut-
22 rumque versāvit, ut alter alterī inimīcus auxiliō salūtīque esset, neque diiū-
23 dicārī posset, uter utrī virtūte anteferendus vidērētur.

9. What happens to Pullo? (13)
10. What problem does Pullo have even though he was not actually injured by
    the spear? (13–14)
11. What happens when Vorenus runs to rescue Pullo? Why? (15–17)
12. How does Vorenus handle the situation at first (two items)? (17–18)
13. Then what happens to him? (18–19)
14. How is Vorenus saved from the Gauls? (19–20)
15. What do Vorenus and Pullo do together? (20–21)
16. How is the ending of this story somewhat ironic, given Pullo and Vorenus'
    previous rivalry? (21–23)

Discussion

1. Why did Caesar use the word order that he did in lines 7–8 (**quae ... irrumpit**)? (Cf. the last Reading Strategy on page 99.)
2. Outline how Caesar moves the focus of the story among Pullo, Vorenus, and
   the Gauls. What impression does this create in the reader's mind?
3. How is the behavior of Pullo and Vorenus yet another contrast with that of
   Sabinus earlier in Book V?
4. Why do you think Caesar included this story when he wrote *De bello
   Gallico*?

Vocabulary

♦ Note the use of the prefix **sub-** in both verbs that mean *come to help*, **subvenit** (5.35:13
  and above: 16) and **succurrit** (above: 15); cf. the English *subvention* and *succor*.

1 **Quantō**: here this word is a correlative with **tantō** (3), lit., *By how much . . . by so much* (abl. of degree of difference, **A5l**); less lit., *The more . . . the more.*
   in diēs, idiom, *day by day, every day.*
   asper, aspera, asperum, *rough, harsh; adverse, unfavorable.*
2 ****cōnficiō, cōnficere, cōnfēcī, cōnfectus**, *to complete; to wear our, exhaust.*
   dēfēnsor, dēfēnsōris, m., *defender.*
3 **crēber, crēbra, crēbrum**, *thick, close; numerous, frequent.*
4 **quōrum pars**: *a part of whom, some of whom;* **pars** is the subject of this clause, so **dēprehēnsa** and **necābātur** are singular, but in English we would use the plural. Although Caesar says that only some of the messengers were caught, it appears from what follows that none of them got through.
   dēprehendō, dēprehendere, dēprehēndī, dēprehēnsus, *to get hold of, catch.*
   ****cōnspectus, -ūs** [< cōnspiciō, to catch sight], m., *sight.*
   ****cruciātus, -ūs**, m., *torture.*
5 **necō, -āre, -āvī, -ātus**, *to kill.*
   intus, adv., *within, inside;* here = *inside* (the Roman camp).
   Verticō, Verticōnis, m., *Vertico, a Nervian.*
   honestus, -a, -um, *honored, respected.*
   locō . . . honestō : an abl. of source (**A5a**) with **nātus**; this phrase indicates that Vertico was a nobleman.
6 **ā prīmā obsidiōne**: *at the beginning of the siege.*
   perfugiō, perfugere, perfūgī, *to flee for refuge;* this word is often used when someone changes sides in a conflict.
   suam eī fidem praestiterat: lit., *had bestowed on him his good faith,* i.e., had offered him his allegiance, had joined the Roman side.
7 **servō**: Vertico had brought some of his slaves with him when he came over to the Romans.
8 **inligō, -āre, -āvī, -ātus**, *to tie inside, fasten inside;* presumably the shaft of the spear was hollowed out and the letter rolled up and slipped inside.
   Gallus: *(as) a Gaul.*
9 **versātus**: remember that **versō**, introduced in line 22 of the previous chapter, has a special meaning in the passive.

Word of the legion's plight finally reaches Caesar.

1 [45] Quantō erat in diēs gravior atque asperior oppugnātiō, et maximē quod,
2 magnā parte mīlitum cōnfectā vulneribus, rēs ad paucitātem dēfēnsōrum
3 pervēnerat, tantō crēbriōrēs litterae nūntiīque ad Caesarem mittēbantur;
4 quōrum pars dēprehēnsa in cōnspectū nostrōrum mīlitum cum cruciātū
5 necābātur. Erat ūnus intus Nervius, nōmine Verticō, locō nātus honestō, quī
6 ā prīmā obsidiōne ad Cicerōnem perfūgerat suamque eī fidem praestiterat.
7 Hic servō spē lībertātis magnīsque persuādet praemiīs ut litterās ad Cae-
8 sarem dēferat. Hās ille in iaculō inligātās effert et Gallus inter Gallōs sine
9 ūllā suspiciōne versātus ad Caesarem pervēnit. Ab eō dē perīculīs Cicerōnis
10 legiōnisque cognōscitur.

Initial Explorations
1. How does Caesar describe the assault at this point? (1)
2. Why had the situation reached this point? (2–3)
3. What was done in response to this situation? (3)
4. How did the Romans know that this effort was not successful? (4–5)
5. Who was Vertico? Why was he in the Roman camp? (5–6)
6. Whom did he persuade to carry a letter? How? (7–8)
7. How did the messenger conceal the letter? (8)
8. Why was the messenger able to reach Caesar? (8–9)
9. What did Caesar learn from him? (9–10)

Discussion
1. What two effects would the Gauls' treatment of the captured messengers (4–5) have had on the Romans?

Reading Strategies

◆ You might think at first that both **servō** and **spē** (7) are ablative. What makes it clear that this is not the case?

◆ Roman authors moved words out of their normal position to create emphasis. In this chapter we have two such instances: **locō nātus honestō** (5–6) and **magnīs persuādet praemiīs** (7). Verbs usually come at the end of their clauses; by moving them out of that position and splitting up the noun-adjective pairs, Caesar stresses not the fact that Vertico was born, but the social position into which he was born, and likewise not the fact that Vertico persuaded his slave, but the great rewards that it took to accomplish this.

1 **ūndecimus, -a, -um**, *eleventh*.
2 **Bellovācī, -ōrum**, m. pl., *the Bellovaci*, a Belgic tribe whose territory lay between the Seine and Somme Rivers. Refer back to the map on page 111 to see the locations of the various Roman **hiberna**.
4 **Exit cum nūntiō**: *leaves with the (arrival of) the messenger*, i.e., with no delay.
5 **iter faciendum**: sc. **esse**.
6 **commodō**: abl. of the noun **commodum**, *convenience, advantage*, used as an adv. with the special meaning *without injury, without detriment* (lit., *with advantage*). For some reason Caesar suspected that it might not be wise for Labienus to leave his camp and therefore ordered him to do so only if he thought it would cause no problems.
8 **quādringentōs**: only a small number of cavalry was available, since Caesar usually required the Gallic tribes to provide cavalry during the campaigning season and sent them home during the winter.
9 **colligō, colligere, collēgī, collectus**, *to collect*.

* * * * * * * *

Memorial to a Centurion

This inscription was found in Athens. The first line of the stone is damaged, so we do not know the man's **cognōmen**, but there seems to be room for about five additional letters. Inscriptions such as this one usually put the highest honor a man received first, with other offices or distinctions in descending order. What does the stone tell us about Numerius Granonius' life and military career? Parentheses indicate abbreviations on the stone that have been expanded.

> N(umerius) Grānōnius N(umerī) f(īlius) Cal(..?..),
> domō Lūceriā, iiiivir, centu
> riō Cornēleī Spin[t]erī
> legiō(ne) xiix et Cn. Pompeī
> Mag(nī) legiōne secundā

Lūceria, -ae: a town in Apulia, southern Italy.
iiiivir: = **quattuorvir**, one of a group of four chief officials in some Italian towns.
Cornēleī Spinterī: Publius Cornelius Lentulus Spinter, consul in 57 BCE. At first he was a friend of Caesar, who helped him attain the consulship. Later he allied himself with Pompey and the **optimātēs** in the political turmoil of the late 50s and fought with Pompey against Caesar at the battle of Pharsalus.

Caesar organizes a relief force.

1 **[46]** Caesar, acceptīs litterīs hōrā circiter ūndecimā diēī, statim nūntium in
2 Bellovācōs ad M. Crassum quaestōrem mittit, cuius hiberna aberant ab eō
3 mīlia passuum xxv; iubet mediā nocte legiōnem proficīscī celeriterque ad
4 sē venīre. Exit cum nūntiō Crassus. Alterum ad C. Fabium lēgātum mittit,
5 ut in Atrebatum fīnēs legiōnem addūcat, quā sibi iter faciendum sciēbat.
6 Scrībit Labiēnō, sī reī pūblicae commodō facere posset, cum legiōne ad fī-
7 nēs Nerviōrum veniat. Reliquam partem exercitūs, quod paulō aberat lon-
8 gius, nōn putat exspectandam; equitēs circiter quādringentōs ex proximīs
9 hibernīs colligit.

Initial Explorations

1. At what time of day did Caesar receive Quintus Cicero's letter? (1)
2. How far away was Marcus Crassus' camp? What orders did Caesar send to Crassus? (1–4)
3. Where did Caesar tell Gaius Fabius to bring his legion, and why? (4–5)
4. What were Caesar's instructions to Labienus? (6–7)
5. Did Caesar think it advisable to summon any other legions? Why or why not? (7–8)
6. How many cavalry did Caesar gather and from where? (8–9)

This coin shows a trophy of Gallic arms. The Romans sometimes set up such trophies after a victory. In addition to the typical oblong Gallic shield, this trophy includes a helmet with horns such as that described by Diodorus (page 108). At the right are a long war trumpet and a battle axe, both decorated with animal heads.

1 **antecursor, antecursōris** [ante + currō], m., *advance guard* (military term; lit.,
    one who runs before). In the days before airplanes and satellites, armies on
    the move normally sent out small groups of soldiers in advance of the main
    body to make sure that the army would not walk into an ambush, that it was
    following the best route, etc.

3 **attribuō, attribuere, attribuī, attribūtus,** *to allot, assign.*
    obsidēs cīvitātum: *hostages of the tribes,* i.e., hostages gives to Caesar by the
    tribes to insure their good behavior.

4 **eō,** adv., *to that place, there.* This adv. is related to the pronoun **is, ea, id** = *this/*
    that, not to the verb **eō, īre.**
    tolerō, -āre, -āvī, -ātus, *to bear, endure.*
    devehō, dēvehere, dēvexī, dēvectus, *to carry down, bring to.*

5 **ut imperātum erat:** note the neuter ending **-um** (remember that intransitive
    verbs are used impersonally in the passive; see **F3e**).
    multum: a neuter form used as an adv.
    nōn ita multum: *not so much,* less lit., *not very much, hardly at all.*

6 **occurrit:** sc. **Caesarī.**
    interitus, -ūs [< interitus, supine of intereō, to die], m., *death.*
    *****caedēs, caedis** [< caedō, to kill] f., *killing, slaughter.*

7 **cognitā:** the particple is feminine because it agrees with the adjacent noun
    caede, but it modifies **interitū** also.
    ad eum: *against him.*
    veritus nē: what is unusual about clauses introduced by the verb **vereor?** (See
    N3e if needed.)

8 **fugae similem profectiōnem:** if the Treveri saw Labienus making a hurried de-
    parture from his winter quarters, they might assume that he had decided to
    flee from fear of them and so attack, believing that the Romans were fright-
    ened and disorganized.

9 **quōs . . . scīret:** a linking **quī,** = **cum eōs . . . scīret;** the subjunctive here has a
    causal sense.
    efferrī: clearly from **ex + ferō,** but with a special meaning in the passive, *to be*
    carried away (by feelings), *be lifted up, made confident, elated.*

10 **rem gestam in Eburōnibus:** i.e., the slaughter of the troops commanded by
    Sabinus and Cotta.

11 **perscrībō, perscrībere, perscrīpsī, perscrīptus,** *to write out, write an account,*
    relate, describe.

12 **tria:** neuter of **trēs.**
    *****cōnsīdō, cōnsīdere, cōnsēdī, cōnsessūrus,** *to sit down, settle;* military term, *to*
    pitch camp, encamp.

The relief force begins to move toward Cicero's camp.

1 [47] Hōrā circiter tertiā ab antecursōribus dē Crassī adventū certior factus,
2 eō diē mīlia passuum xx prōcēdit. Crassum Samarobrīvae praeficit legiō-
3 nemque attribuit, quod ibi impedīmenta exercitūs, obsidēs cīvitātum, lit-
4 terās pūblicās, frūmentumque omne quod eō tolerandae hiemis causā dē-
5 vexerat relinquēbat. Fabius, ut imperātum erat, nōn ita multum morātus in
6 itinere cum legiōne occurrit. Labiēnus, interitū Sabīnī et caede cohortium
7 cognitā, cum omnēs ad eum Trēverōrum cōpiae vēnissent, veritus nē, sī ex
8 hibernīs fugae similem profectiōnem fēcisset, hostium impetum sustinēre
9 nōn posset, praesertim quōs recentī victōriā efferrī scīret, litterās Caesarī
10 remittit: quantō cum perīculō legiōnem ex hibernīs ēductūrus esset; rem
11 gestam in Eburōnibus perscrībit; docet omnēs equitatūs peditātūsque cōpiās
12 Trēverōrum tria mīlia passuum longē ab suīs castrīs cōnsēdisse.

Initial Explorations

1. What did Caesar learn and how? (1)
2. What did he do that day? (2)
3. Why did Caesar leave one legion in Samarobriva under the command of Crassus? (2–5)
4. What did Fabius do in response to Caesar's order? (5–6)
5. What was Labienus' situation? (6–7)
6. What did Labienus fear and why? (7–9)
7. What three points does Labienus make in his reply to Caesar? (10–12)

1 *opīniō, opīniōnis, f., *belief, expectation.*
   dēiectus: when used with emotions this word = *disappointed.* Two legions was
      not very many men, given the size of the Gallic forces. In §49 (not included
      in this book) Caesar gives the figure of 60,000 Gauls and 7,000 in his two
      legions. The number of Gauls may be exaggerated; even if so, it is clear that
      Caesar's army was vastly outnumbered.

2 redierat: deduce from re- + eō, īre.
   commūnis salūtis: lit., *of common safety*; less lit., *of safety for all,* i.e., both the be-
      sieged men and the two legions with him. Note again how Caesar places the
      modifiers inside the two words ūnum . . . auxilium.

3 magnīs itineribus: *by forced marches,* a military term indicating that an army
      is made to march faster than normal. Cf. Caesar's description of his travels
      from Rome to Gaul after hearing of the Helvetians' plans, quam maximīs
      potest itineribus, 1.7:2.

5 epistola, -ae (also spelled epistula), f., *a letter.*

6 Graecīs litterīs: the letter was in Latin, but written in Greek characters.

7 *adeō, adīre, adiī or adīvī, aditūrus, *to go towards, approach, come up to*; less lit.,
      get through.

8 ammentum, -ī, n., *strap.* The trāgula was a spear with a leather strap attached to
      its shaft. The strap enabled a soldier to throw the spear farther and more ac-
      curately, perhaps by putting spin on the spear as it was thrown.

10 retineō, retinēre, retinuī, retentus, *to hold on to, keep.*
   praecipiō, praecipere, praecēpī, praeceptus, *to order, instruct.*

11 cāsū: in the abl. cāsus often = *by chance.*
   turrim: a few i-stem nouns have the acc. ending -im not -em.
   adhaereō, adhaerēre, adhaesī, adhaesitus, *to stick to.*

12 dēmō, dēmere, dēmpsī, dēmptus, *to take away, remove.*

13 perlegō, perlegere, perlēgī, perlēctus, *to read through.*
   conventus, -ūs [< conventus, supine of conveniō], m., *assembly.*
   recitō, -āre, -āvī, -ātus, *to read aloud.*
   perlectam . . . recitat: *he reads it, having been read through, out loud,* less lit., *he
      reads it through (to himself) and (then) reads it aloud.* Polyaenus, a Greek
      author of the 2nd century CE who wrote a book called *Military Strategies,*
      describes this incident and says that the note read: "Caesar to Cicero. Keep
      up your courage. Expect help."

14 laetitia, -ae [< laetus, happy], f., *happiness, joy.*
   fūmus, -ī, m., *smoke*; the plural suggests plumes or clouds of smoke.

15 dubitātiō, dubitātiōnis, f., *hesitation, doubt.*

Word of Caesar's approach is brought to Cicero's camp.

1 [48] Caesar, cōnsiliō eius probātō, etsī opīniōne trium legiōnum dēiectus
2 ad duās redierat, tamen ūnum commūnis salūtis auxilium in celeritāte pō-
3 nēbat. Vēnit magnīs itineribus in Nerviōrum fīnēs. Ibi ex captīvīs cognōscit
4 quae apud Cicerōnem gerantur quantōque in perīculō rēs sit. Tum cuidam
5 ex equitibus Gallīs magnīs praemiīs persuādet utī ad Cicerōnem epistolam
6 dēferat. Hanc Graecīs cōnscrīptam litterīs mittit, nē interceptā epistolā nos-
7 tra ab hostibus cōnsilia cognōscantur. Sī adīre nōn possit, monet ut trāgu-
8 lam cum epistolā ad ammentum dēligātā intrā mūnītiōnem castrōrum abici-
9 at. In litterīs scrībit sē cum legiōnibus profectum celeriter adfore; hortātur ut
10 prīstinam virtūtem retineat. Gallus perīculum veritus, ut erat praeceptum,
11 trāgulam mittit. Haec cāsū ad turrim adhaesit neque ab nostrīs biduō ani-
12 madversa tertiō diē ā quōdam mīlite cōnspicitur, dēmpta ad Cicerōnem
13 dēfertur. Ille perlectam in conventū mīlitum recitat, maximāque omnēs
14 laetitiā adficit. Tum fūmī incendiōrum procul vidēbantur, quae rēs omnem
15 dubitātiōnem adventūs legiōnum expulit.

Initial Explorations

1. Did Caesar accept Labienus' reasoning? What resulted from Labienus' decision? (1–2)
2. What did Caesar believe was the only way to save the situation? (2–3)
3. What did Caesar learn, and how, when he arrived among the Nervii? (3–4)
4. Whom did Caesar persuade to carry a letter to Cicero, and how? (4–6)
5. What detail does Caesar give us about the letter? (6–7)
6. What instructions did Caesar give if the messenger was not able to reach Cicero? (7–8)
7. What was the content of the letter? (9–10)
8. Why was the letter not delivered immediately to Cicero? (11–13)
9. What did Cicero do after reading the letter? What effect did this have? (13–14)
10. What was the final confirmation for the men in the camp that help had arrived? (14–15)

Discussion

1. In what way would the letter's being written in Greek characters prevent the Gauls from learning Caesar's plans? Was this a foolproof method?

2. Most commentators think that **fūmī** (14) refers to Caesar's army ravaging the countryside as they came. Why might this not make sense? What other explanation might there be?

3. Caesar was well known among his contemporaries for his **celeritās**, his ability to respond quickly and decisively as events unfolded. Review §§46–48 and show how Caesar demonstrates that quality when going to the relief of Cicero's legion.

4. Caesar responded quickly and effectively to the crisis. But could it have been prevented? Does Caesar bear any responsibility for the Gallic attacks on his winter camps?

* * * * * * * * *

After hearing of Caesar's arrival, the Gauls abandoned the siege and moved to confront Caesar's two legions. Caesar lured the Gauls into a battle on unfavorable ground and they suffered a major defeat; Caesar then joined Cicero in the camp. Caesar soon returned to Samarobriva and decided to stay there for the winter with three legions, although he sent Fabius and his legion back to their camp among the Morini. Many Gallic tribes had begun to plan revolts against the Roman occupation after hearing about the defeat of Sabinus and Cotta. Caesar was able to keep most of them loyal to the Romans by meeting personally with the leaders of each tribe. The Treveri, however, continued to stir up resistance. They attacked Labienus' camp but were defeated and their leader Indutiomarus killed.

Vocabulary Review: Book V (Second Part)

The following asterisked words were introduced in §§38–48:

adeō, adīre	iaculum	praemium
aditus, -ūs	incolumis	praesidium
adiūtor	intercipiō	quisquam
admodum	intrōeō	sīcutī
caedēs	iūdicō	testūdō
concurrō	laus	turris
cōnficiō	littera	uter
cōnsīdō	metus	versō
cōnspectus, -ūs	mūnītiō	vulnerō
cruciātus, -ūs	opīniō	succendō
dēcēdō	opus	
exanimō	paene	**Proper Names**
excitō	pīlum	Nerviī
fāma	posterus	Pullō
fossa	potestās	Vorēnus

Epitaph for Two Soldiers

The Roman army, like modern militaries, gave soldiers various kinds of decorations to recognize their courage or special service. The most prestigious were **corōnae**, *crowns* or *garlands* of various types. More often, soldiers were awarded **torquēs**, *torques* (see the photograph and caption on page 29), **armillae**, *armbands*, or **phalerae**, disc-shaped medallions.

The inscription shown below was found in Capua. What can you learn about the lives, careers, and family relationships of these men?

> Gāius Canuleius, Quīntī fīlius, legiōnis VII, ēvocātus, mortuus est
> annōrum nātus XXXV, dōnātus torquibus, armillīs, phalerīs, corōnīs.
> Quīntus Canuleius, Quīntī fīlius, legiōnis VII, occīsus in Galliā
> annōrum nātus XVIII. Duo frātrēs.
> Eīs pater monumenum fēcit.

ēvocātus: a soldier whose enlistment was up but who remained in service (5.35:10).
dōnō, -āre, -āvī, -ātus, *to present someone* (acc.) *with something* (abl.)

The centurion in this picture, dressed for a ceremonial occasion, is wearing a leather harness on top of his armor. On the harness are hung his **torquēs** and **phalerae**. He is wearing **armillae** on his wrists and holding a vine stick, which was a symbol of his rank and also used for disciplining soldiers. The crest on his helmet, which was also worn in battle, identifies him as a centurion.

The men shown here belong to one of several groups of historic re-enactors. The first of these groups, the Ermine Street Guard, was created in Britain in 1972. Several others have come into existence since, in Britain, the United States, Europe, and elsewhere.

Such re-enactors carefully study what the ancient evidence, both literary and archaeological, tells us about the Roman army. They then re-create armor and equipment and try out what they have made. Their efforts have led to a greater understanding of many aspects of Roman military life.

Book VI

53 BCE

IN THE SPRING of the following year, many tribes made plans to continue resisting the Roman occupation. The Treveri in particular were active, allying themselves with Ambiorix and persuading some of the German tribes to help them in return for money. To counter this, Caesar first persuaded Pompey to send him the legions that Pompey had recruited in Cisalpine Gaul. By doing so Caesar replaced the cohorts lost under Sabinus and obtained an equivalent number of additional troops. He wanted the Gauls to think that no matter how many men the Romans lost, there were always more available. Caesar then decided that he needed to take steps immediately to counter the plans of the Gauls. Before winter was completely over he took an army into the territory of the Nervii and compelled them to surrender. Then, as he usually did in the spring, Caesar held a council of Gallic leaders. This time, however, he held it in Lutetia (now Paris); only the Treveri, the Senones, and Carnutes did not send representatives. Caesar immediately marched south to the Senones, whose territory was adjacent to the Parisii. Both the Senones and the Carnutes sued for peace. Caesar accepted their request because he wanted to focus his attention on the Treveri and Ambiorix.

* * * * * * * * *

1 The Treveri routed

[1] Caesar had many reasons, however, for expecting still more serious disturbances before long. He therefore charged three of his generals, Marcus Silanus, Gaius Antistius Reginus, and Titus Sextius, with the duty of raising fresh troops. He also sent a message to Pompey—who, though vested as proconsul with military command, was remaining for political reasons in the neighbourhood of Rome—requesting him to mobilize the recruits from northern Italy whom he had sworn in during his consulship and to send them out to him. Caesar considered it very important, with a view to making a permanent impression upon the tribesmen, to let it be seen that the manpower of Italy was sufficient not only to repair speedily any loss sustained in the field, but actually to increase the size of the expeditionary force. Pompey acceded to this request from motives of patriotism as well as of friendship, and Caesar's officers promptly enlisted further recruits, so that before the end of the winter three legions were formed and brought to Gaul, making double the number of the

cohorts lost under Sabinus. This large reinforcement, and the speed with which it was effected, showed what Roman organization and resources were capable of.[1]

[2] After the death of Indutiomarus, related above,[2] his command was transferred by the Treveri to members of his family, who persisted in trying to obtain the support of the nearest German tribes by promises of money. Failing in this, they made overtures to more distant tribes, a number of which consented. The alliance was confirmed by an exchange of oaths, and hostages were given as security for the payment of the money. Ambiorix also was admitted as a partner to the league. Caesar was informed of these intrigues, and saw warlike preparations going on all around. The Nervii, Aduatuci, and Menapii, together with all the tribes of German origin on the west bank of the Rhine, were in arms; the Senones refused to attend at his bidding, and were concerting plans with the Carnutes and others of their neighbours; and the Treveri were sending embassy after embassy to obtain German aid. He therefore decided that he must take the field in advance of the usual season.

[3] Accordingly, before the winter was over, he assembled the four nearest legions and made an unexpected attack on the country of the Nervii. Before they could either concentrate their forces or flee, a large number of cattle and prisoners were captured and handed over as booty to the soldiers; the country was ravaged, and the Nervii forced to surrender and give hostages. After this quick success Caesar took the legions back into winter quarters. In the early spring he convoked the usual Gallic council, which was attended by all those summoned except the Senones, Carnutes, and Treveri. He regarded their non-appearance as the first step towards an armed revolt, and in order to make it clear that he considered its suppression of paramount importance, he decided to transfer the meeting to Lutetia, a town of the Parisii. They inhabited a territory adjoining that of the Senones, and a generation before had united with them to form one state; but they appeared to have had no hand in the present policy of the Senones. After announcing his decision from the platform in his camp, Caesar started with his legions the same day and made his way by forced marches to the country of the Senones.

[4] On learning of his approach, Acco, the ringleader of the conspiracy, ordered the population to gather in their strongholds. Before they had time to complete this operation they heard that the Romans were at hand. The Senones had no choice but

---

[1] From 57 to 54 BCE Caesar had eight legions. The losses under Sabinus were perhaps not much more than the full complement of one legion, which would leave seven. Of the two new legions now enrolled in northern Italy (in the winter of 54 BCE), one took the number of the 14th, destroyed under Sabinus; the other was numbered the 15th. The legion borrowed from Pompey was the 1st, although apparently Caesar renumbered it afterwards. This reinforcement brought the number of his legions up to ten.

Pompey held proconsular command as nominal governor of Spain. In his consulship of 55 BCE he had been invested with special powers which enabled him to levy troops even in provinces under the control of other governors.

[2] This is described in 5.58 (not included in this book). Indutiomarus was leading an attack on the camp of Labienus. He was caught and killed by Roman cavalry while crossing a river. ✎

to abandon their project and send envoys to ask Caesar's pardon. These were introduced by the Aedui, under whose protection their tribe had been from ancient times. Caesar willingly pardoned them at the request of the Aedui and accepted their excuses; for he thought that the summer should be devoted to the impending war, and not wasted in holding an inquest. He ordered them, however, to provide a hundred hostages, whom he entrusted to the custody of the Aedui. The Carnutes, too, sent envoys and hostages while Caesar was in the district, pleading their cause with the support of the Remi, whose dependants they were, and received the same reply. Caesar then completed the business of the council and requisitioned cavalry from the various tribes.

[5] Now that this part of Gaul was tranquillized, Caesar devoted all his energies to the war against the Treveri and Ambiorix. He bade Cavarinus[3] accompany him with the cavalry of the Senones, lest his hasty temper or the hatred that he had earned should cause trouble in the tribe. Then, since he felt certain that Ambiorix did not intend to fight a battle, he cast about to discover what other plans he might have. Close to the Eburones and protected by a continuous line of marshes and forests dwelt the Menapii, the only Gallic people who had never sent envoys to Caesar to sue for peace. He knew that Ambiorix was united to them by ties of hospitality and also that, through the agency of the Treveri, he had formed an alliance with the Germans. He thought it advisable to deprive Ambiorix of these allies before attacking him directly, for fear desperation should make him hide among the Menapii or join the tribes beyond the Rhine. Therefore, after sending the baggage of the entire army to Labienus' camp in the country of the Treveri and ordering two legions to proceed there too, he started himself for the territory of the Menapii with five legions in light marching order. The Menapii did not collect any troops, but relying on the protection of the terrain took refuge with all their belongings in the forests and marshes.

[6] Caesar put Fabius and the quaestor Marcus Crassus in command of detachments, and the three columns advanced with the aid of hastily constructed causeways, burning farms and villages, and taking a large number of cattle and prisoners. By this means the Menapii were compelled to send envoys to sue for peace. Caesar took the hostages they offered and told them that he would treat them as enemies if they admitted Ambiorix or his agents into their territory. With this warning, he left Commius the Atrebatian with a force of cavalry to keep the Menapii under surveillance, while he marched against the Treveri.

[7] Meanwhile the Treveri had collected large forces of infantry and cavalry and were preparing to attack Labienus and the single legion which was wintering in their territory. They were within a two days' march of his camp, when they heard of the arrival of the two legions dispatched to him by Caesar and, encamping at a dis-

---

[3] King of the Senones; Caesar had helped him seize the throne, displacing his brother (5.54, not included in this book). 🦶

tance of fifteen miles, they decided to wait for reinforcements from the Germans. Apprised of their intention, Labienus hoped that their imprudence would give him some opportunity of bringing them to action. He left five cohorts to guard the baggage, marched against the enemy with the other twenty-five and a strong force of cavalry, and entrenched a camp a mile away from them. Between the two camps was a river with steep banks, difficult to cross; Labienus had no intention of crossing it himself and did not think the enemy would. The Gauls' hope of being reinforced was increasing daily, and Labienus purposely let the soldiers hear him say that, since the Germans were said to be approaching, he would not jeopardize their safety and his own by remaining, but would break up the camp next morning at dawn. This remark was soon reported to the enemy, since among the large number of Gallic horsemen it was only natural that there should be some who sympathized with their fellow countrymen's cause. At night Labienus summoned the military tribunes and first-grade centurions and explained his plans; then, to help in making the enemy think they were afraid, he ordered the camp to be broken up with more noise and disturbance than is customary with Roman armies, and so made his departure resemble a flight. This also was reported to the Gauls by their patrols before daybreak, for the camps were very close together.

[8] They urged one another not to let the hoped-for prize slip from their grasp: to wait for German aid when the Romans were panic-stricken would mean unnecessary delay and with such a large army it would be disgraceful to shrink from attacking a mere handful of men, especially men who were running away and hampered by baggage. Accordingly, when the rearguard of the Roman column had barely got outside the entrenchment, they boldly began to cross the river and join battle in an unfavourable position. Labienus had expected this, and enticed them all across by continuing to advance slowly, keeping up the pretence that he was marching away. Then, sending the baggage a short distance ahead and parking it on a piece of rising ground, he said to the soldiers: 'Here is your chance. You have got the enemy where you wanted them—in a bad position, where they are not free to manoeuvre. Fight as bravely under me as you often have under the commander-in-chief; imagine that he is here, watching the battle in person.' With these words he bade the units turn to face the enemy and form a line of battle, sent a few squadrons of cavalry to protect the baggage, and posted the rest on the flanks. The men at once raised a shout and launched their spears. The enemy were amazed to see the enemy that they thought to be in flight advancing to the attack. They had not the courage to face its charge; directly the lines met, they turned tail and made for the nearest woods. Labienus hunted them down with his cavalry, killing many of them and taking a number of prisoners, and a few days later had recovered his hold over the tribe; for the Germans who were coming to aid them returned home when they found the Treveri routed. The relatives of Indutiomarus who had instigated the revolt fled the country

and went along with the Germans. Cingetorix, who had remained loyal right from the outset, was invested with civil and military control of the tribe.

2 The second crossing of the Rhine

[9] After marching from the country of the Menapii to that of the Treveri, Caesar determined to cross the Rhine for two reasons: first, because the Germans had sent the Treveri reinforcements to use against him; secondly, to prevent Ambiorix's finding an asylum in Germany. He therefore proceeded to build a bridge a little above the place where he had crossed before. As the method of construction was familiar to the soldiers from the previous occasion, they were able by energetic efforts to complete the task in a few days. Leaving a strong guard on the Gallic side of the bridge to prevent any sudden rising on the part of the Treveri, he led across the remainder of his forces, including the cavalry. The Ubii, who had previously given hostages and submitted, sent envoys to clear themselves by explaining that they had not broken their word: the aid sent to the Treveri did not come from their state. They begged him to spare them, and not to let an indiscriminate animosity against the Germans make the innocent suffer for the guilty; if he wanted more hostages they should be given. On investigating the matter he found that the reinforcements had been sent by the Suebi. He therefore accepted the Ubii's explanation and made careful inquiry about the routes leading to the territory of the Suebi.

[10] A few days later Caesar was told by the Ubii that the Suebi were concentrating all their forces and calling upon their subject tribes to furnish contingents of infantry and cavalry. Thereupon he arranged for a supply of grain, selected a suitable site for a camp, and directed the Ubii to remove their cattle and transfer all their possessions from the fields into their strongholds, hoping that the ignorant and uncivilized Germans might be induced by shortage of food to fight a battle on unequal terms. He also told the Ubii to keep sending scouts into Suebic territory and find out what the enemy were about. The Ubii carried out these instructions, and a few days later reported that on the receipt of reliable information about the Roman army all the Suebi had retired, with the whole of their forces and those which they had raised from their allies, to the farthest extremity of their country, where there was an immense forest called Bacenis, stretching far into the interior and forming a natural barrier between the Suebi and the Cherusci, which prevented them from raiding and damaging each other's territory. On the edge of this forest, they said, the Suebi had resolved to await the arrival of the Romans.

3 Customs and institutions of the Gauls

[11] At this point, it seems not inappropriate to give an account of the customs of the Gauls and the Germans and the differences between these peoples.

In Gaul, not only every tribe, canton, and subdivision of a canton, but almost every family, is divided into rival factions.[4] At the head of these factions are men who are regarded by their followers as having particularly great prestige, and these have the final say on all questions that come up for judgement and in all discussions of policy. The object of this ancient custom seems to have been to ensure that all the common people should have protection against the strong; for each leader sees that no one gets the better of his supporters by force or by cunning—or, if he fails to do so, is utterly discredited.

The same principle holds good in intertribal politics: all the tribes are grouped in two factions.

[12] At the time of Caesar's arrival, these were headed respectively by the Aedui and the Sequani. As the Aedui had long enjoyed very great prestige and had many satellite tribes, the Sequani were the weaker of the two, depending on their own resources. They therefore secured the alliance of Ariovistus and his Germans, at the cost of heavy sacrifices and the promise of still further concessions [70–65 BCE}. Then, as a result of several victories in which all the Aeduans of rank were killed, the Sequani became so much stronger than their rivals that they were able to bring over to their side a considerable part of the Aeduan dependencies, and to make the Aeduans surrender the sons of their chiefs as hostages and swear to form no hostile designs against the Sequani. They had also seized and retained a part of the Aeduan territory that lay near their own frontier and had in fact established a hegemony over the whole of Gaul. Reduced to this extremity, Diviciacus the Aeduan went to Rome to solicit aid from the Senate,[5] but returned without success [61 BCE].

Caesar's arrival changed the situation: the Aedui had their hostages restored to them, and not only regained their former dependencies but acquired new ones with Caesar's help, because those who became their allies found that they were better off and more equitably governed than before. In other respects, too, their influence and standing were enhanced, and the Sequani lost their supremacy. Their place was taken by the Remi; and as it was known that they stood as high in Caesar's favour as the Aedui, tribes which on account of old feuds could not be induced to join the Aedui were placing themselves under the protection of the Remi, who by taking good care of them were able to maintain the unaccustomed power that they had suddenly acquired. At this time, therefore, the position was that, while the Aedui were acknowledged to be easily ahead of all the other tribes, the Remi came next in importance.

---

[4] There are several instances in Caesar's narrative of factionalism between members of the same family—e.g., Diviciacus and his brother Dumnorix (1.18ff.), Indutiomarus and his son-in-law Cingetorix (5.3–4, 6.8), Vercingetorix and his uncle Gobannitio (7.4).

[5] Cicero mentions in his book *On divination* (I.41) that he had met Diviciacus, whom he describes as a druid. ❧

Questions

1. From what two different sources did Caesar obtain additional troops? How many did he get? With these additions, how did the size of Caesar's army compare with what it had been before the defeat of Sabinus and Cotta?

2. For what reasons was Caesar eager to obtain these reinforcements?

3. Summarize the efforts to resist Roman control that Caesar describes in §2.

4. What was the first step that Caesar took in response to these efforts (see §3)? What was unusual about this?

5. How did Caesar deal with the Senones and the Carnutes after they refused to attend the council of Gallic tribes?

6. How were the Menapii different from other tribes? What was their connection to Ambiorix? By what means did Caesar attempt to prevent them from aiding Ambiorix?

7. How did Labienus forestall the planned attack on his camp by the Eburones and the German mercenaries?

8. Why did Caesar decide to cross the Rhine again? What did the ambassadors from the Ubii tell him?

9. What group of Germans had sent aid to the Treveri? What did Caesar ask the Ubii to do in order to assist him in dealing with this group?

10. What two Gallic tribes were traditionally the most influential? What was the political situation when Caesar arrived in Gaul? How did Caesar's arrival shift the balance of power?

✳ ✳ ✳ ✳ ✳ ✳ ✳ ✳ ✳

Book VI continues in Latin on the following pages.

1 **numerō**: *position, rank* (additional meaning).

   honos, honōris, m., *esteem, honor.* The nom. of this word is often found as **honor**, although Caesar uses the form **honos** in line 16 below.

2 **plēbēs**: here in a fifth decl. form, rather than the common third decl. **plēbs**.

3 **adhibeō, adhibēre, adhibuī, adhibitus** [ad + habeō], *to hold towards, bring, summon.*

   *plērīque, plēraeque, plēraque, *most, very many, a great many.*

   aes aliēnum, aeris aliēnī, n., *debt*; lit., *bronze (= money) belonging to another.*

4 *tribūtum, -ī, n., *taxes, taxation.*

   servitūtem: *service.*

   dicō, -āre, -āvī, -ātus, *to dedicate, consecrate; to give up, give over (to).* This is not the same verb as **dīcō, dīcere**; it is first conj. and the 'i' in the stem is short.

5 **quibus . . . eadem omnia sunt iūra**: dative of possession.

   in hōs: *over them.*

6 *druidēs, druidum, m. pl., *druids,* the priests of Gaul.

   equitum: the cavalry in the Gallic armies was made up of nobles, so **equitēs** here = something like *noble-born cavalrymen* or *mounted nobility.*

   rēbus dīvīnīs: *worship of the gods*; for the case, see **A3c**.

7 **intersum, interesse, interfuī, interfutūrus** [inter + sum], *to be among, be present at*, in this context = *be in charge of.*

   prōcūrō, -āre, -āvī, -ātus, *to take care of, look after, attend to.* Remember to distinguish **cūrāre** from **currere**.

   *religiō, religiōnis, f., *piety, religion*; in pl., *religious matters.*

8 *disciplīna, -ae, f., *teaching(s); training.*

10 **sī quod**: remember the special meaning of **quī** after **sī**; see **E5b** for help.

   *facinus, facinoris [< faciō], n., *action, deed; bad deed, crime* (the latter meaning is more common).

11 **hērēditās, hērēditātis** [< hērēs, heir], f., *inheritance.*

   īdem: *likewise, also* (see the note on 5.42:8, page 152).

   dēcernō, dēcernere, dēcrēvī, dēcrētus, *to judge, decide.*

12 **populus**: i.e., an entire tribe.

   dēcrētum, -ī [< dēcernō], n., *decree, decision.*

13 **stetit**: *observe*, lit., *stand (in)*, from **stō**. The perfect tense here indicates a general condition: *if anyone does not observe.*

   sacrificiīs: an abl. of separation, *from the sacrifices.*

14 **interdīcō, interdīcere, interdīxī, interdictus**, *to forbid, prohibit.*

   Quibus ita est interdictum: *to whom it has been prohibited in this way,* less lit., *against whom such a prohibition has been made*; the antecedent of **Quibus** is **hī** (14). What structure is **est interdictum**?

   numerō: lit., *in the number (of)*, less lit., *among.*

   impius, -a, -um, *wicked.*

   scelerātus, -a, -um, *criminal.*

   habentur: *are considered,* the "thinking" sense of **habeō**, also in line 22 below.

   hīs: abl. with **dēcēdunt** (15); cf. the Structure note on page 81.

15 **contāgiō, contāgiōnis**, f., *contact.*

16 **incommodī**: partitive genitive with **quid** (15).

   *reddō, reddere, reddidī, redditus [re- + dō, dare), *to give back, give.*

The social classes of Gaul.

1 **[13]** In omnī Galliā eōrum hominum, quī aliquō sunt numerō atque honōre,
2 genera sunt duo. Nam plēbēs paene servōrum habētur locō, quae nihil audet
3 per sē, nūllī adhibētur cōnsiliō. Plērīque, cum aut aere aliēnō aut magnitūdine
4 tribūtōrum aut iniūriā potentiōrum premuntur, sēsē in servitūtem dicant
5 nōbilibus, quibus in hōs eadem omnia sunt iūra quae dominīs in servōs. Sed
6 dē hīs duōbus generibus alterum est druidum, alterum equitum. Illī rēbus
7 dīvīnīs intersunt, sacrificia pūblica ac prīvāta prōcūrant, religiōnēs interpre-
8 tantur: ad hōs magnus adulēscentium numerus disciplīnae causā concur-
9 rit, magnōque hī sunt apud eōs honōre. Nam ferē dē omnibus contrōversiīs
10 pūblicīs prīvātīsque cōnstituunt, et, sī quod est admissum facinus, sī caedēs
11 facta, sī dē hērēditāte, dē fīnibus contrōversia est, īdem dēcernunt, prae-
12 mia poenāsque cōnstituunt; sī quī aut prīvātus aut populus eōrum dēcrētō
13 nōn stetit, sacrificiīs interdīcunt. Haec poena apud eōs est gravissima. Qui-
14 bus ita est interdictum, hī numerō impiōrum ac scelerātōrum habentur, hīs
15 omnēs dēcēdunt, aditum sermōnemque dēfugiunt, nē quid ex contagiōne
16 incommodī accipiant, neque hīs petentibus iūs redditur neque honos ūllus
17 commūnicātur.   (continued)

Initial Explorations

1. Of what are there two classes in Gaul? (1–2)
2. Summarize the position of the common people in Gaul. (2–3)
3. For what reasons do ordinary people give themselves in service to the nobles? (3–4)
4. What kind of relationship is this service? (5)
5. Who makes up the two classes mentioned previously? (6)
6. What are the general functions of the druids? (6–8)
7. Cite one piece of evidence that shows the prestige of the druids among the Gauls. (8–9)
8. Give four examples of the types of things about which the druids make rulings. (9–11)
9. What is the penalty for those who do not obey the druids' decrees? How does Caesar describe this punishment? (12–13)
10. Describe five things that can happen to those punished in this way. (13–17)

18　Hīs . . . omnibus druidibus: for the case, see **A3c**.

19　**excellō, excellere, excelluī,** *to rise up, be eminent, excel.*
　　dignitās, dignitātis, f., *prestige.*

20　**suffrāgium, -ī,** n., *ballot, vote.*
　　nōn numquam (often written as one word), adv., *sometimes*; lit., *not never* (cf.
　　　nōn nūllī, *some,* lit., *not none*).

24　**pāreō, pārēre, pāruī** + dat., *to obey.*
　　reperiō, reperīre, repperī, repertus, *to find, discover; to invent, develop.*
　　trānslāta esse: deduce from **trāns** + **ferō.** What is the root meaning of the
　　　English word 'translate'?

26　**illō** [< ille, that], adv., *to that place, there.*
　　*****discō, discere, didicī,** *to learn.*

❖　　❖　　❖　　❖　　❖

2　*****mīlitia, -ae** [< mīles, mīlitis], f., *military service.*
　　vacātiō, vacātiōnis, f., *freedom.*
　　immūnitās, immūnitātis [neg. prefix in- + mūnus, obligation], f., *exemption.*

4　*****propinquus, -a, -um** [< prope, near], *nearby*; as substantive, *relative.*
　　versus, -ūs, m., *verse.* The teachings of the druids were put into poetry so that
　　　they would be easier to remember.

5　**ēdiscō, ēdiscere, ēdidicī** [< ē + discō, to learn], *to learn thoroughly, learn by
　　　heart, memorize.*
　　XX: vīgintī.

6　**fās,** indeclinable, *proper, right*; this word, and its opposite **nefās,** have a religious
　　　connotation.
　　litterīs: *writing.*
　　mandō, -āre, -āvī, -ātus [manus + do, dare], *to hand over, commit, entrust.*
　　cum: remember that you must use the context to determine the best meaning of
　　　the conj. **cum.** See **O4e** for a review of all the possible meanings.

7　**ratiōnibus:** *accounts* (additional meaning).

18 Hīs autem omnibus druidibus praeest ūnus, quī summam inter eōs habet
19 auctōritātem. Hōc mortuō, aut, sī quī ex reliquīs excellit dignitāte, succēdit,
20 aut, sī sunt plūrēs parēs, suffragiō druidum, nōn numquam etiam armīs dē
21 prīncipātū contendunt. Hī certō annī tempore in fīnibus Carnūtum, quae
22 regiō tōtīus Galliae media habētur, cōnsīdunt in locō cōnsecrātō. Hūc omnēs
23 undique quī contrōversiās habent conveniunt eōrumque dēcrētīs iūdiciīsque
24 pārent. Disciplīna in Britanniā reperta atque inde in Galliam trānslāta esse
25 exīstimātur, et nunc quī dīligentius eam rem cognōscere volunt plērumque
26 illō discendī causā proficīscuntur.

11. How are the druids governed? (18–19)
12. By what methods is a successor chosen? (19–21)
13. Where do the druids meet once a year? Why is this an appropriate meeting place? (21–22)
14 Who comes to this meeting and why? (22–24)
15. What do people believe about the origin of the druids' teachings? (24–25)
16. How is the influence of this origin still felt? (25–26)

Privileges and training of the druids.

1 [14] Druidēs ā bellō abesse cōnsuērunt neque tribūta ūnā cum reliquīs
2 pendunt; mīlitiae vacātiōnem omniumque rērum habent immūnitātem.
3 Tantīs excitātī praemiīs et suā sponte multī in disciplīnam conveniunt et
4 ā parentibus propinquīsque mittuntur. Magnum ibi numerum versuum
5 ēdiscere dīcuntur. Itaque annōs nōn nūllī xx in disciplīnā permanent. Neque
6 fās esse exīstimant ea litterīs mandāre, cum in reliquīs ferē rēbus, pūblicīs
7 prīvātīsque ratiōnibus, Graecīs litterīs ūtantur.   (continued)

Initial Explorations
1. What privileges do the druids enjoy? (1–2)
2. What effect does the existence of these privileges have? (3–4)
3. Describe one important part of the druids' training. (4–5)
4. What shows that it is not easy to become a druid? (5)
5. What do the druids believe is wrong? (5–6)
6. Why might this be surprising? (6–7)

8 **mihi**: one of the very few places in *De bello Gallico* where Caesar uses the first person singular.

in vulgum . . . efferī: i.e., the details of the teachings to become widely known.

vulgum: **vulgus** is normally neuter (acc. **vulgus**, same as the nom.), but is sometimes treated as masc. (acc. **vulgum**, as here).

9 **cōnfisōs**: *to rely upon* (additional meaning).

10 **studeō, studēre, studuī** + dat., *to be eager for, be diligent in, apply oneself to.*

ferē: *generally, usually* (additional meaning).

11 **perdiscendō**: deduce; cf. **discendī** (6.13:26) and **ēdiscere** (6.14:5).

remittant: *to slack off, relax* (additional meaning).

In prīmīs: *in the first things, particularly, especially.*

hoc: the indirect statement **nōn interīre animās** is in apposition with, and explains, **hoc**.

12 **ab aliīs . . . ad aliōs**: *from some to others*, less lit., *from (person) one to another*, i.e., from an individual in one lifetime to another in a later incarnation.

13 **excitārī**: an impersonal passive; see **F3d** and esp. **F3f**. This mght be translated *it is inspired*, less lit., *men are inspired.*.

anima, -ae, f., *soul*; do not confuse with **animus, -ī,** *mind, spirit*.

hōc: abl. of means or cause.

14 **sīdus, sīderis, n.,** *constellation*.

mundus, -ī, m., *world* (i.e., the universe, as opposed to **terra**, the earth).

15 **disputō, -āre, -āvī, -ātus,** *to weigh, examine, investigate.*

16 **iuventūs, iuventūtis, f.,** *youth, young people.*

---

1 **alterum**: this picks up the thought from §13:1–2, where Caesar mentioned two classes of people.

ūsus: *need* (additional meaning).

2 **incidō, incidere, incidī,** *to fall upon, happen, occur.*

quotannīs, adv., *every year.*

soleō, solēre, solitus sum + infin., *to be accustomed (to), be in the habit (of).*

3 **inlātās**: what noun is gapped here? How do you know? (Review the Reading Strategy on page 25).

propulsō, -āre, -āvī, -ātus, *to drive back, repel.*

4 **eōrum**: the pronoun comes to the left of its clause marker.

ut: completed by **est**; how does the form **est** affect the meaning of **ut**? (See **O4d**.)

ut . . . ita: correlatives, *as . . so.*

genere: *family* (additional meaning).

amplus, -a, -um, *great, abundant; splendid, distinguished.* The superlative **amplissimus** was often used by the Romans to describe someone holding very high office.

5 **ambactus, -ī, m.,** *retainer* (a Celtic word); the exact meaning is not known, although the **ambactī** seem higher in status than **clientēs**.

grātiam: *(source of) influence* (additional meaning).

potentia, -ae, f., *power.*

6 **nōscō, nōscere, nōvī, nōtus,** *to get to know*; in perfect, *to know* (**F2e**).

8 Id mihi duābus dē causīs īnstituisse videntur, quod neque in vulgum
9 disciplīnam efferri velint neque eōs quī discunt, litterīs cōnfīsōs, minus
10 memoriae studēre; quod ferē plērīsque accidit, ut praesidiō litterārum
11 dīligentiam in perdiscendō ac memoriam remittant. In prīmīs hoc vo-
12 lunt persuādēre, nōn interīre animās, sed ab aliīs post mortem trānsīre ad
13 aliōs, atque hōc maximē ad virtūtem excitārī putant, metū mortis neglectō.
14 Multa praetereā dē sīderibus atque eōrum mōtū, dē mundī ac terrārum
15 magnitūdine, dē rērum nātūrā, dē deōrum immortālium vī ac potestāte dis-
16 putant et iuventūtī trādunt.

7. For what two reasons does Caesar believe this custom was established?
   (8–10)
8. What general statement does Caesar make about learning? (10–11)
9. What is one of the primary teachings of the druids? (11–13)
10. What effect do they think this belief has, and why? (13)
11. What are some other things that the druids investigate and teach? (14–16)

The nobility: prestigious warriors.

1 [15] Alterum genus est equitum. Hī, cum est ūsus atque aliquod bellum
2 incidit (quod ferē ante Caesaris adventum quotannīs accidere solēbat, utī
3 aut ipsī iniūriās īnferrent aut inlātās prōpulsārent), omnēs in bellō versan-
4 tur; atque eōrum ut quisque est genere cōpiīsque amplissimus, ita plūrimōs
5 circum sē ambactōs clientēsque habet. Hanc ūnam grātiam potentiamque
6 nōvērunt.

Initial Explorations
1. What is the other class of important people in Gaul? (1)
2. Under what circumstances are the services of this class needed? How often
   did this happen before Caesar arrived in Gaul? (1–2)
3. What function do members of this class perform? (3–4)
4. What determines the number of retainers and dependents a man has? (4–5)
5. Why is having many retainers and dependents important in Gallic society?
   (5–6)

1 **dēdō, dēdere, dēdidī, dēditus**, *to hand over, devote.*

2 ***morbus, -ī**, m., *disease, illness.*

  in proeliīs perīculīsque: HENDIADYS, reinforced by ALLITERATION.

3 **victima, -ae**, f., *(sacrificial) victim,* usually an animal killed to please the gods in a religious ritual.

  ***immolō, -āre, -āvī, -ātus**, *to slay, sacrifice.*

  sē immolātūrōs: sc. **esse**, and **hominēs** as object.

4 **voveō, vovēre, vōvī, vōtus**, *to pledge, vow.*

  administer, administrī, m., *attendant, assistant.*

  administrīs: *as assistants.*

  prō vītā hominis nisi hominis vīta reddātur: note the CHIASMUS. The religion of the Gauls, like that of the Romans, was based on the notion of exchange; the worshipper gave something to the god in order to get something in return. Among the Romans a sacrifice might be something as small as pouring out some wine (called a libation). Animals of various sizes were sacrificed if the situation was important and the worshipper could afford to do so; the more valuable a gift one gave the god, the more one was entitled to expect in return. The custom of human sacrifice takes this concept to its logical, albeit horrifying, conclusion. It is not certain that human sacrifice was still practiced when Caesar arrived in Gaul, although it clearly had been before then.

  nūmen, nūminis, n., *divinity, divine power.*

6 **placō, -āre, -āvī, -ātus**, *to placate, appease.*

  pūblicē: this word indicates that not only were some such sacrifices held in public, but that they were meant to benefit the whole community (as opposed to the sacrifices by individuals mentioned previously).

  īnstitūta: *established,* i.e., carried out, performed.

7 **immānis, -is, -e**, *enormous, huge.*

  ***simulācrum, -ī**, n., *image, figure.*

  contexō, contexere, contexuī, contextus, *to weave together, to weave.*

  vīmen, vīminis, n., *twig, small branch.*

8 ***vīvus, -a, -um**, *alive, living.*

9 **exanimantur**: *killed* (additional meaning).

  ***supplicium, -ī**, n., *punishment, execution.*

  fūrtum, -ī, n., *theft.*

  lātrōcinium, -ī, n., *robbery.*

10 **noxia, -ae**, f., *crime.*

  sint comprehēnsī: subjunctive in a relative clause of characteristic.

  grātus, -a, -um + dat., *pleasing (to).*

12 **dēscendunt**: *resort to,* lit., *sink down to.*

Human sacrifice.

1 [16] Nātiō est omnium Gallōrum admodum dēdita religiōnibus, atque ob
2 eam causam quī sunt adfectī graviōribus morbīs quīque in proeliīs perīcu-
3 līsque versantur aut prō victimīs hominēs immolant aut sē immolātūrōs
4 vovent, administrīsque ad ea sacrificia druidibus ūtuntur; quod, prō vītā
5 hominis nisi hominis vīta reddātur, nōn posse deōrum immortālium nū-
6 men placārī arbitrantur, pūblicēque eiusdem generis habent īnstitūta sac-
7 rificia. Aliī immānī magnitūdine simulacra habent, quōrum contexta vīmi-
8 nibus membra vīvīs hominibus complent; quibus succēnsīs circumventī
9 flammā exanimantur hominēs. Supplicia eōrum quī in fūrtō aut in lātrō-
10 ciniō aut aliquā noxiā sint comprehēnsī grātiōra dīs immortālibus esse arbi-
11 trantur; sed, cum eius generis cōpia dēficit, etiam ad innocentium supplicia
12 dēscendunt.

Initial Explorations

1. What does Caesar say about the Gallic people? (1)
2. What types of men might make a human sacrifice? (2–4)
3. How do they carry out these sacrifices? (4)
4. What is the justification for such sacrifices? (4–6)
5. Describe the figures mentioned by Caesar. (7–8)
6. How are these figures used? (8–9)
7. What individuals are usually executed? How do the Gauls regard such
   executions? (9–11)
8. What happens if none of these people are available? (11–12)

Discussion

1. What is the effect of the CHIASMUS in line 5?

1 **deum**: contracted form for **deōrum**.

   Mercurium: this is not the actual Roman god but a Celtic deity who was thought to have some of the same powers as Mercury; the same is true of the other gods mentioned in this chapter. The habit of identifying a god of one group with that of another, called syncretism, existed throughout the ancient world. For instance, at Bath, England there are dedications to Sulis Minerva. Sulis was a native Celtic goddess identfied with Minerva, even though she seems not to have been particularly a goddess of wisdom or crafts. The popularity of 'Mercury' is attested by the hundreds of dedications to this god found throughout the old Celtic lands. We do not know his Celtic name for certain, although he may have been the god Lugus (for whom the city of Lugdunum, now Lyon, was named).

   colō, colere, coluī, cultus, *to pay attention to; to cultivate; to worship.*

2 **ferunt**: *they say.* This verb of thinking governs an indirect statement, which you can recognize from the combination of **ferunt** and **hunc inventōrem**; supply **esse** here and in the next phrase. The indirect statement continues, although the third phrase (**hunc . . . maximam**) is governed by **arbitrantur** (3). Note the ASYNDETON between the first/second and third parts of the indirect statement: *they say . . . (and) they think . . . .*

   ducem: *guide* (additional meaning).

3 **ad**: *for.*

   quaestus, -ūs [< quaestus, perf. part. of quaerō, to seek], m., *gain, acquisition.*

   mercātūra, -ae, f., *business, trade.*

4 **Post hunc**: sc. **colunt**. How do you know that this verb is gapped?

5 **gēns, gentis**, f., *clan; people.*

6 **artificium, -ī** [ars + faciō], n., *craft* (here contrasted with **opus**, *art*).

7 **caelestis, -is, -e** [< caelum, sky], *of the sky, of heaven.*

   caelestium: genitive plural; a substantive, *of the heavenly ones*, i.e., *of the gods.*

   dīmicō, -āre, -āvī, -ātus, *to fight.*

8 **dēvoveō, dēvovēre, dēvōvī, dēvōtus**, *to vow, dedicate.*

10 **exstruō, exstruere, exstrūxī, exstrūctus**, *to build.*

   tumulus, -ī, m., *mound.*

   cōnspicor, -ārī, -ātus sum, *to catch sight of.*

11 **neque saepe accidit**: LITOTES.

12 *****occultō, -āre, -āvī, -ātus**, *to conceal, hide.*

Text

♦ The Oxford Classical Text, following all the manuscripts, reads **quae superāverint** (8). Many editors believe that **quae** does not make sense (why not?) and replace it with **cum**, as is done here.

The gods of the Gauls.

1 [17] Deum maximē Mercurium colunt. Huius sunt plūrima simulacra,
2 hunc omnium inventōrem artium ferunt, hunc viārum atque itinerum du-
3 cem, hunc ad quaestūs pecūniae mercātūrāsque habēre vim maximam ar-
4 bitrantur. Post hunc Apollinem et Mārtem et Iovem et Minervam. Dē hīs
5 eandem ferē quam reliquae gentēs habent opīniōnem: Apollinem morbōs
6 dēpellere, Minervam operum atque artificiōrum initia trādere, Iovem im-
7 perium caelestium tenēre, Mārtem bella regere. Huic, cum proeliō dīmicāre
8 cōnstituērunt, ea quae bellō cēperint plērumque dēvovent: cum superāverint,
9 animālia capta immolant; reliquāsque rēs in ūnum locum cōnferunt. Multīs
10 in cīvitātibus hārum rērum exstrūctōs tumulōs locīs cōnsecrātīs cōnspicārī
11 licet; neque saepe accidit ut neglectā quispiam religiōne aut capta apud sē
12 occultāre aut posita tollere audēret, gravissimumque eī reī supplicium cum
13 cruciātū cōnstitūtum est.

Initial Explorations

1. Who is the chief god of the Gauls? What is one sign of his popularity? (1)
2. Describe three powers that the Gauls believe he has. (2–4)
3. What other gods are worshipped most frequently? (4)
4. How do the beliefs of the Gauls about these gods compare with the beliefs of other peoples about them? (4–5)
5. What are the powers of these various gods? (5–7)
6. What do the Gauls do when they have decided to fight a war? (7–8)
7. What happens to captured animals? (8–9)
8. What happens to other things that are captured? (9)
9. What can be seen among many tribes? (10–11)
10. What happens on rare occasions? (11–12)
11. What is the penalty for this? (12–13)

Discussion

1. What is the effect of the LITOTES in line 11?

1   **Dīs, Dītis,** m., *Dis* or *Dis Pater*, another name for Pluto, god of the underworld; it is from the same root as **dīves,** *rich,* since the god of the underworld controlled the gold, silver, and precious stones that are found in the ground.

    prōgnātus, -a, -um [cf. nātus, perf. part. of nāscor, to be born], *sprung from, born from.*

    prōgnātōs: sc. **esse,** and also with **prōditum** in the next line.

2   **nōn numerō diērum sed noctium:** because Dis/Pluto was the god of the dark underworld.

3   **fīniunt:** *they measure.*

    diēs nātālēs: *birthdays.*

5   **quod suōs līberōs:** the causal clause begins with these two words. Then an *if*-clause, **nisi cum adolēvērunt,** and a result clause, **ut . . . possint,** are nested inside; the causal clause resumes with **palam** (6). The **-que** (**fīliumque,** 6) shows that the causal clause has two parts to it; the main verb in the second part is **dūcunt** (7).

    adolēscō, adolēscere, adolēvī, adultus, *to grow up.*

    mūnus, mūneris, n., *duty, obligation; burden.*

6   **puerīlis, -is, -e** [< puer, boy, child], *childish, youthful.*

7   **aetās, aetātis,** f., *age* (do not confuse with **aestās,** *summer*).

    puerīlī aetāte: abl. of description (**A5n**).

    adsistō, adsistere, astitī, *to stand nearby.*

    turpe: sc. **esse.** The infinitive phrase **fīlium . . . adsistere** serves as the subject of the indirect statement introduced by **dūcunt,** although it can be conveniently translated as *they consider it disgraceful for a son. . . .*

    fīlium . . . dūcunt: this custom must have seemed very strange to the Romans. In Rome fathers regularly took their sons, even at a relatively young age, with them as they went about their business; in the early period of Roman history senators even brought their sons into sessions of the Senate.

Discussion

1. Look carefully at the illustration opposite. What impression did the artist want to give of the druids and the Gauls? Explain your answer by referring to specific details in the illustration. To what extent is this later view similar to, or different from, the ideas held by the Romans about the Gauls?

Some unusual customs.

1 **[18]** Gallī sē omnēs ab Dīte patre prōgnātōs praedicant, idque ab druidibus
2 prōditum dīcunt. Ob eam causam spatia omnis temporis nōn numerō diē-
3 rum sed noctium fīniunt; diēs nātālēs et mēnsum et annōrum initia sīc ob-
4 servant ut noctem diēs subsequātur. In reliquīs vītae īnstitūtīs hōc ferē ab
5 reliquīs differunt, quod suōs līberōs, nisi cum adolēvērunt, ut mūnus mīli-
6 tiae sustinēre possint, palam ad sē adīre nōn patiuntur filiumque puerīlī
7 aetāte in pūblicō in cōnspectū patris adsistere turpe dūcunt.

Initial Explorations

1. What do the Gauls say about the origin of their people? How do they know
   this? (1–2)
2. What custom do they observe as a result? (2–4)
3. What do the Gauls not allow children to do until they are grown up? (5–6)
4. How is 'grown up' defined? (5–6)
5. What do they think is disgraceful? (6–7)

Gallic warriors seeking the blessings of the gods from a druid, as imagined by a 19th century artist.

1 **quantās**: a correlative with **tantās**; men contribute *as much* (**tantās**) *as* (**quantās**) they receive.

 dōs, dōtis, f., *dowry*.

 dōtis nōmine: *under the name of dowry, as a dowry*.

2 **bonīs**: **bona**, a n. pl., substantive, *goods, possessions*. How would you know this is a substantive if the note were not here?

 aestimātiō, aestimātiōnis, f., *assessment, accounting*.

3 **coniūnctim**, adv., *together, jointly*.

 frūctus, -ūs, m., *fruit; profit*.

 superārit: what would be the uncontracted form of this verb? (See **F2g**.)

4 **vītā superārit**: *has survived in life*, i.e., has outlived the other.

5 **nex, necis**, f., *killing, death*.

6 **inlūstris, -is, -e**, *bright, clear; famous, distinguished*.

 inlūstrī locō: for the use of the abl., see the note on 5.25:1 or **A5a**.

 dēcessit: *has gone away* = *has died* (additional meaning).

7 **dē morte**: this phrase appears to the left of its clause marker **sī**.

 dē uxōribus: note that Caesar uses the plural here, although he spoke of **pater** (singular) at the beginning on the sentence. Was this just an inconsistency caused by hasty writing, or did the Gauls practice polygamy? The Germans clearly did; recall the mention of Ariovistus' two wives in Book I.

 in servīlem modum: *in the manner of slaves*, i.e., with torture; Roman law forbade the torture of citizens but permitted slaves to be questioned this way.

8 **quaestiō, quaestiōnis**, f., *inquiry, investigation*; **quaestiōnem habēre** is a term from Roman law.

 comperiō, comperīre, comperī, compertus, *to find out, discover*.

 compertum est: an impersonal passive.

9 **excruciō, -āre, -āvī, -ātus** [ex + crux, crucis, cross], *to torture*.

 fūnus, fūneris, n., *funeral*.

10 **sumptuōsus, -a, -um**, *expensive, costly*.

 cor, cordis, n., *heart*; **cordī** is a dative of purpose, so **cordī esse** = *to be (dear) to the heart, to be loved*. **cordī** is used with **vīvīs** in a double dative (**A3i**).

11 **paulō suprā hanc memoriam**: i.e., just a short time before people living in Gaul when Caesar was governor could remember.

12 **dīligō, dīligere, dīlēxī, dīlēctus**, *to value highly, to love*.

 iūstīs fūneribus: *the funeral proper*, i.e., the actual funeral ritual, which would be followed by cremation of the body.

Marriages and funerals.

1   [19] Virī, quantās pecūniās ab uxōribus dōtis nōmine accēpērunt, tantās
2   ex suīs bonīs, aestimātiōne factā, cum dōtibus commūnicant. Huius om-
3   nis pecūniae coniūnctim ratiō habētur frūctūsque servantur: uter eōrum
4   vītā superārit, ad eum pars utrīusque cum frūctibus superiōrum temporum
5   pervenit. Virī in uxōrēs, sīcutī in līberōs, vītae necisque habent potestātem;
6   et cum pater familiae inlustriōre locō nātus dēcessit, eius propinquī con-
7   veniunt et, dē morte sī rēs in suspiciōnem venit, dē uxōribus in servīlem
8   modum quaestiōnem habent et, sī compertum est, ignī atque omnibus tor-
9   mentīs excruciātās interficiunt. Fūnera sunt prō cultū Gallōrum magnifica
10 et sumptuōsa; omniaque quae vīvis cordī fuisse arbitrantur in ignem īnfe-
11 runt, etiam animālia; ac paulō suprā hanc memoriam servī et clientēs, quōs
12 ab eīs dīlēctōs esse cōnstābat, iūstis fūneribus cōnfectīs ūnā cremābantur.

Initial Explorations

1. What do men receive when they get married? (1)
2. What must the men do in return? (1–2)
3. How is this property handled (2–3)
4. What happens to it in the end? (3–5)
5. What power do men have within their families? (5)
6. When do relatives assemble? (6)
7. What do they do if circumstances of the death are suspicious? (7–8)
8. What happens if they decide that the wife was responsible for her husband's death? (8–9)
9. How does Caesar describe Gallic funerals? (9–10)
10. What happens at the funeral? (10–11)
11. How has this custom changed in recent times? (11–12)

Discussion

1. If you translated the first sentence in this chapter, you probably had to rearrange the order of words considerably. How is the Latin order effective in showing what actually happened in such a situation? (Review the Reading Strategy on page 125.)
2. Do you find the financial arrangements described in this chapter surprising? What effects might these arrangements have had during a marriage or after one partner died?

1 **cīvitātēs**: the antecedent appears inside the relative clause.
2 **sanciō, sancīre, sānxī, sānctus**, *to make holy; to appoint, establish.*
  habent lēgibus sānctum: *have established by law, that* . . . . **sānctum** is neuter because it describes the indirect command begun by **utī** (3); the *if*-clause **sī** . . . **accēperit** is nested between the main clause **habent lēgibus sānctum** and the **ut** clause that completes it.
3 **nēve** [nē + -ve]: *and not*; the **nē** introduces a second part of the indirect command begun by **utī**. Because of the **nē**, **quō** (4) = **aliquō** (see **E1**).
4 **temerārius, -a, -um**, *reckless.*
5 **ad facinus . . . cōnsilium capere**: i.e., people do bad things or make inappropriate decisions because they are afraid.
6 **quae**: n. pl.; what antecedent must be supplied? (Cf. the Structure note on page 27.)
  quaeque: **quae** (n. pl.) with **-que** (not a form of **quisque**).
7 **ex ūsū**: *of use, useful.*

✳ ✳ ✳ ✳ ✳ ✳ ✳ ✳ ✳

Vocabulary Review: Book VI

The following asterisked words were introduced in §§13–20:

disciplīna	plērīque
discō	propinquus
druidēs	reddō
facinus	religiō
immolō	simulācrum
mīlitia	supplicium
morbus	tribūtum
occultō	vīvus

Good government among the Gauls.

1 [20] Quae cīvitātēs commodius suam rem pūblicam administrāre exīsti-
2 mantur habent lēgibus sānctum, sī quis quid dē rē pūblicā ā fīnitimīs ru-
3 mōre aut fāmā accēperit, utī ad magistrātum dēferat nēve cum quō aliō
4 commūnicet: quod saepe hominēs temerāriōs atque imperītōs falsīs rumō-
5 ribus terrērī et ad facinus impellī et dē summīs rēbus cōnsilium capere
6 cognitum est. Magistrātūs quae vīsa sunt occultant quaeque esse ex ūsū
7 iūdicāvērunt multitūdinī prōdunt. Dē rē pūblicā nisi per concilium loquī
8 nōn concēditur.

Initial Explorations
1. What tribes is Caesar describing in this chapter? (1–2)
2. What rules have these tribes enacted through laws? (2–4)
3. Why did they make this rule? (4–6)
4. How do the officials deal with the information they get? (6–7)
5. What additional piece of information does Caesar give about the government of the Gallic tribes? (7–8)

Discussion
1. Do you agree that rules such as those described in 1–4 are justified?
2. What might result from some tribes' rule that public affairs could not be discussed except at a council? Who would benefit from this?
3. Caesar refers to the Gauls as "barbarians" (**barbarī**). To what extent was Caesar's use of this term justified? Consider everything you have learned about the Gauls from Caesar's own writings in Book VI and previous books of *De bello Gallico*, from the the Introduction and the selection from Diodorus (page 108), and from any additional research you may have done.
4. What did Caesar gain by referring to the Gauls this way?

* * * * * * * * *

The remainder of Book VI appears in English starting on the following page, where Caesar describes the life and customs of the Germans. Then Caesar resumes his military narrative, telling how he exacted vengeance from the Eburones for their massacre of the cohorts commanded by Sabinus and Cotta. However, Ambiorix, leader of the Eburones and the chief target of Caesar's wrath, managed to escape.

* * * * * * * * *

4 Customs and institutions of the Germans

[21] The customs of the Germans are entirely different. They have no Druids to control religious observances and are not much given to sacrifices. The only beings they recognize as gods are things that they can see, and by which they are obviously benefited, such as Sun, Moon, and Fire; the other gods they have never even heard of. They spend all their lives in hunting and warlike pursuits, and inure themselves from childhood to toil and hardship. Those who preserve their chastity longest are most highly commended by their friends; for they think that continence makes young men taller, stronger, and more muscular. To have had intercourse with a woman before the age of twenty is considered perfectly scandalous. They attempt no concealment, however, of the facts of sex: men and women bathe together in the rivers, and they wear nothing but hides or short garments of hairy skin, which leave most of the body bare.

[22] The Germans are not agriculturalists, and live principally on milk, cheese, and meat. No one possesses any definite amount of land as private property; the magistrates and tribal chiefs annually assign a holding to clans and groups of kinsmen or others living together, fixing its size and position at their discretion, and the following year make them move on somewhere else. They give many reasons for this custom: for example, that their men may not get accustomed to living in one place, lose their warlike enthusiasm, and take up agriculture instead; that they may not be anxious to acquire large estates, and the strong be tempted to dispossess the weak; to prevent their paying too much attention to building houses that will protect them from cold and heat, or becoming too fond of money—a frequent cause of division and strife; and to keep the common people contented and quiet by letting every man see that even the most powerful are no better off than himself.

[23] The various tribes regard it as their greatest glory to lay waste as much as possible of the land around them and to keep it uninhabited. They hold it a proof of a people's valour to drive their neighbours from their homes, so that no one dare settle near them, and also think it gives them greater security by removing any fear of sudden invasion. When a tribe is attacked or intends to attack another, officers are chosen to conduct the campaign and invested with powers of life and death. In peacetime there is no central magistracy; the chiefs of the various districts and cantons[1] administer justice and settle disputes among their own people. No discredit attaches to plundering raids outside the tribal frontiers; the Germans say that they serve to keep the young men in training and prevent them from getting lazy. When a chief announces in an assembly his intention of leading a raid and calls for volunteers, those who like the proposal, and approve of the man who makes it, stand up and promise their assistance amid the applause of the whole gathering; anyone who backs out afterwards is looked on as a deserter and a traitor and no one will ever

---

[1] Small local areas. 🐾

trust him again. To wrong a guest is impious in their eyes. They shield from injury all who come to their houses for any purpose whatever, and treat their persons as sacred; guests are welcomed to every man's home and table.

[24] There was a time when the Gauls were more warlike than the Germans, when they actually invaded German territory, and sent colonists across the Rhine because their own country was too small to support its large population. It was in this way that the most fertile district of Germany, in the neighbourbood of the Hercynian forest (which I see was known to Eratosthenes and other Greeks, who call it Orcynia) was seized and occupied by the Volcae Tectosages, who remain there to this day and have a high reputation for fair dealing and gallantry. Nowadays, while the Germans still endure the same life of poverty and privation as before, without any change in their diet or clothing, the Gauls, through living near the Roman Province and becoming acquainted with sea-borne products,[2] are abundantly supplied with various commodities. Gradually accustomed to inferiority and defeated in many battles, they do not even pretend to compete with the Germans in bravery.

[25] This Hercynian forest is so wide that it takes a lightly equipped traveller nine days to cross it; this is the only way the Germans have of estimating its size, as they know nothing of measures of length. Starting from the frontiers of the Helvetii, Nemetes, and Rauraci, it runs straight along the Danube to the country of the Dacians and the Anartes. At this point it turns north-east away from the river, and in its huge length extends through the territories of many different peoples. No western German claims to have reached its eastern extremity, even after travelling for two months, or to have heard where it ends. The forest is known to contain many kinds of animals not seen elsewhere, some of which seem worthy of mention because they differ greatly from those found in other countries.

[26] There is an ox shaped like a deer, with a single horn in the middle of its forehead between the ears, which sticks up higher and straighter than those of the animals we know, and at the top branches out widely like a man's hand or a tree. The male and female are alike, and their horns are of the same shape and size.

[27] There are also animals called elks, which resemble goats in shape and in their piebald colouring, but are somewhat larger, and have stunted horns and legs without joints or knuckles. They do not lie down to rest, and if they fall by accident, cannot get up or raise themselves from the ground. Trees serve them as resting-places: they support themselves against the trunks and rest in that way, leaning over only slightly. When the hunters have found out their usual retreats by following their tracks, they either sever the roots of all the surrounding trees or cut nearly through the trunks, so that they only look as if they are still standing firm. When

---

[2] Merchants from Massilia for a long time had been in the habit of trading up the rivers of Gaul, such as the Rhône. Recall also Caesar's comment in §1.1 about the Belgae being furthest from the luxuries of the Province and therefore the fiercest fighters. 🐾

the elks lean against them as usual, they push over the insecure trunks with their weight, and fall down with them.[3]

[28] A third species is the aurochs, an animal somewhat smaller than the elephant, with the appearance, colour, and shape of a bull. They are very strong and agile, and attack every man and beast they catch sight of. The natives take great pains to trap them in pits, and then kill them. This arduous sport toughens the young men and keeps them in training; and those who kill the largest number exhibit the horns in public to show what they have done, and earn high praise. It is impossible to domesticate or tame the aurochs, even if it is caught young. The horns are much larger than those of our oxen, and of quite different shape and appearance. The Germans prize them greatly: they mount the rims with silver and use them as drinking-cups at their grandest banquets.

Questions

1. How did the Germans obtain a living? How was this different from the tribes of Gaul?
2. What practices show that the Germans were a warlike people?
3. Do you agree with the idea that people who have a higher standard of living become less fierce? Why or why not?
4. What seemed to impress Caesar most about the Hercynian forest (the forest itself, not its wildlife)?
5. Why might Caesar have included the account he gives of the elks?
6. Compare and contrast the customs of the Gauls and the Germans. Which were more civilized by Roman standards and why?
7. S. A. Handford, whose translation of *De bello Gallico* is used in this book, suggests that Caesar might have added the discussion of the customs of Gaul and Germany at this point to distract his readers from thinking about how little the expedition to Germany had accomplished (note 6, page 201 opposite). Can you think of other reasons why Caesar might have included the material, in general or at this point in particular?

---

[3] The 'ox shaped like a deer' is apparently the reindeer; but in reality it has two antlers. The idea that the elk had no joints in is legs and slept against trees is of course a fairy-tale. As for the alleged method of catching the animal, it is hard to believe that Caesar took such a traveller's tale seriously.

5 Devastation of the country of the Eburones[4]

[29] Learning from the scouts of the Ubii that the Suebi had retired into the forests, Caesar was afraid that if he followed them he might run short of corn,[5] since, as already said, none of the Germans pay much attention to agriculture. He therefore decided to advance no farther.[6] However, so as not to let the natives think they had seen the last of him, he left the greater part of the bridge standing. In order to hold up any reinforcements which they might try to send to Gaul, after withdrawing his army he broke down the end that touched the Ubian bank for a distance of two hundred feet, and at the Gallic end erected a four-storeyed tower, posted a detachment of twelve cohorts to protect the bridge and fortified the position with strong defence works. A young officer named Gaius Volcacius Tullus was placed in command of it. When the crops were beginning to ripen Caesar set out through the Ardennes[7] to fight Ambiorix. He sent Lucius Minucius Basilus in advance with all the cavalry, to see if he could gain any advantage by travelling quickly and striking at a favourable opportunity. Caesar told him to forbid fires to be lighted in his camps, so as not to give the enemy warning of his approach from a distance, and promised to follow him immediately.

[30] Basilus duly carried out his instructions. Completing the journey more quickly than anyone had thought possible, he surprised a number of Eburones working in the fields, and following their directions hurried on to a place where Ambiorix, guarded only by a few horsemen, was said to be. Much depends on fortune, in war, as in all other things. It was a lucky chance that enabled Basilus to catch Ambiorix unprepared and off his guard and to appear on the scene before his approach was reported or even rumoured. But by an equally great stroke of luck Ambiorix escaped alive, although he lost all the military equipment that he had with him, his carriages, and his horses. His house was in a wood, like most Gallic houses—for they generally choose sites near woods and rivers, to avoid the heat. So, fighting in a confined space, his attendants and friends were able to resist the attack of Basilus' cavalry for a time. Meanwhile, one of them mounted him on a horse, and his flight was covered by the wood. In this way he was first brought into danger, and then delivered from it, by the all-prevailing power of fortune.

[31] Ambiorix did not assemble his troops—either on purpose, because he thought it better not to give battle, or through lack of time, because his plans were upset by the sudden arrival of the Roman cavalry, which he assumed would be fol-

---

[4] At this point Caesar resumes the narrative he interrupted at the end of §10 in order to describe the customs of Gaul and Germany. Review §10 if you have forgotten what was happening. 🏳

[5] Grain. 🏳

[6] This incursion into Germany had achieved as little as the former one. Perhaps to distract his readers' attention from its insignificant results, Caesar inserted at this point a long digression (6.11–28) on the customs and institutions of Gaul and Germany.

[7] A large forest located in the area where France, Belgium, and Luxemburg meet. 🏳

lowed up by the rest of the army. At all events he sent out messengers through the countryside, bidding every man shift for himself. Some fled into the Ardennes, others into a continuous belt of marshes, while those who lived nearest the sea hid in places cut off from the mainland at high tide. Many left their own country and entrusted their lives and all their possessions to complete strangers. Catuvolcus, who as king of one half of the Eburones[8] had joined in Ambiorix's enterprise, was now a weak old man, unable to face the hardships of war or flight; solemnly cursing Ambiorix for having suggested the plan, he poisoned himself with yew, a tree which is very common in Gaul and Germany.

[32] The Segni and Condrusi, peoples of Germanic origin and generally counted as Germans, living between the Eburones and the Treveri, sent ambassadors to ask Caesar not to regard them as enemies and not to assume that all the Germans in Gaul were leagued together against him. They said that they had never thought of making war upon him, and had not sent any help to Ambiorix. After confirming their statements by interrogating prisoners, Caesar ordered them to bring to him any Eburonian fugitives who had come to their country; if they obeyed, he would respect their territory.

He then separated his forces into three divisions and took all the heavy baggage to Aduatuca, a fortress situated about in the middle of the country of the Eburones, where Sabinus and Cotta had had their winter quarters. He had several reasons for selecting this place: the principal one was that the fortifications constructed in the previous year were still intact, which would save the soldiers the labour of building new ones. He left the baggage under the protection of the 14th legion, one of the three which he had recently brought from Italy, where they had been levied. He placed this legion and the camp in charge of Cicero, assigning him also two hundred cavalry.

[33] After dividing the army, Caesar ordered Labienus to advance with three legions towards the coast, into the region bordering on the country of the Menapii, and sent Trebonius with three more to ravage the district lying on the frontiers of the Aduatuci. He took the remaining three himself, and decided to march to the river Scheldt, which flows into the Meuse,[9] and to the western end of the Ardennes, where he heard Ambiorix had gone with a small number of cavalry. Before setting out he promised to return in a week, when a distribution of rations to the legion left at the fortress would be due. He asked Labienus and Trebonius to return by the same date if the military situation allowed, so that after holding a further discussion they might be able to restart the campaign on new lines, in the light of what they would have learnt by that time of the enemy's plans.

---

[8] That is, as leader of one of the two factions within the tribe.

[9] The Scheldt does not flow into the Meuse, but there is some reason for thinking that these rivers did at one time communicate with each other near their mouths.

[34] It has been explained that the Eburones had no regular force assembled, no stronghold, and no garrison capable of armed resistance: their population was scattered in all directions. Each man had installed himself in any remote glen, any wooded spot, or impenetrable morass, that offered a chance of protection or escape. These hiding-places were known to the natives living in the neighbourhood, and great care was needed to ensure the safety of the Roman troops. So long as they kept together, they were in no danger from a panic-stricken and scattered enemy; but losses severe enough to weaken the army might easily be sustained by the waylaying of individual soldiers, who were tempted far afield by the hope of plunder, or got separated from the rest because the illdefined and half-concealed paths through the woods were not practicable for columns in close formation. The only way to make an end of the business, and exterminate this race of criminals, would have been to break up the army into a large number of detachments which could be sent out separately. But it was safer to keep the companies in their regular formation, according to the established practice of the Roman army, although this meant that they could not injure the Gauls in such country. Even so, any men who strayed apart from the main body were liable to be ambushed and surrounded by some of the bolder spirits among them. In these difficult circumstances the most careful precautions were taken; Caesar thought it better to let the enemy off comparatively lightly, in spite of the men's burning desire for revenge, than to punish them severely at the cost of serious loss to his own troops. He preferred to expose Gauls, instead of Roman legionaries, to the dangers of fighting in the forests, and also wanted to envelop the Eburones with a great multitude of men, in order to punish their heinous crime with total annihilation. Large numbers soon assembled from every side.

[35] While the whole of the Eburonian territory was being plundered, it was getting near the day on which Caesar had intended to return to the legion left in charge of the baggage. At this moment an instance occurred of the important part played in war by accident, which can have far-reaching consequences. After the panic-stricken flight of the enemy, already described, there was no hostile force in the field to give the slightest occasion for alarm. But the Germans across the Rhine heard that the Eburones were being plundered, and that all comers were invited to share the spoil. Immediately a force of two thousand cavalry was raised by the Sugambri, who live close to the Rhine—the people who, as said above, sheltered the fugitive Tencteri and Usipetes.[10] They crossed the river on boats and rafts, some thirty miles below the place where Caesar's bridge had been built and the garrison left, entered the territory of the Eburones, caught a number of the scattered fugitives and seized a quantity of cattle—a prize much sought after by the barbarians. Lured on by the hope of more plunder, they advanced farther; for these born fight-

---

[10] These were two Germanic tribes who, under pressure from the more powerful Suebi, had crossed the Rhine into Gaul seeking land; Caesar drove them back. 🦶

ers and bandits were not to be stopped by marshes or forests. On asking their prisoners where Caesar was, they were told that he had started on a campaign some distance away, and that all the army had left the district. One of the prisoners added: 'Why go after this paltry miserable loot, when you have the chance of making your fortunes right away? In three hours you can reach Atuatuca, where the Romans have stored all their property. The garrison is so small that they can't even man the wall, and not a man dare set foot outside the entrenchments.' The offer of such a chance decided the Germans. They hid the booty they had got, and guided by their informant made straight for Atuatuca.

[36] Throughout the previous week Cicero had been most careful to keep the soldiers in camp according to Caesar's instructions, not allowing even a single servant to go outside the entrenchment. But on the seventh day he began to fear that Caesar would not keep his appointment; it was said that he had advanced a long way, and there was no news of his return. The soldiers, too, were grumbling at Cicero's patient acceptance of the situation: to be cooped up like this in camp, they said, was almost as bad as a blockade. With nine legions and a strong cavalry force in the field, and the enemy scattered and very nearly destroyed, he had no reason to expect a serious accident within three miles of his camp. Accordingly he sent five cohorts to get corn from the nearest fields, which were separated from the camp by only a single hill. A number of sick men had been left behind by the legions; from these there went with the cohorts, as a separate detachment, some three hundred men who had recovered from illness during the week, and permission to accompany them was granted also to a large number of servants, who took out a great many of the animals that were being kept in the camp.

[37] It happened that just at this moment the German cavalry appeared and, riding right on without slackening speed, tried to break in by the back gate. As the view was obstructed by woods on that side, they were not seen until they were quite close to the camp—so close that the traders who had their tents at the foot of the rampart had no time to get away. The suddenness of the attack upset the soldiers, and the cohort on guard had difficulty in withstanding the first rush. The enemy spread out all round, trying to find a way in. The soldiers had hard work to defend the gates; elsewhere the lie of the land and the entrenchments gave protection. The whole camp was in a state of alarm; the men were asking one another the cause of the disturbance, and could not tell where to assemble or in which direction to advance. Some said the camp was already taken; others maintained that the Germans had come in triumph after destroying the Roman army and its commander-inchief. Most of them were filled with strange superstitious fancies suggested by the spot on which they stood, and saw in imagination the disaster that had befallen Cotta and Sabinus, who perished not far from that same fort. Everyone was so paralysed by fear that the Germans believed the prisoner had spoken the truth when he told

them that there was no garrison in the camp. They strove hard to force their way in, calling on one another not to let such a piece of luck slip through their fingers.

[38] Among the sick men left with the garrison was Baculus, who had served under Caesar as chief centurion of his legion, and has been mentioned in connection with earlier engagements. For five days he had been too ill to eat. Feeling anxious for his own and his comrades' safety, he walked unarmed out of his tent, and, on seeing the enemy close at hand and the situation extremely critical, borrowed arms from the nearest soldiers and posted himself in the gateway. He was joined by the centurions of the cohort on guard, and for a time they fought together to hold the enemy's attack. Baculus was severely wounded and fainted, and the others just managed to save him by passing him back from hand to hand. This respite gave the rest of the troops time to recover courage enough to man the fortifications and make a show of defence.

[39] Meanwhile the reaping party, which had finished its work, heard the shouting at the camp. The horsemen hurried on, and discovered how serious the peril was. Out there in the open there was no fortification to shelter the frightened men—raw recruits without any experience—and they turned to the military tribune and centurions, waiting to be told what to do; even the bravest were unnerved by the emergency. The Germans caught sight of the standards in the distance, and desisted from their attack on the camp. At first they thought it was the legions, returned from the distant expedition on which the prisoners said they had gone; but when they saw how small the force was, they regarded it with contempt and attacked from all sides.[11]

[40] The servants ran forward to the nearest rising ground, from which they were quickly dislodged and, by rushing to the standards round which the companies were formed up, increased the nervous soldiers' alarm. Since the camp was so near, some were for adopting a wedge formation and making a quick dash through, feeling confident that, though a few might be surrounded and killed, the rest could escape. Others preferred to make a stand on the hill, and all take their chance together. The latter plan was rejected by the detachment of veterans which had gone out with the cohorts. The veterans, therefore, with words of mutual encouragement, advanced under their commander Gaius Trebonius, a Roman knight,[12] broke right through the enemy, and reached the camp without a single casualty. Close behind them, in the gap made by their courageous charge, the servants and the cavalry got safely through. But those who had taken their stand on the hill showed that they had still learnt nothing of the art of war: they failed either to stick to the

---

[11] The two thousand cavalry of the Sugambri must have been accompanied, according to the German custom (1.48, 7.65), by a similar number of infantry, since they regarded with contempt a Roman force which must have considerably exceeded two thousand.

[12] I.e., a member of the equestrian class, wealthy businessmen, second to the senatorial class in power and prestige. 🀫

plan they had chosen of defending themselves on the high ground, or to imitate the swift and vigorous action which they could see had saved their comrades. Instead, in an attempt to regain the camp, they let themselves be caught in a bad position on low-lying ground. The centurions, some of whom had been promoted for gallantry from lower grades in other legions to the higher grades in this one, were determined not to forfeit the reputation they had won in previous actions, and fell fighting with the utmost courage. Some of the soldiers were saved by the centurions' brave stand, which made the enemy fall back, and—to their surprise—reached the camp in safety. The rest were surrounded by the enemy and killed.

[41] As the Germans saw that the Roman troops had now manned the fortifications, they gave up hope of taking the camp by storm, and retired across the Rhine with the booty that they had hidden in the woods. Even after their departure, the defenders were still so frightened that Volusenus, who was sent ahead by Caesar with the cavalry and arrived that night in the camp, could not make them believe that Caesar was close at hand, with his army safe and sound. Fear had so completely possessed them all that they nearly took leave of their senses, and would have it that the whole army had been cut to pieces, and that the cavalry had managed to escape by flight: if the army were not destroyed, they maintained, the Germans would never have attacked the camp. The panic was eventually stopped by Caesar's arrival.

[42] He was well aware of the way things happen in war, and on his return made only one criticism—that the cohorts had been allowed to leave their post in the garrison: Cicero should have avoided running even the slightest risk.[13] For the rest, he recognized that what had happened was largely the result of accident: it was a strange chance that had brought the enemy to the camp so suddenly, and a still stranger chance that had sent them away when they were almost masters of the rampart and gates. And the strangest thing of all was that although their object in crossing the Rhine was to plunder Ambiorix's country, circumstances had led them to attack the Roman camp instead, and thus render Ambiorix the greatest service he could have desired.

[43] Setting out once more to harass the Eburones, Caesar sent out in all directions a large force of cavalry that he had collected from the neighbouring tribes. Every village and every building they saw was set on fire; all over the country the cattle were either slaughtered or driven off as booty; and the crops, a part of which had already been laid flat by the autumnal rains, were consumed by the great numbers of horses and men. It seemed certain, therefore, that even if some of the inhabitants had escaped for the moment by hiding, they must die of starvation after the retirement of the troops. With such a large number of horsemen scouring the country

---

[13] Caesar treats Quintus Cicero very tenderly whenever he refers to him in the *Gallic War*, wishing to gratify his brother Marcus Cicero, whose friendship was useful to Caesar. In the present passage he lets him off with a reprimand much less severe than he deserved and mentions all the extenuating circumstances he can think of. Cicero had certainly been incautious and disobedient.

in separate parties, it happened time and again that prisoners were taken who had just seen Ambiorix in flight; they would actually look round to see where he was, insisting that he was barely out of sight. This raised his pursuers' hopes of running him down, and so standing high in Caesar's favour. They took endless pains and made almost superhuman efforts. But they always seemed just to have missed what they so ardently desired; Ambiorix would escape by hiding in a wood or ravine, and under cover of night would make off in some new direction, escorted only by four horsemen—for to no one else did he dare entrust his life.

[44] After ravaging the country in this way, Caesar withdrew his army—minus the two cohorts of Cicero's legion which had been lost—to Durocortorum, a town of the Remi, where he convened a Gallic council and held an inquiry into the conspiracy of the Senones and Carnutes. Acco, the instigator of the plot, was condemned to death and executed in the ancient Roman manner.[14] Some others, who fled in fear of being brought to trial, were outlawed. Caesar then distributed the legions in winter quarters—two on the frontier of the Treveri, two among the Lingones, and the other six at Agedincum in the country of the Senones—and after provisioning them, since Gaul was quiet, set out for northern Italy as usual to hold his assizes.[15]

Questions

1. What was the first phase of Caesar's operation agains the Eburones after returning from Germany? Was it successful?
2. What was the plan that Caesar adopted during the second part of his campaign?
3. What problem did he encounter? How did he react to it?
4. Why did the Sugambri cross the Rhine? What unexpected event happened when they did?
5. How did each of the following groups react to the arrival of the Germans? What happened to each group?
   a. the soldiers in the camp
   b. the cohorts sent to gather grain
   c. the veterans who went with the cohorts
   d. the servants
6. In what two ways did unexpected turns of fate play a part in Caesar's campaign against the Eburones? How did fate also play havoc with his decision to leave the 14th Legion to guard the baggage?
7. Would you describe Caesar's actions as described in the second half of Book VI as overly cautious, appropriate, or too aggressive? Why or why not? What might have motivated Caesar to behave as he did?

---

[14] The 'ancient Roman manner' of execution was by scourging [whipping to death] and beheading. By thus setting himself up as a judge over the Gauls, Caesar is quite openly treating them as the inhabitants of a conquered province.

[15] Assizes: see note 14, §1.54, page 70. 🔆

A Political Survivor: L. Munatius Plancus

You met Lucius Munatius Plancus as one of Caesar's legates (5.24–25). Scion of an aristocratic family, Plancus (ca. 85–ca. 15 BCE), like some Roman nobles, survived the tumultuous times of the late Republic by knowing when to change sides. His tomb, a large cylindrical structure, still survives near Naples with the following inscription:

L(ūcius) · Munātius · L(ūciī) · f(īlius) · L(ūciī) · n(epōs) · L(ūciī) · prōn(epōs)
Plancus · cō(n)s(ul) · cēns(or) · (imp)erātor · iter(um) · viivir
Epulōn(um) · triump(hātor) · ex · Raetīs · aedem · Saturnī
fēcit · dē · manubiīs · agrōs · dīvīsit · in · Italiā
Beneventī · in · Galliā · colōniās · dēdūxit
Lugdūnum · et · Rauricam

Lucius Munatius, son of Lucius, grandson of Lucius, great-grandson of Lucius, Plancus, consul, censor, twice **imperātor, septemvir epulonum**, *triumphed over the Raeti, (re)built the temple of Saturn from the spoils, divided lands in Italy at Beneventum, in Gaul founded the colonies (of) Lugdunum and Raurica.*

Plancus was serving as governor of Gallia Transalpina when Caesar was assassinated. This was a common pattern: a man served as a young officer in a particular province, and later was sent back to that province as a high-level official who could take advantage of his acquaintance with the province and some of its leaders. As governor, Plancus founded two important Roman colonies at Lugdunum and Raurica. He also defeated the Raeti, a tribe in the Alps not conquered by Caesar. After Caesar's murder, Plancus declared his allegiance to the Republic and worked with Decimus Junius Brutus who led the senatorial forces in northern Italy, fighting against Mark Antony. Plancus soon deserted Brutus and allied himself with Antony and Lepidus, two other former officers of Caesar, and he held the consulship with Lepidus in 42 BCE.

Bust of Plancus found at Lyon.

During the proscriptions carried out by Antony and Octavian, he allowed (or even arranged) the death of his own brother. Plancus served under Antony in various capacities, including stints as governor of Asia and of Syria. After Antony's campaign against the Parthians failed, Plancus shifted his allegiance to Octavian in 32 BCE. He justified this action by saying that he could not fight for Cleopatra, although he probably sensed that Octavian would win the impending conflict between the two rivals. According to Suetonius, it was Plancus who proposed granting Octavian the title Augustus in 27 BCE. In 22 Augustus appointed him censor with Aemilius Paullus. He did a poor job in that office, however, and it marked the end of his public career.

Book VII

52 BCE

BOOK VII OF DE BELLO GALLICO, which is presented here complete in English, is one of the best-known parts of Caesar's commentaries. In the early spring of 52, the Gauls, believing (incorrectly) that Caesar was unable to return to his army due to the political situation in Rome, organized a general revolt. Vercingetorix, a charismatic young chieftain of the Arverni, emerged as the leader. Caesar did return to Gaul and in one season had to conduct three difficult siege operations, one of which turned out badly for the Romans, and fight battles in the field as well. This revolt represented the most serious challenge that Caesar had faced in several years, since so many of the tribes took part—even the Aedui, who were normally faithful allies of Rome, joined the uprising. The Gauls raised a huge army, far outnumbering Caesar's legions, to come to the rescue of Vercingetorix who was beseiged in the fortified town of Alesia. Caesar ultimately prevailed, and this year marked the end of serious Gallic resistance to Roman rule.

A statue of Vercingetorix in the main square of Clermont-Ferrand, France. The modern city of Clermont-Ferrand occupies the site of the capital of the Arverni, of whom Vercingetorix was a chief. The statue was created in 1903 by Frédéric Bartholdi, who also designed the Statue of Liberty.

1 The opening stage

[1] On his arrival in Italy Caesar was told of the assassination of Publius Clodius,[1] and of a senatorial decree ordering all Italians of military age to be sworn in.[2] He proceeded to enrol recruits in all parts of the Cisalpine Province. The news of these events soon reached Gaul; and the Gauls, drawing what they thought was the natural inference, invented a story that Caesar was detained by the disturbances in Rome, where political strife was so acute, they said, that he could not rejoin his army. The prospect of such a chance spurred them into action. They were already smarting under their subjection to Rome, and now began to plan war with greater confidence and boldness. The leading men arranged meetings at secluded spots in the woods, where they spoke bitterly of the execution of Acco[3] and pointed out that the same fate might befall them next. They complained of the miserable condition of the whole country and offered tempting rewards to induce some of their hearers to open hostilities and risk their lives for the liberty of Gaul. The first step, they said, was to contrive means of cutting Caesar off from his army before their plot was divulged. This could easily be done, because the legions would not dare to leave their winter quarters in the absence of their commander-in-chief, and he would not be able to reach them without an escort. In any case it was better to die in battle than to resign themselves to the loss of their ancient military glory and the liberty inherited from their ancestors.

[2] These discussions ended with a declaration by the Carnutes that they were prepared to face any danger for the common cause, and would undertake to strike the first blow. As it was not possible at the moment to give mutual guarantee by exchange of hostages, for fear their design should be betrayed, the Carnutes called upon the others to stack their military standards together—a most solemn rite, according to Gallic custom—and to bind themselves by an oath not to desert them when once hostilities were begun. The Carnutes were warmly congratulated by the assembly; all present took the oath and before separating fixed a date for the rising.

[3] When the appointed day arrived, the Carnutes, led by two desperadoes named Gutuater and Conconnetodumnus, swooped down at a given signal on Cenabum, killed the Romans who had settled there for purposes of commerce—including Gaius Fufius Cita, a Roman knight of high standing, whom Caesar had put in charge of the commissariat—and plundered their property. Tidings of these events sped swiftly to all the tribes of Gaul; for when anything specially important or remarkable occurs, the people shout the news to one another through the countryside and villages, and others in turn take up the cry and pass it on to their neigh-

---

[1] P. Clodius Pulcher was a prominent **populāris**, whose murder in January of 52 BCE increased unrest among the people in Rome, many of whom had supported him politically.

[2] This was similar to registering for the draft. Men between the ages of 18 and 46 had to take the oath, but only a very small number of them ended up actually serving in the army.

[3] See §6.44, page 207.

bours. Thus, on the present occasion, what happened at Cenabum at dawn was known before eight o'clock at night in the country of the Arverni, about a hundred and fifty miles away.

[4] There, the lead given by the Carnutes was followed by Vercingetorix, a very powerful young Arvernian, whose father Celtillus had held suzerainty over all Gaul, and had been put to death by his compatriots for seeking to make himself king. Assembling his retainers, Vercingetorix had no difficulty in exciting their passions, and the news of what was afoot soon brought others out in arms. An effort to restrain him was made by his uncle Gobannitio and other chiefs, who thought the enterprise too risky, and he was expelled from the town of Gergovia. Undeterred, however, he went round the countryside raising a band of vagabonds and beggars. With these at his back he was able to win over all the Arvernians whom he approached. Calling upon them to take up arms for the freedom of Gaul, he assembled a large force and succeeded in expelling the opponents by whom, not long before, he had been driven out himself. He was proclaimed king by his adherents, and sent embassies in every direction adjuring the tribes to keep faith. In a short time he had secured the support of the Senones, Parisii, Cadurci, Turoni, Aulerci, Lemovices, Andes, Pictones, and all the other tribes of the west coast, who unanimously elected him commander-in-chief. Armed with this power, he ordered each tribe to give hostages, to bring a specified quota of troops at once, and to manufacture a specified quantity of arms by a certain date—paying particular attention to the cavalry arm. Himself a man of boundless energy, he terrorized waverers with the rigours of an iron discipline. Serious cases of disaffection were punished by torture and death at the stake, and even for a minor fault he would cut off a man's ears or gouge out one of his eyes and send him home to serve as warning to others of the severe chastisement meted out to offenders.

[5] By this terrorism he quickly raised an army, part of which he sent into the territory of the Ruteni under a Cadurcan of great daring named Lucterius. Vercingetorix himself marched against the Bituriges, who at his approach sent envoys to their overlords the Aedui, asking for help to enable them to offer a more effective resistance. On the advice of the generals whom Caesar had left with the army, the Aedui sent cavalry and infantry to aid the Bituriges. When these reached the Loire, however, the boundary between the Bituriges and the Aedui, they halted and after a few days turned back without venturing to cross it. The explanation they gave to the generals was that they were afraid of treachery on the part of the Bituriges, who, according to information they had received, had concerted a plan with the Arverni to cut them off on both sides if once they crossed the river. Whether they really acted for the reason they alleged, or from motives of treachery, I do not know for certain, and therefore do not feel justified in making a positive statement. On the departure of the Aedui, the Bituriges immediately joined forces with the Arverni.

[6] By the time news of these events reached Caesar in Italy, the situation in Rome had improved, thanks to the resolute action of Pompey; and accordingly he set out for Gaul. On arriving he was faced with a difficult problem: how was he to rejoin his army? If he summoned the legions to the Transalpine Province, they would clearly have to fight a pitched battle on the march without him; and to travel across Gaul without an escort would mean risking his own life, since in the circumstances even the tribes that were apparently quiet could not be relied upon.

[7] In the meantime Lucterius, the Cadurcan who had been sent to the Ruteni, induced them to join the Arverni. Advancing into the territories of the Nitiobroges and Gabali, he took hostages from both, and after assembling a strong force attempted to make a raid into the Province in the direction of Narbonne. Caesar decided that he must let everything else wait. Marching at once to the town, he reassured the frightened inhabitants and posted detachments of the garrison troops in the districts that lay near the point of attack, i.e. the part of the Province inhabited by the Ruteni, Volcae Arecomici, and Tolosates and the neighbourhood of Narbonne itself. He also ordered a part of the Provincial garrison and a fresh draft that he had brought from Italy to concentrate in the territory of the Helvii,[4] which adjoins that of the Arverni.

[8] These measures checked Lucterius and made him keep his distance, because he was afraid to venture into the area encircled by the Roman detachments. Accordingly Caesar joined the forces assembled in the country of the Helvii. The Cevennes mountains, which form a barrier between the Helvii and the Arverni, were at this season—the severest part of the winter—covered with very deep snow, and the passes blocked. But the soldiers cleared stretches of the path by shovelling away drifts up to six feet deep, and by prodigious exertions enabled Caesar to get across into the land of the Arverni. Taking them completely by surprise—for they thought that the Cevennes gave them as secure protection as a solid wall, since the passes had never been considered practicable even for single travellers at that time of year[5]—Caesar ordered his cavalry to scour the widest possible area and frighten the Gauls as much as they could. Rumours and dispatches soon brought the news to Vercingetorix, and in the greatest alarm all his Arvernian supporters came running to him, begging him to save them from ruin and not to let their country be pillaged by the enemy; they had a right to claim protection, they said, since it was obvious that they were now bearing the brunt of the attack. In response to their entreaties he moved his camp from the country of the Bituriges and marched towards that of the Arverni.

---

[4] Not the same tribe as the Helvetii. ✦

[5] Caesar's unexpected march across the Cevennes in midwinter disorganized Vercingetorix's strategical plan, which was to start a widespread revolt in central and western Gaul before Caesar could rejoin his army after his usual winter visit to northern Italy, and at the same time to threaten an invasion of the Province.

[9] But Caesar stayed there only two days, because he had anticipated Vercingetorix's move. Then, on the pretext of collecting reinforcements and cavalry, he went away, leaving the troops under the command of the young Brutus.[6] He instructed him to send out the cavalry as far as possible in every direction, and announced that he would try not to be away from the camp longer than three days. After making these arrangements, to the great surprise of his escort he made his way post-haste to Vienne. There he picked up some fresh cavalry which he had sent on some time before, and without stopping night or day pushed on through the country of the Aedui into that of the Lingones, where two legions were wintering—for he thought it possible that the Aedui might go so far as to make an attempt on his life, and wished to forestall this by making all the speed he could. Directly he arrived at the winter camp, he sent word to the other legions, and had them all concentrated before the news of his coming could reach the Arverni. When he did get to know of it Vercingetorix led his army back into the country of the Bituriges, and from there marched to attack Gorgobina, a stronghold of the Boii, whom Caesar, after defeating them in the battle with the Helvetii, had established there under the suzerainty of the Aedui.

[10] This move greatly embarrassed Caesar. If he kept the legions all together until the end of the winter and allowed a people subject to the Aedui to be overpowered without interference, it was only too likely that the whole of Gaul would desert his cause, since it would be evident that his friends could not look to him for protection. On the other hand, if he withdrew the troops from their quarters so early in the year, he might be hard put to it to supply them with food, owing to the difficulties of transport. He thought it better, however, to face any risk, rather than alienate all his supporters by submitting to such a loss of prestige. Accordingly he asked the Aedui to send up supplies, and sent forward a message to the Boii saying that he was on his way to their relief, and urging them to remain loyal and resist the enemy's attack courageously. Then, leaving two legions at Agedincum with the heavy baggage of the entire army, he set out for the country of the Boii.

[11] The next day he reached Vellaunodunum, a stronghold of the Senones, and in order to facilitate the movement of supplies by ensuring that he left no enemy in his rear, laid siege to it. In two days he had encircled it with entrenchments, and on the third day the garrison sent out envoys to surrender. Caesar ordered them to deposit all their arms in one place, bring out their horses, and give six hundred hostages. As he wanted to complete his journey to Gorgobina as soon as possible, he left Trebonius to see to the execution of these orders and himself set out for Cenabum, in the territory of the Carnutes. The Carnutes, who had only just heard of the siege of Vellaunodunum and expected that it would last some time, were engaged in collecting troops to send to the defence of Cenabum. Caesar reached

---

[6] This refers Decimus Junius Brutus Albinus, who later participated in Caesar's murder along with his cousin, the more famous Marcus Junius Brutus. ❧

this town in two days, but by the time he had encamped in front of it, it was too late to attack that city. He therefore directed the necessary preparations to be made for an assault on the next day, and as there was a bridge over the Loire right under the town walls, and he was afraid that the inhabitants might escape under cover of night, he ordered two legions to remain under arms all night. Shortly before midnight the people of Cenabum moved silently out of the town and began to cross the river. Apprised of this by the patrols, Caesar set the gates on fire and sent inside the legions he had kept ready for action. The town was captured, and all but a very few of the enemy taken prisoner—for the narrow streets and bridge were blocked by the crowd of fugitives. After plundering and burning Cenabum and distributing among his soldiers the booty it contained and the prisoners, Caesar marched across the Loire and made his way into the territory of the Bituriges.

[12] At his approach Vercingetorix raised the siege of Gorgobina and marched to meet him. Caesar had laid siege to a stronghold of the Bituriges called Noviodunum, which lay upon his line of march, when envoys came to him from the garrison, begging him to pardon them and spare their lives. As he wanted to complete the campaign with the same speed that had already brought him so many successes, he granted their petition, ordering them to collect all their arms in one place, bring out their horses, and furnish hostages.

A part of the hostages had already been delivered up, and some centurions had been sent into the town with a small party of soldiers to collect the arms and horses, when the cavalry preceding Vercingetorix's main body was seen in the distance. Directly the besieged townsmen caught sight of it and thought there was a chance of being relieved, they raised a cheer and began to snatch up their arms, shut the gates, and man the wall. The centurions inside the town, realizing from the cheering that some fresh scheme was afoot, seized the gates sword in hand and got their men away without a single casualty.

[13] Caesar ordered his Gallic cavalry out of camp and engaged Vercingetorix's horse; when the cavalry got into difficulties, he reinforced it with four hundred German horsemen whom he had kept with his army from the start of this campaign. Their charge overpowered the enemy, who were put to flight and fell back with heavy loss on their main body. Their defeat made the defenders of Noviodunum change their minds once more. Terror-stricken, they laid hands on those they thought responsible for instigating the people against the Romans, hauled them off to Caesar, and surrendered. Noviodunum being thus disposed of, Caesar advanced on Avaricum, a very large and strongly defended town situated in a particularly fertile part of the Biturigan country, as he felt sure that its capture would secure the submission of the whole tribe.

Questions

1. Why did the Gauls decide to revolt? What was the general outline of their plan?
2. What tribe took the lead in the revolt? What did this tribe do?
3. Who was Vercingetorix and how did he come to be leader of the Arverni?
4. How did Vercingetorix prepare for war after being elected commander-in-chief?
5. How did the Bituriges react when Vercingetorix marched toward their territory? What did they do in the end?
6. Why did Caesar not rejoin his army in Gaul? What did he do instead?
7. Outline the steps by which Caesar was able to return to his legions.
8. In what way did Vercingetorix's attack on the Boii cause problems for Caesar? What did he decide to do, and why?
9. What **oppida** did Caesar capture on his way to Avaricum?
10. How do the events in §§7–13 illustrate Caesar's **celeritās**, his ability to move more quickly and more decisively than most commanders?

2 Siege and capture of Avaricum

[14] After this series of reverses at Vellaunodunum, Cenabum, and Noviodunum, Vercingetorix summoned his followers to a council of war and told them that their plan of campaign must be completely changed.

'We must strive by every means,' he said, 'to prevent the Romans from obtaining forage and supplies. This will be easy, since we are strong in cavalry and the season is in our favour. There is no grass to cut; so the enemy will be forced to send out parties to get hay from the barns, and our cavalry can go out every day and see that not a single one of them returns alive. What is more, when our lives are at stake we must be prepared to sacrifice our private possessions. Along the enemy's line of march we must burn all the villages and farms within the radius that their foragers can cover. We ourselves have plenty of supplies, because we can rely upon the resources of the· people in whose territory the campaign is conducted; but the Romans will either succumb to starvation or have to expose themselves to serious risk by going far from their camp in search of food. We can either kill them or strip them of their baggage—which will be equally effective, since without it they cannot keep the field. We should also burn all the towns except those which are rendered impregnable by natural and artificial defences; otherwise they may serve as refuges for shirkers among our own numbers, and give the enemy the chance of looting the stores of provisions and other property that they contain. You may think these measures harsh and cruel, but you must admit that it would be a still harsher fate to have your wives and children carried off into slavery and be killed yourselves—which is what will inevitably befall you if you are conquered.'

[15] This proposal was unanimously approved and in a single day more than twenty of the Bituriges' towns were fired. The same was done in the territory of the neighbouring tribes, until fires were visible in every direction; and. although this

was a grievous sorrow to all Gauls, they found consolation in the thought that victory was practically assured and that they would soon repair the loss. In a second joint council of war the question was debated whether Avaricum was to be burnt or defended. The Bituriges went down on their knees and implored the representatives of the other tribes not to compel them to set fire with their own hands to a town that was almost the finest in Gaul, the chief defence and pride of their state. It could easily be held, they said, in view of its natural strength; for it was almost completely surrounded by river and marsh, in which there was only one narrow opening. Their petition was granted—Vercingetorix, though he opposed it at first, was at length prevailed upon by their entreaties and by the general sympathy felt for them—and a careful choice was made of officers to defend the town.[7]

[16] Following Caesar's march by easy stages, Vercingetorix selected for his encampment a spot sixteen miles from Avaricum protected by marshes and forests. By an organized liaison service he was informed hourly of events at Avaricum and transmitted his orders accordingly. He was constantly on the watch for parties going out for forage or corn, and by attacking them when they were isolated—for they were obliged to go far afield—he inflicted heavy losses, although they tried everything they could think of to baffle him, setting out at irregular intervals and by different routes.

[17] Caesar encamped on the side of the town where there was a narrow gap in the marshes and watercourses surrounding it, and began to build a siege terrace,[8] form lines of mantlets, and erect two towers upon the terrace; for the lie of the land made it impossible to invest the place. To maintain a supply of corn he kept importuning the Boii and the Aedui; but the Aedui were lukewarm and gave little help, while the Boil, a small and feeble tribe, had only slender resources, which were quicky exhausted. The troops were brought to such straits by the inability of the Boii to relieve them and the indifference of the Aedui, as well as by the burning of the granaries, that for several days they had no grain and saved themselves from starvation only by bringing in cattle from distant villages. Yet not a word were they heard to utter that was unworthy of Roman soldiers with successful campaigns to their credit. Indeed, when Caesar addressed the men of each legion at their work, and told them that if they found their privations unbearable he would abandon the siege, with one voice they begged him not to do so, saying that they had served under him for many years without suffering any humiliation or ever being forced to relinquish a task that they had set their hands to. They would feel it a humiliation to abandon the siege now, and would rather suffer any hardship than fail in avenging

---

[7] Vercingetorix saw now that it was useless either to fight pitched battles or to try holding one fortress after another, and decided on the one strategy that might have been successful—to starve the Roman army by means of a 'scorched earth' policy. But his followers could not see that, to be effective, the work of destruction must be persisted in ruthlessly, and he had no means of compelling them.

[8] A ramp of logs and earth built up to the wall of the beseiged city, through which the attackers could gain access to the walls, either directly or though a siege tower. See the reconstruction on p. 157. ⚘

the Romans who had fallen victims to Gallic treachery at Cenabum. They said the same to their centurions and military tribunes, asking them to pass it on to Caesar.

[18] The siege towers had already been moved close to the wall, when Caesar learnt from prisoners that Vercingetorix, having run out of forage, had moved nearer Avaricum, and had taken command in person of the cavalry and the light-armed infantry who regularly fought among the cavalry, in order to ambush the place where he expected our men would go the next day to forage. Accordingly Caesar set out silently at midnight and reached the enemy's camp in the morning. But they received speedy warning of his approach from their patrols, hid their wagons and baggage in the densest parts of the woods, and drew up all their forces on open rising ground. On hearing of this Caesar at once ordered his men to pile their packs and get their arms ready.

[19] The hill that the enemy occupied had a gentle gradient at the bottom, and was almost surrounded by a marsh which was extremely difficult to negotiate, although only fifty feet wide. The Gauls had broken down the causeways leading over the marsh, and relying on the strength of their position refused to budge from the hill. Formed up in tribal groups, they held all the fords and the thickets that bordered the marsh, determined, if the Romans tried to force a passage, to overpower them by running down to the attack while they were stuck fast in the mud. Awaiting us at such a short distance, they looked as if they were prepared to fight a battle on more or less equal terms; but their position was so much stronger than ours that this show of courage was clearly a mere pretence. The legionaries were indignant at the enemy's daring to face them at such close range, and clamoured for the signal to attack. But Caesar pointed out how costly a victory would be in these conditions, how many brave men's lives must be sacrificed; when they showed such steadfast loyalty and were willing to face any danger for his honour, he would be guilty of the grossest injustice if he did not consider their lives before his own interests. After addressing them in this way to alleviate their disappointment, he led them back to camp the same day and proceeded to complete his preparations for the siege of the town.

[20] On returning to his main body Vercingetorix was accused of treachery for having moved his camp nearer the Romans, for going off with all the cavalry, and for leaving such a large army without anyone in supreme command, with the result that the Romans had taken advantage of his departure to make a swift move against it. All this could not have happened by chance, they said, but must have been deliberately planned; evidently he would rather become king of Gaul by Caesar's favour than by the gift of his fellow countrymen. To these charges Vercingetorix replied that he moved camp because he was short of forage, and they themselves had pressed him to do so; he went nearer the Romans because he had found a very favourable position, so well protected by nature that no defence works were required.

'I knew,' he continued, 'that the cavalry would not be missed on this marshy ground, whereas it was very useful in the place to which I took it. I purposely did not delegate the command to anyone when I went away, for fear the person I chose might be induced by the enthusiasm of the rank and file to give battle; for I could see that that was what they all desired, because they were soft and incapable of prolonged exertion. If the arrival of the Romans during my absence was an accident, it was a stroke of luck for us; if it was the result of information conveyed by a traitor, you ought to be grateful to him for enabling you to see from your commanding position how weak are their forces and how contemptible is their cowardice, since they slunk back ignominiously to their camp without daring to fight. I have no need to obtain from Caesar by treachery the power that I can secure by victory—a victory already in my grasp, and to be shared by the whole Gallic people. You may take back the command you entrusted me with, if you imagine that you are conferring a favour on me when in reality you owe your lives to me. To satisfy yourselves that what I say is true, hear what these Roman soldiers have to say.'

With these words he brought forward some camp servants whom he had captured on a foraging expedition some days previously and had subjected to the tortures of chains and starvation. These he had carefully primed beforehand with the answers they were to make when questioned. They said that they were legionaries, and that the hunger and want they had suffered made them steal out of camp to see if they could find any corn or cattle in the fields. The whole army, they added, was in the same plight; every man was at the end of his strength and unfit for work, and their commander had decided to raise the siege in three days' time unless some progress was made.

'That,' cried Vercingetorix, 'is what you owe to me, whom you charge with treachery. Thanks to me, without shedding a drop of your own blood, you see a great and victorious army almost destroyed by starvation; and when it is routed and retreats in disgrace, I have taken good care that no people shall admit it into their territory.'

[21] The whole concourse cheered and clashed their weapons, as the Gauls are accustomed to do when they approve of what a speaker says. Vercingetorix was a great leader, they declared, his loyalty above suspicion, and no one could conduct the campaign with greater skill. They determined to send into Avaricum ten thousand men picked from all the contingents, not wishing to entrust the national cause to the Bituriges alone, because they realized that if the Bituriges saved the town the victory would be entirely theirs.

[22] To baffle the extraordinary bravery of our troops the Gauls resorted to all kinds of devices; for they are a most ingenious people and very clever at borrowing and applying ideas suggested to them. They pulled aside our wall hooks[9] with lassoes, for example, and when they had made them fast hauled them inside with windlasses. They made our terraces fall in by undermining, at which they were expert because they have extensive iron mines in their country and are thoroughly fa-

---

[9] For wall hooks, cf. 5.42:8, page 153. ✒

miliar with every kind of underground working. They had also equipped the whole circuit of the wall with towers, furnished with platforms and protected by hides. They made frequent sorties by day and night, either to set fire to the terrace or to attack our soldiers at work. As our towers were raised higher by the material added each day to the terrace, they increased the height of theirs correspondingly by inserting floors between the upright posts forming the framework. They countermined the subterranean galleries that we were digging towards the walls, and prevented their continuation by throwing into them stakes sharpened and hardened in a fire, boiling pitch, and very heavy stones.

[23] Gallic walls are always built more or less on the following plan. Balks of timber are laid on the ground at regular intervals of two feet along the whole line on which the wall is to be built, at right angles to it. These are made fast to one another by long beams running across them at their centre points, and are covered with a quantity of rubble; and the two-foot intervals between them are faced with large stones fitted tightly in. When this first course has been placed in position and fastened together, another course is laid on top. The same interval of two feet is kept between the balks of the second course, but they are not in contact with those of the first course, being separated from them by a course of stones two feet high; thus every balk is separated from each of its neighbours by one large stone, and so held firmly in position. By the addition of further courses the fabric is raised to the required height. This style of building presents a diversified appearance that is not unsightly, with its alternation of balks and stones each preserving their own straight lines. It is also very serviceable and well adapted for defending a town: the masonry protects it from fire, the timber from destruction by the battering-ram, which cannot either pierce or knock to pieces a structure braced internally by beams running generally to a length of forty feet in one piece.

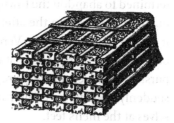

Method of building walls around Gallic towns.

[24] The besiegers were continually hampered, not only by these various devices; but also by incessant rain following a thaw. By unremitting toil, however, they overcame all these hindrances and in twenty-five days raised a terrace three hundred and thirty feet wide and eighty feet high. It was now almost touching the wall; and one night when Caesar was staying up as usual with the working parties, urging them not to lose an instant, smoke was noticed rising from the terrace shortly before midnight. The enemy had dug a tunnel under it and set it on fire. At the same moment the Gauls raised a cheer all along the wall and came pouring out of two gates on either side of our towers. Others flung torches and dry wood on to the terrace from their position on the wall and dropped pitch and other inflammable material, so that it was hard to decide which points to defend or which attack to

counter first. It was Caesar's practice, however, to have two legions on duty all night in front of the camp, while a larger number laboured at the works by shifts. So the defence was quickly organized: some checked the sorties while others pulled back the towers and made a gap in the terrace, and all the rest of the troops ran from the camp to extinguish the flames.

[25] The fight went on everywhere throughout the remainder of the night, and the enemy's hope of victory was continually renewed, especially as they saw that the sheds used to protect the men who moved the towers were burnt and that it was not easy for our soldiers to advance without cover to help their comrades, while in their own ranks fresh men kept relieving those who were worn out. They felt that the fate of Gaul depended entirely on what happened at that moment, and performed before our eyes an exploit so memorable that I felt I must not leave it unrecorded.

There was a Gaul standing before one of the gates and throwing into the flames, opposite one of our towers, lumps of tallow and pitch that were passed along to him. An arrow from a catapult pierced his right side and he fell dead. Another near him stepped over his prostrate body and took over his job. When he likewise was killed by the catapult, a third took his place, and so they went on. The post was not abandoned by the defenders until the fire on the terrace was extinguished, the Gauls repulsed all along the line, and the battle at an end.

[26] The enemy had now tried everything without success, and the next day determined to abandon the town, a course to which Vercingetorix was urgently pressing them. By making the attempt when all was quiet at night they hoped to bring it off without serious loss; Vercingetorix's camp was not far away, and the continuous stretch of marshland that lay between the town and the Romans would hinder pursuit. They were already preparing to execute this plan the following night, when suddenly their wives came running out into the streets and in tears threw themselves at the men's feet.

'Do not abandon us,' they begged, 'and the children who are yours as much as ours, to a cruel enemy. We cannot fly with you because we have not the strength.'

When they saw that their minds were made up—for men who stand in extreme peril are generally too scared to feel pity—they started shrieking and gesticulating to the Romans to warn them of the men's intention. This frightened the Gauls into giving up the idea; for they were afraid that the Roman cavalry would have seized the roads before they could get away.

[27] The next day Caesar completed the siege works which he had under construction and moved forward one of the towers. It began to rain heavily and he thought this a good opportunity to attempt an assault, especially as he saw that the guards on the wall had been carelessly posted. He told the men to go about their work in a half-hearted fashion and explained his plan to them. The legions were got ready for action, as far as possible under cover of mantlets, and Caesar, calling upon them to seize the chance of victory and reap at long last the fruit of all their

toil, promised rewards to those who were first to mount the wall. He then gave the signal for the assault. The soldiers suddenly darted out everywhere and quickly lined the wall.

[28] Taken by surprise and panic-stricken, the enemy were dislodged from the wall and towers, but re-formed in the market place and other open spaces in wedge-shaped masses, determined to fight a pitched battle against attackers from any direction. But when they saw the Romans occupying the entire circuit of the wall around them, and not a man coming down to meet them on level ground, they were afraid of being cut off from all chance of escape, and throwing down their arms ran without stopping to the farthest corners of the town. There, some were cut down by our infantry as they jammed the narrow gateways and others by the cavalry after making their way out. None of our soldiers thought about making money by taking prisoners. They were exasperated by the massacre of Romans at Cenabum and the labour of the siege and spared neither old men nor women nor children. Of the whole population—about forty thousand—a bare eight hundred who rushed out of the town at the first alarm got safely through to Vercingetorix. He took them in silently, late at night. Afraid that if numbers of them entered the camp together the compassion they would arouse among the rank and file of his army might cause a riot, he stationed his trusted friends and the tribal leaders some distance along the road, with orders to sort them out and convey them to the various parts of the camp allotted to each tribe at the start of the campaign.

[29] The next day Vercingetorix called a council of war and encouraged his followers, telling them not to be unduly disheartened or upset by this reverse.

'The Romans have not won by superior courage or in fair fight,' he said, 'but by their expert knowledge of siegecraft, a special technique that we were unacquainted with. It is idle to expect invariable success in war. I personally was never in favour of defending Avaricum, as you yourselves can testify. It was the imprudence of the Bituriges and the too ready acquiescence of the rest that caused this setback. However, the successes that I shall soon gain will more than make up for it. I am working hard to bring over the tribes which are standing aloof from us. The whole of Gaul will then be united, and when we are all of one mind the entire world cannot stand against us. I have already nearly succeeded in this. Meanwhile it is only fair that you should do what I ask for the safety of us all—fortify the camp, so that we can more easily resist any sudden attack.'

[30] This speech was well received by the Gauls, who were especially pleased to find that Vercingetorix had not lost heart after such a serious defeat, and faced them instead of hiding himself. They credited him with extraordinary foresight and prudence because, while there was still time, he had twice given them good advice about Avaricum—in the first place to burn it, later to evacuate it. And so, unlike most commanders, whose position is weakened by failure, Vercingetorix gained reputation with every day that followed the reverse. Their hopes were raised by his

assurances that other tribes could be induced to join them. They even built a fortified camp—an unheard-of thing in Gaul. The shock had been so severe that, unused to hard work though they were, they felt they must submit to anything that was demanded of them.

[31] Vercingetorix kept his promise and used every means he could think of to gain the adherence of the tribes outside the alliance. He tried to entice their chiefs by presents and offers of reward, employing the agents whom he thought best qualified for the purpose; some were personal friends of the chiefs, other were chosen for their powers of subtle speech. The refugees who came in after the fall of Avaricum were provided with arms and clothes, and to bring his army up to its former strength Vercingetorix called for reinforcements from the various tribes, fixing the precise number of each quota and the date by which it was to arrive at the camp. He also ordered all the archers who could be found (there were a very large number of them in Gaul) to be sent to him. By these measures he quickly repaired the losses at Avaricum, and Teutomatus, king of the Nitiobroges (son of Ollovico, who was granted the title of 'Friend' by the Roman Senate), now joined him with a strong force of cavalry from his own tribe and some mercenaries whom he had raised in Aquitania.

Questions

1. What strategy did Vercingetorix persuade the other Gallic leaders to adopt?
2. Why was an exception made for the **oppidum** of Avaricum?
3. Describe Caesar's camp outside Avaricum and the activities his men were performing there.
4. What problem did the Romans have? What was the attitude of the soldiers? How was this same attitude in evidence when the Romans approached Vercingetorix's camp outside Avaricum?
5. How did Vercingetorix respond to the challenge to his leadership and simultaneously improve the morale of the Gauls?
6. What steps did the Gauls in Avaricum take to counter the Roman siege?
7. How large was the siege terrace as it approached completion? What final attempt did the Gauls make to prevent its completion?
8. When this last attempt failed, what did the Gauls decide to do? Why was this plan not carried out?
9. How did Caesar get control of the town? What happened to its people?
10. In what way did Vercingetorix respond to the capture of Avaricum? How did the Gauls make up for the men they lost when the town was captured?

3 Roman reverse at Gergovia

[32] Caesar stayed several days at Avaricum, where he found abundance of grain and other provisions, so that the troops were able to recover from their fatigue and undernourishment. It was now near the end of the winter and the start of the cam-

paigning season; and Caesar had just decided to march against the enemy, in the hope of either manoeuvring them out of the marshes and forests or blockading them where they were, when some of the leading men of the Aedui came to ask for his help in a serious emergency. The situation, they said, was critical. Their old-established practice was to elect a single magistrate to hold sovereign power for a year. Now, however, there were two magistrates in office, each of whom claimed to have been legally appointed. One was Convictolitavis, a young man of wealth and distinction; the other was Cotus, a descendant of a very old house and a man with great personal influence and numerous family connections whose brother Valetiacus had held the same office the year before. The country had become an armed camp; both council and people were divided in their loyalty and each claimant was supported by his retainers. If the quarrel was kept up much longer it would mean civil war. The only way of preventing this was for Caesar to intervene and exert his authority.

[33] It was most unfortunate for Caesar to have to leave the fighting front, but he knew what serious harm such disputes often cause. The Aedui were a powerful tribe, bound by the closest ties to Rome. He himself had done all in his power to strengthen them and had shown them every mark of favour; and now that there was a prospect of their coming to blows with each other, and a risk that the side which felt itself the weaker might call in help from Vercingetorix, he thought it was his first duty to prevent such a catastrophe. As Aeduan law forbade the chief magistrate to leave the country and Caesar wished to avoid the appearance of violating this rule of its constitution, he decided to go there in person, and summoned the whole council and the two disputants to meet him at Decetia. Almost all the councillors assembled there, and informed Caesar that the announcement of Cotus' election had been made by his brother, the magistrate of the previous year, in the presence of a mere handful of people called together in secret, neither in the proper place nor at the proper time. It was further pointed out that Aeduan law forbade the election, not merely to the magistracy but even to a seat on the council, of a near relation of a person previously elected and still living. Caesar therefore made Cotus resign his claims and told Convictolitavis, who had been appointed constitutionally, under the presidency of the priests and at a time when the magistracy was vacant, to continue in office.

[34] After deciding the matter in this way, Caesar advised the Aedui to forget their disputes and quarrels and allow nothing to distract them from the war they had on hand. They might look forward to receiving from him the rewards they deserved when the conquest of Gaul was completed. In the meantime they must send him without delay all their cavalry, and ten thousand infantry to be distributed at various places for the protection of his convoys. He then divided his army into two parts. Four legions and a part of the cavalry were assigned to Labienus to lead against the Senones and Parisii. Caesar himself took the other six legions and the rest of the cavalry, and marched into the country of the Arverni towards Gergovia,

following the course of the Allier. On learning this, Vercingetorix broke down all the bridges over that river and began to march along the opposite bank.

[35] The two armies were within sight of one another and Vercingetorix was generally encamped opposite Caesar, placing patrols to prevent the Romans from making a bridge anywhere and getting across. Thus Caesar found himself in a very difficult position: it looked as if his progress might be barred by the river for most of the summer, since it is not usually fordable until autumn. To get out of this impasse he encamped in a wooded spot opposite one of the bridges destroyed by the enemy and next day stayed there in concealment with two legions, sending on the rest as usual with all the baggage, and breaking up some of the cohorts into companies so as to make it appear that the number of legions was unchanged. He ordered them to march on as far as they could, and when he had allowed enough time for them to reach their next encampment, he began to rebuild the bridge on the original piles, the lower parts of which were still intact. The work was quickly completed and the legions were taken across. Then, choosing a suitable site for a camp, Caesar recalled the other legions. When Vercingetorix heard of it, he was afraid of being compelled to fight a pitched battle, and therefore pushed on ahead by forced marches.

[36] Five days' march brought Caesar to Gergovia, where on the day of his arrival he fought a cavalry skirmish and reconnoitred the position of the town. As it was situated on a high mountain and difficult of access on every side, he decided that it was hopeless to attempt an assault and that it would be better not to start a siege until he had secured his food supply. Vercingetorix, who had encamped near the town, placed the various tribal contingents at short distances round his headquarters; they occupied all the mountain heights within view and presented a terrifying appearance. The chieftains whom he had chosen to form his council of war were summoned every morning at daybreak to exchange intelligence or make arrangements, and almost daily the cavalry were sent into action with archers dispersed among their ranks, to test each man's courage and fighting spirit. Opposite the town, there projected from the foot of the mountain a very steep hill of great natural strength. Once in possession of this, we should clearly be able to deprive the enemy of a considerable part of his water supply and restrict the movements of his foragers; but it was held by a fairly strong garrison. By starting out of camp at dead of night, however, Caesar dislodged the garrison before relief could come from the town, and making himself master of the position installed two legions there in a camp connected with his larger camp by a double trench twelve feet wide,[10] so that men could pass to and fro even singly, without fear of being surprised by the Gauls.

[37] While these events were taking place at Gergovia, Convictolitavis, the Aeduan in whose favour, as told above, Caesar had decided the dispute about the magistracy, was bribed by the Arverni and entered into negotiation with certain young

---

[10] Excavations carried out in 1861–5 on the instructions of the Emperor Napoleon III revealed remains of the two Roman camps and the double trench connecting them.

men of his tribe, chief among whom were Litaviccus and his brothers, members of a very illustrious family. He shared the money with them and bade them remember that they were free men and born to rule. It was the Aedui alone, he said, who hindered the Gallic victory which, but for them, would be certain. Their influence kept the other tribes loyal to Rome; and if they changed sides, the Romans would be unable to maintain their position in Gaul.

'It is true,' he went on, 'that I am under some obligation to Caesar—though the justice of my case was so apparent that he could hardly help deciding in my favour. But the cause of national liberty outweighs any such consideration. Why should we call Caesar in to adjudicate questions involving our rights and the interpretation of our laws? We do not expect him to submit questions of Roman law to our arbitration.'

The young men soon yielded to the combined persuasions of Convictolitavis' eloquence and gold, and professed themselves ready to take the lead in the enterprise; but how to put it into execution required some thought, since they knew that it would be no easy task to induce the Aeduan people to take up arms against Rome. It was decided that Litaviccus should march at the head of the ten thousand men who were to be sent to Caesar as reinforcements, while his brothers hurried on ahead to Caesar; and the remainder of their programme was agreed upon.

[38] On taking command of the army Litaviccus marched to a point within thirty miles of Gergovia, and then suddenly halted and paraded his troops.

'Soldiers,' he said with tears in his eyes, 'where are we going? All our cavalry and all our men of high rank have perished. Two of our leading citizens, Eporedorix and Viridomarus, have been accused of treason and put to death by the Romans without trial. Learn the facts from these men who have escaped from the actual scene of the massacre. I cannot bear to describe what has happened myself; for my brothers and all my other relations have been killed.'

He then produced some men whom he had carefully coached and they repeated to the troops the tale that he had already told. All the Aeduan cavalry, they said, had been butchered because it was alleged that they had entered into negotiation with the Arverni; they themselves had hidden among the crowd of soldiers and escaped while the slaughter was still going on. With shouts of indignation all the Aedui begged Litaviccus to consider what they were to do.

'It needs no consideration,' he replied. 'Obviously we must march straight to Gergovia and join the Arverni. After such a crime, can we doubt that the Romans are even now hastening here to kill us too? So if we have a spark of courage in us, let us avenge this foul murder by wiping out these ruffians.' With these words he indicated some Romans who had been travelling with him in reliance on his protection. The Gauls cruelly tortured and killed them and plundered a large quantity of grain and other supplies that they had with them. Litaviccus then sent messengers into every part of the Aeduan country and inflamed the people by the same propaganda about the massacre of cavalrymen and chiefs, calling on them to avenge their wrongs by doing the same as he had done.

[39] The two Aeduans who were alleged to have been killed were serving in the contingent of Gallic cavalry, having been called up by a special summons from Caesar. Eporedorix was a young man of the noblest birth and very powerful in his own country; Viridomarus, a man of the same age and equally influential, though not of good birth, had been raised by Caesar, on Diviciacus' recommendation, from a humble position to the highest honour. They were rivals for power; and in the recent struggle for the magistracy Eporedorix had been a strong supporter of Convictolitavis, and Viridomarus of Cotus. On hearing of Litaviccus' project, Eporedorix came about midnight to inform Caesar of it, and begged him not to allow the misguided counsels of raw youths to detach the tribe from its friendship with Rome—which must happen if Litaviccus' army joined Vercingetorix, since neither their relations nor the tribal authorities could be indifferent to the safety of so many thousand men.

[40] Caesar was much perturbed by the news that the Aedui were turning disloyal in spite of the special favour that he had always shown them. Without a moment's hesitation he started out with four legions in light marching order and all his cavalry.[11] There was no time to reduce the size of the camp,[12] since in such an emergency everything depended on prompt action, but he left Fabius to guard it with two legions. He ordered Litaviccus' brothers to be arrested, but found that he was just too late; they had already deserted to the enemy. Urged by Caesar to submit without complaint to the laborious march that the crisis necessitated, all ranks followed him with enthusiasm, and an advance of twenty-four miles brought him within sight of the Aeduan army. By sending forward the cavalry he forced them to halt and prevented them from resuming their march. Orders were given that no one was to kill any of them, and Eporedorix and Viridomarus, who were believed by the Aedui to have been put to death, were told to go to and fro among the cavalrymen and speak to their fellow countrymen. As soon as the Aedui recognized them and realized that Litaviccus had imposed upon them, they stretched out their hands in token of surrender and throwing down their arms begged for quarter. Litaviccus escaped to Gergovia, accompanied by his retainers; for Gallic custom regards it as a crime, even in a desperate situation, for retainers to desert their lord.

[41] Caesar sent a message to the Aeduan authorities informing them that by an act of grace he had spared men whom the laws of war entitled him to put to the

[11] Caesar had six legions at Gergovia (7.34). Two of these were placed in the small camp on the hill when it was first occupied (7.36); but the major part of this garrison was evidently withdrawn later, since in the final stage of the siege the small camp had a garrison only some cohorts strong (7.49, 51). So Caesar could take approximately four legions to deal with the Aedui and leave two with Fabius to guard the main camp.

[12] I.e., to make it smaller in size; it would be difficult for two legions, if attacked, to defend a camp designed to house six because the defenders would be stretched so thin. ✢

sword; and after giving his army three hours' rest he started for Gergovia. When he had covered about half the distance he met a party of horse sent by Fabius, who told him that a dangerous situation had arisen. The enemy, they said, had assaulted the camp in full force, and, by continually sending in fresh troops to relieve their tired comrades, had exhausted our men, who on account of the size of the camp had to remain hard at work on the rampart without relief. Showers of arrows and every other kind of missile had wounded many of the defenders, but the artillery was of great use in helping them to hold out. The enemy had at length retired, and Fabius was now blocking up all but two of the camp gates, strengthening the rampart with breastworks, and preparing to meet a similar attack the next day. At this Caesar accelerated his march and the soldiers made such exertions that they reached the camp before sunrise.

[42] In the meantime Litaviccus' first messages reached the country of the Aedui. Without waiting for confirmation they accepted an idle rumour as an established fact, some excited by greed, others carried away by anger and impetuosity— the most striking characteristic of the Gallic race. All the Romans in their power were killed or enslaved and their property was plundered. Convictolitavis added fuel to the fire and goaded the people to frenzy, in the hope that if once they committed a serious crime they would be ashamed to return to reason. Marcus Aristius, a military tribune on his way to rejoin his legion, was ejected from the town of Chalon-sur-Saône with the promise of safe conduct, and the Roman merchants living there were also compelled to leave. Directly they started the Gauls set on them and stripped them of all their baggage. As the Romans resisted, they continued harassing them all that day and the following night, and when many had been killed on both sides, called a larger number of their countrymen to arms.

[43] Meanwhile news arrived that the whole Aeduan army was in Caesar's power. At this the tribal leaders came running to Aristius, saying that the government had no hand in what had occurred. They ordered an inquiry into the robberies, confiscated the property of Litaviccus and his brothers, and sent a deputation to make their excuses to Caesar. The object of these moves was to secure the release of their army. But the number of people involved in the outrages was large. Fascinated by the profits of the plunder, yet at the same time dreading retribution for their crimes, they began to make secret preparation for war and sent envoys to obtain the support of other tribes. Caesar understood this perfectly well, but answered the deputation in the most conciliatory terms: in spite of the ignorance and irresponsibility of the populace, he still felt the same goodwill towards the Aedui and would not judge them too harshly. Anticipating a widespread rising, however, and afraid of being surrounded by rebellious tribes, he began to consider how he could draw off from Gergovia and reunite the whole army without making his departure look like a flight occasioned by the fear of revolt.

[44] He was still occupied with this problem when he thought he saw a chance of striking an effective blow. On going to inspect the defence works at the smaller of his two camps, he noticed that a hill within the enemy's lines was completely deserted, although previously they had been so thick upon it that the ground was scarcely visible. He inquired the reason for this surprising circumstance from the deserters who daily flocked to him. They all confirmed what he had already discovered from his patrols—that the heights adjoining this hill formed a ridge that was almost level, but narrow and wooded where it gave access to the farther side of the town. The Gauls, they said, were very anxious for the safety of this ridge, feeling sure that if they lost a second height in addition to the one already occupied by the Romans, it would be obvious to everyone that they were all but imprisoned and unable to get away or to send out foraging parties; so every man who could be spared had been summoned by Vercingetorix to fortify the ridge.

[45] About midnight, therefore, Caesar sent several squadrons of cavalry in that direction with orders to scour the whole district and make as much disturbance as possible. At daybreak he had a large number of packhorses and mules brought out of camp, unsaddled them, and ordered the drivers to put on helmets and ride round over the high ground masquerading as cavalry. A few cavalrymen who were sent with them were told to range over a wide area with the object of letting themselves be seen. All were to make a long circuit and converge upon the same place. These movements could be seen from the town, which commanded a view of the camp, but at such a distance it was impossible to make out with certainty what was going on. Next, a single legion was sent along the same line of heights by which the horsemen had gone, and after advancing a short way was stationed on lower ground, concealed in a wood. The Gauls now became even more alarmed and the whole of their forces were transferred to the threatened ridge to aid in the work of fortification. When he saw their camps empty, Caesar told his soldiers to cover the crests of their helmets, hide their standards, and move across in small parties—so as not to attract the defenders' attention—from the larger to the smaller camp. He explained his plan to the generals in command of the various legions, warning them above all to keep their men well in hand and not let them be tempted to advance too far by over-eagerness for battle or hope of plunder. He pointed out that their inferior position placed them at a disadvantage which could be remedied only by quick action: it was a case for a surprise attack, not a regular battle. He then gave the signal to advance, at the same time sending the Aedui up the hill by another route on the right.

[46] The distance, as the crow flies, between the town ramparts and the point on the plain from which the ascent began was a little over a mile; but the turns that had to be made in order to ease the ascent increased its length. About half way up the Gauls had built a six-foot wall of large stones, which followed the contour of the mountain and was intended to impede any attack. All the lower part of the slope

was left unoccupied, while the higher part, between this wall and the town ramparts, was covered with their camps, placed close together. Advancing at the signal, the Romans soon reached the wall, climbed over, and captured three of the camps—so quickly that Teutomatus, king of the Nitiobroges, was surprised in his tent, where he was taking his siesta, and only just managed to escape, naked to the waist and riding a wounded horse, from the soldiers who entered in search of plunder.

[47] As his purpose had now been achieved, Caesar ordered the recall to be sounded[13] and the 10th legion, which was with him, immediately halted. The other legions did not hear the trumpet, because a fairly wide hollow intervened; but the military tribunes and the generals did their best, in accordance with Caesar's orders, to hold them back. The soldiers, however, elated by the hope of a quick victory, by the enemy's flight, and by the recollection of their past triumphs, thought that nothing was too hard for their valour to achieve, and continued their pursuit until they got close to the ramparts and gates of the town. Then shouts came from every part of the fortress, and those of the defenders who were farthest away, alarmed by the sudden uproar, thought that the attackers were inside the gates and rushed out. The married women threw clothes and money down from the ramparts and leaning over with bared breasts and outstretched hands besought the Romans to spare them, and not to kill the women and children as they had done at Avaricum. Some were lowered from the rampart by their companions and gave themselves up to the soldiers. Lucius Fabius, a centurion of the 8th legion, who had said that day in the hearing of his men that he meant to win a reward such as Caesar had offered at Avaricum, by mounting the rampart before any other man, got three men of his company to hoist him up, and after clambering to the top himself, pulled up each of the others after him.

[48] Meanwhile the Gauls who had assembled, as related above, on the other side of the town to construct defence works had heard the shouting and were recalled by a succession of messengers telling them that the town was in the Romans' hands. Their cavalry loped up first, with the whole horde of infantrymen racing after them. Every man as he arrived took his stand under the ramparts and swelled the ranks of fighters. When a great crowd of them had gathered, the women who a moment before had been holding out their hands in supplication to the Romans began to appeal to their own folk, leaning over the wall with their hair flung loose in Gallic fashion, and bringing out their children for the men to see. It was an unequal struggle for the Romans, with both position and numbers against them; tired out with hurrying uphill and fighting a long engagement, they found it difficult to hold their own against troops just come fresh into action.

---

[13] It is difficult to believe Caesar's statement that his only objective in this battle was the capture of three half-empty Gallic camps. It seems much more likely that he hoped to take the town by a surprise attack and sounded the recall only when he saw that this could not be done.

[49] Seeing his men harassed on such unfavourable ground by continually increasing numbers, Caesar became anxious for their safety, and sent orders to Titus Sextius, the general left in charge of the small camp, to lead his cohorts out immediately and station them at the foot of the hill, facing the enemy's right flank, where he could cover the legions' retreat, if he saw them driven from their position, by frightening off their pursuers. Caesar also moved his own legion to a slightly more forward position and there awaited the issue of the battle.

[50] Fierce hand-to-hand fighting was in progress, the Gauls relying on their superior numbers and position, while our men trusted in their courage to see them through, when suddenly the Aedui, whom Caesar had sent up by another route on the right to create a diversion, appeared on our right flank. The similarity of their arms to those of the enemy gave our soldiers a bad fright; for although they could see that the newcomers had their right shoulders uncovered—the sign always agreed upon to mark friendly troops—they imagined that this was a ruse employed by the enemy to trick them. At the same moment the centurion Fabius and the others who had climbed with him on to the rampart were surrounded and killed, and their bodies pitched down. Marcus Petronius, another centurion of the same legion, tried to break down the gate, but was overwhelmed by a host of assailants, and realizing that he was a doomed man—he was already covered with wounds—shouted to the men of his company who had followed him: '1 can't save myself and you. It's my fault you're in this tight corner, because I was so keen to distinguish myself. So at least I'll help you to get away with your lives. Now's your chance: look after yourselves.'

With these words he charged into the middle of the enemy, killed two of them and forced the rest a short way back from the gate. The men still tried to rescue him.

'It's no use,' he cried, 'trying to save me. I've lost too much blood and haven't any strength left. So get away while you have the chance and fall back to your legion.' So he went on fighting and a few moments later fell dead. But he had saved his men.

[51] Harassed on every side, our men held their ground till they had lost forty-six centurions. When eventually they were driven back, the Gauls began to pursue relentlessly, but were checked by the 10th legion, which was posted in reserve on fairly level ground; and the 10th in turn supported by the cohorts of the 13th under Sextius, which after leaving the small camp had moved forward to higher ground. As soon as they reached the plain, all the legions halted and re-formed facing the enemy, and Vercingetorix withdrew his men from the foot of the hill and led them within his entrenchments. Our losses that day amounted to nearly seven hundred.

[52] The next day Caesar paraded the troops and reprimanded them for their rashness and impetuosity.[14] They had decided for themselves, he said, to advance

---

[14] This was the only defeat that Caesar himself suffered at the hands of the Gauls. Both he and his troops were to blame—Caesar, for sounding a vital trumpet signal in a place where it was inaudible

farther and attack the town, neither halting when the retreat was sounded nor obeying the military tribunes and generals who tried to restrain them. He stressed the disadvantage of an unfavourable position, explaining the motives which had dictated his action at Avaricum, when, although he had caught the enemy without their general or their cavalry, he preferred to sacrifice a certain victory rather than incur even light casualties by fighting on unfavourable ground.

'Much as I admire the heroism that you showed,' he went on, 'in refusing to be daunted by a fortified camp, a high mountain, and a walled fortress, I cannot too strongly condemn your bad discipline and your presumption in thinking that you know better than your commander-in-chief how to win a victory or to foresee the results of an action. I want obedience and self-restraint from my soldiers, just as much as courage in the face of danger.'

[53] He concluded his speech with words of encouragement, telling the men not to be upset by a reverse which was due to their unfavourable position and not to the enemy's fighting quality.

As he had not changed his mind regarding the advisability of a retirement, Caesar then led the legions out of camp and formed line of battle in a strong position. Vercingetorix, however, still remained within his entrenchments and would not come down into the plain; and after a cavalry skirmish which resulted in favour of the Romans Caesar marched the army back into camp. After offering battle again the next day he decided that he had done enough to humble the conceit of the Gauls and restore the confidence of his own troops, and he therefore set out for the country of the Aedui. Still the enemy did not follow; and on the third day Caesar reached the river Allier, repaired a broken-down bridge, and marched his army across.

Questions

1. What problem was brought to Caesar, and how did he deal with it?
2. How did Caesar use his trip to the Aedui to strengthen his army?
3. Why did Convictolitavis the Aeduan change sides? Whom did he recruit to help him?
4. What steps did Convictolitavis and his supporters take to get the Aedui to join the revolt against Caesar?
5. How did Caesar find out what was happening? What happened when he went to meet the Aeduan army?
6. What happened after Litaviccus' messages reached the Aeduans?
7. How did the leaders of the Aedui react after they learned that Caesar had control of the Aeduan troops? What was Caesar's response to the Aeduan leaders?
8. Why were the Gauls eager to fortify the ridge described by Caesar in §44? How did Caesar fool the enemy into thinking that he was planning to take the

---

to most of those whom it was intended to reach; the soldiers, for disobeying the orders of the generals and military tribunes on the spot.

take the ridge? What did the Gauls do in response?

9. What did Caesar tell his generals before starting the engagement?

10. What did the Romans accomplish initially?

11. Why did only the 10th legion stop its advance when Caesar sounded the recall? What did the other legions do?

12. How did the people in the town react when they thought that the Romans were going to capture Gergovia? How did their response change when they saw the large number of Gauls who came to fight the Romans?

13. What was the final outcome of the battle? How many centurions were killed, and how many Romans in total?

14. What did Caesar say to his troops on the following day?

15. What did Caesar do before heading back to the territory of the Aedui? Why?

4 Vercingetorix's defeat in open warfare

[54] At the Allier the Aeduans Viridomarus and Eporedorix asked for an interview with Caesar and informed him that Litaviccus had gone with all the Gallic cavalry to try to seduce the Aedui from their allegiance; it was essential, they said, for them to get there before him in order to keep the tribe loyal. By this time Caesar had many proofs of the treachery of the Aedui, and felt sure that the result of letting these men go would be to make them revolt all the sooner. However, he thought it unwise to detain them, lest he should be accused of high-handed action or give an impression of being afraid. Before they went he briefly reminded them of his services to the Aedui—in what a feeble state they were when he received them into alliance, cooped up in their strongholds, stripped of their lands, deprived of all their allies, forced to pay tribute and submit to humiliating demands for hostages; and how he had not merely restored them to their previous position, but had raised them to a height of prosperity, prestige, and power that they had never reached before. Bidding them pass on this reminder to their countrymen he let them go.

[55] Situated in a strategic position on the Loire was an Aeduan town called Noviodunum, to which Caesar had sent all his hostages from the various Gallic states, his stores of grain, public funds, a large part of his personal luggage and that of his troops, and numbers of horses that he had bought in Italy and Spain for use in the war. On reaching this town Eporedorix and Viridomarus heard the latest news about the Aedui—that Litaviccus had been received at Bibracte, one of their most important towns, and visited by the chief magistrate Convictolitavis and a large number of councillors; and that an official embassy had been sent to Vercingetorix to conclude a treaty of peace and alliance. This was too good a chance, they thought, to be missed. Accordingly they massacred the garrison of Noviodunum and the merchants who lived there, shared the money and horses, had all the hostages taken to the magistrates at Bibracte, and carried away as much grain as they had time to stow into boats, the rest being thrown into the river or burnt. The town

itself they thought they could not possibly hold, so they burnt it to prevent its being of use to the Romans. Then they set about collecting troops from the neighbourhood, placing detachments and pickets along the Loire, and making demonstrations here and there with their cavalry to intimidate the Romans. In this way they hoped either to starve them out or to force them by stress of famine to retire into the Province. They were greatly encouraged in this hope by the swollen state of the river—the result of melting snow—which made it to all appearance quite unfordable.

[56] Caesar decided that he must act quickly. If he had to build bridges, a battle might be forced upon him; and in that case it would be better to fight before enemy reinforcements arrived. The only alternative was to alter his whole plan of campaign and retire to the Province, a course which some of his frightened officers thought unavoidable. But there were many reasons against it. It was undignified and humiliating; the route was a difficult one leading over the Cevennes; above all he was anxious about the legions under command of Labienus, who was separated from him. Accordingly he made a series of extraordinarily long marches, by day and night, and astonished everyone by appearing on the bank of the Loire. The cavalry found a ford good enough for an emergency—all that was needed for the men to be able to keep their shoulders and arms above water, so as to carry their shields and weapons. Cavalrymen waded in upstream to break the force of the current; and, as the shock of Caesar's appearance unnerved the enemy, the crossing was effected without loss. After provisioning the army with some grain and a quantity of cattle that were found in the neighbouring fields, he marched towards the country of the Senones.

[57] Meanwhile Labienus,[15] leaving the draft recently arrived from Italy at Agedincum to protect the baggage, started with his four legions for Lutetia, a town of the Parisii situated on an island in the Seine. When the Gauls knew of his approach, large forces assembled from the neighbouring tribes and the chief command was given to an Aulercan named Camulogenus, who although enfeebled by age was called out of retirement to this post of honour on account of his unrivalled knowledge of warfare. Camulogenus noticed a long stretch of marsh which drained into the Seine and rendered a wide area almost impassable. Encamping near-by he prepared to prevent the Roman troops from crossing it.

[58] Labienus first tried, under cover of a line of mantlets, to make a causeway across the marsh on a foundation of fascines and other material. Finding this too difficult, he silently quitted his camp some time after midnight and retraced his steps to Metlosedum, a town of the Senones situated like Lutetia on an island in the river. He seized some fifty boats, quickly lashed them together to form a bridge, and sent troops across to the island. Such of the inhabitants as were left in the town—many had been called up to the war—were terrified by this unex-

---

[15] Labienus had been sent with four legions against the Parisii and Senones soon after the fall of Avaricum (7.34).

pected attack and surrendered the place without a fight. After repairing a bridge recently broken down by the enemy, Labienus crossed to the right bank of the river, marched downstream to Lutetia, and encamped near it. The enemy, informed of this by refugees from Metlosedum, sent orders to burn Lutetia and destroy its bridges; they then moved from their position by the marsh and encamped on the left bank opposite Labienus.

[59] By this time people were saying that Caesar had retreated from Gergovia and rumours were circulating about the insurrection of the Aedui and the success of the general Gallic rising. Gauls who got into conversation with Roman soldiers said that Caesar had been prevented from continuing his march across the Loire and compelled by famine to return to the Province. The news of the Aeduan rebellion encouraged the Bellovaci, who had already been meditating revolt, to mobilize and make open preparations for war. Now that the situation was so much changed, Labienus saw that he must completely revise his plans; he no longer had any idea of making conquests or attacking, but was only concerned to get his army safely back to Agedincum. On one side he was threatened by the Bellovaci, reputed the bravest fighters in Gaul; on the other, Camulogenus had a well-equipped army ready for action: and Labienus' own legions were separated from their reserves and their baggage by a great river. Confronted suddenly by such formidable difficulties, he realized that only resolute courage could save him.

[60] Towards evening he assembled his officers. Urging them to execute his orders with energy and care, he placed a Roman knight in charge of each of the boats which he had brought from Metlosedum, and ordered them to move silently four miles downstream in the early part of the night and wait for him there. He detailed to guard the camp the five cohorts which he considered least reliable in action, and told the remaining five of the same legion to start upstream with all the luggage shortly after midnight, making as much commotion as possible. He also requisitioned some smaller boats, which he sent in the same direction at high speed, with loud splashing of the oars, and then himself moved quietly out of camp with the other three legions and marched downstream to the place where he had ordered the main flotilla to put in.

[61] The enemy patrols posted all along the river were taken by surprise, because a sudden heavy storm concealed the approach of the legions, and both infantry and cavalry were quickly ferried across under the superintendence of the knights in charge of the boats. Just before dawn the enemy received several reports almost simultaneously—that there was an unusual commotion in the Roman camp, that a strong force was marching upstream, that the sound of oars was audible from the same direction, and that a little way downstream soldiers were being ferried across. This news made them think that the Romans were crossing at three different places and preparing for a general retreat in alarm at the revolt of the Aedui. They therefore divided their own troops into three sections. One section re-

mained on guard opposite the Roman camp; a small force was dispatched towards Metlosedum with orders to advance upstream as far as the boats had gone; and the remainder were led against Labienus.

[62] By dawn the whole of the three Roman legions had been taken across and were in sight of the enemy. Labienus urged them to remember their long-standing tradition of courage and brilliant successes, and to imagine that Caesar, who had so often led them to victory, was present in person. He then gave the signal to attack. At the first onset the right wing, where the 7th legion was posted, drove back the enemy and put them to flight; on the left, where the 12th legion was, the enemy's front rank were killed or disabled by missiles, but the rest put up a determined resistance, and it was clear that not a single one of them had any thought of flight. Camulogenus was there in person encouraging his men. The issue still hung in the balance, when the 7th legion, whose military tribunes had received a report of what was happening on the left wing, appeared in the enemy's rear and charged. Even then not a single Gaul gave ground; all of them, including Camulogenus, were surrounded and killed. The detachment left on guard opposite Labienus' camp, on hearing that a battle was being fought, went to lend a hand and occupied a hill, but could not withstand the charge of the victorious Romans and joined their fleeing comrades. All who could not escape into woods or hills were killed by the cavalry. On the completion of this action Labienus returned to Agedincum, where he had left all the baggage, and then rejoined Caesar with his entire force.

[63] The defection of the Aedui was the signal for a further extension of the war. They sent embassies into every part of Gaul and used all their influence, prestige, and money to induce other tribes to join them. The possession of the hostages whom Caesar had left in their keeping gave them another means of exerting pressure; by threatening to kill them they could intimidate tribes which hesitated. They asked Vercingetorix to visit them and arrange a plan of campaign, and when he came claimed the chief command for themselves. He refused their demand, and a pan-Gallic council was summoned at Bibracte. There was a full attendance of tribesmen from all parts. The matter was referred to their decision and they unanimously confirmed the appointment of Vercingetorix. The chief absentees were the Remi and Lingones, who stuck to their alliance with Rome, and the Treveri, who remained neutral throughout because they lived at a distance and were harassed by German attacks. It was a bitter disappointment to the Aedui to have their claim to leadership rejected. It was with great reluctance that Eporedorix and Viridomarus—young men who regarded themselves as having a great future—took orders from Vercingetorix.

[64] The various tribes were required to send hostages to Vercingetorix by a certain date, and the whole of the cavalry, numbering fifteen thousand, was ordered to concentrate immediately at Bibracte. He said that he would content himself with the infantry which he had in the previous campaign, and would not tempt fortune

by fighting a pitched battle. With his great cavalry strength it would be quite easy to prevent the Romans from getting corn and forage.

'All you have to do,' he concluded, 'is to destroy your corn crops without hesitation and burn your granaries, knowing that this sacrifice will make you free men for ever and rulers over others.'

He then commanded the Aedui and the Segusiavi—a tribe living on the Provincial frontier—to supply ten thousand infantry, which together with eight hundred cavalry were placed under command of Eporedorix's brother and detailed to attack the Allobroges. At the same time, however, hoping that the memory of their recent defeat by Rome [61 BCE] still rankled in the minds of the Allobroges, Vercingetorix tried to seduce them from their allegiance by sending secret agents and envoys, who offered bribes to their chiefs and promised the tribesmen that they should be made rulers of the whole Province. In another direction, the Gabali and the southernmost clans of the Arverni were sent to attack the Helvii, while the Ruteni and Cadurci were to devastate the country of the Volcae Arecomici.

[65] To meet these various assaults, a force of militiamen amounting to twenty-two cohorts had been raised in the Province itself by the general Lucius Caesar[16] and was posted all along the threatened frontier. The Helvii, who chose to offer battle to the invaders advancing across their borders, were defeated with heavy loss—their chief magistrate Gaius Valerius Domnotaurus, son of Valerius Caburus, being among the casualties—and were compelled to take shelter behind the walls of their strongholds. The Allobroges posted a closely linked chain of pickets along the Rhône and protected their frontier with great vigilance.

Meanwhile Caesar found a way of remedying his inferiority in cavalry. Since all the roads were blocked and no reinforcements could be got from the Province or from Italy, he sent across the Rhine to the German tribes which he had subdued in previous campaigns and obtained some of their cavalry, attended by the light infantrymen who always fought among them. As their horses were unsuitable for the service required of them, he mounted the Germans on horses requisitioned from the military tribunes and other Roman knights serving with him, and from the time-expired volunteers.

[66] During all this time the Gauls were concentrating the troops which had been operating in the country of the Arverni and the cavalry levied from all over Gaul. A large number of cavalry had now been assembled; and while Caesar was marching through the southeastern part of the Lingones' territory into that of the Sequani, so as to be in a better position for reinforcing the Provincial troops, Vercingetorix established himself in three camps about ten miles from the Romans, summoned his cavalry officers to a council, and addressed them.

'The hour of victory,' he said, 'has come. The Romans are fleeing to the Province and abandoning Gaul. But although this will assure our liberty for the moment, for

---

[16] A distant cousin of Julius Caesar. ♟

future peace and security we need more than that; otherwise they will return in increased force and continue the war indefinitely. So let us attack them on the march while they are encumbered with their baggage. If the whole column of infantry halts to come to the rescue, they cannot continue their march; if—which I feel sure is more likely—they abandon the baggage and try to save their own skins, they will be stripped of the supplies without which they cannot live, and disgraced into the bargain. As for their cavalry, not a man of them will dare even to stir outside the column; you ought to know that as well as I do. To encourage your men I will draw up all my troops in front of the camps and overawe the enemy.'

The cavalrymen cried that they should all swear a solemn oath not to allow any man who had not ridden twice through the enemy's column to enter his home again or to see his wife, children or parents.

[67] This proposal was approved and every man was duly sworn. Next day their cavalry was divided into three sections, two of which made a demonstration on either flank of the Roman column while the third barred the way of the vanguard. Caesar also divided his cavalry into three sections and ordered them to advance against the enemy. Simultaneous engagements took place all along the column, which halted and formed a hollow square with the baggage inside. If Caesar saw the cavalry in difficulties anywhere or especially hard pressed, he moved up some of the infantry and formed line of battle, which hindered the enemy's pursuit and encouraged the cavalry by the assurance of support. At length the German horse gained the top of some rising ground on the right, dislodged some of the enemy, and chased them with heavy loss to a river where Vercingetorix's infantry was posted. At this the rest of his cavalry fled, afraid of being surrounded, and were cut down in numbers all over the field. Three Aeduans of the highest rank were brought to Caesar as prisoners: the cavalry commander Cotus, who had been Convictolitavis' rival at the recent election; Cavarillus, who after Litaviccus deserted the Roman cause had been placed in command of the Aeduan infantry; and Eporedorix,[17] leader of the Aedui in their war with the Sequani before Caesar's arrival in Gaul [70–65 BCE].

Questions

1. What happened at Noviodunum, and why? What did the Gauls hope to achieve?
2. Why was Caesar unwilling to retreat to the Province? How did he manage to cross to the north bank of the Loire?
3. Labienus had marched on Lutetia and had gone to great lengths to cross the River Seine. Why did this end up putting his troops in danger?
4. How did Labienus manage to get his army back across the Seine? What was the outcome of the battle between the Romans and the Gauls?

---

[17] The Eporedorix who had led the Aedui against the Sequani was evidently a different person from the Aeduan of that name mentioned several times earlier in this chapter.

5. What general strategy did Vecingetorix adopt (§64)?
6. How did the Gauls try to take the battle into the Province? What was the result?
7. How did Caesar obtain additional cavalry?
8. What plan of battle did Vercingetorix adopt? What was the outcome?

5 Siege and capture of Alesia

[68] After the rout of his cavalry Vercingetorix withdrew his troops from their position in front of the camps and marched straight for Alesia, a stronghold of the Mandubii, leaving orders for the heavy baggage to be packed up immediately and brought after him. Caesar, after removing the army's baggage with a guard of two legions to the nearest hill, followed the enemy as long as daylight lasted and killed some three thousand of their rearguard. The next day he encamped near Alesia. The Gauls were terrified by the defeat of their cavalry, the arm on which they placed the greatest reliance. Accordingly, after reconnoitring the position of the town, Caesar called on the soldiers to undertake the heavy task of investing it with siege works.

[69] It was clearly impregnable except by blockade; for it stood at a high altitude on top of a hill washed by streams on the north and south, and closely surrounded by other hills as high as itself on every side except the west, where a plain extended for some three miles. The whole of the slope below the town ramparts on the east was occupied by a camp crowded with Gallic troops, who had fortified it with a trench and a six-foot wall. The siege works that the Romans were starting to make had a circumference of ten miles. Eight camps were placed in strategic positions, linked together by fortifications along which twenty-three redoubts were built.[18] The redoubts were occupied in the daytime by pickets, to prevent a surprise attack at any point; at night strong garrisons bivouacked in them with sentries on duty.

[70] During the construction of these works a hard fought cavalry battle took place in the three-mile stretch of plain between the hills. Seeing his men in difficulties, Caesar reinforced them with the German cavalry and drew up the legions in front of their camps. Encouraged by their support the cavalry routed the enemy, whose flight was impeded by their own numbers. Hotly pursued by the Germans right up to the fortifications of Vercingetorix's camp, they got jammed in the narrow entrances and suffered heavy losses. Some let their horses go and tried to scramble over the trench and climb the wall. Caesar then ordered the legions posted in front of their camp ramparts to be moved forward a little, whereupon the Gauls inside the camp became as frightened as their fleeing cavalry and expecting an immediate attack shouted a call to arms. Some in their terror rushed right into the town, and Vercingetorix had the town gates shut for fear the camp should be left unguarded. Before retiring the Germans killed many of the fugitives and captured a number of horses.

---

[18] The sites of the eight Roman camps and five of the twenty-three redoubts were discovered by Napoleon III's excavations.

[71] Vercingetorix now decided to send out all his cavalry in the night, before the Roman entrenchments were completed. He bade them go every man to his own country and impress for service all the men of military age. He pointed out how much they owed him and urged them to consider his safety; after all he had done for the cause of national liberty they ought not to abandon him to the cruel vengeance of the enemy. Moreover, if they were slack in doing their duly, they would condemn eighty thousand picked men to perish with him. He had taken stock of the corn, he said, and by strict rationing would have enough for a month—even a little longer, if the ration were reduced. With these instructions the cavalry was sent out in silence through a gap in the entrenchments shortly before midnight. Vercingetorix now ordered all the garrison, on pain of death, to surrender to him all the corn they had, and proceeded to dole it out a little at a time; the large quantity of livestock which had been brought in by the Mandubii was shared out individually at once. All the troops posted outside the town were taken inside. In this way Vercingetorix prepared to continue the struggle until the arrival of reinforcements.

[72] On being informed of this by deserters and prisoners, Caesar started to construct more elaborate siege works. He dug a trench twenty feet wide, which, having perpendicular sides, was as broad at the bottom as at the top. The other works were kept some six hundred and fifty yards behind this trench, to protect them against surprise attacks; for as such a vast extent of ground had to be enclosed, and it was difficult to man the whole circuit, there would be a danger of the enemy's swooping down in force on the lines at night, or hurling javelins in the daytime when the men were tied down to their work. At this distance, therefore, Caesar dug two trenches of equal depth, each fifteen feet wide, and filled the inner one, where it crossed the low ground of the plain, with water diverted from the streams. Behind the trenches a palisaded rampart twelve feet high was erected, strengthened by a battlemented breastwork, with large forked branches projecting where it joined the rampart to hinder the enemy if they tried to climb over. Towers were placed at intervals of a hundred and thirty yards along the entire circuit of fortifications.

[73] Parties had to be sent out constantly in search of timber and corn; and as this duty took them far afield, it seriously reduced the number of men available for the construction of the huge fortifications. Moreover, the Gauls tried many times to attack the works, making furious sorties from several of the town gates at once. Caesar decided, therefore, that he must strengthen them still further, to render them defensible by a smaller force. Accordingly tree trunks or very stout boughs were cut and their tops stripped of bark and sharpened; they were then fixed in long trenches dug five feet deep, with their lower ends made fast to one another to prevent their being pulled up and the branches projecting. There were five rows in each trench, touching one another and interlaced, and anyone who went among them was likely to impale himself on the sharp points. The soldiers called them bound-

ary posts. In front of them, arranged in diagonal rows forming quincunxes,[19] were pits three feet deep, tapering gradually towards the bottom, in which were embedded smooth logs as thick as a man's thigh, with the ends sharpened and charred, and projecting only three inches above ground. To keep the logs firmly in position, earth was thrown into the pits and trodden down to a depth of one foot, the rest of the cavity being filled with twigs and brushwood to hide the trap. These were planted in groups, each containing eight rows three feet apart, and they were nicknamed lilies from their resemblance to that flower. In front of these again were blocks of wood a foot long with iron hooks fixed in them, called goads by the soldiers. These were sunk right into the ground and strewn thickly everywhere.

[74] When these defences were completed, Caesar constructed a similar line of fortifications facing outwards instead of inwards. This line described a circuit of fourteen miles, running along the flattest ground that could be found, and its purpose was to hold off attacks from outside, so that, even if Vercingetorix's cavalry assembled a very large force, the troops defending the siege works could not be surrounded. To avoid the danger of having to send out foraging parties when the relieving force was near, every man was ordered to provide himself with a month's supply of corn and fodder.

---

[19] An arrangement of five objects in a square or rectangle, one at each corner and one in the center. ⚜

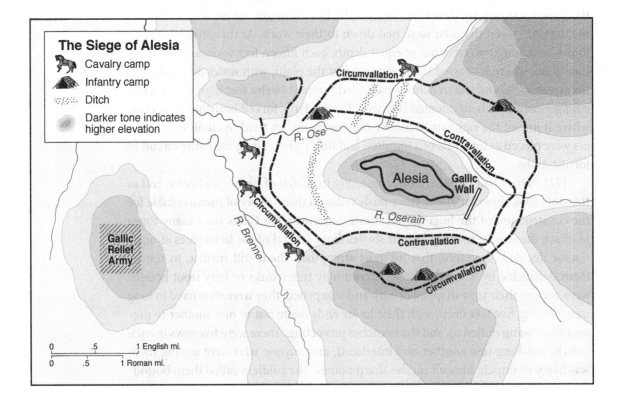

240

[75] Meanwhile the Gallic tribes convened a council of their leaders, who decided not to adopt Vercingetorix's plan of calling up everyone able to bear arms, as they were afraid that in such a vast mixed host they would be unable to control their contingents or keep them separate, or to organize an adequate supply of corn. They therefore demanded a specified number of men from each tribe as follows: Aedui (with their dependent tribes the Segusiavi, Ambivareti, Aulerci Brannovices, and Blannovii)—35,000; Arverni (with their dependent tribes the Eleuteti, Cadurci, Gabali, and Vellavii)—35,000; Sequani, Senones, Bituriges, Santoni, Ruteni, Carnutes—12,000 each; Bellovaci, Lemovices—10,000 each; Pictones, Turoni, Parisii, Helvetii—8,000 each; Suessiones, Ambiani, Mediomatrici, Petrocorii, Nervii, Morini, Nitiobroges, Aulerci Cenomani—5,000 each; Atrebates—4,000; Veliocasses, Aulerci Eburovices—3,000 each; Rauraci, Boii—1,000 each; Aremorican tribes (i.e., all the maritime tribes—Coriosolites, Redones, Ambibarii, Caleti, Osismi, Vendi, Lexovii, Venelli)—20,000.

The Bellovaci did not send their full contingent, because they said they intended to fight the Romans on their own account and in their own way, and would not take orders from anyone. At the request of Commius, however, and in consideration of their friendship with him, they sent 2,000 men along with the other contingents.

[76] In former years Commius had rendered Caesar loyal and useful service in Britain, as described above, and in return Caesar had ordered that his tribe should be immune from taxation and have its independence restored and had made Commius suzerain over the Morini. But the whole Gallic people were so united in their determination to liberate themselves and recover their former prestige that they allowed no favours or recollection of friendship to influence them, and all devoted their energies and resources to the prosecution of the war.

When eight thousand horse and about two hundred and fifty thousand infantry had been assembled in the country of the Aedui, a start was made to the task of reviewing and counting them and choosing officers. The chief command of this relieving army was entrusted to Commius the Atrebatian, the Aeduans Viridomarus and Eporedorix, and the Arvernian Vercassivellaunus, a cousin of Vercingetorix. With them were associated representatives of the various tribes, to act as an advisory committee for the conduct of the campaign. They all started for Alesia full of enthusiasm and confidence. Every single man believed that the mere sight of such an enormous host of infantry and cavalry would be enough to make the enemy turn tail, especially as he would be attacked on two fronts—for the besieged would sally out from the town at the same time as the relieving force came into view.

[77] In Alesia, however, they knew nothing of these preparations; the time by which they had expected relief was past and their corn was exhausted. So they summoned an assembly and considered what their fate was to be. Among the various speeches that were made—some advising capitulation, others recommending a sortie while they still had the strength—the speech of Critognatus, a noble Arver-

nian whose opinion commanded great respect, deserves to be recorded for its unparalleled cruelty and wickedness.

'I do not intend,' he said, 'to make any comment on the views of those who advise "capitulation"—the name they give to the most shameful submission to enslavement; in my opinion they ought not to be regarded as citizens or allowed in the assembly. I will concern myself only with those who advocate a sortie. You all approve their suggestion, as showing that we have not forgotten our traditional courage. But it is not courage, it is weakness, to be unable to endure a short period of privation. It is easier to find men who will voluntarily risk death than men who will bear suffering patiently. Even so, I would support their proposal—so much do I respect their authority—if it involved no loss beyond that of our own lives. But in making our decision we must consider all our fellow countrymen, whom we have called to our aid. If eighty thousand of us are killed in one battle, what heart do you suppose our relatives and kinsmen will have when they are compelled to fight almost over our corpses? Do not leave them to continue the struggle alone when for your sakes they have counted their own danger as nothing, and do not by folly and rashness, or by lack of resolution, ruin all Gaul and subject it to perpetual servitude. Because they have not come on the appointed day, do you doubt their loyalty

Napoleon III of France was very interested in Julius Caesar and his battles in Gaul. He ordered excavations at the site of Alesia, and archaeology has confirmed much of Caesar's account of the battle. The site is now occupied by an archaeological park, including reconstructions of the circumvallation works, shown here. In the background are the towers and the parapet with the merlons projecting upwards from it. In the foreground are the various traps that Caesar describes to slow down attackers; the two ditches are between the wall and the traps but are not visible in this photograph.

or constancy to our cause? What? Do you suppose the Romans are working day after day on those outer fortifications to amuse themselves? Since our countrymen cannot get messengers through the cordon that is drawn round us, to assure you that they are coming soon, believe what the enemy are telling you by their actions: for. it is the fear of their coming that keeps the Romans hard at work night and day.

'What counsel, then, have I to offer? I think we should do what our ancestors did in a war that was much less serious than this one [109–102 BCE]. When they were forced into their strongholds by the Cimbri and Teutoni, and overcome like us by famine, instead of surrendering they kept themselves alive by eating the flesh of those who were too old or too young to fight. Even if we had no precedent for such an action, I think that when our liberty is at stake it would be a noble example to set to our descendants. For this is a life and death struggle, quite unlike the war with the Cimbri, who, though they devastated Gaul and grievously afflicted her, did eventually evacuate our country and migrate elsewhere, and left us free men, to live on our own land under our own laws and in possession of our rights. The Romans, we know, have a very different purpose. Envy is the motive that inspires them. They know that we have won renown by our military strength, and so they mean to install themselves in our lands and towns and fasten the yoke of slavery on us for ever. That is how they have always treated conquered enemies. You do not know much, perhaps, of the condition of distant peoples; but you need only look at the part of Gaul on your own borders that has been made into a Roman province, with new laws and institutions imposed upon it, ground beneath the conqueror's iron heel in perpetual servitude.'

[78] At the conclusion of the debate it was decided to send out of the town those whom age or infirmity incapacitated for fighting. Critognatus' proposal was to be adopted only as a last resort—if the reinforcements still failed to arrive and things got so bad that it was a choice between that and surrendering, or accepting dictated peace terms. So the Mandubian population, who had received the other Gauls into their town, were compelled to leave it with their wives and children. They came up to the Roman fortifications and with tears besought the soldiers to take them as slaves and relieve their hunger; but Caesar posted guards on the ramparts with orders to refuse them admission.[20]

[79] Meanwhile Commius and the other commanders arrived before Alesia with the whole of their relief force and encamped on a hill outside the Roman lines, not more than a mile away. Next day they brought out their cavalry and occupied all the plain—three miles long, it will be remembered. Their infantry was moved away a short distance and posted on the slopes of the hill. As the town command-

---

[20] The story of the starving Mandubii is made terribly dramatic by what it does not say. Of course Caesar had not enough food to relieve them without the risk of running short himself. According to a later historian, he hoped that they would be re-admitted to the town and so hasten the time when it must surrender; but they were left outside to die of starvation.

ed a view over the plain, the besieged saw the troops who had come to their relief, and all crowding together in excitement rejoiced and congratulated one another on their deliverance. Then they brought out their forces, posted them in front of the town, and filled the nearest trench wIth fascines and earth, ready for a sortie and all the perils it would entail.

[80] Caesar placed the whole of his infantry along the two lines of entrenchments, so that in case of need every man could know his post and hold it. He then ordered out the cavalry to battle. The plain was visible from all the camps on the surrounding hilltops and the whole army was intently watching to see the result of the engagement. The Gauls had placed archers and light-armed infantrymen here and there among their cavalry, to support them if they had to give ground and to help them meet our cavalry charges; These took a number of our men by surprise and forced them to retire wounded from the battle. Feeling confident that their cavalry was winning, since it was obvious that our force was heavily outnumbered, the Gauls on every side—both the besieged and the relieving force—encouraged them with shouts and yells. As the action was taking place in full view of everyone, so that no gallant exploit and no act of cowardice could pass unnoticed, the thirst for glory and the fear of disgrace was an incentive to both sides. They had fought from midday till near sunset and the issue was still in doubt, when the German horse massed all their squadrons at one point, charged the Gauls, and hurled them back. When the cavalry broke and fled, the archers were surrounded and killed. The rest of our horsemen advanced from other points, pursued the fugitives right up to their camp, and gave them no chance of rallying. At this the Gauls who had come out of the town went back in, bitterly disappointed and now almost despairing of success.

[81] After an interval of only one day, however, during which they prepared a great quantity of fascines, ladders, and grappling-hooks, the relieving army moved silently out of camp at midnight and advanced towards the entrenchments in the plain. Suddenly raising a shout to inform the besieged of their approach, they began to throw fascines into the trenches, drove the Romans from the rampart with arrows and stones discharged from slings or by hand, and employed every other method of assault.

Meanwhile, hearing the distant shouting, Vercingetorix sounded the trumpet and led his men out of the town. The Roman troops moved up to the posts previously allotted to them at the entrenchments and kept the Gauls at a distance with slingstones, bullets, large stones, and stakes which were placed ready at intervals along the rampart, while the artillery pelted them with missiles. It was too dark to see, and casualties were heavy on both sides. The generals Mark Antony and Gaius Trebonius, who had been detailed for the defence of this particular sector, reinforced the points where they knew the troops were hard pressed with men brought up from redoubts well behind the fighting line.

[82] As long as the Gauls were at a distance from the entrenchments, the rain of javelins which they discharged gained them some advantage. But when they came nearer they suddenly found themselves pierced by the goads or tumbled into the pits and impaled themselves, while others were killed by heavy siege spears discharged from the rampart and towers. Their losses were everywhere heavy and when dawn came they had failed to penetrate the defences at any point. Afraid, therefore, of having their right flank turned by an attack from the camps on higher ground, they fell back upon their remaining troops. The besieged lost much time in bringing out the implements that Vercingetorix had prepared for the sortie and in filling up the first stretches of trench, and before they reached the main fortifications heard of the retreat of the relief force, so they returned into the town without effecting anything.

[83] After this second costly repulse the Gauls held a council of war. By calling in men familiar with the ground they ascertained the positions of the higher camps and the nature of their defences. There was a hill on the north which had such a wide sweep that the Romans were unable to include it within the circuit of the siege works and were compelled to place the camp there on a slight slope, in what would ordinarily be considered a bad position. It was garrisoned by two legions under the generals Gaius Antistius Reginus and Gaius Caninius Rebilus. After sending out scouts to reconnoitre the ground, the enemy commanders selected from their whole force sixty thousand men belonging to the tribes with the highest reputation for courage, secretly decided on their objective and plan of action, and ordered them to begin an attack at noon under Vercassivellaunus the Arvernian, one of their four generals and a relative of Vercingetorix. Leaving camp in the early evening, he almost completed his march before daybreak, and ordered his troops to rest under cover of the hill after their hard night's work. When he saw that it was getting on for midday, he marched towards the Roman camp referred to above, while at the same time the Gallic cavalry moved up to the fortifications in the plain and the rest of the army made a demonstration in front of their own camp.

[84] On seeing these troop movements from the citadel of Alesia, Vercingetorix sallied out with the fascines, poles, sappers' huts, grappling-hooks, and other implements which he had prepared for the purpose. There was fighting simultaneously all over the field and the Gauls tried every expedient, concentrating on the weakest point of the defences. Distributed as they were along lines of such length, the Romans found it difficult to meet simultaneous attacks in many different places. They were unnerved, too, by the shouts they could hear behind them as they fought, which indicated that their lives were not in their own hands but depended on the bravery of others. It is nearly always invisible dangers that are most terrifying.

[85] Caesar found a good observation point, from which he could follow the actions in every part of the field, and sent help where it was needed. Both sides realized that this was the time, above all others, for a supreme effort. The Gauls knew

that unless they broke through the lines they were lost; the Romans, if they could hold their ground, looked forward to the end of all their hardships. The danger was greatest at the fortifications on the hill where, as said above, Vercassivellaunus had been sent. The unfavourable downward slope of the ground told heavily against the Romans. Some of the Gauls flung javelins, while others advanced to the attack with shields locked together above their heads, fresh troops continually relieving them when they were tired. All of them threw earth on to the fortifications, which enabled them to climb the rampart and covered the obstacles hidden in the ground.

[86] At length, when Caesar saw that his men were weakening and running short of weapons, he sent Labienus to their relief with six cohorts, telling him to remain on the defensive if possible; but if he could not hold the camp by any other means, he must withdraw some cohorts from their positions and counter-attack. Caesar himself visited other parts of the lines, urging the men to hold out: on that day, he said, on that very hour, depended the fruits of all their previous battles.

The besieged Gauls despaired at last of penetrating the huge fortifications in the plain and attempted to storm one of the steep ascents. Carrying there all the implements they had provided themselves with, they dislodged the defenders of the towers with a hail of missiles, filled the trenches with earth and fascines, and tore down the palisade and breastwork with their hooks.

[87] Caesar first sent some cohorts to the rescue under young Brutus, then others under the general Gaius Fabius; finally, as the struggle grew fiercer, he led up a fresh detachment in person. These troops renewed the fight and succeeded in repulsing the attack.

Caesar now started for the sector to which he had sent Labienus, taking four cohorts from the nearest redoubt, and ordering a part of the cavalry to follow him; another detachment was to ride round the outer lines and attack the enemy in the rear. Labienus, when he found that neither ramparts nor trenches could check the Gauls' furious onslaught, had fortunately been able to collect eleven cohorts from the nearest posts, and at this moment sent to tell Caesar that he considered the time for decisive action was at hand. Caesar put on speed to get there in time for the fight.

[88] The enemy knew that he was coming by the scarlet cloak which he always wore in action to mark his identity; and when they saw the cavalry squadrons and cohorts following him down the slopes, which were plainly visible from the heights on which they stood, they joined battle. Both sides raised a cheer, which was answered by the men on the rampart and all along the entrenchments. The Romans dropped their spears and fought with their swords. Suddenly the Gauls saw the cavalry in their rear and fresh cohorts coming up in front. They broke and fled, but found their retreat cut off by the cavalry and were mown down. Sedullus, chieftain and commander of the Lemovices, was killed, Vercassivellaunus was taken prisoner in the rout, seventy-four standards were brought in to Caesar, and only a few men of all the large army got back unhurt to their camp. When the Gauls in the town

saw their countrymen being slaughtered in flight, they gave up hope and recalled their troops from the entrenchments. The relieving forces immediately fled from their camps; and if the Romans had not been tired out after a long day's work, during which they had been repeatedly summoned to the relief of hard-pressed comades, the enemy's army might have been annihilated. As it was, a large number were taken or killed by the cavalry, which was sent in pursuit and came up with their rear soon after midnight. The survivors dispersed to their homes.

[89] The next day Vercingetorix addressed an assembly. 'I did not undertake the war,' he said, 'for private ends, but in the cause of national liberty. And since I must now accept my fate, I place myself at your disposal. Make amends to the Romans by killing me or surrender me alive as you think best.' A deputation was sent to refer the matter to Caesar, who ordered the arms to be handed over and the tribal chiefs brought out to him. He seated himself at the fortification in front of his camp, and there the chiefs were brought; Vercingetorix was delivered up,[21] and the arms laid down. Caesar set apart the Aeduan and Arvernian prisoners, in the hope that he could use them to regain the allegiance of their tribes; the rest he distributed as booty to the entire army, allotting one to every man.[22]

[90] He then went to the country of the Aedui and received their submission. Envoys from the Arverni waited upon him there, undertaking to obey any orders he gave, and were commanded to supply a large number of hostages. Some twenty thousand prisoners were restored to the Aedui and Arverni. Finally, the legions were distributed in winter quarters. Two legions and some cavalry were sent to the Sequani under the charge of Labienus, with Marcus Sempronius Rutilus under him; two were placed under Fabius and Basilus among the Remi, to protect them from injury at the hands of their neighbours the Bellovaci; Reginus was sent to the Ambivareti, Titus Sextius to the Bituriges, and Caninius to the Ruteni, each with one legion; and Cicero and Sulpicius Rufus were quartered in Aeduan territory at Chalon-sur-Saône and Mâcon, to collect grain. Caesar himself decided to winter at Bibracte. When the results of this year's campaign were reported in his dispatches, a thanksgiving of twenty days was celebrated in Rome.

---

[21] So ended the brief but brilliant career of a great patriot. Caesar pays a fine tribute to the qualities of leadership which enabled Vercingetorix to strengthen his hold upon his followers and re-animate them in the hour of defeat (7.29–30), but either could not or would not protect him from the fate which Roman custom demanded for a vanquished barbarian. Six years after his capture Vercingetorix was exhibited at Rome in Caesar's triumph and then executed.

[22] Most of the soldiers probably sold their captives to the slave dealers who accompanied the army. ✿

Questions

1. Describe the siege works that Caesar began to build at Alesia.
2. Why did Vercingetorix send his cavalry out of Alesia? What instructions did he give them?
3. How did Vercingetorix prepare to hold out as long as possible in the town?
4. Why did Caesar decide to construct more elaborate fortifications around Alesia? Describe these additional works.
5. What was the final step in the construction of the siege works (§74)? Why did Caesar build these?
6. How large was the relief army that the Gauls assembled? Who were their leaders? Why were they confident of success?
7. What problem did Vercingetorix and those in Alesia face?
8. What solution to the problem did Critognatus suggest? What did the Gauls decide to do?
9. Describe the cavalry battle (§80).
10. What happened one day later? Why were the Gauls not able to accomplish much against the Romans?
11. During the final assault by the Gauls (§§84–85), why did the Romans find it difficult to withstand the attack? Why did both sides regard this as a crucial time?
12. What actions of Caesar show that the Gallic attack on one of the hill camps was almost successful (§87)?
13. How did the Romans finally win a decisive victory?
14. What happened to Vercingetorix? To most of the Gauls taken prisoner? Why did Caesar spare the Aeduan and Arvernian captives?

Outline of De bello Gallico

Portions contained in this book, whether in Latin or in English, are indicated by a double asterisk (**).

Book I: 52 BCE **
  Helvetii driven back to Switzerland
  Ariovistus forced out of Gaul

Book II: 57 BCE
  Belgae attempt unsuccessfully to unite
  Belgae are defeated separately

Book III: 56 BCE
  Veneti defeated and destroyed in a naval campaign
  Caesar defeats the Aquitani
  Caesar fights the Morini and the Menapii

Book IV: 55 BCE
  Usipetes and Tencteri suffer severe defeat
  Caesar crosses the Rhine into Germany
  Caesar makes a brief expedition to Britain **

Book V: 54 BCE
  Caesar invades Britain for the second time
  Eburones destroy Sabinus' army **
  Nervii attack the winter quarters of Quintus Cicero **
  Treveri attack Labienus' camp but are defeated

Book VI: 53 BCE **
  Treveri suffer a severe defeat
  Caesar crosses the Rhine again
  Caesar describes the society and customs of the Gauls
  Caesar describes the society and customs of the Germans
  Eburones punished for attack on Sabinus' army, but Ambiorix escapes

Book VII: 52 BCE **
  Vercingetorix becomes leader of a widespread revolt
  Caesar besieges and captures Avaricum
  Romans defeated at Gergovia
  Vercingetorix suffers a defeat and Gallic army moves to Alesia
  Vercingetorix besieged at Alesia and forced to surrender

Book VIII: 51–50 BCE
  Aulus Hirtius introduces his continuation of Caesar's work
  Bituriges, Carnutes, and Bellovaci rise against Roman rule
  Romans capture Uxellodunum
  Caesar's opponents work to weaken his position; Caesar returns to Italy

Summary of Forms

I. Nouns

Number Case	1st Declension Fem.	2nd Declension Masc.	Masc.	Masc.	Neut.
Singular					
Nominative	puell*a*	servus	puer	ager	bacul*um*
Genitive	puell*ae*	serv*ī*	puer*ī*	agr*ī*	bacul*ī*
Dative	puell*ae*	serv*ō*	puer*ō*	agr*ō*	bacul*ō*
Accusative	puell*am*	serv*um*	puer*um*	agr*um*	bacul*um*
Ablative	puell*ā*	serv*ō*	puer*ō*	agr*ō*	bacul*ō*
Vocative	puell*a*	serv*e*	puer	ager	bacul*um*
Plural					
Nominative	puell*ae*	serv*ī*	puer*ī*	agr*ī*	bacul*a*
Genitive	puell*ārum*	serv*ōrum*	puer*ōrum*	agr*ōrum*	bacul*ōrum*
Dative	puell*īs*	serv*īs*	puer*īs*	agr*īs*	bacul*īs*
Accusative	puell*ās*	serv*ōs*	puer*ōs*	agr*ōs*	bacul*a*
Ablative	puell*īs*	serv*īs*	puer*īs*	agr*īs*	bacul*īs*
Vocative	puell*ae*	serv*ī*	puer*ī*	agr*ī*	bacul*a*

N.B.: In 2nd decl. nouns that end -**ius**, the voc. sing. is -**ī** (e.g., **nūntī**, voc. of **nūntius**).

Number Case	3rd Declension M./F.	Neut.	M./F.	Neut.	4th Declension Masc.	Neut.	5th Declension Masc.	Fem.
Singular								
Nominative	dux	nōmen	cīv*is*	mare	arc*us*	gen*ū*	di*ēs*	r*ēs*
Genitive	duc*is*	nōmin*is*	cīv*is*	mar*is*	arc*ūs*	gen*ūs*	di*ēī*	re*ī*
Dative	duc*ī*	nōmin*ī*	cīv*ī*	mar*ī*	arc*uī*	gen*ū*	di*ēī*	re*ī*
Accusative	duc*em*	nōmen	cīv*em*	mare	arc*um*	gen*ū*	diem	rem
Ablative	duce	nōmine	cīve	mar*ī*	arc*ū*	gen*ū*	di*ē*	r*ē*
Vocative	dux	nōmen	cīv*is*	mare	arc*us*	gen*ū*	di*ēs*	r*ēs*
Plural								
Nominative	duc*ēs*	nōmin*a*	cīv*ēs*	mar*ia*	arc*ūs*	gen*ua*	di*ēs*	r*ēs*
Genitive	duc*um*	nōmin*um*	cīv*ium*	mar*ium*	arc*uum*	gen*uum*	di*ērum*	r*ērum*
Dative	duc*ibus*	nōmin*ibus*	cīv*ibus*	mar*ibus*	arc*ibus*	gen*ibus*	di*ēbus*	r*ēbus*
Accusative	duc*ēs*	nōmin*a*	cīv*ēs*	mar*ia*	arc*ūs*	gen*ua*	di*ēs*	r*ēs*
Ablative	duc*ibus*	nōmin*ibus*	cīv*ibus*	mar*ibus*	arc*ibus*	gen*ibus*	di*ēbus*	r*ēbus*
Vocative	duc*ēs*	nōmin*a*	cīv*ēs*	mar*ia*	arc*ūs*	gen*ua*	di*ēs*	r*ēs*

N.B.: **cīvis** and **mare** are typical of 3rd decl. i-stem nouns.

5th decl. nouns have gen. & dat. sing. in -**ēī** if the stem ends -**i**-; otherwise -**eī**.

II. Adjectives

Number Case	1st and 2nd Declensions			3rd Declension		
	Masc.	Fem.	Neut.	Masc.	Fem.	Neut.
Singular						
Nominative	magn**us**	magn**a**	magn**um**	omn**is**	omn**is**	omn**e**
Genitive	magn**ī**	magn**ae**	magn**ī**	omn**is**	omn**is**	omn**is**
Dative	magn**ō**	magn**ae**	magn**ō**	omn**ī**	omn**ī**	omn**ī**
Accusative	magn**um**	magn**am**	magn**um**	omn**em**	omn**em**	omn**e**
Ablative	magn**ō**	magn**ā**	magn**ō**	omn**ī**	omn**ī**	omn**ī**
Vocative	magn**e**	magn**a**	magn**um**	omn**is**	omn**is**	omn**e**
Plural						
Nominative	magn**ī**	magn**ae**	magn**a**	omn**ēs**	omn**ēs**	omn**ia**
Genitive	magn**ōrum**	magn**ārum**	magn**ōrum**	omn**ium**	omn**ium**	omn**ium**
Dative	magn**īs**	magn**īs**	magn**īs**	omn**ibus**	omn**ibus**	omn**ibus**
Accusative	magn**ōs**	magn**ās**	magn**a**	omn**ēs**	omn**ēs**	omn**ia**
Ablative	magn**īs**	magn**īs**	magn**īs**	omn**ibus**	omn**ibus**	omn**ibus**
Vocative	magn**ī**	magn**ae**	magn**a**	omn**ēs**	omn**ēs**	omn**ia**

III. Comparative Adjectives

Number Case	Masc.	Fem.	Neut.
Singular			
Nominative	laetior	laetior	laetius
Genitive	laetiōr**is**	laetiōr**is**	laetiōr**is**
Dative	laetiōr**ī**	laetiōr**ī**	laetiōr**ī**
Accusative	laetiōr**em**	laetiōr**em**	laetius
Ablative	laetiōr**e**	laetiōr**e**	laetiōr**e**
Plural			
Nominative	laetiōr**ēs**	laetiōr**ēs**	laetiōr**a**
Genitive	laetiōr**um**	laetiōr**um**	laetiōr**um**
Dative	laetiōr**ibus**	laetiōr**ibus**	laetiōr**ibus**
Accusative	laetiōr**ēs**	laetiōr**ēs**	laetiōr**a**
Ablative	laetiōr**ibus**	laetiōr**ibus**	laetiōr**ibus**

Adjectives have positive, comparative, and superlative forms. You can usually recognize the comparative by the letters *-ior(-)* and the superlative by *-issimus, -errimus*, or *-illimus*:

Positive	Comparative	Superlative
ignāvus, -a, -um, *lazy*	ignāvior, ignāvius	ignāvissimus, -a, -um
pulcher, pulchra, pulchrum, *beautiful*	pulchrior, pulchrius	pulcherrimus, -a, -um
facilis, -is, -e, *easy*	facilior, facilius	facillimus, -a, -um

Some very common adjectives are irregular in the comparative and superlative:

Positive	Comparative	Superlative
bonus, -a, -um, *good*	**melior, melius,** *better*	**optimus, -a, -um,** *best*
malus, -a, -um, *bad*	**peior, peius,** *worse*	**pessimus, -a, -um,** *worst*
magnus, -a, -um, *big*	**maior, maius,** *bigger*	**maximus, -a, -um,** *biggest*
parvus, -a, -um, *small*	**minor, minus,** *smaller*	**minimus, -a, -um,** *smallest*
multus, -a, -um, *much*	**plūs,** *more*	**plūrimus, -a, -um,** *most, very much*
multī, -ae, -a, *many*	**plūrēs, plūra,** *more*	**plūrimī, -ae, -a,** *most, very many*

N.B.: The singular **plūs** is not an adjective but a neuter substantive, usually found with a partitive genitive, e.g., **Titus plūs vīnī bibit.** *Titus drank **more** (of the) wine.*

IV. Present Participles

Number / Case	Masc.	Fem.	Neut.
Singular			
Nominative	portāns	portāns	portāns
Genitive	portant*is*	portant*is*	portant*is*
Dative	portant*ī*	portant*ī*	portant*ī*
Accusative	portant*em*	portant*em*	portāns
Ablative	portant*ī/e*	portant*ī/e*	portant*ī/e*
Plural			
Nominative	portant*ēs*	portant*ēs*	portant*ia*
Genitive	portant*ium*	portant*ium*	portant*ium*
Dative	portant*ibus*	portant*ibus*	portant*ibus*
Accusative	portant*ēs*	portant*ēs*	portant*ia*
Ablative	portant*ibus*	portant*ibus*	portant*ibus*

V. Numbers

Case	Masc.	Fem.	Neut.	Masc.	Fem.	Neut.	Masc.	Fem.	Neut.
Nom.	ūn*us*	ūn*a*	ūn*um*	duo	du*ae*	duo	tr*ēs*	tr*ēs*	tr*ia*
Gen.	ūn*īus*	ūn*īus*	ūn*īus*	du*ōrum*	du*ārum*	du*ōrum*	tr*ium*	tr*ium*	tr*ium*
Dat.	ūn*ī*	ūn*ī*	ūn*ī*	du*ōbus*	du*ābus*	du*ōbus*	tr*ibus*	tr*ibus*	tr*ibus*
Acc.	ūn*um*	ūn*am*	ūn*um*	du*ōs*	du*ās*	duo	tr*ēs*	tr*ēs*	tr*ia*
Abl.	ūn*ō*	ūn*ā*	ūn*ō*	du*ōbus*	du*ābus*	du*ōbus*	tr*ibus*	tr*ibus*	tr*ibus*

	Cardinal	**Ordinal**
I	ūnus, -a, -um, *one*	prīmus, -a, -um, *first*
II	duo, -ae, -o, *two*	secundus, -a, -um, *second*
III	trēs, trēs, tria, *three*	tertius, -a, -um, *third*
IV	quattuor, *four*	quārtus, -a, -um, *fourth*
V	quīnque, *five*	quīntus, -a, -um, *fifth*
VI	sex, *six*	sextus, -a, -um, *sixth*
VII	septem, *seven*	septimus, -a, -um, *seventh*
VIII	octō, *eight*	octāvus, -a, -um, *eighth*
IX	novem, *nine*	nōnus, -a, -um, *ninth*
X	decem, *ten*	decimus, -a, -um, *tenth*
XI	ūndecim, *eleven*	ūndecimus, -a, -um, *eleventh*
XII	duodecim, *twelve*	duodecimus, -a, -um, *twelfth*
XIII	trēdecim, *thirteen*	tertius decimus, -a, -um, *thirteenth*
XIV	quattuordecim, *fourteen*	quārtus decimus, -a, -um, *fourteenth*
XV	quīndecim, *fifteen*	quīntus decimus, -a, -um, *fifteenth*
XVI	sēdecim, *sixteen*	sextus decimus, -a, -um, *sixteenth*
XVII	septendecim, *seventeen*	septimus decimus, -a, -um, *seventeenth*
XVIII	duodēvīgintī, *eighteen*	duodēvīcēsimus, -a, -um, *eighteenth*
XIX	ūndēvīgintī, *nineteen*	ūndēvīcēsimus, -a, -um, *nineteenth*
XX	vīgintī, *twenty*	vīcēsimus, -a, -um, *twentieth*
L	quīnquāgintā, *fifty*	quīnquāgēsimus, -a, -um, *fiftieth*
C	centum, *a hundred*	centēsimus, -a, -um, *hundredth*
D	quīngentī, -ae, -a, *five hundred*	quīngentēsimus, -a, -um, *five hundredth*
M	mīlle, *a thousand;* mīlia, *thousands*	mīllēsimus, -a, -um, *thousandth*

N.B.: The cardinal numbers from **quattuor** to **centum** do not change their form to indicate case and gender. **Mīlle** is also indeclinable in the singular, but the plural declines as a neuter and takes a partititve genitive: e.g., **mīlle virī**, *a thousand men;* **duo mīlia virōrum**, *two thousand(s) of) men.*

The following adjectives have -**īus** in the gen. sing. and -**ī** in the dat. sing., just as does **ūnus** above: **alius, -a, -ud,** *other;* **alter, altera, alterum,** *another;* **ūllus, -a, -um,** *any;* **nūllus, -a, -um,** *no;* **sōlus, -a, -um,** *alone;* **tōtus, -a, -um,** *all;* **uter, utra, utrum,** *which (of two);* **neuter, neutra, neutrum,** *neither;* and **uterque, utraque, utrumque,** *both.*

VI. Personal Pronouns

Number / Case	1st Person	2nd Person	3rd Person Masc.	Fem.	Neut.
Singular					
Nominative	ego	tū	is	ea	id
Genitive	meī	tuī	eius	eius	eius
Dative	mihi	tibi	eī	eī	eī
Accusative	mē	tē	eum	eam	id
Ablative	mē	tē	eō	eā	eō
Plural					
Nominative	nōs	vōs	eī	eae	ea
Genitive	nostrī	vestrī	eōrum	eārum	eōrum
	nostrum	vestrum			
Dative	nōbīs	vōbīs	eīs	eīs	eīs
Accusative	nōs	vōs	eōs	eās	ea
Ablative	nōbīs	vōbīs	eīs	eīs	eīs

N.B.: The forms of **is, ea, id** may also serve as demonstrative adjectives, meaning either *this* or *that*.

VII. Reflexive Pronoun

Number / Case	Singular	Plural
Singular		
Nominative	—	—
Genitive	suī	suī
Dative	sibi	sibi
Accusative	sē	sē
Ablative	sē	sē

VIII. Relative Pronoun

Number / Case	Masc.	Fem.	Neut.
Singular			
Nominative	quī	quae	quod
Genitive	cuius	cuius	cuius
Dative	cui	cui	cui
Accusative	quem	quam	quod
Ablative	quō	quā	quō
Plural			
Nominative	quī	quae	quae
Genitive	quōrum	quārum	quōrum
Dative	quibus	quibus	quibus
Accusative	quōs	quās	quae
Ablative	quibus	quibus	quibus

IX. Interrogative Pronoun

Number Case	Masc.	Fem.	Neut.
Singular			
Nominative	quis	quis	quid
Genitive	cuius	cuius	cuius
Dative	cui	cui	cui
Accusative	quem	quem	quid
Ablative	quō	quō	quō
Plural	Same as the plural of the relative pronoun in chart VIII above.		

X. Indefinite Adjectives and Pronouns

Number Case	Masc.	Fem.	Neut.	Masc.	Fem.	Neut.
Singular						
Nominative	quīdam	quaedam	quoddam	aliquī	aliqua	aliquod
Genitive	cuiusdam	cuiusdam	cuiusdam	alicuius	alicuius	alicuius
Dative	cuidam	cuidam	cuidam	alicui	alicui	alicui
Accusative	quendam	quandam	quoddam	aliquem	aliquam	aliquod
Ablative	quōdam	quādam	quōdam	aliquō	aliquā	aliquō
Plural						
Nominative	quīdam	quaedam	quaedam	aliquī	aliquae	aliqua
Genitive	quōrundam	quārundam	quōrundam	aliquōrum	aliquārum	aliquōrum
Dative	quibusdam	quibusdam	quibusdam	aliquibus	aliquibus	aliquibus
Accusative	quōsdam	quāsdam	quaedam	aliquōs	aliquās	aliqua
Ablative	quibusdam	quibusdam	quibusdam	aliquibus	aliquibus	aliquibus

N.B.: The indefinite pronoun **quīdam, quaedam, quiddam**, *a certain*, pl., *certain, some*, has the same forms as the indefinite adjective, except for **quiddam** in the neuter nominative and accusative singular.

The indefinite pronoun **aliquis, aliquis, aliquid**, *someone, anyone*, has the regular forms of the interrogative pronoun **quis, quis, quid**, as do the indefinite pronouns **quisque, quisque, quidque**, *each one, every one*, **quispiam, quispiam, quidpiam**, *someone, anyone*, and **quisquam, quisquam, quidquam (quicquam)**, *someone, anyone*.

Quisque and **quispiam** are used as adjectives as well as pronouns. When they are adjectives, they decline like the relative pronoun **quī, quae, quod** (i.e., **quī** rather than **quis** in the masc. nom. sing., and **quod** rather than **quid** in the neuter sing.).

The indefinite pronoun **quisquis, quisquis, quidquid**, *whoever*, also has the same forms as **quis, quis, quid**, but note that both halves of this word are declined.

XI. Demonstrative Adjectives and Pronouns

Number Case	Masc.	Fem.	Neut.	Masc.	Fem.	Neut.
Singular						
Nominative	hic	haec	hoc	ille	illa	illud
Genitive	huius	huius	huius	illīus	illīus	illīus
Dative	huic	huic	huic	illī	illī	illī
Accusative	hunc	hanc	hoc	illum	illam	illud
Ablative	hōc	hāc	hōc	illō	illā	illō
Plural						
Nominative	hī	hae	haec	illī	illae	illa
Genitive	hōrum	hārum	hōrum	illōrum	illārum	illōrum
Dative	hīs	hīs	hīs	illīs	illīs	illīs
Accusative	hōs	hās	haec	illōs	illās	illa
Ablative	hīs	hīs	hīs	illīs	illīs	illīs

Number Case	Masc.	Fem.	Neut.
Singular			
Nominative	ipse	ipsa	ipsum
Genitive	ipsīus	ipsīus	ipsīus
Dative	ipsī	ipsī	ipsī
Accusative	ipsum	ipsam	ipsum
Ablative	ipsō	ipsā	ipsō
Plural			
Nominative	ipsī	ipsae	ipsa
Genitive	ipsōrum	ipsārum	ipsōrum
Dative	ipsīs	ipsīs	ipsīs
Accusative	ipsōs	ipsās	ipsa
Ablative	ipsīs	ipsīs	ipsīs

Number Case	Masc.	Fem.	Neut.	Masc.	Fem.	Neut.
Singular						
Nominative	is	ea	id	īdem	eadem	idem
Genitive	eius	eius	eius	eiusdem	eiusdem	eiusdem
Dative	eī	eī	eī	eīdem	eīdem	eīdem
Accusative	eum	eam	id	eundem	eandem	idem
Ablative	eō	eā	eō	eōdem	eādem	eōdem
Plural						
Nominative	eī	eae	ea	eīdem	eaedem	eadem
Genitive	eōrum	eārum	eōrum	eōrundem	eārundem	eōrundem
Dative	eīs	eīs	eīs	eīsdem	eīsdem	eīsdem
Accusative	eōs	eās	ea	eōsdem	eāsdem	eadem
Ablative	eīs	eīs	eīs	eīsdem	eīsdem	eīsdem

N.B.: Nom. pl. **iī** is sometimes found instead of **eī**, and dat./abl. pl. **iīs** instead of **eīs**.

XII. Adverbs

Latin adverbs may be formed from adjectives of the 1st and 2nd declensions by adding *-ē* to the base of the adjective, e.g., **strēnuē**, *strenuously*, from **strēnuus, -a, -um**. To form an adverb from a 3rd declension adjective, add *-(i)ter* to the base of the adjective or *-er* to bases ending in **-nt-**, e.g., **breviter**, *briefly*, from **brevis, -is, -e**, and **prūdenter**, *wisely*, from **prūdēns, prūdentis**.

laetē, *happily*	laetius	laetissimē
audācter, boldly	audācius	audācissimē
fēlīciter, *luckily*	fēlīcius	fēlīcissimē
celeriter, *quickly*	celerius	celerrimē
prūdenter, *wisely*	prūdentius	prūdentissimē

Note the following as well:

diū, *for a long time*	diūtius	diūtissimē
saepe, *often*	saepius	saepissimē
sērō, *late*	sērius	sērissimē

Some adverbs are irregular:

bene, *well*	**melius**, *better*	**optimē**, *best*
male, *badly*	**peius**, *worse*	**pessimē**, *worst*
facile, *easily*	**facilius**, *more easily*	**facillimē**, *most easily*
magnopere, *greatly*	**magis**, *more*	**maximē**, *most*
paulum, *little*	**minus**, *less*	**minimē**, *least*
multum, *much*	**plūs**, *more*	**plūrimum**, *most*

XIII. Regular Verbs Active: Infinitive, Imperative, Indicative

			1st Conjugation	2nd Conjugation	3rd Conjugation		4th Conjugation
	Infinitive		port*āre*	mov*ēre*	mitt*ere*	iac*ere* (-iō)	aud*īre*
	Imperative		port*ā*	mov*ē*	mitt*e*	iac*e*	aud*ī*
			port*āte*	mov*ēte*	mitt*ite*	iac*ite*	aud*īte*
Present	Sing.	1	port*ō*	move*ō*	mitt*ō*	iaci*ō*	audi*ō*
		2	port*ās*	mov*ēs*	mitt*is*	iac*is*	aud*īs*
		3	porta*t*	move*t*	mitti*t*	iaci*t*	audi*t*
	Pl.	1	port*āmus*	mov*ēmus*	mitt*imus*	iac*imus*	aud*īmus*
		2	port*ātis*	mov*ētis*	mitt*itis*	iac*itis*	aud*ītis*
		3	porta*nt*	move*nt*	mitt*unt*	iaci*unt*	audi*unt*
Imperfect	Sing.	1	port*ābam*	mov*ēbam*	mitt*ēbam*	iac*iēbam*	aud*iēbam*
		2	port*ābās*	mov*ēbās*	mitt*ēbās*	iac*iēbās*	aud*iēbās*
		3	port*ābat*	mov*ēbat*	mitt*ēbat*	iac*iēbat*	aud*iēbat*
	Pl.	1	port*ābāmus*	mov*ēbāmus*	mitt*ēbāmus*	iac*iēbāmus*	aud*iēbāmus*
		2	port*ābātis*	mov*ēbātis*	mitt*ēbātis*	iac*iēbātis*	aud*iēbātis*
		3	port*ābant*	mov*ēbant*	mitt*ēbant*	iac*iēbant*	aud*iēbant*
Future	Sing.	1	port*ābō*	mov*ēbō*	mitt*am*	iac*iam*	aud*iam*
		2	port*ābis*	mov*ēbis*	mitt*ēs*	iac*iēs*	aud*iēs*
		3	port*ābit*	mov*ēbit*	mitt*et*	iaci*et*	audi*et*
	Pl.	1	port*ābimus*	mov*ēbimus*	mitt*ēmus*	iac*iēmus*	aud*iēmus*
		2	port*ābitis*	mov*ēbitis*	mitt*ētis*	iac*iētis*	aud*iētis*
		3	port*ābunt*	mov*ēbunt*	mitt*ent*	iaci*ent*	audi*ent*
Perfect	Sing.	1	portāv*ī*	mōv*ī*	mīs*ī*	iēc*ī*	audīv*ī*
		2	portāv*istī*	mōv*istī*	mīs*istī*	iēc*istī*	audīv*istī*
		3	portāv*it*	mōv*it*	mīs*it*	iēc*it*	audīv*it*
	Pl.	1	portāv*imus*	mōv*imus*	mīs*imus*	iēc*imus*	audīv*imus*
		2	portāv*istis*	mōv*istis*	mīs*istis*	iēc*istis*	audīv*istis*
		3	portāv*ērunt*	mōv*ērunt*	mīs*ērunt*	iēc*ērunt*	audīv*ērunt*
Pluperfect	Sing.	1	portāv*eram*	mōv*eram*	mīs*eram*	iēc*eram*	audīv*eram*
		2	portāv*erās*	mōv*erās*	mīs*erās*	iēc*erās*	audīv*erās*
		3	portāv*erat*	mōv*erat*	mīs*erat*	iēc*erat*	audīv*erat*
	Pl.	1	portāv*erāmus*	mōv*erāmus*	mīs*erāmus*	iēc*erāmus*	audīv*erāmus*
		2	portāv*erātis*	mōv*erātis*	mīs*erātis*	iēc*erātis*	audīv*erātis*
		3	portāv*erant*	mōv*erant*	mīs*erant*	iēc*erant*	audīv*erant*
Future Perfect	Sing.	1	portāv*erō*	mōv*erō*	mīs*erō*	iēc*erō*	audīv*erō*
		2	portāv*eris*	mōv*eris*	mīs*eris*	iēc*eris*	audīv*eris*
		3	portāv*erit*	mōv*erit*	mīs*erit*	iēc*erit*	audīv*erit*
	Pl.	1	portāv*erimus*	mōv*erimus*	mīs*erimus*	iēc*erimus*	audīv*erimus*
		2	portāv*eritis*	mōv*eritis*	mīs*eritis*	iēc*eritis*	audīv*eritis*
		3	portāv*erint*	mōv*erint*	mīs*erint*	iēc*erint*	audīv*erint*

XIV. Regular Verbs Passive: Infinitive, Imperative, Indicative

			1st Conjugation	2nd Conjugation	3rd Conjugation		4th Conjugation
	Infinitive		port*ārī*	mov*ērī*	mitt*ī*	iac*ī* (-iō)	aud*īrī*
	Imperative		port*āre*	mov*ēre*	mitt*ere*	iac*ere*	aud*īre*
			port*āminī*	mov*ēminī*	mitt*iminī*	iac*iminī*	aud*īminī*
Present	Sing.	1	port*or*	move*or*	mitt*or*	iac*ior*	aud*ior*
		2	port*āris*	mov*ēris*	mitt*eris*	iac*eris*	aud*īris*
		3	port*ātur*	mov*ētur*	mitt*itur*	iac*itur*	aud*ītur*
	Pl.	1	port*āmur*	mov*ēmur*	mitt*imur*	iac*imur*	aud*īmur*
		2	port*āminī*	mov*ēminī*	mitt*iminī*	iac*iminī*	aud*īminī*
		3	port*antur*	mov*entur*	mitt*untur*	iac*iuntur*	aud*iuntur*
Imperfect	Sing.	1	port*ābar*	mov*ēbar*	mitt*ēbar*	iac*iēbar*	aud*iēbar*
		2	port*ābāris*	mov*ēbāris*	mitt*ēbāris*	iac*iēbāris*	aud*iēbāris*
		3	port*ābātur*	mov*ēbātur*	mitt*ēbātur*	iac*iēbātur*	aud*iēbātur*
	Pl.	1	port*ābāmur*	mov*ēbāmur*	mitt*ēbāmur*	iac*iēbāmur*	aud*iēbāmur*
		2	port*ābāminī*	mov*ēbāminī*	mitt*ēbāminī*	iac*iēbāminī*	aud*iēbāminī*
		3	port*ābantur*	mov*ēbantur*	mitt*ēbantur*	iac*iēbantur*	aud*iēbantur*
Future	Sing.	1	port*ābor*	mov*ēbor*	mitt*ar*	iac*iar*	aud*iar*
		2	port*āberis*	mov*ēberis*	mitt*ēris*	iac*iēris*	aud*iēris*
		3	port*ābitur*	mov*ēbitur*	mitt*ētur*	iac*iētur*	aud*iētur*
	Pl.	1	port*ābimur*	mov*ēbimur*	mitt*ēmur*	iac*iēmur*	aud*iēmur*
		2	port*ābiminī*	mov*ēbiminī*	mitt*ēminī*	iac*iēminī*	aud*iēminī*
		3	port*ābuntur*	mov*ēbuntur*	mitt*entur*	iac*ientur*	aud*ientur*

		Perfect Passive		Pluperfect Passive		Future Perfect Passive	
Sing.	1	portātus, -a	sum	portātus, -a	eram	portātus, -a	erŏ
	2	portātus, -a	es	portātus, -a	erās	portātus, -a	eris
	3	portātus, -a, -um	est	portātus, -a, -um	erat	portātus, -a, -um	erit
Pl.	1	portātī, -ae	sumus	portātī, -ae	erāmus	portātī, -ae	erimus
	2	portātī, -ae	estis	portātī, -ae	erātis	portātī, -ae	eritis
	3	portātī, -ae, -a	sunt	portātī, -ae, -a	erant	portātī, -ae, -a	erunt

N.B.: The perfect passive, pluperfect passive, and future perfect passive are formed the same way for all conjugations (fourth principal part with a form of **esse**).

XV. Deponent Verbs

Deponent verbs are conjugated in the same way as passive verbs of the same conjugation; e.g., **cōnārī** is conjugated like the passive of **portāre** (cōnor ≈ portor, cōnāris ≈ portāris, etc.).

XVI. Regular Verbs Active: Subjunctive

			1st Conjugation	2nd Conjugation	3rd Conjugation		4th Conjugation
Present	Sing.	1	portem	moveam	mittam	iaciam	audiam
		2	portēs	moveās	mittās	iaciās	audiās
		3	portet	moveat	mittat	iaciat	audiat
	Pl.	1	portēmus	moveāmus	mittāmus	iaciāmus	audiāmus
		2	portētis	moveātis	mittātis	iaciātis	audiātis
		3	portent	moveant	mittant	iaciant	audiant
Imperfect	Sing.	1	portārem	movērem	mitterem	iacerem	audīrem
		2	portārēs	movērēs	mitterēs	iacerēs	audīrēs
		3	portāret	movēret	mitteret	iaceret	audīret
	Pl.	1	portārēmus	movērēmus	mitterēmus	iacerēmus	audīrēmus
		2	portārētis	movērētis	mitterētis	iacerētis	audīrētis
		3	portārent	movērent	mitterent	iacerent	audīrent
Perfect	Sing.	1	portāverim	mōverim	mīserim	iēcerim	audīverim
		2	portāveris	mōveris	mīseris	iēceris	audīveris
		3	portāverit	mōverit	mīserit	iēcerit	audīverit
	Pl.	1	portāverimus	mōverimus	mīserimus	iēcerimus	audīverimus
		2	portāveritis	mōveritis	mīseritis	iēceritis	audīveritis
		3	portāverint	mōverint	mīserint	iēcerint	audīverint
Pluperfect	Sing.	1	portāvissem	mōvissem	mīsissem	iēcissem	audīvissem
		2	portavissēs	mōvissēs	mīsissēs	iēcissēs	audīvissēs
		3	portāvisset	mōvisset	mīsisset	iēcisset	audīvisset
	Pl.	1	portāvissēmus	mōvissēmus	mīsissēmus	iēcissēmus	audīvissēmus
		2	portāvissētis	mōvissētis	mīsissētis	iēcissētis	audīvissētis
		3	portāvissent	mōvissent	mīsissent	iēcissent	audīvissent

See note on perf. subjunct., bottom of p. 261 opposite.

XVII. Regular Verbs Passive: Subjunctive

			1st Conjugation	2nd Conjugation	3rd Conjugation		4th Conjugation
Present	Sing.	1	porter	movear	mittar	iaciar	audiar
		2	portēris	moveāris	mittāris	iaciāris	audiāris
		3	portētur	moveātur	mittātur	iaciātur	audiātur
	Sing.	1	portēmur	moveāmur	mittāmur	iaciāmur	audiāmur
		2	portēminī	moveāminī	mittāminī	iaciāminī	audiāminī
		3	portentur	moveantur	mittantur	iaciantur	audiantur
Imperfect	Sing.	1	portārer	movērer	mitterer	iacerer	audīrer
		2	portārēris	movērēris	mitterēris	iacerēris	audīrēris
		3	portārētur	movērētur	mitterētur	iacerētur	audīrētur
	Sing.	1	portārēmur	movērēmur	mitterēmur	iacerēmur	audīrēmur
		2	portārēminī	movērēminī	mitterēminī	iacerēminī	audīrēminī
		3	portārentur	movērentur	mitterentur	iacerentur	audīrentur
Perfect		1	portātus sim etc.	mōtus sim etc.	missus sim etc.	iactus sim etc.	audītus sim etc.
Pluperfect		1	portātus essem etc.	mōtus essem etc.	missus essem etc.	iactus essem etc.	audītus essem etc.

XVIII. Irregular Verbs: Infinitive, Imperative, Indicative

	Infinitive	esse	posse	velle	nōlle	mālle
	Imperative	es	—	—	nōlī	—
		este	—	—	nōlīte	—
Present	Sing. 1	sum	possum	volō	nōlō	mālō
	2	es	potes	vīs	nōn vīs	māvīs
	3	est	potest	vult	nōn vult	māvult
	Pl. 1	sumus	possumus	volumus	nōlumus	mālumus
	2	estis	potestis	vultis	nōn vultis	māvultis
	3	sunt	possunt	volunt	nōlunt	mālunt
Imperfect	Sing. 1	eram	poteram	volēbam	nōlēbam	mālēbam
	2	erās	poterās	volēbās	nōlēbās	mālēbās
	3	erat	poterat	volēbat	nōlēbat	mālēbat
	Pl. 1	erāmus	poterāmus	volēbāmus	nōlēbāmus	mālēbāmus
	2	erātis	poterātis	volēbātis	nōlēbātis	mālēbātis
	3	erant	poterant	volēbant	nōlēbant	mālēbant
Future	Sing. 1	erō	poterō	volam	nōlam	mālam
	2	eris	poteris	volēs	nōlēs	mālēs
	3	erit	poterit	volet	nōlet	mālet
	Pl. 1	erimus	poterimus	volēmus	nōlēmus	mālēmus
	2	eritis	poteritis	volētis	nōlētis	mālētis
	3	erunt	poterunt	volent	nōlent	mālent
Perfect	Sing. 1	fuī	potuī	voluī	nōluī	māluī
	2	fuistī	potuistī	voluistī	nōluistī	māluistī
	3	fuit	potuit	voluit	nōluit	māluit
	Pl. 1	fuimus	potuimus	voluimus	nōluimus	māluimus
	2	fuistis	potuistis	voluistis	nōluistis	māluistis
	3	fuērunt	potuērunt	voluērunt	nōluērunt	māluērunt
Pluperfect	Sing. 1	fueram	potueram	volueram	nōlueram	mālueram
	2	fuerās	potuerās	voluerās	nōluerās	māluerās
	3	fuerat	potuerat	voluerat	nōluerat	māluerat
	Pl. 1	fuerāmus	potuerāmus	voluerāmus	nōluerāmus	māluerāmus
	2	fuerātis	potuerātis	voluerātis	nōluerātis	māluerātis
	3	fuerant	potuerant	voluerant	nōluerant	māluerant
Future Perfect	Sing. 1	fuerō	potuerō	voluerō	nōluerō	māluerō
	2	fueris	potueris	volueris	nōlueris	mālueris
	3	fuerit	potuerit	voluerit	nōluerit	māluerit
	Pl. 1	fuerimus	potuerimus	voluerimus	nōluerimus	māluerimus
	2	fueritis	potueritis	volueritis	nōlueritis	mālueritis
	3	fuerint	potuerint	voluerint	nōluerint	māluerint

(Irregular verbs continued on next page.)

N.B.: In the perfect subjunctive active (chart XVI opposite), the -i- in the tense marker may be either long or short in the 2nd person, sing. and pl., and in the 1st person pl.: mōveris or mōverīs, iēcerimus or iēcerīmus, etc. Long and short -i- are both regularly found when scanning poetry.

XVIII. Irregular Verbs: Infinitive, Imperative, Indicative (cont.)

		Infinitive			fierī	īre
		ferre	ferrī			
	Imperative	fer ferte	ferre feriminī	— —	ī īte	
Present	Sing. 1	ferō	feror	fīō	eō	
	2	fers	ferris	fīs	īs	
	3	fert	fertur	fit	it	
	Pl. 1	ferimus	ferimur	fīmus	īmus	
	2	fertis	feriminī	fītis	ītis	
	3	ferunt	feruntur	fīunt	eunt	
Imperfect	Sing. 1	ferēbam	ferēbar	fīēbam	ībam	
	2	ferēbās	ferēbāris	fīēbās	ībās	
	3	ferēbat	ferēbātur	fīēbat	ībat	
	Pl. 1	ferēbāmus	ferēbāmur	fīēbāmus	ībāmus	
	2	ferēbātis	ferēbāminī	fīēbātis	ībātis	
	3	ferēbant	ferēbantur	fīēbant	ībant	
Future	Sing. 1	feram	ferar	fīam	ībō	
	2	ferēs	ferēris	fīēs	ībis	
	3	feret	ferētur	fiet	ībit	
	Pl. 1	ferēmus	ferēmur	fīēmus	ībimus	
	2	ferētis	ferēminī	fīētis	ībitis	
	3	ferent	ferentur	fīent	ībunt	
Perfect	Sing. 1	tulī	lātus sum	factus sum	īvī	or, more usually iī
	2	tulistī	lātus es	factus es	īvistī	iistī > īstī
	3	tulit	lātus est	factus sit	īvit	iit
	Pl. 1	tulimus	lātī sumus	factī sumus	īvimus	iimus
	2	tulistis	lātī estis	factī estis	īvistis	iistis > īstis
	3	tulērunt	lātī sunt	factī sunt	īvērunt	iērunt
Pluperfect	Sing. 1	tuleram	lātus eram	factus eram	īveram	ieram
	2	tulerās	lātus erās	factus erās	īverās	ierās
	3	tulerat	lātus erat	factus erat	īverat	ierat
	Pl. 1	tulerāmus	lātī erāmus	factī erāmus	īverāmus	ierāmus
	2	tulerātis	lātī erātis	factī erātis	īverātis	ierātis
	3	tulerant	lātī erant	factī erant	īverant	ierant
Future Perfect	Sing. 1	tulerō	lātus erō	factus erō	īverō	ierō
	2	tuleris	lātus eris	factus eris	īveris	ieris
	3	tulerit	lātus erit	factus erit	īverit	ierit
	Pl. 1	tulerimus	lātī erimus	factī erimus	īverimus	ierimus
	2	tuleritis	lātī eritis	factī eritis	īveritis	ieritis
	3	tulerint	lātī erunt	factī erunt	īverint	ierint

XIX. Irregular Verbs: Subjunctive

Present	Sing.	1	sim	possim	velim	nōlim	mālim
		2	sīs	possīs	velīs	nōlīs	mālīs
		3	sit	possit	velit	nōlit	mālit
	Pl.	1	sīmus	possīmus	velīmus	nōlīmus	mālīmus
		2	sītis	possītis	velītis	nōlītis	mālītis
		3	sint	possint	velint	nōlint	mālint
Imperfect	Sing.	1	essem	possem	vellem	nōllem	māllem
		2	essēs	possēs	vellēs	nōllēs	māllēs
		3	esset	posset	vellet	nōllet	māllet
	Pl.	1	essēmus	possēmus	vellēmus	nōllēmus	māllēmus
		2	essētis	possētis	vellētis	nōllētis	māllētis
		3	essent	possent	vellent	nōllent	māllent
Perfect	Sing.	1	fuerim	potuerim	voluerim	nōluerim	māluerim
		2	fueris	potueris	volueris	nōlueris	mālueris
		3	fuerit	potuerit	voluerit	nōluerit	māluerit
	Pl.	1	fuerimus	potuerimus	voluerimus	nōluerimus	māluerimus
		2	fueritis	potueritis	volueritis	nōlueritis	mālueritis
		3	fuerint	potuerint	voluerint	nōluerint	māluerint
Pluperfect	Sing.	1	fuissem	potuissem	voluissem	nōluissem	māluissem
		2	fuissēs	potuissēs	voluissēs	nōluissēs	māluissēs
		3	fuisset	potuisset	voluisset	nōluisset	māluisset
	Pl.	1	fuissēmus	potuissēmus	voluissēmus	nōluissēmus	māluissēmus
		2	fuissētis	potuissētis	voluissētis	nōluissētis	māluissētis
		3	fuissent	potuissent	voluissent	nōluissent	māluissent

Present	Sing.	1	feram	ferar	fiam	eam
		2	ferās	ferāris	fiās	eās
		3	ferat	ferātur	fiat	eat
	Pl.	1	ferāmus	ferāmur	fiāmus	eāmus
		2	ferātis	ferāminī	fiātis	eātis
		3	ferant	ferantur	fiant	eant
Imperfect	Sing.	1	ferrem	ferrer	fierem	īrem
		2	ferrēs	ferrēris	fierēs	īrēs
		3	ferret	ferrētur	fieret	īret
	Pl.	1	ferrēmus	ferrēmur	fierēmus	īrēmus
		2	ferrētis	ferrēminī	fierētis	īrētis
		3	ferrent	ferrentur	fierent	īrent
Perfect	Sing.	1	tulerim	lātus sim	factus sim	ierim
		2	tuleris	lātus sīs	factus sīs	ieris
		3	tulerit	lātus sit	factus sit	ierit
	Pl.	1	tulerimus	lātī sīmus	factī sīmus	ierimus
		2	tuleritis	lātī sītis	factī sītis	ieritis
		3	tulerint	lātī sint	factī sint	ierint
Pluperfect	Sing.	1	tulissem	lātus essem	factus essem	īssem
		2	tulissēs	lātus essēs	factus essēs	īssēs
		3	tulisset	lātus esset	factus esset	īsset
	Pl.	1	tulissēmus	lātī essēmus	factī essēmus	īssēmus
		2	tulissētis	lātī essētis	factī essētis	īssētis
		3	tulissent	lātī essent	factī essent	īssent

N.B.: The perfect subjunctive of eō may be ierim, etc., as shown in the chart, or īverim.

The pluperfect subjunctive of eō may be īssem, as shown in the chart, or īvissem.

XX. Participles

		Active	Passive
Present	1	portāns, portantis	
	2	movēns, moventis	
	3	mittēns, mittentis	
	-iō	iaciēns, iacientis	
	4	audiēns, audientis	
Perfect	1		portātus, -a, -um
	2		mōtus, -a, -um
	3		missus, -a, -um
	-iō		iactus, -a, -um
	4		audītus, -a, -um
Future	1	portātūrus, -a, -um	portandus, -a, -um
	2	mōtūrus, -a, -um	movendus, -a, -um
	3	missūrus, -a, -um	mittendus, -a, -um
	-iō	iactūrus, -a, -um	iaciendus, -a, -um
	4	audītūrus, -a, -um	audiendus, -a, -um

N.B.: The perfect participles of deponent verbs have active, not passive, meanings: e.g., **portātus** = *having been carried*, vs. **ēgressus** (deponent) = *having gone out.*

N.B.: The future passive participle is also known as the gerundive.

XXI. Infinitives

		Active	Passive
Present	1	portāre	portārī
	2	movēre	movērī
	3	mittere	mittī
	-iō	iacere	iacī
	4	audīre	audīrī
Perfect	1	portāvisse	portātus, -a, -um esse
	2	mōvisse	mōtus, -a, -um esse
	3	mīsisse	missus, -a, -um esse
	-iō	iēcisse	iactus, -a, -um esse
	4	audīvisse	audītus, -a, -um esse
Future	1	portātūrus, -a, -um esse	portātum īrī
	2	mōtūrus, -a, -um esse	mōtum īrī
	3	missūrus, -a, -um esse	missum īrī
	-iō	iactūrus, -a, -um esse	iactum īrī
	4	audītūrus, -a, -um esse	audītum īrī

N.B.: The present and perfect infinitives of deponent verbs have passive forms with active meanings: e.g., **cōnārī** = *to try*, **cōnātus esse, -a, -um** = *to have tried.* The future active infinitive of deponents is the same as for non-deponent verbs, e.g., **cōnātūrus, -a, -um esse.**

N.B.: the future passive infinitive is extremely rare.

XXII. Gerunds

Case Singular	1st Conjugation	2nd Conjugation	3rd Conjugation	3rd -iō Conjugation	4th Conjugation
Genitive	porta**ndī**	move**ndī**	mitte**ndī**	iacie**ndī**	audie**ndī**
Dative	porta**ndō**	move**ndō**	mitte**ndō**	iacie**ndō**	audie**ndō**
Accusative	porta**ndum**	move**ndum**	mitte**ndum**	iacie**ndum**	audie**ndum**
Ablative	porta**ndō**	move**ndō**	mitte**ndō**	iacie**ndō**	audie**ndō**

N.B.: Gerunds have only singular forms and have no nominative case.

Summary of Grammar

Note: most examples are taken from Caesar and are identified by book and chapter: *DbG* 1.3 = *De bello Gallico* Book 1, chapter 3. Some are from Vergil's *Aeneid*: *Aen.* 1.4 = *Aeneid* Book 1, line 4. Examples with no source were written to illustrate the point under discussion.

I. Basic Forms and Functions

A. Nouns

A1. Nominative Case

A1a. Subject
A noun or pronoun in the nominative is used as the subject of a conjugated verb:
Ea rēs <u>est</u> Helvētiīs <u>ēnūntiāta</u>.
This matter <u>was reported</u> to the Helvetians. (*DbG* 1.4)

A1b. Complement or predicate nominative
A linking verb may be completed by a COMPLEMENT in the nominative (also called a PREDICATE NOMINATIVE). **Esse** and **fierī** are the most common linking verbs; some verbs in the passive can also take a complement:
fortissimī <u>sunt</u> Belgae, *the bravest <u>are</u> the Belgae* (*DbG* 1.1)
quī **Celtae** <u>appellantur,</u> *who <u>are called</u> Celts* (*DbG* 1.1)

A2. Genitive Case

Note: the basic function of the genitive is to make one noun modify or describe another noun, i.e., to act as an adjective. The first five uses of the genitive listed here all serve that function, although they are labeled in different ways.

A2a. Genitive of description
prō <u>glōriā</u> **bellī**, *in proportion to their glory in (lit., of) war* (*DbG* 1.2)
<u>mūrum</u> in altitūdinem **pedum sēdecim**, *a wall of sixteen feet in height* (*DbG* 1.8)

A2b. Partitive Genitive
A word or phrase in the genitive may indicate the whole of which something is a part:
Hōrum omnium fortissimī sunt Belgae.
Of all these the bravest are the Belgae. (*DbG* 1.1)

The partitive genitive is used with some words that Romans considered nouns but which are often adjectives in English, e.g., **mīlia, nimis, plūs,** and **satis,** and with pronouns:
<u>mīlia</u> **passuum**, *<u>thousands</u> of paces* (*DbG* 1.2)
quid **incommodī**, *some damage*, lit., *something of damage* (*DbG* 6.13)

Note that **ē/ex** with the abl., not a partitive gen., is usually used with numbers and with the words **complūrēs** and **quīdam**:
<u>complūrēs</u> ex eīs, *<u>several</u> of them* (*DbG* 4.37)
<u>quīdam</u> ex mīlitibus, *<u>some</u> of the soldiers* (*DbG* 1.42)

A2c. Genitive of possession

A noun in the genitive often indicates possession:

decimae legiōnis aquilam, *the eagle of the tenth legion* (*DbG* 4.25)

A2d. Genitive of characteristic or predicate genitive

A phrase in the genitive may express a quality or charateristic that is typical of the noun modified; the verb in the clause is usually a form of **esse**:

<u>est</u> enim hoc **Gallicae cōnsuētūdinis**

for this <u>is</u> (typical of) the custom(s) of Gaul (*DbG* 4.5)

A2e. Genitive expressing indefinite value

A noun in the genitive may express the general value of something (compare the ablative of price, which is used for a specific amount):

cuius auctōritās in hīs regiōnibus **magnī** habēbātur

whose prestige in these regions was considered of great value (*DbG* 4.21)

A2f. Genitive with impersonal verbs of feeling

Impersonal verbs that express feelings use the genitive to show the source or cause of the feeling, with the person who feels in the accusative:

cōnsilia **quōrum** <u>eōs</u> <u>paenitēre</u> necesse est

plans of which it is necessary that <u>they repent</u> (*DbG* 4.5)

A2g. Genitive with certain adjectives

The genitive is used to complete the meaning of certain adjectives, notably **cupidus**, *desirous*, **perītus/imperītus**, *experienced/inexperienced*, and **plēnus**, *full*:

hominēs **bellandī** <u>cupidī</u>, *men <u>desirous</u> of making war* (*DbG* 1.2)

A2h. Genitive as object of intransitive verbs

The genitive is used as the object of a small number of intransitive verbs: **meminī**, *to remember*, **misereor**, *to pity*, **oblīvīscor**, *to forget*, and **potior**, *to get control*:

<u>miserēre</u> **domūs lābentis**, *<u>take pity on</u> (my) failing house* (*Aen.* 4.318)

A2i. Genitive of specification

The genitive is used to indicate the respect in which something is true:

dīves **opum**, *rich in* (lit., *of*) *resources* (*Aen.* 1.14)

A3. Dative Case

A3a. Indirect object of transitive verbs

A word or phase in the dative may indicate the indirect object of transitive verbs (**F1e**), especially verbs of "giving," "telling," or "showing":

Is **sibi** lēgātiōnem suscēpit.

He took for himself a diplomatic mission. (*DbG* 1.3)

Some transitive verbs can be used without a direct object (although one is usually understood):

lēgātīs respondit, *he answered (to) the ambassadors* (*DbG* 1.7)

A3b. Dative with intransitive verbs

Special intransitive (**E1f**) verbs such as **crēdere**, **favēre**, **imperāre**, **nocēre**, **pārēre**, **studēre**, etc., take an object in the dative:

cīvitātī <u>persuāsit</u>, *<u>he persuaded</u> the tribe* (*DbG* 1.2)

A3c. Dative with compound verbs

Some intransitive compound verbs can be completed by word(s) in the dative; note that all compounds of **esse** fall into this category:

cum **omnibus** virtūte <u>praestārent</u>, *since <u>they surpassed</u> all in courage (DbG 1.2)*

hostibus <u>appropinquārunt</u>, *<u>they approached</u> the enemy (DbG 4.25)*

eīs **mīlitibus** <u>praeesse</u>, *<u>to be in charge of</u> these soldiers (DbG 5.24)*

A3d. Dative with impersonal verbs

The dative is found with impersonal verbs (**F1d**) such as **necesse est** and **licet**:

ut id **sibi** facere <u>liceat</u>, *that <u>it be allowed</u> for them to do this (DbG 1.7)*

A3e. Dative with verbs of taking or depriving

A word in the dative may show the person from whom something is taken away:

Rōmānī arma **Gallīs** captīs <u>adēmērunt</u>.

The Romans <u>took away</u> the weapons from the captured Gauls.

A3f. Dative of possession

A dative case noun may be used with the verb **esse** to indicate possession; the thing owned is the subject of the form of **esse** and the person who has it is in the dative:

sibi <u>esse</u> in animō iter facere, *that **they had** in mind to travel (DbG 1.7)*

A3g. Dative of purpose

A noun in the dative, used with the verb **esse**, may express purpose or function:

quae ad reficiendās nāvēs erant **ūsuī**

*which were **of use/useful** for rebuilding the ships (DbG 4.29)*

rem esse **testimōniō**

*(he said that) the fact served (lit., was) **as a proof** (DbG 5.28)*

A3h. Dative of reference

A noun in the dative may indicate the person or thing to whom events refer. The connection between such a dative and other parts of the sentence is less direct than with a verb of telling or showing (ind. obj.) or with a special intransitive verb.

intellēgebat magnō cum perīculō **prōvinciae** futūrum [esse]

*he understood that this would be very dangerous **for the Province** (DbG 1.10)*

Sometimes the best English equivalent is a possessive:

trānsfīgitur scūtum **Pullōnī**, ***Pullo's** shield is pierced through (DbG 5.44)*

A3i. Double dative

Two datives may be used together in a construction called the DOUBLE DATIVE. A dative of purpose is combined with a dative of reference:

quae rēs **magnō ūsuī** <u>nostrīs</u> fuit

*which action was **very useful** <u>to our men</u> (DbG 4.25)*

populum ventūrum **excidiō** <u>Libyae</u>

*that a people would come **as a (source of) destruction** <u>for Libya</u> (Aen. 1.21–22)*

A3j. Dative with certain adjectives

The dative is used to complete the meaning of certain adjectives, including **aequus/inīquus**, *fair/unfair (to)*, **amīcus/inimīcus**, *friendly/unfriendly (to)*, **grātus**, *pleasing (to)*, **idōneus**, *suitable (for)*, and **similis**, *similar (to)*:

<u>proximī</u> sunt Germānīs, *they are <u>closest to</u> the Germans (DbG 1.1)*

Note however that the genitive is used with pronouns:

meī [not **mihi**] <u>similis</u>, *similar to me*

A3k. Dative of agent

In the passive periphrastic construction (**H2**), the person by whom something must be done is expressed by the dative (not by the ablative with ā or **ab**):

> **mīlitibus . . . dē nāvibus** <u>dēsiliendum erat</u>,
>
> *the soldiers <u>had to jump down</u> from the ships (DbG 4.24)*

In poetry the dative of agent is found with regular passive verbs also:

> nec <u>cernitur</u> **ūllī**, *nor <u>is he seen</u> by anyone (Aen. 1.440)*

A4. Accusative Case

A4a. Direct object

A word or phrase in the accusative may be the direct object of a transitive verb:

> **coniūrātiōnem** nōbilitātis <u>fēcit</u>, *<u>he made</u> a conspiracy of the nobles (DbG 1.2)*

A4b. Double or predicate accusative

Verbs of naming, making, and asking can take two accusatives, one the direct object and the other a predicate to that object:

> cotīdiē Caesar **Aeduōs frūmentum** <u>flāgitāre</u>
>
> *every day Caesar <u>demanded</u> **grain from the Haedui** (DbG 1.16)*

A4c. Accusative with certain prepositions

The accusative is used as the object of many prepositions:

> <u>per</u> **indicium**, *<u>through</u> information (DbG 1.4)*

A4d. Accusative of duration of time or extent of space

Words or phrases in the accusative without a preposition may indicate duration of time or extent of space:

> **multōs annōs**, *for many years (DbG 1.3)*
>
> **mīlia** passuum **xxv**, *for 25 miles (DbG 5.46)*

A4e. Adverbial accusative

A word in the accusative may be used as an adverb:

> cum **plūrimum** possent, *because they were the **most** powerful (DbG 1.3)*
>
> nec **mortāle** sonāre, *not sounding **human** (Aen. 6.50)*

A4f. Accusative of exclamation

The accusative is used in exclamations:

> **Ō fortūnātam rem pūblicam!** *O fortunate state! (Cicero, In Cat. 2.7)*

Sometimes an accusative of exclamation is accompanied by an infinitive:

> **Mēne** <u>dēsistere</u> **victam?** *Am I <u>to give up</u> defeated? (Aen. 1.37)*

A4g. Subject of infinitive

For this use of the accusative, see **Q2**.

A4h. Accusative of respect

The accusative may tell in respect to what something occurs. This is a Greek construction particularly common with body parts:

> lacrimīs **oculōs** suffūsa **nitentēs**,
>
> *filled with tears **in respect to her shining eyes** / with her shining eyes filled with tears (Aen. 1.228)*

A5. Ablative Case

Note: the ablative case as used in classical Latin represents a fusion of three separate cases found in early Indo-European languages. The original ablative expressed separation (hence the name **ablātīvus** from **ab** + **lātus**, perf. part. of **ferre**); use **A5a** is a survival of this, as is the the ablative of place from which, **B3**. The majority of ablative nouns in Latin, however, perform an adverbial function; that is, they modify a verb and answer the questions *how, where, when,* or *why*.

A5a. Ablative of separation or source
A word in the ablative may indicate the source from which something comes or from which it is separated:

> cum suīs fīnibus eōs <u>prohibent</u>
> *when they <u>keep them away</u> from their territory* (DbG 1.1)
> summō locō <u>nātus</u> Tasgetius
> *Tasgetius, <u>born</u> from a very high rank* (DbG 5.25)

A5b. Ablative of time when or within which
A word or phrase in the ablative, without a preposition, may indicate the time when or within which something happens:

> eādem nocte, **on the same night** (DbG 4.29)

A5c. Ablative of means, instrument, or route
A noun referring to a physical object may be used in the ablative without a preposition to tell how something is done:

> ferē **cotīdiānīs proeliīs** contendunt, *they struggle in almost **daily battles*** (DbG 1.1)
> **eōdem itinere** contendit, *he hurries **along the same route*** (DbG 1.21)

A5d. Ablative of cause or reason
A noun in the ablative without a preposition may state the cause or reason for which something is done:

> hīs rēbus fīēbat, **because of these things** *it happened* (DbG 1.2)
> eius **adventū**, **because of** *his **arrival*** (DbG 4.34)

A5e. Ablative of specification or respect
A word or phrase in the ablative may specify the way in which something exists or is done:

> Hī omnēs **linguā, īnstitūtīs, lēgibus** inter sē differunt.
> *They all differ from each other **in languge, in customs, (and) in laws.*** (DbG 1.1)

A5f. Ablative of price
A phrase in the ablative may indicate the price of something:

> **parvō pretiō** redēmpta, *redeemed **for a small price*** (DbG 1.18)

A5g. Ablative of manner
A noun in the ablative with the preposition **cum** may be used to indicate the manner in which something is done:

> pars **cum cruciātū** necābātur, *some were killed **with torture*** (DbG 5.45)

If the noun is modified by an adjective, the preposition may be omitted:

> **maximō clāmōre, with very loud shouting** (DbG 5.43)

A5h. Ablative of accompaniment
Accompaniment is expressed by the ablative with the preposition **cum**:

> ut <u>cum</u> **omnibus cōpiīs** exīrent, *to leave <u>with</u> **all their forces*** (DbG 1.2)

A5i. Ablative absolute

An ablative absolute is an adverbial phrase grammatically separate from the rest of the sentence (and therefore often set off by commas in modern books). It consists of a noun (or pronoun) plus a participle, both in the ablative; the best translation is usually an English clause introduced by *when, since, although,* or *if:*

> **oppidīs suīs vīcīsque exustīs**
> *when all their towns and villages had been burned* (DbG 1.5)
> **nostrīs** fortiter in aciē **resistentibus**
> *because our (men) were fighting back bravely in the battle*

Since there is no present participle for the verb **esse** in classical Latin, an ablative absolute may consist of two nouns, or a noun and an adjective, with the verb "to be" understood:

> **Sēquanīs invītīs** īre nōn poterant
> *if the Sequani (were) unwilling they could not go* (DbG 1.9)

A5j. Ablative of personal agent

A noun in the ablative with the preposition **ā** or **ab** is used to tell the person by whom something is done:

> exercitum **ab Helvētiīs** pulsum (esse)
> *that the army had been beaten **by the Helvetians*** (DbG 1.7)

A5k. Ablative of comparison

A noun in the ablative may be used with a comparative adjective or adverb:

> nōn <u>amplius</u> **quīnis aut senīs mīlibus** passuum
> *not <u>more</u> **than five or six miles*** (DbG 1.15)

A5l. Ablative of degree of difference

A word or phrase in the ablative is used to express the degree of difference with comparative adjectives and adverbs and other words implying comparison:

> **multō** facilius, *easier **by much**, **much** easier* (DbG 1.6)

A5m. Ablative with certain prepositions

A noun in the ablative may be used as object of the prepositions **ā/ab, cum, dē, ē/ex, in, prae, prō, sine,** and **sub:**

> <u>ex</u> agrīs, <u>*out of*</u> *the fields* (DbG 1.4)

A5n. Ablative of description

A noun and an adjective in the ablative, without a preposition, may be used to describe a noun. This is the only construction in which the ablative case acts as an adjective rather than an adverb:

> hominēs **inimīcō animō**, *men **of hostile mind*** (DbG 1.4)

A5o. Ablative with special deponent verbs

A noun in the ablative is used as the object of five deponent verbs and their compounds: **fruor, fungor, potior, ūtor,** and **vēscor:**

> **quō genere** in proeliīs <u>ūtī</u> cōnsuērunt
> *which type they are accustomed <u>to use</u> in battles* (DbG 4.24)

Note: **potior** can also take the genitive.

A6. Vocative Case

A6a. Direct address

The vocative case is used when addressing a person directly:

'Dēsilīte,' inquit, '**mīlitēs**,' *Jump down, **soldiers**' he said* (*DbG* 4.25)

B. Place Constructions

B1. The <u>special words</u> referred to in this section are the names of cities and towns plus **domus**, *house, home,* and **rūs**, *countryside.*

B2. Place to which

This is normally expressed by **ad** or **in** + the accusative, but with special words the preposition is omitted.

lēgātōs **ad eum** mittunt, *they send ambassadors **to him*** (*DbG* 1.7)
domum reditiōnis spē, *the hope of returning **home*** (*DbG* 1.5)

In poetry **ad** is sometimes omitted with other words:

Lāvīniaque vēnit **lītora**, *and he came **to the shores** of Lavinium* (*Aen.* 1.2)

In poetry a dative of direction is also used to indicate place to which:

ventūraque dēsuper **urbī**, *and to come down **upon the city** from above* (*Aen.* 2.47)

B3. Place from which

This is normally expressed by **ā/ab** or **ē/ex** + the ablative, but with special words the preposition is omitted:

<u>ab</u> urbe, <u>*from* **the city**</u> (*DbG* 1.7)
domō exīre, *to go out **from home** / to leave **home*** (*DbG* 1.6)

B4. Place in which or on which

B4a. This is normally expressed by **in** + the ablative, but with special words the LOCATIVE CASE is used:

<u>in</u> Galliā ulteriōre, <u>*in* **further Gaul**</u> (*DbG* 1.7)
neque sōlum **domī**, *not only **at home*** (*DbG* 1.18)

In poetry the use of the locative case is extended to other words:

nōn **Libyae**, nōn ante **Tyrō**, *not **in Libya**, not previously **in Tyre*** (*Aen.* 4.36)

B4b. Sometimes the preposition is omitted, particularly in poetry (see example in **B4a** above, **Tyrō**). In prose the preposition is omitted with the word **locus** when it is modified by an adjective, or with any word when modified by **tōtus**:

nōn nūllīs **locīs**, *in several places* (*DbG* 1.6)
tōtā **aciē**, *throughout the whole line of battle* (*DbG* 5.34)

B4c. Forms of the locative: in first and second declension singular, the locative has the same ending as the genitive (**Rōmae**, *in Rome*, **Brundisiī**, *in Brundisium*); in third declension and in all plural names it looks like the ablative or dative (**Carthāginī** or **Carthāgine**, *in Carthage*; **Gadibus**, *in Gades*, **Athēnīs**, *in Athens*).

C. Adjectives

C1. Adjectives modify nouns or pronouns and must agree with the word modified in gender, number, and case:

ab **extrēmīs** Galliae <u>fīnibus</u>, *from the **furthermost** <u>territory</u> of Gaul* (*DbG* 1.1)

C2. Adjectives, usually in the plural, may be used by themselves with no noun to modify; in this situation they function as nouns in the sentence and are called SUBSTANTIVES. In Caesar the possessive adjectives are very often used this way:

(Labiēnus) **nostrōs** expectābat, *(Labienus) was waiting for **our men*** (*DbG* 1.22)
Caesar **suōs** ā proeliō continēbat, *Caesar kept **his men** from battle* (*DbG* 1.15)

Participles can also be used as substantives:

cōnāta perficere, *to complete **the things begun** / **the undertakings*** (*DbG* 1.3)

C3. Adjectives are sometimes used in Latin with adverbial force:

Invītī adulēscentēs Vercingetorīgī pārent.
*The young men **unwilling(ly)** obey Vercingetorix.* (*DbG* 7.63)

C4. Adjectives have POSITIVE, COMPARATIVE, and SUPERLATIVE degrees. See chart III, page 251, and the examples following it. Comparative adjectives decline in the third declension and superlatives in the first and second.

C4a. The comparative may be translated *-er* (e.g., *higher*) or *more* (e.g., *more difficult*), or by expressions such as *rather . . .* , *quite . . .* , or *too . . .* :

ad **īnferiōrem** partem, *to the **lower** part* (*DbG* 1.1)

C4b. Superlatives may be translated *-est* (e.g., *highest*) or *most* (e.g., *most difficult*) or by expressions such as *very . . .* or *extremely . . .* :

monte Iūrā **altissimō**, *by the **very high** Jura mountain(s)* (*DbG* 1.2)

When preceded by **quam**, superlatives mean *as . . . as possible*:

quam plūrimās cīvitātēs, *as many tribes **as possible*** (*DbG* 1.9)

C5. A comparison can be expressed with an ablative of comparison (**A5k**) or with **quam**:

pulverem **maiōrem** <u>quam</u> cōnsuētūdō ferret
*a larger cloud of dust **than** usual* (lit., ***than** custom brought*) (*DbG* 4.32)

C6. The superlative is often found with a partitive genitive:

<u>hōrum omnium</u> **fortissimī**, ***the bravest** <u>of all these</u>* (*DbG* 1.1)

D. Adverbs

D1. Adverbs modify verbs, adjectives, or other adverbs.

D2. Many adverbs are formed from adjectives; see chart XII, page 257, for the rules.

D3. Adverbs have positive, comparative and superlative degrees; see chart XII, page 257. The comparative adverb is identical to the neuter comparative adjective, usually ending in **-ius**, while superlative adverbs usually end in **-ē**.

E. Pronouns

E1. Pronouns take the place of nouns, referring to a noun the reader already knows.

E2a. The REFLEXIVE PRONOUN **sē** or its alternative form **sēsē** = *himself, herself, itself, them-*

selves. This pron. makes no distinction of gender or number; see chart VII, page 254.

E2b. The pronoun **sē** or **sēsē** in indirect commands, indirect statements, and some other situations refers back to the subject of the main verb when it indicates the thinking of the subject (called an INDIRECT REFLEXIVE):

Cotta **sē** ad armātum hostem itūrum negat.
*Cotta says that **he** will not go to an armed enemy.* (*DbG* 5.36)
Caesar questus quod, cum pācem ab **sē** petīssent
*Caesar complained that, after they had asked for peace from **him*** (*DbG* 4.27)

E3. For the RELATIVE PRONOUN, see chart VIII, page 254 above, and **O2c–e** and **N7** below.

E4. The INTERROGATIVE PRONOUN **quis, quid** asks a question; see chart IX, page 255.

E5. Latin has several INDEFINITE PRONOUNS, which are also used as adjectives.

E5a. The basic indefinite word in Latin is **aliquis**, *someone, anyone*; see chart X and the note below it, page 255. The indefinite **quispiam** also means *someone, anyone* but is quite rare. **Quisquam** means the same as **aliquis** but is used in a negative context (e.g., with a word such as **numquam**, *never*, or **negāre**, *to deny*).

E5b. After **sī, nisi, num**, and **nē**, the pronoun **quis/quid** means *someone/anyone* (i.e., is equivalent to **aliquis**):

s̲ī̲ **quid** vellent, *i̲f̲ they wanted **anything** (else)* (*DbG* 1.7)
n̲ē̲ **quis** ēnūntiāret, *t̲h̲a̲t̲ **anyone** should not (= no one should) report* (*DbG* 1.30)

E5c. Likewise, **quī, quae, quod** = *some/any* is used instead of the adjective **aliquī, aliqua, aliquod** after **sī, nisi, num**, and **nē**.

E6. DEMONSTRATIVE PRONOUNS point out something out. They are also used as adjectives. See chart XI, page 256.

F. Conjugated Verbs

F1. Definitions.

F1a. A CONJUGATED verb has a personal ending that agrees with the subject (as opposed to an infinitive or a gerund): e.g., **habēbā̲m̲u̲s̲, dabu̲n̲t̲**, and **reppulissē̲s̲**.

F1b. Latin has three MOODS: the INDICATIVE, that states a fact or asks a simple question; the SUBJUNCTIVE, that indicates uncertainty and is also used in many kinds of subordinate clauses; and the IMPERATIVE, that expresses a command.

F1c. The subject of a Latin verb may be expressed with a noun or pronoun, or shown through the PERSONAL ENDING:

Is sibi lēgātiōnem suscēpit. *He took for himself the diplomatic mission.* (*DbG* 1.3)
ut suprā dēmōnstrāvimus, *as we have pointed out previously* (*DbG* 5.3)

F1d. Some verbs and phrases are IMPERSONAL; that is, they are never found with a person as the subject. Sometimes no subject is expressed (e.g., **lūcet**, *it is light*), or an infinitive phrase or a clause may serve as the subject. We often use the English pronoun 'it' to translate such verbs:

poenam sequī **oportēbat**
*for the punishment to be inflicted (on him) **was proper** / **it was proper** for the punishment to be inflicted (on him)* (*DbG* 1.4)

F1e. A TRANSITIVE verb must be completed by a direct object in the accusative case:
coniūrātiōnem nōbilitātis fēcit, *he made a conspiracy of the nobles* (*DbG* 1.2)

F1f. An INTRANSITIVE verb may have no object or may be completed by an object in the genitive, dative, or ablative case (the dative is by far the most common of the three):
Rhodanus fluit, *the Rhône flows* (*DbG* 1.6)
persuādet Casticō, *he persuades Casticus* (*DbG* 1.3)

F1g. A LINKING VERB connects a subject with a predicate noun or adjective. Esse and fierī are the most common linking verbs; some verbs in the passive can also be linking:
quī Celtae appellantur, *who are called Celts* (*DbG* 1.1)

F2. Tenses of the indicative.

F2a. The present tense describes an action or a state of being in present time:
Gallōs ab Aquitānīs Garumna flūmen dīvidit
the Garonne River divides the Gauls from the Aquitani (*DbG* 1.1)

The present tense may also describe an action begun in the past and continuing into the present:
iam septem annōs hīc habitant, *they have been living here for seven years now*

F2b. Sometimes writers, particularly historians, use the present tense even though they are describing events in the past. This is called the HISTORIC PRESENT or VIVID PRESENT and is intended to make the action more vivid for the reader:
ad eās rēs cōnficiendās Orgetorīx dēligitur,
Orgetorix is chosen to complete these things (*DbG* 1.3)

F2c. The imperfect tense describes an ongoing, repeated, or habitual action in the past:
quī eō tempore prīncipātum obtinēbat
who at that time was holding the leadership (*DbG* 1.3)

The imperfect can indicate the beginning of an action in past time:
Gallī cōnsilia faciēbant, *the Gauls began to make plans*

The imperfect can also describe an action begun in the past and continuing up to a certain point in the past:
Cum trēs hōrās iam nāvigābāmus, magna temptestās orta est.
When we had been sailing now for three hours, a great storm arose.

F2d. The future tense indicates an action that will take place subsequent to the present:
Caesar ad castra mox adveniet. *Caesar will arrive soon at the camp.*

F2e. The perfect tense indicates an action that occurred in past time (without the idea of ongoing or repetitive action that is expressed by the imperfect):
coniūrātiōnem nōbilitātis fēcit, *he made a conspiracy of the nobles* (*DbG* 1.2)

The perfect may indicate a state or condition at the present time resulting from actions that were completed in the past:
Frūmentum distribūtum est.
The grain has been distributed (and so the soldiers now have their rations).
quod plērumque accidere cōnsuēvit
which usually is accustomed to happen (*DbG* 5.33)

F2f. The pluperfect tense describes an action completed prior to some other event in the past:
id quod cōnstituerant facere, *that which they had decided to do* (*DbG* 1.5)

F2g. The future perfect describes an action that will have been completed before another action in the future begins:

> Tribus hōrīs mīlitēs castra **mūnīverint.**
> *Within three hours the soldiers **will have fortified** the camp.*

Note that Latin uses the future perfect in clauses introduced by **cum** and **sī** if the action must logically be completed before something else in the future happens, although in English we use the present in such situations:

> Vōbīs, sī labōrem **cōnfēceritis,** abīre licēbit.
> *If you finish (lit., **will have finished**) your work, you will will be allowed to leave.*

F2h. Verbs whose perfect stem ends in the letter 'v' may form contractions by dropping the 'v' syllable in any tense of the perfect system (those tenses formed from the third principal part—perfect, pluperfect, and future perfect); these are sometimes called SYNCOPATED forms:

> **oppugnārant = oppugnāverant** (*DbG* 1.5)

F2i. In poetry and sometimes in prose the ending -**ēre** is found instead of -**ērunt** in the third person plural of the perfect tense. Distinguish this from a present infinitive by noting that the -**ēre** is attached to the perfect stem (third prin. part minus -ī).

> Tyriī **tenuēre** colōnī, *settlers from Tyre **held** (the city)* (*Aen.* 1.12)

F2j. In the perfect, pluperfect, and future perfect passive, the helping verb usually comes after the perfect participle. Caesar often reverses this order and sometimes separates the two pieces of the verb:

> unde **erant profectae,** *from where they **had set out*** (*DbG* 4.28)
> sī **essent** hostēs **pulsī,** *if the enemy **had been driven back*** (*DbG* 4.35)

F2k. In sentences that express a generalization or a repeated action, the perfect and pluperfect are used in subordinate clauses to refer to present and past time respectively:

> sī quī eōrum dēcrētō nōn **stetit,** sacrificiīs interdīcunt
> *if anyone **does** not **obey** their decree, they prohibit (him) from sacrifices* (*DbG* 6.13)
> ubi singulārēs **cōnspexerant,** adoriēbantur
> *when(ever) they **caught sight of** individuals, they attacked (them)* (*DbG* 4.26)

F2l. Roman authors frequently omit **esse** from the perfect passive and future active infinitives, and sometimes from the perfect passive indicative (such omission is called ELLIPSIS). Caesar almost always does so with future infinitives:

> intellēgebat magnō cum perīculō prōvinciae <u>futūrum</u> (esse)
> *he understood that this **would be** very dangerous for the Province* (*DbG* 1.10)

F3. Voice.

F3a. Verbs may be either active or passive in voice.

F3b. In the ACTIVE voice, the subject performs the action:

> <u>Aeduī</u> lēgātōs ad Caesarem **mittunt**
> *the <u>Aedui</u> **send** ambassadors to Caesar* (*DbG* 1.11)

F3c. In the PASSIVE voice, the subject is acted upon rather than performing the action:

> locī nātūrā <u>Helvētiī</u> **continentur**
> *the <u>Helvetians</u> **are hemmed in** by the nature of the terrain* (*DbG* 1.2)

Note that the passive voice represents a transformation of an underlying active verb;

for this reason many ideas can be expressed in the active or in the passive with the same meaning (although with a different emphasis):

legiō castra cōnficit ⇨ castra ā legiōne cōnficiuntur

the legion completes the camp ⇨ *the camp is completed by the legion*

F3d. A verb may be used impersonally (**F1d**) in the passive when the writer wishes to emphasize the action, not the person who performed it; this is called an IMPERSONAL PASSIVE. Look for an English equivalent that stresses process or action; sometimes the only good option is to translate an impersonal passive actively.

pugnātum est ācriter, *there **was** fierce **fighting** / **they fought** fiercely* (DbG 4.26)

F3e. Intransitive verbs (**F1e**) are never used personally in the passive in Latin; if an author wishes to use such a verb in the passive, it must be made impersonal. If such a verb takes a dative object, that object stays in the dative:

<u>quibus</u> esset persuāsum

<u>*to whom*</u> ***it had been persuaded***, less lit., *who had been persuaded* (DbG 5.31)

F3f. If an impersonal passive is put into indirect statement, it appears as a passive infinitive with no subject in the accusative:

ācriter **pugnātur**, ***the fighting is*** *fierce* ⇨

<u>dīcunt</u> ācriter **pugnārī**, <u>*they say that*</u> ***the fighting is*** *fierce*

F3g. Some verbs, called DEPONENTS, have passive forms but active meanings:

angustōs sē fīnēs habēre **arbitrantur**

they think *that they have a small territory* (DbG 1.2)

eōdem ūsī cōnsiliō, ***having adopted*** (lit., ***made use of***) *the same plan* (DbG 1.5)

If you see what looks like a passive verb that is clearly accompanied by a direct object (acc. case), then you are dealing with a deponent:

hostēs <u>impedītōs</u> **adoriēbantur**

*the enemy **attacked** <u>the hindered (men)</u>* (DbG 4.26)

Verbs of motion that appear in passive forms are normally deponent:

Ambiorīx statim in Aduātucōs **proficīscitur**

*Ambiorix immediately **sets out** into (the territory of) the Aduatuci* (DbG 5.38)

Otherwise you have to check the principal parts if you are uncertain whether a verb is deponent or a true passive.

F3h. A few verbs are SEMI-DEPONENT, with active forms in the present, imperfect, and future tenses but passive forms with active meanings in the perfect, pluperfect, and future perfect:

quae nihil **audet** per sē, *which **dares** nothing on its own* (DbG 6.13)

cīvitātem ignōbilem populō Rōmānō bellum facere **ausam** (**esse**)

*that an obscure tribe **had dared** to make war on the Roman people* (DbG 5.28)

Semi-deponent verbs include **audeō**, *to dare*, **cōnfīdō**, *to trust*, **gaudeō**, *to rejoice*, and **soleō**, *to be accustomed*.

F4. Commands

F4a. The IMPERATIVE mood expresses a command:

'Dēsilīte,' inquit, 'mīlitēs,' ***'Jump down,*** *soldiers' he said* (DbG 4.25)

F4b. A negative command is usually expressed by **nōlī** (sing.) or **nōlīte** (pl.) with an infinitive. A more gentle or polite command can be given by **nē** with the present or perfect subjunctive:

> **Nōlīte** tantum dēdecus <u>admittere</u>! *Do not commit such a disgraceful crime!*
> **Nē** Rōmānīs <u>resistātis</u>. *Do not resist the Romans.*
> **Nē** hoc <u>dīxeris</u>. *Don't say this.*

In poetry negative commands are sometimes expressed by **nē** plus the imperative:

> equō **nē** <u>crēdite</u>, *do not trust the horse* (*Aen.* 2.48)

F5. The subjunctive mood

F5a. Forms

See charts XVI and XVII (page 260) and chart XIX (page 263) for the forms of the subjunctive. Note that in the present subjunctive, you must know to which conjugation a verb belongs in order to identify the forms correctly:

> **habitet** = present subjunctive (first conjugation);
> **videt** = present indicative (second conjugation);
> **dūcet** = future indicative (third conjugation)

Note also that two common verbs, **esse** and **velle**, along with their compounds, use the letter 'i' to mark the present subjunctive:

> **sīmus, velint** (cf. **sumus, volunt** in the pres. indic.)

F5b. The subjunctive as main verb

In contrast to the indicative, which states a simple fact, the subjunctive conveys uncertainty. The subjunctive as a main verb can express something that the speaker would like to happen (but that may not):

> **Abeāmus!**
> *Let's go!* (called HORTATORY subjunctive; first person plural)
> **Nōbīscum veniat!**
> *Let him come with us!* (called JUSSIVE subjunctive; third person)

The subjunctive is used in a rhetorical question if a speaker is unsure what to do:

> Quō **eam**? Quid **faciam**?
> *Where should I go? What am I to do?* (called DELIBERATIVE subjunctive)

For the POTENTIAL subjunctive, see **P5**.

F5c. There are many types of subordinate clauses that use the subjunctive (hence the name 'subjunctive' from **subiungere**, *to join under*). These are tabulated in §O and §P beginning on page 284 below.

G. Participles

G1. Definition

A participle is a VERBAL ADJECTIVE, that is, an adjective formed from a verb. Because it comes from a verb, it has tense and voice. Since it is an adjective, it must agree with a noun (unless it is used as a substantive [**C2**]). Latin has four participles. See chart XX, page 264, for the forms.

G2. Present participles

The present participle is built on the present stem with the markers -ns (nom. sing.) and -nt- (all other forms); it belongs to the third declension (see chart IV, page 252). The present participle describes an action taking place at the same time as the main verb; its literal translation is —*ing*:

> nostrīs mīlitibus **cūnctantibus**, "Dēsilīte," inquit
> *to our **hesitating** soldiers he said, "Jump down"* (*DbG* 4.25)

G3. Perfect participles

G3a. The perfect passive participle is the fourth principal part of transitive verbs and uses first/second declension endings. It describes an action taking place prior to the main verb; its literal translation is *(having been)* —*ed*:

> rēgnī cupiditāte **inductus**
> *(having been) **influenced** by a desire for supreme power* (*DbG* 1.2)

G3b. The perfect participle of deponent verbs is active in meaning, not passive:

> eōdem **ūsī** cōnsiliō, ***having adopted*** (lit., ***made use of***) *the same plan* (*DbG* 1.5)

G3c. Poets sometimes use a perfect passive participle with a reflexive sense (imitating a Greek construction called the middle voice, which shows that the subject is personally involved in the action):

> lacrimīs oculōs **suffūsa** nitentēs, ***filled** with tears in respect to her shining eyes /*
> *with her shining eyes **filled** with tears* (*Aen.* 1.228)

G4. Future participles

G4a. The future active participle is formed by taking the fourth principal part and adding -ūr- to the stem, plus a first/second declension ending: e.g., **datūrus** from **datus**, perf. part. of **dare**. In this book future participles are given as the fourth principal part of intransitive verbs since such verbs do not have perfect passive participles. The future active participle describes an action taking place after the main verb and can be translated *about to* —, *going to* —, or *intending to* —:

> quod sēcum **portātūrī** erant, *what they were **going to** carry with them* (*DbG* 1.5)

G4b. In poetry the future participle occasionally expresses purpose:

> īnspectūra domōs **ventūra**que dēsuper urbī
> *to look into (our) homes and to come down upon the city from above* (*Aen.* 2.47)

G4c. See **H1** below for the future passive participle.

G5. Alternative translations of participles

Participles may be translated in a variety of ways in addition to their literal meanings. They are often translated as relative clauses (*who, which, that*) or as subordinate clauses, using the conjunctions *since, because, when, although,* or *if*; present participles can also be translated *while*, and perfect participles *after*. The best choice depends upon the context.

> Hunc illī ē nāve ēgressum comprehenderant
> *They had seized him after he had left the ship* (*DbG* 4.27)
> Damnātum poenam sequī oportēbat
> *It was proper that the punishment be inflicted on him if found guilty* (*DbG* 1.4)

G6. Participial phrases

A participle and any words whose meaning goes closely with it make up a PARTICIPIAL PHRASE. Be careful about where such phrases start and end; they very often come after the noun they modify and end with the participle:

partem <u>ex longinquiōribus locīs</u> **arcessītam**

*a part, **summoned** from more distant places* (*DbG* 4.27)

G7. Participles as substantives

Participles may be used as substantives (**C2**):

cōnāta perficere

*to complete (their) **undertakings*** (lit., ***things undertaken***) (*DbG* 1.3)

H. Gerundive and Gerund

H1. A GERUNDIVE, or future passive participle, is formed on the present stem with the marker -**nd**-; it has the same case endings as **magnus, -a, -um**. See chart xx, page 264. Its lit. translation is *to be —ed* and it is sometimes used this way as a simple participle:

ūnam in Morinōs **dūcendam** dedit

*he assigned one **to be lead** into (the territory of) the Morini* (*DbG* 5.24)

H2. Gerundives may be combined with a form of **esse** to express obligation or necessity, a construction called the PASSIVE PERIPHRASTIC or GERUNDIVE OF OBLIGATION. The tense of **esse** determines whether the expression refers to the past, the present, or the future. The dative (not **ā** with the ablative) may be used to indicate the person by whom the action must be performed. A passive periphrastic may be translated actively if the literal translation is awkward English.

<u>Caesarī</u> omnia ūnō tempore **erant agenda**

*everything **had to be done** <u>by Caesar</u> at the same time* (*DbG* 2.20)

Caesar nōn **exspectandum** <u>sibi</u> (**esse**) statuit, *Caesar decided that <u>he</u> **should** not wait*, lit., ***it should not be waited** <u>by him</u>* (*DbG* 1.11)

Note: if the verb is intransitive (**F3d**), the passive periphrastic becomes an impersonal construction, as in the second example above.

H3. A GERUND is a verbal noun in the neuter singular only, using the same marker -**nd**- as the gerundive, with second declension neuter endings (but no nominative). See chart XXII, page 264.

H4a. The Romans normally used a gerundive rather than a gerund with a direct object. One could say **in cōnsilia capiendō**, *at making plans*, with **cōnsilia** as an acc. direct object of the gerund **capiendō**, but usually one finds **in cōnsiliīs capiendīs** (*DbG* 4.5) with the noun **cōnsiliīs** in the ablative and a gerundive modifying it. Remember that a gerund<u>ive</u> is an adject<u>ive</u>.

H4b. Neuter plural pronouns are an exception to the above: e.g., **haec dīcendō**, *by saying these things*, where **haec** is kept as a direct object in the acc. of the gerund **dīcendō**.

H5a. In general, gerunds and gerundives may be used in the same way as other nouns in various cases; e.g., **pīlīs coiciendīs**, *by throwing spears*, is an ablative of means. But gerunds are never used in the nom.; the infinitive is used instead (see **Q2a**).

H5b. Gerunds and gerundives may be used with **ad** + acc. to express purpose:

ad eās rēs **cōnficiendās**, *to accomplish these things* (*DbG* 1.3)

H5c. Gerunds and gerundives may be used with **causā** or **grātiā** to express purpose; note that **causā** or **grātiā** comes after the gerund(ive):

bellī īnferendī <u>causā</u>
<u>for the sake</u> of making war, (in order) to make war (DbG 4.30)

I. Supine

I1. A supine is a verbal noun, formed from the same stem as the perfect passive participle (the 4th principal part). It has only two cases and two uses.

I2. In the abl., with the fourth declension ending -ū, the supine is used as an ablative of respect or specification (**A5e**) to complete the meaning of some adjectives:

<u>perfacile</u> **factū**, <u>very easy</u> **to do** (DbG 1.3)

I3a. In the acc. (ending -**um**), the supine is used with a verb of motion to express purpose:

lēgātōs ad Caesarem <u>mittunt</u> **rogātum** auxilium
they <u>send</u> ambassadors to Caesar **to request** help (DbG 1.11)

I3b. At first glance you might think a supine in the accusative was a perfect participle. To distinguish the two forms, check whether the clause contains a verb of motion and whether there is an acc. sing. noun that the word might agree with (in which case it is a perfect participle, not a supine).

II. Sentence Structure (Syntax)

J. Basic Sentence Patterns

All Latin clauses and sentences are built on one of the following six patterns:

J1. A subject and an intransitive verb:

Caesar mox <u>adveniet</u>. *Caesar <u>will arrive</u> soon.*

J2. A subject, an intransitive verb, and an object in the genitive, dative, or ablative:

Gallī <u>imperiō</u> Caesaris <u>pārēbunt</u>. *The Gauls <u>will obey</u> Caesar's <u>command</u>.*

J3. A subject, a linking verb, and a complement:

Caesar <u>creātus erat</u> <u>prōcōnsul</u>. *Caesar <u>had been chosen</u> <u>governor</u>.*

J4. The verb **esse** (usually first in the sentence) stating the existence of something:

Erant omnīnō itinera duo, *There were in all two routes* (DbG 1.6)

J5a. A subject, a transitive verb, and a direct object:

Orgetorīx <u>omnem suam familiam</u> <u>coēgit</u>
Orgetorix <u>gathered</u> <u>all his household</u>. (DbG 1.4)

J5b. Pattern 5a may be expanded by adding an indirect object in the dative:

Is **sibi** lēgātiōnem suscēpit
*He took **for/upon himself** a diplomatic mission* (DbG 1.3)

J5c. Pattern 5a may be modified by being put into the passive voice (see **F3c**):

Ea rēs **est** Helvētiīs **ēnūntiāta**
*This matter **was revealed** to the Helvetians* (DbG 1.4)

J6. An impersonal passive (**F3d–F3e**):

Cōnsurgitur ex cōnsiliō, *They rise from the council* (DbG 5.31)

J7. A sentence must contain at least one main clause of the types listed in **J1–J6** above. It may contain two or more main clauses connected by **et, sed**, or another coordinating conjunction; this is called a COMPOUND SENTENCE. A sentence may also contain a main clause and one or more subordinate clauses, called a COMPLEX SENTENCE. The types of subordinate clauses are tabulated in **§O** below; like main clauses, all subordinate clauses are built using one of the six patterns listed above.

K. Agreement

K1. A verb must agree with its subject in person and in number:
> <u>Helvētiī</u> reliquōs Gallōs virtūte **praecēdunt**
> *The Helvetians* **surpass** *the other Gauls in courage* (*DbG* 1.1)

K2. An adjective (or a participle) must agree with the noun it describes in gender, number, and case:
> **fortissimī** sunt <u>Belgae</u>, *the bravest are* <u>*the Belgae*</u> (*DbG* 1.1)
> **Belgae** is masc. pl. nom. and therefore **fortissimī** is also masc. pl. nom.

K3. Roman authors sometimes use the first person plural rather than the singular:
> ut suprā **dēmōnstrāvimus**, *as we (= I) have pointed out previously* (*DbG* 2.1)

K4. A plural noun is often found in Latin where English uses a singular. This is particularly common in poetry and is sometimes called the POETIC PLURAL:
> hīs **subsidia** submittēbat, *he sent* **help(s)** *to these men* (*DbG* 4.26)
> et **terrīs** iactātus et altō, *tossed about* **on land(s)** *and sea* (*Aen.* 1.3)

L. Modifiers

L1. Nouns can be modified by adjectives, nouns in the genitive, or relative clauses:
> nāvēs **onerāriae**, *transport ships*
> nāvēs **Caesaris**, *ships of Caesar / Caesar's ships*
> nāvēs **quae equitēs sustulerant**, *ships which had picked up cavalry* (*DbG* 4.28)

L2. Verbs can be modified by adverbs and by other elements that function as adverbs (nouns in the ablative, ablative absolutes, and adverbial clauses):
> **statim** lēgātōs mīsērunt, *they* **immediately** *sent ambassadors* (*DbG* 4.27)
> hostēs **proeliō** superātī, *the enemy defeated* **in battle** (*DbG* 4.27)

L3. Adjectives and adverbs may be modified by adverbs and by nouns in the ablative:
> **paulō** maior, *a little bigger* (lit., *bigger* **by a little**)

M. Expectations

M1. Basic Expectations.

M1a. A noun or pronoun in the nominative creates the expectation of a conjugated verb.

M1b. A transitive verb creates the expectation of a direct object (acc.).

M1c. A preposition creates the expectation of an object in the acc. or the abl.

M1d. A subordinating conjunction (**postquam, cum, ut**, etc.) or a relative pronoun (**O2b**) creates the expectation of a conjugated verb.

M1e. An adjective or a noun in the genitive creates the expectation of a noun to modify.

M1f. Paying attention to expectations helps you comprehend Latin better because they alert you to the elements that you may find later in a sentence. Most importantly, they often help you know when a phrase or clause is complete. As you get more experienced at reading Latin, you will respond more automatically to the expectations created by various types of words—as you already do subconsciously in English.

M1g. We sometimes must revise our expectations when we come to the end of a clause or a sentence. E.g., an adjective creates the expectation of a noun to be modified; but if it turns out there is no such noun, then the adjective is a substantive (**C2**).

M2. Enclosing word order

Roman authors often combined the principle of expectation with word order to show what words go together to make a phrase:

in hōrum hominum **terrā**, *in the land of these men*

in begins the phrase, but since prepositions are never completed by the genitive we know that the phrase does not end at **hominum**; the ablative **terrā** completes the expectation created by the preposition. The author is clearly indicating that the genitive phrase belongs with **terrā**. If it were written **in terrā hōrum hominum**, the likelihood would be greater that **hōrum hominum** could modify another noun later in the sentence. We use the term ENCLOSING WORD ORDER is used to describe such expressions.

M3. Nested clauses

M3a. A clause may begin and then, before it is complete, be interrupted by another clause. We say that the second or inner clause is NESTED or EMBEDDED inside the outer one:

ut aliae eōdem <u>unde erant profectae</u> referrentur
that some (ships) were carried back to the same place <u>from where they had set out</u> (*DbG* 4.28)

M3b. Rule: the first clause, the interrupted one, cannot resume until the second or inner clause is complete.

N. Word Order and Flow of Ideas

N1a. Adjectives (in prose) and relative clauses usually come after the nouns they modify:

dē <u>fīnibus</u> suīs, *from their <u>territory</u>* (*DbG* 1.2)
<u>Germānīs</u>, quī trāns Rhēnum incolunt
the <u>Germans</u>, who live across the Rhine (*DbG* 1.1)

N1b. On occasion a relative clause comes before its antecedent:

et, quōs labōrantēs cōnspexerat, <u>hīs</u> subsidia submittēbat
and he sent help(s) <u>to these</u> whom he had seen struggling (*DbG* 4.26)
The word order in this example reflects the order of events (cf. **N5** below); first Caesar noticed the men in difficulty, then he sent them help.

N1c. Adjectives of size and quantity, most demonstrative adjectives, and numbers usually come before the noun they describe:

tantus subitō <u>timor</u>, *suddenly such a great <u>fear</u>* (*DbG* 1.39)
ob hās <u>causās</u>, *for these <u>reasons</u>* (*DbG* 4.24)

N1d. If a prepositional phrase includes an adjective and a noun, the preposition is often placed in the middle of the phrase:

quā ex parte, *for this reason* (*DbG* 1.2)

N1e. In poetry, adjs. often come before their nouns and are often separated from them:

Iovis **rapidum** iaculāta ē nūbibus ignem
*having hurled the **swift** fire of Jupiter from the clouds* (*Aen.* I.42)
aeternum servāns sub pectore vulnus
*preserving the **never-ending** wound under her heart* (*Aen.* 1.26)

N2. Adverbial modifiers generally come in front of their head words:

neque **longius** prōsequī potuērunt, *they could not follow farther* (*DbG* 4.26)

N3. The most common and neutral word order in Latin is subject–object–verb:

Helvētiī reliquōs Gallōs virtūte praecēdunt.
The Helvetians surpass the other Gauls in courage. (*DbG* 1.1)

N4. The statements about Latin word order above are generally true, but Roman writers took full advantage of the fact that the noun and verb endings of Latin allow for considerable variety in word order. They used word order to structure the ideas that they wanted to communicate to the reader. In particular, the topic of conversation, information that is already known, or something that relates to a previous thought is often put first, with new information or the writer's comment on old information at the end:

proptereā quod aliud iter habērent **nūllum**
*because they had **no** other route* (*DbG* 1.7)

The Helvetian envoy is making the point that they really had no other way to leave their homeland and so places **nūllum** at the end because it is the essence of the point he wants to make.

Hōc proeliō factō reliquās cōpiās Helvētiōrum ut cōnsequī posset, pontem in Arare faciendum cūrat atque ita exercitum trādūcit.
After this battle had taken place, in order to pursue the remaining forces of the Helvetians, he arranges for a bridge to be built on the (River) Arar and so leads his army across. (*DbG* 1.13)

Immediately before the sentence quoted here, Caesar described the defeat of one part of the Helvetian forces. The following sentence begins by recapitulating this information (**Hōc proeliō factō**) then moves to what was probably already in the reader's mind: what about the rest of the Helvetians? The words **reliquās cōpiās** appear to the left of their clause marker **ut** in order to preserve this flow of ideas. Caesar next reveals in a purpose clause **ut cōnsequī posset** his intention to pursue them, which is new information (since he might have let them go or handled the situation in some other way). Then Caesar finishes with two simple statements about building a bridge and crossing the river, which are also new information to the reader.

N5. Narrative prose (i.e., that tells a story) usually presents events in the order that they occur, but may use sophisticated sentence structure and word order unlike that of English:

Ambiorīx prōnūntiārī iubet quam in partem Rōmānī impetum fēcerint cēdant, rūrsus sē ad signa recipientēs īnsequantur.
Ambiorix orders the word to be passed that they should withdraw where (lit., *in what direction*) *the Romans attacked (and) should pursue them as they returned to their standards.* (*DbG* 5.34)

To make a normal English sentence, we need to put *withdraw* and *pursue* before the clauses that depend on them, but in Latin the order of the words shows the exact sequence of events: Ambiorix gives an order; the Romans attack; the Gauls withdraw from that section; the Romans start back; the Gauls pursue them.

N6. Adverbs that show the logical relationship between sentences or clauses are used more often than they are in English. **Enim** and **nam,** *for,* explain the reason for what was said in the previous clause or sentence; **ergō** and **igitur,** *therefore,* show the logical consequence of the previous statement; **tamen,** *however, nevertheless,* shows a contrast with what was just said; and **autem,** *moreover, and now,* can also indicate a contrast or can mark the transition into a different idea.

N7. The Romans often used a relative pronoun (**quī, quae, quod**) at the beginning of a sentence to tie the new thought closely to the preceding one; this is called a CON-NECTING RELATIVE or LINKING QUĪ. Such connecting relatives can be translated by an English demonstrative (*this, that*) or by a personal pronoun introduced by a conjunction (e.g., *and he, but they*):

> **Quibus** rēbus nostrī perterritī, *Terrified by **these** things, our men* . . . (*DbG* 4.24)
> **Quae** cum appropinquārent Britanniae
> *And while **they** were approaching Britain* (*DbG* 4.28)

In the first example **Quibus rēbus** refers back to the tactics of the British discussed in the previous sentence. The second example comes immediately after Caesar's statement that the ships (**nāvēs,** fem. pl., which explains the form **quae**) carrying the cavalry set sail from Gaul.

N8. In phrases or clauses with parallel structure, a word may be expressed only once but mentally supplied by the reader in another phrase or clause, a usage called GAPPING:

> longās **nāvēs** aestūs complēverat, et onerāriās tempestās adflīctābat
> *the tide had filled the long **ships**, and the storm was damaging the cargo (**ships**)*
> (*DbG* 4.29)

O. Subordinate Clauses

O1. Beginnings and ends of clauses

O1a. Subordinate clauses are introduced by a relative pronoun (**quī, quae, quod**) or by a subordinating conjunction or question word (**O4b–d**); they end when the meaning of the clause is complete, which is often—in Caesar, almost always—marked by a verb:

> ut rēgnum in cīvitāte suā <u>occupāret</u>
> *that <u>he should seize</u> power in his tribe* (*DbG* 1.3)

O1b. On occasion words appear to the left of their clause marker:

> Tyriās ōlim <u>quae</u> verteret arcēs
> <u>*who*</u> *would overturn **at some time** the **Tyrian** citadel(s)* (*Aen.* 1.20)

O2. Adjectival clauses

O2a. An ADJECTIVAL CLAUSE acts like an adjective, i.e., it describes a noun or pronoun.

O2b. There is only one type of adjectival clause in Latin, the RELATIVE CLAUSE. A relative clause usually begins with a form of the relative pronoun **quī, quae, quod**; it ends when its meaning is complete, often marked by the verb at the end of the clause. Most relative clauses have their verbs in the indicative; see **O2f–O2i** below for less common situations where the verb is in the subjunctive. (For the relative pronoun used to make a transition from one sentence to another, see **N7**.)

O2c. A relative pronoun takes its gender and number from the noun it describes, called the ANTECEDENT; its case depends on how it is used in the relative clause:

Allobrogum, **quī** nūper pācātī erant

*of the Allobroges, **who** recently had been pacified* (*DbG* 1.6)

quī is masc. pl. because its antecedent **Allobrogēs** is masc. pl.; it is nom. since it is the subject of the rel. clause (the fact that **Allobrogum** is gen. does not matter).

partēs trēs, **quārum** ūnam incolunt Belgae

*three parts, **of which** the Belgae inhabit one* (*DbG* 1.1)

quārum is fem. pl. because **partēs** is fem. pl.; it is gen. since it is a partitive with **ūnam**

O2d. The antecedent is sometimes repeated or put inside the relative clause:

diem dīcunt, quā **diē** omnēs conveniant

*they fix a day, on which **(day)** all would assemble* (*DbG* 1.6)

quī diēs maritimōs aestūs maximōs efficere cōnsuēvit

the day which is accustomed to bring about the most extreme tides (*DbG* 4.39)

O2e. The pronoun **is** often serves as the antecedent of a rel. pron.; such combinations may be translated *he/she who, the one(s) who, those who* (pl.), *the things which* (n. pl.):

eī **quī** in statiōne erant, *those **who** were on guard* (*DbG* 4.32)

The form of **is** is sometimes omitted and must be supplied in translation:

quī erant in agrīs relictī discessērunt

*(those) **who** had been left behind in the fields departed* (*DbG* 4.34)

O2f. A relative clause with its verb in the subjunctive may characterize someone or something as belonging to a class, i.e., as being a type of person or thing rather than just one particular example; this is a RELATIVE CLAUSE OF CHARACTERISTIC:

vix **quā** singulī carrī **dūcerentur**

*along which carts scarcely **could be taken** one at a time* (*DbG* 1.5)

O2g. A relative clause with its verb in the subjunctive may express CAUSE:

quī nihil ante **prōvīdisset**,

***because he had anticipated** nothing beforehand* (*DbG* 5.33)

O2h. A relative clause with its verb in the subjunctive may express PURPOSE:

mittunt nōbilissimōs cīvitātis, **quī dīcerent**

*they sent the noblest (men) of the tribe **to say*** (*DbG* 1.7)

O2i. A relative clause with its verb in the subjunctive may express RESULT:

Secūtae sunt tempestātēs **quae** nostrōs in castrīs **continērent**

*There followed storms **which kept** our men in camp* (*DbG* 4.34)

O2j. It is sometimes difficult to distinguish the various usages of the subjunctive in relative clauses. You may consider any such clause as a clause of characteristic unless the context clearly indicates cause, purpose or result. Also remember that a relative clause inside indirect statement will have its verb in the subjunctive (**Q4e**) in any case.

O3. **Noun clauses**

O3a. A NOUN CLAUSE acts in the same way that a noun does; e.g., it can be the subject or direct object of a verb.

O3b. Indirect commands

Verbs such as **imperāre**, *to order*, **monēre**, *to warn*, **ōrāre**, *to beg*, **persuādēre**, *to persuade*, etc., may be completed by a clause introduced by **ut** (negative **nē**) with its verb in the subjunctive. In English we normally use an infinitive to express such commands, whereas Latin uses a conjugated verb in the subjunctive:

cīvitātī <u>persuāsit</u> ut dē fīnibus suīs **exīrent**

*<u>he persuaded</u> the tribe **to leave** its territory* (DbG 1.2)

The common verb **iubēre**, *to order*, is used with an acc. and infin. phrase (**Q3b**), not with an indirect command:

pontem <u>iubet</u> **rescindī**, *<u>he orders</u> the bridge to be cut down* (DbG 1.7)

O3c. Noun clauses of result

The verb **efficere** is completed by an **ut** clause telling what was accomplished:

commeātūs **ut** ad eum portārī **posset** <u>efficiēbat</u>

<u>he brought it about</u> that it was possible for supplies to be brought to him (DbG 2.5)

Impersonal expressions such as **accidit**, *it happens*, **ēvenit**, *it turns out*, and forms of **fīō** are also followed by noun clauses of result:

hīs rēbus <u>fīēbat</u> **ut vagārentur**

because of these things <u>it happened</u> that they wandered (DbG 1.2)

O3d. Indirect questions

A DIRECT QUESTION repeats the exact words of the speaker (e.g., *"When will you go?"*). If a question is expressed INDIRECTLY (e.g., *He asked when you would go*), it becomes a noun clause introduced by the question word with its verb in the subjunctive:

quanta praedae faciendae facultās **darētur** <u>dēmōnstrāvērunt</u>

<u>they showed</u> what a great opportunity of seizing loot was being offered (DbG 4.34)

O3e. Fear clauses

The verbs **timēre**, **verērī**, and **metuere**, as well as other expressions of fear (e.g., **est metus, est perīculum**) are followed by a subjunctive clause. Affirmative fear clauses are introduced by **nē** and negative ones by **ut** or **ut . . . nōn**:

neque <u>timērent</u> **nē** ab hostibus **circumvenīrentur**

and <u>they did</u> not <u>fear</u> that they would be surrounded by the enemy (DbG 2.26)

O3f. Expressions of doubt

Expressions of doubt in the negative are completed by **quīn** with the subjunct.:

<u>nōn esse dubium</u> **quīn** plūrimum Helvētiī **possent**

<u>there was no doubt</u> that the Helvetians were the most powerful (DbG 1.3)

O4. **Adverbial clauses**

O4a. ADVERBIAL CLAUSES modify the verb or the whole predicate.

O4b. There are many conjunctions that introduce adverbial clauses with verbs in the indicative: **antequam**, *before*, **dum**, *while*, **etsī**, *although*, **postquam**, *after*, **quamquam**, *although*, **quandō**, *when*, **quod**, *because*, **quoniam**, *since*, **ubi**, *when*, **ut**, *as*. These are similar to English usage and usually cause no particular problems in comprehension.

O4c. The conjunction **dum** is used with a present tense verb to describe an action going on at the same time as something in the past:

Dum haec in colloquiō **geruntur**, nūntiātum est . . .
*While these things **were being done** at the conference, it was reported . . .*

O4d. Note that the common conjunction **ut** or **utī** means *when* or *as* if completed by a verb in the indicative, but has other meanings if its verb is subjunctive:

ut Helvētiī **arbitrantur**, <u>*as*</u> *the Helvetians **think*** (*DbG* 1.4)

O4e. The conjunction **cum** with the subjunctive may express cause (**cum** = *since, because*), circumstances (**cum** = *when, while, after*), or concession (**cum** = *although*); you must use the context to determine the meaning of **cum**:

<u>cum</u> virtūte omnibus **praestārent**
<u>*since*</u> *they **surpassed** everyone in courage* (*DbG* 1.2)
<u>Cum</u> cīvitās iūs suum exsequī **cōnārētur**
<u>*While*</u> *the tribe **was trying** to carry out its law* (*DbG* 1.4)

When **cum** is concessive, it is often accompanied by **tamen** in the main clause:

mīlitēs, <u>cum</u> magnopere **timērent**, fugere **tamen** nōn coepērunt
<u>*although*</u> *the soldiers **were very frightened**, **nevertheless** they did not start to flee*

Less frequently, **cum** is used with the indicative to express a particular time (not the general circumstances under which something happens); translate *when*:

<u>cum</u> suīs fīnibus eōs **prohibent**
<u>*when*</u> *(the Belgae) **keep** them (the Germans) away from their territory* (*DbG* 1.1)

O4f. Clauses of anticipation

Antequam and **priusquam** (*before*) and **dum** and **quoad** (*until*) with the subjunctive express anticipation (note that **dum** with the indicative means *while*, the more common meaning of this word):

<u>dum</u> mīlitēs **convenīrent**, <u>*until*</u> *the soldiers **could assemble*** (*DbG* 1.7)

O4g. Result clauses

A subjunctive clause introduced by **ut** (negative **ut . . . nōn**) may express the result of an action. Such clauses are signaled by the presence of a key word in the main clause (**adeō** *to such an extent*, **ita** or **sīc** *in such a way*, **tālis** *such*, **tam** *so*, **tantopere** *so much*, **tantus** *so large, so great, such a great*, **tot** *so many*):

<u>tanta</u> tempestās coorta est **ut** nūlla eārum cursum tenēre **posset**
<u>*such a great*</u> *storm arose **that** none of them **could** hold its course* (*DbG* 4.28)

O4h. Purpose clauses

Purpose is often expressed by a clause introduced by **ut** (negative **nē**) with its verb in the subjunctive. In English we very often use an infinitive to express purpose. This does not happen in Latin, although purpose clauses may be translated as English infinitives, with or without the phrase *in order*:

ut parātiōrēs **essent**,
(in order) to be / so that they would be more ready (*DbG* 1.5)

Negative purpose clauses may be translated *(in order) that . . . not, lest*, or, less literally, *to prevent . . . , to avoid . . .* :

nē causam **dīceret** sē ēripuit
*(Orgetorix) rescued himself **to avoid** pleading his case* (*DbG* 1.4)

A purpose clause that contains a comparative adj. or adv. is introduced by **quō** (not **ut**):

> **quō** <u>facilius</u> prohibēre **possit**
> *in order to be able to stop (the Helvetians) <u>more easily</u>* (*DbG* 1.8)

Other ways to express purpose include gerunds and gerundives (see **H5b, H5c**), the supine in the accusative (**I3**), or a relative clause with the subjunctive (**O2h**).

O5. Sequence of tenses

O5a. The rule that tells a speaker or writer which tense of the subjunctive to use in a subordinate clause is called SEQUENCE OF TENSES. Understanding of sequence is necessary to speak or to write Latin, but it is not usually essential for reading; the rules are given here for the sake of completeness.

O5b. If the main verb in a sentence is in the present, the future, or the perfect expressing a mental state in present time, this is called PRIMARY SEQUENCE. If the main verb is in any of the past tenses—imperfect, perfect (usually), or pluperfect—then we have SECONDARY SEQUENCE.

O5c. The present and imperfect subjunctive show an action that is taking place at the same time as the main verb or after it, while the perfect and pluperfect subjunctive show actions that take place prior to that of the main verb.

	MAIN VERB (INDICATIVE)	SUBORDINATE VERB (SUBJUNCTIVE)
Primary sequence	Rogat	quandō Caesar adveniat, *is arriving, will arrive* quandō Caesar advēnerit, *arrived*
Seconday sequence	Rogābat	quandō Caesar advenīret, *was arriving, would arrive* quandō Caesar advēnisset, *had arrived*

O5d. The perfect subjunctive is occasionally found in result clauses in secondary sequence to emphasize the fact that the action really did take place:

> Gallī tam temerāriī erant ut castra mūnītissima **oppugnāverint**.
> *The Gauls were so reckless that **they attacked** the very well fortified camp.*

O5e. If the main verb is in the historic present (see **F2b**, second half), subordinate clauses in the subjunctive may remain in secondary sequence or be put in primary:

> <u>persuādet</u> Casticō ut rēgnum **occupāret** [secondary]
> *he <u>persuades</u> (or <u>persuaded</u>) Casticus **to seize** power* (*DbG* 1.3)

> omnia <u>excōgitantur</u> quārē nec sine perīculō **maneātur** [primary]
> *all sorts of reasons <u>are imagined</u> (or <u>were imagined</u>) why they **cannot (could not)** stay without danger* (*DbG* 5.31)

P. Conditional Sentences

P1. A CONDITIONAL SENTENCE contains two clauses, a subordinate clause (the PROTASIS) that begins with sī or nisi, and a main clause (the APODOSIS). Conditional sentences come in two types, factual and hypothetical.

P2. FACTUAL or SIMPLE conditions have their verbs in the indicative and usually are easy to understand. Note however that Latin uses the future or future perfect in *if*-clauses referring to the future, while English uses the present:

> Caesar, sī magnīs itineribus iter **faciet**, tribus diēbus cum exercitū **adveniet**.
> *If Caesar **travels** by forced marches, he **will arrive** in three days with the army.*
> Gallī, sī victōrēs **fuerint**, omnia spolia Mārtī **cōnsecrābunt**.
> *If the Gauls **are** victorious, they **will consecrate** all the spoils to Mars.*

P3. HYPOTHETICAL conditions have their verbs in the subjunctive.

P3a. Conditions with the present subjunctive express something that is possible (but not likely) in future time:

> Sī Gallī Caesarem **vincant**, Rōmānī dolōre **afficiantur**. *If the Gauls **were to** defeat/should defeat Caesar, the Romans **would be filled** with grief.*

P3b. Conditions with the imperfect subjunctive express something that is contrafactual, that is, hypothetical or not actually true, at the present time:

> Sī Caesar ipse **adesset**, Gallī rebellāre nōn **audērent**.
> *If Caesar **were here** in person, the Gauls **would** not **dare** to revolt.*

P3c. Conditions with the pluperfect subjunctive express something that is contrafactual in reference to past time:

> Gallī, nisi inter sē tantopere **dissēnsissent**, facilius Caesarī **restitissent**.
> *If the Gauls **had** not **argued** with each other so much, they **would have resisted** Caesar more easily.*

P4. Conditional sentences may be MIXED, i.e., have their verbs in different tenses, as the sense requires:

> Sī Caesar in Italiam **redīsset**, Gallī hiberna nunc **obsidērent**.
> *If Caesar **had gone back** to Italy, the Gauls now **would be besieging** the winter camps.*

P5. Sometimes a main clause with the subjunctive is found that implies, but does not actually state, an *if*-clause; this is called the POTENTIAL SUBJUNCTIVE:

> **Intellegās** Gallōs fortiter restitisse.
> *You **would understand** that the Gauls resisted bravely.*

An *if*-clause such as "If you were to get more information" is implied.

Q. Infinitives

Q1. An infinitive is a VERBAL NOUN, i.e., a noun formed from a verb. It functions in the sentence as any noun would, as a subject, direct object, etc. Note that Latin has two other verbal nouns, the gerund and the supine (see §H and §I); the infinitive is used much more often and in a greater variety of ways than these other verbal nouns.

Q2. Infinitive as subject.

Q2a. An infinitive may serve as the subject of a verb. Often we translate such infinitives by adding the pronoun 'it' in English:

> Latīnē **scīre** est ūtile.
> *To know Latin is useful. It is useful to know Latin.*

Q2b. With impersonal verbs and expressions (**F1d**), the infinitive serves as the subject; but more often we translate such verbs by inserting 'it':

> ut eius voluntāte id sibi **facere** <u>liceat</u>
> *that **to do** this with his permission <u>would be allowed</u> for them*
> *that <u>it would be allowed</u> for them **to do** this with his permission* (DbG 1.7)

Q3. Infinitive as object

Q3a. An infinitive may serve as the object of a verb; this is often called a COMPLEMENTARY infinitive since it completes the meaning of the verb:

> cōnstituērunt ea **comparāre**, *they decided **to prepare** those things* (DbG 1.3)

Q3b. An accusative and infinitive phrase can also serve as the object of certain verbs (e.g., **iubēre**, *to order*, and **vetāre**, *to forbid*):

> **Orgetorīgem ex vinclīs causam dīcere** <u>coēgērunt</u>
> *They forced **Orgetorix to plead** his case in chains* (DbG 1.4)

Q4. Indirect statement

Q4a. DIRECT STATEMENT reproduces the exact words of the speaker: *John said, "We will leave tomorrow."* INDIRECT STATEMENT gives the speaker's word as reported by someone else, introduced by a verb of saying, thinking, etc.: *John said (that) we would leave tomorrow.* In English we sometimes include the conjunction 'that' and sometimes omit it; including 'that' if you translate a Latin sentence may help you to remember that you are dealing with indirect statement, but it is not required.

Q4b. A subject (nom. case) and its conjugated verb become an accusative and infinitive when put into indirect statement; this is the most common type of indirect speech:

> cum nūntiātum esset <u>eōs</u> per prōvinciam nostram iter facere **cōnāri**, *when it had been reported (that) <u>they</u> **were trying** to travel through our Province* (DbG 1.7)

In direct speech, the verb would be **cōnantur** with the subject 'they' probably understood from the personal ending; in indirect statement, the subject must be specified, and put in the acc. case.

Q4c. In indirect statement, an impersonal passive (**F3d**) becomes an infinitive; no subject accusative is expressed, so such sentences may require careful reading in order to understand that an impersonal passive is being used:

> Videt ācriter **pugnārī**. *He sees that **the fighting is fierce**.*

In direct statement the impersonal passive would be **ācriter pugnātur**.

Q4d. A command (imperative) in direct statement becomes subjunctive in indirect:

> (Lēgātīs respondit) ad Īd. Aprīl. **reverterentur**. (DbG 1.7)
> *(He answered the ambassadors) that **they should return** about April 13th.*

Caesar would have said **revertiminī**, *return*, (imperative) when speaking directly to the ambassadors.

Q4e. Any subordinate clause inside indirect statement has its verb in the subjunctive, even if the verb would be indicative in direct speech:

> **quod** nōndum bonō animō in populum Rōmānum **vidērentur**
> *because they **did** not yet **seem** well disposed toward the Romans* (DbG 1.6)

Clauses with **quod** = *because* normally have the indicative, but this clause is found inside the indirect statement **Allobrogibus sēsē persuāsūrōs (esse) exīstimābant**.

Q4f. The pronoun **sē** or **sēsē** in indirect statement always refers back to the person who did the saying, thinking, etc.:

> Cotta **sē** ad armātum hostem itūrum negat.
> *Cotta says that **he** will not go to an armed enemy.* (DbG 5.36)

In the example above *he* = Cotta himself. Compare the following, where *he* = some other person (exactly who would depend on the context):

> Cotta **eum** ad armātum hostem itūrum negat.
> *Cotta says that **he** will not go to an armed enemy.*

Q4g. Infinitives, like participles, do not express an absolute time of their own, but are relative to the time of the main verb.

> i) The present infinitive shows an action taking place at the same time as that of the main verb:

> <u>Arbitrātur</u> Caesarem benignum **esse**. *He <u>thinks</u> that Caesar **is** kind.*
> <u>Arbitrābātur</u> Caesarem benignum **esse**. *He <u>thought</u> that Caesar **was** kind.*

> ii) The perfect infinitive shows an action taking place prior to that of the main verb:

> Caesar <u>scit</u> Helvētiōs populō Rōmānō multīs ante annīs **nocuisse**.
> *Caesar <u>knows</u> that the Helvetians **hurt** the Romans many years earlier.*
> Caesar <u>sciēbat</u> Helvētiōs populō Rōmānō multīs ante annīs **nocuisse**.
> *Caesar <u>knew</u> that the Helvetians **had hurt** the Romans many years earlier.*

> iii) The future infinitive shows an action taking place after that of the main verb:

> Gallī <u>putant</u> Caesarem mox **adventūrum esse**.
> *The Gauls <u>think</u> that Caesar **will arrive** soon.*
> Gallī <u>putābant</u> Caesarem mox **adventūrum esse**.
> *The Gauls <u>thought</u> that Caesar **would arrive** soon.*

In the examples above, note how the translation of the infinitive changes to keep the time relationship correct in relation to the main verb.

Q4h. Indirect statement may be introduced by a context which shows that someone is speaking rather than by a specific verb. E.g., at the beginning of *DbG* 1.2 Caesar explains that Orgetorix persuaded the Helvetians to leave their territory. This is followed by **perfacile esse**, *(and he said) that it was very easy*; this is clearly something that Orgetorix said while talking to the Helvetians.

Q4i. Once begun, indirect statement may continue even though the verb of saying or thinking is not repeated, as long as the context shows that the same speaker is continuing. E.g., *DbG* 5.29 begins with the general Quintus Titurius Sabinus speaking (**Titūrius clāmitābat**), and the rest of the chapter is all expressed in Latin in indirect statement, reporting what Titurius said at the council, but no additional verb of saying is present.

Q5. Historic infinitive

Sometimes an infinitive is used instead of a conjugated verb in one of the past tenses; this is particularly common in the writing of historians. It often conveys a sense of speed or urgency:

cotīdiē Caesar Aeduōs frūmentum **flāgitāre**
*every day Caesar **demanded** grain from the Aedui* (DbG 1.16)
hinc semper Ulixēs / crīminibus **terrēre** novīs
for this reason Ulysses always frightened (me) with new charges (Aen. 2.97–98)

Latin to English Vocabulary

This list includes all basic words that do not appear in the running vocabularies. It also includes all words that appear more than once in this book, i.e., are printed with an asterisk in the running vocabularies. The passage where each word first appears is indicated: 1.1 = Book I, chapter 1. Comparative and superlative adjectives are listed under the positive form (even if the positive does not occur in the selections in this book), unless they are irregular; likewise, adverbs formed regularly from adjectives are not listed separately.

A

ā or ab, prep. + abl., *from, by* (1.1)

abiciō, abicere, abiēcī, abiectus, *to throw away* (5.37)

absum, abesse, āfuī, āfutūrus, irreg., *to be away, be absent, be distant* (1.1)

ac, conj., *and*; after a word implying a comparison, *than, as* (1.3)

accēdō, accēdere, accessī, accessūrus, *to approach* (5.37)

*accidit, accidere, accidit, *it happens* (4.29)

accipiō, accipere, accēpī, acceptus, *to take, receive, accept; to endure* (1.3)

*aciēs, aciēī, f., *line of battle* (4.35)

*ācriter, adv., *fiercely* (4.26)

ad, prep. + acc., *to, toward, at, near*; with numbers, *about, approximately* (1.1)

*addūcō, addūcere, addūxī, adductus, *to lead forward, lead on, influence* (1.3)

adeō, adīre, adiī or adīvī, aditūrus, *to go forward, approach, come up to* (5.48)

*adficiō, adficere, adfēcī, adfectus, *to do, treat, affect* (1.2)

*adflictō, -āre, -āvī, -ātus, *to shatter, damage severely* (4.29)

adfore: = adfutūrus esse; see adsum

*aditus, -ūs, m., *approach; access* (5.41)

*adiūtor, adiūtōris, m., *helper, assistant* (5.38)

*administrō, -āre, -āvī, -ātus, *to administer, manage* (4.29)

*admittō, admittere, admīsī, admissus, *to let in; to become guilty, commit (crime)* (4.25)

*admodum, adv., *to full measure, completely, absolutely* (5.40)

*adorior, adorīrī, adortus sum, *to rise up against, attack* (4.26)

*adsum, adesse, adfuī, adfutūrus, *to be present, be here* (5.27)

*Aduātucī, -ōrum, m. pl., *the Aduatuci (a tribe of Germanic origin in Gallia Belgica)* (5.27)

adulēscēns, adulēscentis, m., *young man* (6.13)

*adventus, -ūs, m., *arrival* (1.7)

aedificium, -ī, n., *building* (1.5)

aeger, aegra, aegrum, *sick* (5.40)

*aegrē, adv., *uncomfortably, with dislike, with difficulty* (4.32)

*aes, aeris, n., *bronze* (4.31)

ager, agrī, m., *field, land; territory* (1.2)

*agmen, agminis, n., *column, line of march* (5.31)

agō, agere, ēgī, āctus, *to move, push forward, drive; to do, act* (5.28)

*aliēnus, -a, -um, *belonging to another, foreign; inappropriate, unfavorable* (4.34)

*aliquī, aliquae, aliquod, *some, any* (4.26)

aliquis, aliquis, aliquid, *someone, anyone* (4.32)

*aliter, adv., *in another way, differently* (5.24)

alius, alia, aliud, *other, another* (1.1)

alius . . . alius, *one . . . another*, pl., *some . . . others*

*Allobrogēs, Allobrogum, m. pl., *the Allobroges (*a tribe of southeastern Gaul)* (1.6)

alter, altera, alterum, *one (of two), the other (of two), the second* (1.2)

*altitūdō, altitūdinis, f., *height; depth* (4.25)

*altus, -a, -um, *tall, high; deep* (1.2)

*altum, -ī, n., *the deep, the sea* (4.24)

*Ambiorīx, Ambiorīgis, m., *Ambiorix (a chieftain of the Eburones)* (5.24)

*amīcitia, -ae, f., *friendship* (1.3)

amīcus, -a, -um, *friendly*; as substantive, *friend* (1.3)

*āmittō, āmittere, āmīsī, āmissus, *to lose* (4.29)

*ancora, -ae, f., *anchor* (4.28)

*angustus, -a, -um, *compressed, narrow; small, scanty* (1.2)

*animadvertō, animadvertere, animadvertī, animadversus, *to observe, notice, perceive* (4.25)

animal, animālis, n., *animal* (6.17)

*animus, -ī, m., *soul, spirit, mind* (1.1)

annus, -ī, m., *year* (1.3)

ante, adv., *previously, before*; prep. + acc., *before, in front of* (1.3)

*apertus, -a, -um, *open; unprotected* (4.25)

Apollō, Apollinis, m., *Apollo (god of the sun, medicine, and prophecy)* (6.17)

appellō, -āre, -āvī, -ātus, *to call, name* (1.1)

appropinquō, -āre, -āvī, -ātūrus + dat. or + ad with acc., *to approach, draw near* (4.25)

*apud, prep. + acc., *at the house of, near, with, among* (1.2)

aqua, -ae, f., *water* (4.24)

*aquila, -ae, f., *eagle* (4.25)

*arbitror, -ārī, -ātus sum, *to think* (1.2)

*āridum, -ī, n., *dry land, land* (4.24)

*arma, -ōrum, n. pl., *weapons, arms; force of arms* (1.4)

*armō, -āre, -āvī, -ātus, *to arm* (4.32)

*Arpineius, -ī, m., *Gaius Arpineius (friend of Titurius, sent to speak with the Eburones)* (5.27)

ars, artis, f., *skill, art* (6.17)

ascendō, ascendere, ascendī, ascēnsus, *to climb* (5.26)

at, conj., *but* (4.24)

atque, conj., *and, and also* (1.1)

*Atrebās, Atrebatis, m., *Atrebatian, member of the tribe of the Atrebates* (4.27)

*auctor, auctōris, m., *promoter, advocate, creator, instigator* (5.25)

*auctōritās, auctōritātis, f., *prestige* (1.3)

audācter, adv., *bravely, boldly* (4.24)

*audeō, audēre, ausus sum, semi-deponent + infin., *to dare (to)* (5.28)

audiō, audīre, audīvī or audiī, audītus, *to hear* (5.28)

Aurunculeius: see Cotta

aut, conj., *or* (1.1)

aut . . . aut, conj., *either . . . or*

autem, conj., *however, but; moreover* (1.2)

auxilium, -ī, n., *help* (4.34)

B

barbarus, -a. -um, *foreign, barbaric*; as substantive, *foreigner, barbarian* (4.24)

*Belgae, -ārum, m. pl., *the Belgae (a large group of tribes in northeastern Gaul)* (1.1)

bellum, -ī, n., *war* (1.1)

*bellum īnferre, *to make war upon someone (dat.)* (1.2)

bellum gerere, *to wage war*

*biduum, -ī, n., *space of two days, two days* (5.27)

bonus, -a, -um, *good* (1.6)

bona, -ōrum, n. pl. substantive, *goods, possessions*

brevis, -is, -e, *brief, short* (4.33)

Britannia, -ae, f., *Britain* (4.27)

C

*caedēs, caedis, f., *killing, slaughter* (5.47)

Caesar, Caesaris, m., *Gaius Julius Caesar (Roman general and dictator)* (1.7)

capiō, capere, cēpī, captus, *to take, capture; to reach* (4.26)

captīvus, -ī, m., *captive* (5.42)

*Carnūtēs, Carnūtum, m. pl., *the Carnutes (a tribe of central Gaul)* (5.25)

*carrus, -ī, m., *wagon, cart* (1.3)

casa, -ae, f., *small house, hut, cabin* (5.43)

castra, -ōrum, n. pl., *camp* (4.28)

*cāsus, cāsūs, m., *accident, misfortune, emergency, difficult situation, disaster* (4.31)

*Catuvolcus, -ī, m., *Catuvolcus* (a leader of the Eburones) (5.24)

causa, -ae, f., *reason* (1.1)

　genitive + causā, *for the sake of, for the purpose of* (4.30)

　quā dē causā, *for this reason* (1.1)

*cēdō, cēdere, cēssī, cessūrus, *to go, move; to give way, yield* (5.34)

*celeritās, celeritātis, f., *quickness, speed* (4.35)

celeriter, adv., *quickly* (4.34)

centum, *one hundred* (5.24)

*centuriō, centuriōnis, m., *centurion* (commander of a hundred men)

certus, -a, -um, *certain, sure* (1.7)

　*certior fierī, *to be made more certain, be informed* (1.7)

*Cicerō, Cicerōnis, m., *Quintus Cicero* (one of Caesar's legates, brother of the orator Marcus Cicero) (5.24)

*circiter, adv., *about, approximately* (4.35)

circum, prep. + acc., *around* (5.37)

*circumsistō, circumsistere, circumstetī, *to take a stand around; to surround* (4.26)

circumspiciō, circumspicere, circumspexī, circumspectus, *to look around* (5.31)

*circumveniō, circumvenīre, circumvēnī, circumventūrus, *to surround* (5.35)

*cīvitās, cīvitātis, f., *citizenship; state, tribe* (1.2)

*clam, adv., *secretly* (4.30)

clāmor, clāmōris, m., *shouting* (5.33)

*cliēns, clientis, m., *client, dependent* (1.4)

coāctus: see cōgō

*coepī, coepisse, coeptus, *to begin* (4.25)

cognōscō, cognōscere, cognōvī, cognitus, *to find out, learn, hear of; to get to know, become acquainted with, recognize* (4.24)

*cōgō, cōgere, coēgī, coāctus, *to force, compel; to gather, collect* (1.3)

*cohors, cohortis, f., *cohort* (one-tenth of a legion) (4.32)

*cohortor, -ārī, -ātus sum, *to encourage* (4.25)

*coiciō, coicere, coiēcī, coiectus, *to throw* (4.24)

*collocō, -āre, -āvī, -ātus, *to locate, place, position* (4.33)

colloquor, colloquī, collocūtus sum, *to talk together, talk, converse, confer* (4.30)

*committo, committere, commīsī, commissus, *to bring together, join; to enter into, engage in, begin* (4.34)

*commodē, adv., *suitably, properly, appropriately, well* (4.31)

*commūnicō, -āre, -āvī, -ātus, *to communicate, share; to take counsel with, consult* (5.36)

*commūnis, -is, -e, *common* (5.26)

comparō, -āre, -āvī, -ātus, *to buy, obtain; to get ready, prepare* (1.3)

*compleō, complēre, complēvī, complētus, *to fill* (4.26)

*complūrēs, -ēs, -a, *several* (4.29)

comportō, -āre, -āvī, -ātus, *to bring together, to bring* (4.31)

*comprehendō, comprehendere, comprehendī, comprehēnsus, *to seize, catch* (4.27)

*concēdō, concēdere, concessī, concessūrus, *to yield, submit; to allow, grant* (1.7)

*concilium, -ī, n., *council* (5.24)

*concitō, -āre, -āvī, -ātus, *to put in motion, incite, stir up* (5.26)

conclāmō, -āre, -āvī, -ātus, *to shout together* (5.26)

*concurrō, concurrere, concurrī, concursūrus, *to rush together, rush; to assemble, gather* (5.39)

*condiciō, condiciōnis, f., *condition* (5.37)

*condūcō, condūcere, condūxī, conductus, *to lead together, lead, gather; to hire* (1.4)

cōnferō, cōnferre, contulī, collātus, *to bring together, gather* (4.31)

*cōnfertus, -a, -um, *pressed together, dense, closely packed* (4.32) *cōnfestim, adv., *immediately, without delay* (4.32)

*cōnficiō, cōnficere, cōnfēcī, cōnfectus, *to complete; to wear our, exhaust* (5.45)

*cōnfidō, cōnfidere, cōnfisus sum + dat., *to trust confidently, be assured, believe* (4.30)

*cōnfirmō, -āre, -āvī, -ātus, *to strengthen, establish; to declare, assert* (1.3)

*coniūrātiō, coniūrātiōnis, f., *conspiracy* (1.2)

cōnor, -ārī, -ātus sum, *to try, attempt* (1.3)

cōnsecrātus, -a, -um, *consecrated, sacred* (6.13)

*cōnscrībō, cōnscrībere, cōnscrīpsī, cōnscrīptus, *to write down; to sign up, enlist* (5.24)

*cōnsīdō, cōnsīdere, cōnsēdī, cōnsessūrus, *to sit down, settle; military term, to pitch camp, encamp* (5.47)

cōnsilium, -ī, n., *plan; council (of war); advice* (1.5)

cōnsilium capere, *to form a plan, adopt a plan*

*cōnsistō, cōnsistere, cōnstitī, *to halt, stand, take a stand; of soldiers, to take a position* (4.24)

cōnspiciō, cōnspicere, cōnspexī, cōnspectus, *to catch sight of* (4.25)

*cōnspectus, -ūs, m., *sight* (5.45)

cōnstituō, cōnstituere, cōnstituī, cōnstitūtus, *to establish, set up, arrange; to station, deploy; to decide, determine* (1.3)

*cōnstō, cōnstāre, cōnstitī, cōnstatūrus, *to stand together, stand firm, agree; impersonal, it is agreed* (4.29)

*cōnsuēscō, cōnsuēscere, cōnsuēvī, cōnsuētus, *to accustom; in perfect, to be accustomed, to be in the habit* (4.24)

*cōnsuētūdō, cōnsuētūdinis, f., *custom, habit* (4.32)

cōnsul, cōnsulis, m., *consul*, one of the two chief magistrates elected annually in Rome (1.2)

*cōnsulō, cōnsulere, cōnsuluī, cōnsultus, *to consider, reflect upon; + dat., to take care for, be mindful of, look out for* (5.27)

cōnsūmō, cōnsūmere, cōnsūmpsī, cōnsūmptus, *to use up, consume* (5.31)

cōnsurgō, cōnsurgere, cōnsurrēxī, cōnsurrēctūrus, *to arise, stand up* (5.31)

contemptiō, contemptiōnis, f., *contempt, disdain* (5.29)

*contendō, contendere, contendī, contentus, *to stretch, strain; to strive, struggle; to compete* (1.1)

*continēns, continentis, f., *continent, mainland* (4.27)

*contineō, continēre, continuī, contentus, *to hold together, contain, enclose, hem in, border* (1.1)

continuus, -a, -um, *continuous, without a break* (4.34)

contrā, adv. and prep. + acc., *against, opposite; on the other hand; in reply* (5.29)

*contrōversia, -ae, f., *quarrel, dispute, disagreement* (5.26)

conveniō, convenīre, convēnī, conventūrus, *to come together, meet* (1.6)

*coorior, coorīrī, coortus sum, *to arise* (4.28)

*cōpia, -ae, f., *supply, abundance*; pl., *resources, forces, troops* (1.2)

*cotīdiānus, -a, -um, *daily* (1.1)

*Cotta, -ae, m., *Lucius Aurunculeius Cotta* (one of Caesar's legates) (5.24)

*Crassus, -ī, m., *Marcus Crassus* (one of Caesar's quaestors, son of Caesar's partner in the First Triumvirate) (5.24)

crēdō, crēdere, crēdidī, crēditus + dat., *to trust, believe* (5.28)

cremō, -āre, -āvī, -ātus, *to burn* (1.4)

*cruciātus, -ūs, m., *torture* (5.45)

*cultus, -ūs, m., *care; culture, civilization* (1.1)

cum, conj., *when, since, although* (1.1)

cum, prep. + abl., *with* (1.1)

*cupidus, -a, -um, *desirous* (of + gen.), *eager (to)* (1.2)

*cursus, -ūs, m., *course* (4.26)

D

dē, prep. + abl., *down from, from, concerning, about* (1.1) dēbeō, dēbēre, dēbuī, dēbitus, *to owe;* + infin., *ought, should, must* (5.27)

*dēcēdō, dēcēdere, dēcessī, dēcessūrus, *to go away, depart* (5.43)

dedī: see dō

dēdūcō, dēdūcere, dēdūxī, dēductus, *to lead down, lead out, bring* (4.30)

*dēferō, dēferre, dētulī, dēlātus, irreg., *to carry down; to report; to deliver* (4.27)

*dēficiō, dēficere, dēfēcī, dēfectus, *to fail; to withdraw, desert, revolt* (5.25)

dēfugiō, dēfugere, dēfūgī, *to run away from, shun, avoid* (6.13)

*dēiciō, dēicere, dēiēcī, dēiectus, *to throw down; (of a ship) to drive off course* (4.28)

deinde, adv., *then, next* (4.35)

dēlīberō, -āre, -āvī, -ātus, *to think, ponder, deliberate* (1.7)

*dēligō, -āre, -āvī, -ātus, *to bind, tie up* (4.29)

*dēmōnstrō, -āre, -āvī, -ātus, *to point out, show, mention* (4.27)

dēpellō, dēpellere, dēpepulī, dēpulsus, *to drive off, drive away* (6.17)

dēpōnō, dēpōnere, dēposuī, dēpositus, *to put down* (4.32)

dēscendō, dēscendere, dēscendī, dēscēnsūrus, *to go down, descend; to resort to* (5.29)

*dēsiliō, dēsilīre, dēsiluī, dēsultus, *to leap down, jump down* (4.24)

dēspērātiō, dēspērātiōnis, f., *lack of hope, despair* (5.33)

*dēspērō, -āre, -āvī, -ātus, *to give up hope* (5.26)

*dēsum, dēesse, dēfuī, dēfutūrus + dat., *to be missing, be lacking* (4.26)

deus, -ī, m., *god* (4.25)

*dicō, -āre, -āvī, -ātus, *to dedicate, consecrate; to give up, give over (to)* (6.13)

dīcō, dīcere, dīxī, dictus, *to say, tell* (4.25)

diēs, diēī, m.; f. when referring to a specific date, *day* (1.6)

   *diem dīcere, *to fix a day, name a day* (1.6)

differō, differre, distulī, dīlātus, irreg., *to differ* (1.1)

difficilis, -is, -e, *difficult* (1.6)

difficultās, difficultātis, f., *difficulty* (4.24)

dīligēns, dīligentis, *diligent, careful* (5.35)

dīligentia, -ae, f., *diligence* (6.14)

*dīmittō, dīmittere, dīmīsī, dīmissus, *to send away* (4.34)

*discēdō, discēdere, discessī, discessūrus, *to go away, depart, leave* (4.30)

*disciplīna, -ae, f., *teaching(s); training* (6.13)

*discō, discere, didicī, *to learn* (6.13)

*disputātiō, disputātiōnis, f., *argument, debate* (5.30)

dissentiō, dissentīre, dissēnsī, dissēnsūrus, *to disagree* (5.29)

distribuō, distribuere, distribuī, distribūtus, *to distribute* (5.24)

dīvidō, dīvidere, dīvīsī, dīvīsus, *to divide* (1.1)

dīvīnus, -a, -um, *divine* (6.13)

dō, dare, dedī, datus, *to give* (1.7)

*doceō, docēre, docuī, doctus, *to teach, inform, show* (5.28)

*dolor, dolōris, m., *pain; grief* (1.2)

dominus, -ī, m., *master* (6.13)

domus, -ūs, f., *house, home* (1.6)

*druidēs, -um, m. pl., *druids* (the priests of Gaul) (6.13)

dūcō, dūcere, dūxī, ductus, *to lead; to think, consider* (1.6)

dum, conj., *while;* with subjnct., *until* (1.7)

duo, duae, duo, *two* (1.6)

duodecim, *twelve* (1.5)

*dux, ducis, m., *leader, commander* (5.34)

E

ē or ex, prep. + abl., *from, out of* (5.30)

*Eburōnēs, Eburōnum, m. pl., *the Eburones* (a Belgic tribe) (5.24)

ēdūcō, ēdūcere, ēdūxī, ēductus, *to lead out, lead away* (5.27)

efferō, efferre, extulī, ēlātus, *to carry out* (1.5)

*efficiō, efficere, effēcī, effectus, *to bring about, cause, make* (4.29)

effugiō, effugere, effūgī, *to run away, escape* (4.35)

ego, *I* (4.25)

ēgredior, ēgredī, ēgressus sum, *to go out; to get off* (a ship), *disembark* (4.24)

eiusmodī: = eius modī

ēmittō, ēmittere, ēmīsī, ēmissus, *to send out* (5.26)

enim, conj., *for, because* (4.29)

eō, īre, iī or īvī, itūrus, irreg., *to go* (1.6)

*eōdem, adv., *to the same place* (1.3)

*eques, equitis, m., *cavalryman, horseman; equestrian* (member of the class of wealthy businessman) (4.26)

*equitātus, -ūs, m., *cavalry* (4.24)

equus, -ī, m., *horse* (4.24)

*essedum, -ī, n., *chariot* (used by the Britons) (4.32)

et, conj, *and, also* (1.1)

et . . . et, conj., *both . . . and*

etiam, adv., *also, even* (4.30)

*etsī, conj., *even if, although* (4.31)

*ēventus, -ūs, *occurrence, event; consequence, result* (4.31)

*exanimō, -āre, -āvī, -ātus, *to knock unconscious* (5.44)

*excēdō, excēdere, excessī, excessūrus, *to go out* (4.33)

*excitō, -āre, -āvī, -ātus, *to wake up, rouse up; to incite, inspire;* (of things) *to raise up, build, construct* (5.40)

exeō, exīre, exiī or exīvī, exitūrus, irreg., *to go out* (1.2)

*exercitātiō, exercitātiōnis, f., *training, practice* (4.33)

exercitus, -ūs, m., *army* (1.3)

*exīstimō, -āre, -āvī, -ātus, *to evaluate, think, judge, consider* (1.6)

*expedītus, -a, -um, *unimpeded, unobstructed; available, convenient* (1.6)

expellō, expellere, expulī, expulsus, *to drive out, drive off, drive away* (4.34)

exspectō, -āre, -āvī, -ātus, *to wait for* (5.32)

exstinguō, exstinguere, exstīnxī, exstīnctus, *to put out, exstinguish, destroy* (5.29)

extrā, prep. + acc., *outside* (5.44)

*extrēmus, -a, -um, *outermost, farthest* (1.1)

F

*Fabius, -ī, m., *Gaius Fabius* (one of Caesar's legates) (5.24)

facilis, -is, -e, *easy* (1.2)

facile, adv., *easily*

*facinus, facinoris, n., *action, deed; bad deed, crime* (6.13)

faciō, facere, fēcī, factus, *to make, do* (1.2)

*facultās, facultātis, f., *opportunity* (1.7)

falsus, -a, -um, *false* (6.20)

*fāma, -ae, f., *rumor; report* (5.39)

*famēs, famis, f., *hunger, starvation* (5.29)

familia, -ae, f., *household* (1.3)

*ferē, adv., *almost, approximately* (1.1)

ferō, ferre, tulī, lātus, irreg., *to bring, carry, bear* (4.25)

*fidēs, fideī, f., *faith, good faith, pledge* (1.3)

fīlia, -ae, f., *daughter* (1.3)

fīlius, -ī, m., *son* (1.3)

*fīnis, fīnis, m., *end, boundary;* pl., *territory* (1.1)

*fīnitimus, -a, -um, *neighboring;* as substantive, *neighbor* (1.2)

fiō, fierī, factus sum, irreg., *to become, be made, be done, happen* (1.2)

flamma, -ae, f., *flame* (5.43)

*flūctus, -ūs, m., *wave* (4.24)

*flūmen, flūminis, n., *river* (1.1)

*fore: = futūrus esse; see sum (4.31)

*fortis, -is, -e, *brave* (1.1)

fortūna, -ae, f., *fortune, fate; good fortune, luck* (4.26)

*fossa, -ae, f., *ditch, trench* (5.40)

frāter, frātris, m., *brother* (1.3)

*frūmentārius, -a, -um, *having to do with grain, of grain* (5.24)

*frūmentum, -ī, n., *grain* (1.3)

fuī: see sum

*fuga, -ae, f., *flight* (4.26)

in fugam dare, *to give into flight, put to flight*

*funda, -ae, f., *slingshot* (4.25)

G

*Gallia, -ae, f., *Gaul* (1.1)

*Gallus -a, -um, *of Gaul, Gaulish, Gallic;* as pl. substantive, *the Gauls in general;*

the Celts (distinguished from the Belgae and Aquitani) (1.1)

**Genāva, -ae, f., *Genava* (a town, now Geneva, Switzerland) (1.6)

**genus, generis, n., *type, class* (4.24)

**Germānī, -ōrum, m. pl, *the Germans* (1.1)

gerō, gerere, gessī, gestus, *to carry on, perform, do, manage; to wear* (clothing) (1.1)

bellum gerere, *to wage war* (1.1)

gladius, -ī, m., *sword* (5.42)

glōria, -ae, f., *glory* (1.2)

Graecus, -a, -um, *Greek* (5.48)

**grātia, -ae, f., *favor, regard; thanks* (5.27)

gravis, -is, -e, *heavy, serious* (4.24)

H

habeō, habēre, habuī, habitus, *to have, hold* (1.2)

**Helvētiī, -ōrum, m. pl., *the Helvetii* (a Gallic tribe) (1.1)

**hiberna, -ōrum, n. pl., *winter quarters* (5.24)

hic, haec, hoc, *this; the latter* (1.1)

**hiemō, -āre, *to spend the winter* (4.29)

**hiems, hiemis, f., *winter* (4.29)

Hispānia, -ae, f., *Spain* (1.1)

homō, hominis, m., *man* (1.2)

hōra, -ae, f., *hour* (5.35)

hortor, -ārī, -ātus sum, *to encourage* (5.38)

hostis, hostis, m., *enemy* (4.24)

**hūc, adv., *to this place, here* (4.32)

I

iaciō, iacere, iēcī, iactus, *to throw* (4.28)

**iaculum, -ī, n., *javelin* (5.43)

iam, adv., *now, already* (1.5)

ibi, adv., *there* (5.25)

īdem, eadem, idem, *the same* (1.3)

Īdūs, Īduum, f. pl., *the Ides* (thirteenth day of the month, fifteenth in March, May, July, and October) (1.7)

ignis, ignis, m., *fire* (1.4)

ille, illa, illud, *that; he, she, it; the former* (1.3)

immittō, immittere, immīsī, immissus, *to send into, throw into* (5.44)

**immolō, -āre, -āvī, -ātus, *to slay, sacrifice* (6.16)

immortālis, -is, -e, *immortal* (6.14)

**impedīmenta, -ōrum, n. pl., *baggage* (4.30)

**impedītus, -a, -um, *obstructed, impeded, hindered, burdened* (4.24)

**impellō, impellere, impulī, impulsus, *to push against, strike; to set in motion, urge on, persuade* (5.26)

**imperātor, imperātōris, m., *commander, general* (4.25)

**imperītus, -a, -um, *inexperienced, unskilled* (4.24)

**imperium, -ī, n., *power, rule* (1.2)

imperō, -āre, -āvī, -ātus, *to demand, give orders for, requisition something* (acc.) *from someone* (dat.); *to give orders to* (dat.) (1.7)

**impetrō, -āre, -āvī, -ātus, *to accomplish, bring to pass; to get, obtain, procure; to obtain a request* (5.36)

**impetus, -ūs, m., *attack* (4.26)

importō, -āre, -āvī, -ātus, *to bring in, import* (1.1)

in, prep. + abl., *in, on, among* (1.3)

in, prep. + acc., *into, toward, against, among* (1.6)

incendium, -ī, n., *fire* (5.48)

**incendō, incendere, incendī, incēnsus, *to burn, set fire to* (1.5)

**incertus, -a, -um, *uncertain; disorganized* (4.32)

**incitō, -āre, -āvī, -ātus, *to set in motion; to spur on, stir up* (1.4)

**incolō, incolere, incoluī, incultus, *to live in, inhabit* (1.1)

**incolumis, -is, -e, *unhurt, safe* (5.41)

**incommodum, -ī, n., *inconvenience; trouble, misfortune* (5.35)

incrēdibilis, -is, -e, *unbelievable, incredible* (5.40)

**inde, adv., *from there, then* (4.25)

**ineō, inīre, iniī or inīvī, initūrus, irreg., *to go into, enter; to enter upon, begin, undertake* (4.32)

**īnferior, īnferiōris, *lower* (1.1)

*īnferō, īnferre, intulī, inlātus, irreg., *to bring in, carry on, inflict on* (1.2)
  *bellum īnferre, *to make war upon someone* (dat.) (1.2)
*inimīcus, -a, -um, *hostile*; as substantive, *enemy* (1.7)
*initium, -ī, n., *beginning* (1.1)
  iniūria, -ae, f., *injury, wrongdoing* (1.7)
  innocēns, innocentis, *innocent* (6.16)
  inquit, *(he/she) says, said* (4.25)
*īnsistō, īnsistere, īnstitī, *to stand on; to push forward, advance* (4.26)
*īnstituō, īnstituere, īnstituī, īnstitūtus, *to put in place, establish; to fabricate, construct; to undertake, begin* (5.37)
*īnstitūtum, -ī, n., *custom* (1.1)
  īnsula, -ae, f., *island* (4.26)
*intellegō, intellegere, intellēxī, intellēctus, *to understand* (4.30)
  inter, prep. + acc., *between, among* (1.1)
*intercipiō, intercipere, intercēpī, interceptus, *to intercept, cut off* (5.39)
  intereā, adv., *meanwhile* (4.27)
*intereō, interīre, interiī or interīvī, interitūrus, *to perish, die* (5.30)
  interficiō, interficere, interfēcī, interfectus, *to kill* (4.32)
*interim, adv., *meanwhile* (4.33)
*intermittō, intermittere, intermīsī, intermissus, *to leave off, neglect; to pause, cease, stop*; of time, *to go by, pass* (4.31)
*interpōnō, interpōnere, interposuī, interpositus, *to put between, insert, introduce* (4.32)
  interpretor, -ārī, -ātus sum, *to interpret* (6.13)
*intrā, adv. and prep. + acc., *within* (5.37)
  inventor, inventōris, m., *inventor* (6.17)
  Iovem: see Iuppiter
  ipse, ipsa, ipsum, *himself, herself, itself*, pl., *themselves; very* (1.4)
  is, ea, id, *he she, it; this, that* (1.1)
  ita, adv., *thus, so, in this way, in such a way* (4.29)
  Italia, -ae, f., *Italy* (5.29)
  itaque, adv., *and so, therefore* (4.30)
*item, adv., *likewise* (1.3)
  iter, itineris, n., *journey, route* (1.3)

  iter facere, *to make a journey, travel* (4.32)
  magnum iter, *forced march*
  iubeō, iubēre, iussī, iussus, *to order* (1.7)
*iūdicium, -ī, n., *judgment; trial, court* (1.3)
*iūdicō, -āre, -āvī, -ātus, *to judge, decide* (5.44)
*iugum, -ī, n., *yoke* (for oxen; symbol of humiliation for a defeated army) (1.7)
*Iūnius, -ī, m., *Quintus Junius* (Roman officer sent to speak with the Eburones) (5.27)
  Iuppiter, Iovis, m., *Jupiter* (god of the sky and king of the gods, Roman equivalent of Zeus) (6.17)
*Iūra, -ae, m., *the Jura mountains* (1.2)
*iūs, iūris, n., *right; rightness, justice; legal power, authority* (1.3)
  *iūs iūrandum, iūris iūrandī, n., *oath* (1.3)

L

*Labiēnus, -ī, m., *Titus Labienus* (one of Caesar's legates) (5.24)
  labor, labōris, m., *labor, work* (5.40)
  labōrō, -āre, -āvī, -ātus, *to work; to suffer, be in difficulty, struggle* (4.26)
*lātus, -a, -um, *broad, wide* (1.2)
*latus, lateris, n., *side* (4.25)
*lēgātus, -ī, m., *legate, deputy, assistant; envoy, ambassador* (1.7)
  legiō, legiōnis, f., *legion* (military unit of about 6000 men) (1.7)
*lēx, lēgis, f., *law* (1.1)
  līberī, -ōrum, m. pl., *children* (6.18)
  līberō, -āre, -āvī, -ātus, *to set free, free, liberate* (4.34)
  lībertās, lībertātis, f., *liberty, freedom* (5.27)
  licet, licēre, licuit + dat., *it is allowed* (1.7)
*littera, -ae, f., *letter* (of the alphabet); in pl., *letter, writing* (5.40)
  locus, locī, m.; usually n. in pl., *place, position*; pl., *region; social position, rank* (1.2)
*longinquus, -a, -um, *far away, distant; long, prolonged* (4.27)
*longitūdō, longitūdinis, f., *length* (1.2)
  longus, -a, -um, *long* (4.25)
  *longē, adv., *far away; by far* (1.1)

loquor, loquī, locūtus sum, *to speak* (4.30)

lūna, -ae, f., *moon* (4.29)

lūx, lūcis, f., *light* (5.31)

  prīmā lūce, *at dawn* (5.31)

M

*magistrātus, -ūs, m., *official, magistrate* (1.4)

magnificus, -a, -um, *magnificent* (6.19)

*magnitūdō, magnitūdinis, f., *large size, size* (4.24)

magnus, -a, -um, *big, great, large* (1.2)

maior, maior, maius, *bigger, larger, greater*; in pl., *ancestors* (4.32)

maleficium, -ī, n., *evil deed, offense, harm* (1.7)

maneō, manēre, mānsī, mānsūrus, *to stay, remain* (5.31)

manus, -ūs, f., *hand; band, group* (4.24)

mare, maris, n., *sea* (4.25)

Mārs, Mārtis, m., *Mars* (god of war) (6.17)

*mātēria, -ae, f., *matter, material; timber* (4.31)

mātrimōnium, -ī, n., *motherhood; marriage* (1.3)

maximus, -a, -um, *biggest, greatest, largest* (1.3)

  maximē, adv., *most, very much, very; particularly* (1.3)

medius, -a, -um, *mid-, middle of* (5.31)

*membrum, -ī, n., *limb* (4.24)

memoria, -ae, f., *memory* (1.7)

  memoriā tenēre, *to hold in memory, remember* (1.7)

*mēnsis, mēnsis, m., *month* (1.5)

mercātor, mercātōris, m., *merchant* (1.1)

Mercurius, -ī, m., *Mercury* (god of merchants, messenger of the gods) (6.17)

*metus, -ūs, m., *fear* (5.41)

meus, -a, -um, *my, mine* (4.25)

mīles, mīlitis, m., *soldier* (1.7)

*mīlitia, -ae, f., *military service* (6.14)

*mīlle, indeclinable; neuter in pl., mīlia, *a thousand* (1.2)

  mīlle passūs, *a mile* (1.2)

Minerva, -ae, f., *Minerva* (goddess of wisdom and crafts) (6.17)

minor, minus, *smaller, less* (1.2)

*minuō, minuere, minuī, minūtus, *to make smaller, lessen; to settle* (a dispute) (5.26)

mittō, mittere, mīsī, missus, *to send* (1.7)

mōbilitās, mōbilitātis, f., *mobility* (4.33)

modo, adv., *only* (4.25)

modus, -ī, m., *way, method, manner* (4.27)

moneō, monēre, monuī, monitus, *to advise, warn* (5.27)

mōns, montis, m., *mountain* (1.2)

*morbus, -ī, m., *disease, illness* (6.16)

morior, morī, mortuus sum, *to die* (1.4)

*moror, -ārī, -ātus sum, *to remain, stay, delay* (5.24)

mors, mortis, f., *death* (5.29)

*mōs, mōris, m., *habit, custom* (1.3)

*mōtus, -ūs, m., *movement* (4.25)

*multitūdō, multitūdinis, f., *large number; crowd; common people* (1.2)

multus, -a, -um, *much*; pl., *many* (1.3)

  multō, adv., *greatly, by much, very* (5.40)

*mūniō, mūnīre, mūnīvī, mūnītus, *to build, fortify* (5.24)

*mūnītiō, mūnītiōnis, f., *fortification* (5.39)

N

nam, conj., *for* (4.25)

*nāscor, nāscī, nātus sum, *to be born* (5.25)

nātiō, nātiōnis, f., *people, nation* (6.16)

nātūra, -ae, f., *nature* (1.2)

nāvigō, -āre, -āvī, -ātus, *to sail* (4.29)

nāvis, nāvis, f., *ship* (4.24)

  nāvis longa, *galley, warship*

  nāvis onerāria, *transport ship*

nē, conj. + subj., *not to, so that . . . not, to prevent, to avoid*; introducing clause of fearing, *that* (4.25)

nē . . . quidem, adv., *not even* (5.40)

nec, conj., *and . . . not, but . . . not, nor* (5.31)

necesse, adv. or indecl. adj., *necessary* (4.29)

neglegō, neglegere, neglēxī, neglēctus, *to nelgect, ignore, disregard* (5.28)

*negō, -āre, -āvī, -ātus, *to deny, say no* (5.27)

*negōtium, -ī, n., *business, task; trouble, difficulty* (5.33)

nēmō, nēminis, m./f., *no one* (4.30)

neque, conj., *and . . . not* (1.4)

neque . . . neque, conj., *neither . . . nor*

*Nerviī, -ōrum, m. pl., *the Nervii (a Belgic tribe)* (5.24)

nihil, pron., *nothing*; as adv., *in no way, not* (5.29)

nisi, conj., *if . . . not, unless; except* (4.24)

nōbilis, -is, -e, *noble* (1.2)

noceō, nocēre, nocuī, nocitūrus + dat., *to harm* (5.34)

*noctū, adv., *at night* (4.32)

*nocturnus, -a, -um, *during the night, at night* (5.32)

nōlō, nōlle, nōluī, irreg., *to not want, not wish, be unwilling, refuse* (5.40)

nōmen, nōminis, n., *name* (5.45)

nōn, adv., *not* (1.3)

*nōn nūllus, -a, -um, *often written as one word* nōnnūllus, *some, several* (1.6)

*nōndum, adv., *not yet* (1.6)

nōs, *we, us* (5.29)

noster, nostra, nostrum, *our* (1.1)

nostrī, substantive, *our men, our soldiers* (4.24)

*nōtus, -a, -um, *well known, familiar* (4.24)

novus, -a, -um, *new* (4.32)

nox, noctis, f., *night* (4.28)

nūllus, -a, -um, *no, none* (1.7)

numerus, -ī, m., *number; position, rank* (1.3)

nunc, adv., *now* (5.27)

nūntiō, -āre, -āvī, -ātus, *to announce, report* (1.7)

*nūntius, -ī, m., *messenger; message* (4.34)

O

*ob, prep. + acc., *because of, on account of* (1.4)

observō, -āre, -āvī, -ātus, *to observe* (5.35)

*obses, obsidis, m., *hostage* (4.27)

*obsidiō, obsidiōnis, f., *seige* (5.29)

obtineō, obtinēre, obtinuī, obtentus, *to hold, control* (1.3)

*occāsiō, occāsiōnis, f., *opportunity* (5.29)

occīdō, occīdere, occīsī, occīsus, *to kill* (1.7)

*occultō, -āre, -āvī, -ātus, *to conceal, hide* (6.17)

occupātus, -a, -um, *busy* (4.32)

*occupō, -āre, -āvī, -ātus, *to seize* (1.3)

*occurrō, occurrere, occurrī, occursūrus + dat., *to meet* (4.26)

*Ōceanus, -ī, m., *the Ocean (a body of water believed to surround the entire world)* (1.1)

*officium, -ī, n., *duty, service* (4.25)

*omnīnō, adv., *altogether, in all* (1.6)

omnis, -is, -e, *all, the whole, every, each* (1.1)

*onerārius, -a, -um, *designed for cargo* (4.25)

nāvis onerāria, *cargo ship, transport ship*

*opera, -ae, f., *exertion, efforts, service* (5.25)

*opīniō, opīniōnis, f., *belief, expectation* (5.48)

*oportet, oportēre, oportuit, *it is fitting, it is proper, ought* (1.4)

*oppidum, -ī, n., *town* (1.5)

*opportūnus, -a, -um, *convenient, suitable, advantageous, helpful* (4.34)

opprimō, opprimere, oppressī, oppressus, *to overwhelm, oppress, weigh down* (4.24)

*oppugnātiō, oppugnātiōnis, f., *attack, assault* (5.26)

*oppugnō, -āre, -āvī, -ātus, *to attack, assault* (1.5)

optimus, -a, -um, *best, very good, excellent* (4.30)

*opus, operis, n., *work* (5.40)

*ōrātiō, ōrātiōnis, f., *oration, speech* (1.3)

*orbis, orbis, m., *circle* (5.33)

*ōrdō, ōrdinis, m., *order; (military) formation, rank* (4.26)

*orior, orīrī, ortus sum, *to rise, arise, begin* (1.1)

*ōrō, -āre, -āvī, -ātus, *to beg* (5.27)

ostendō, ostendere, ostendī, ostentus, *to show* (5.32)

P

*paene, adv., *almost* (5.43)

*palam, adv., *openly* (5.25)

*pār, paris, *equal* (5.34)

parātus, -a, -um, *prepared* (1.5)

*parcō, parcere, pepercī + dat., *to spare* (5.36)

parēns, parentis, m., *parent* (6.14)

parō, -āre, -āvī, -ātus, *to prepare, get ready* (5.42)

pars, partis, f., *part, direction, region* (1.1)

passus, -ūs, m., *pace, step* (1.2)

   *mīlle passūs, pl., mīlia passuum, *mile* (1.2)

*pateō, patēre, patuī, *to lie open, be accessible; stretch out, extend* (1.2)

pater, patris, m., *father* (1.3)

patior, patī, passus sum, *to suffer; to allow* (1.6)

*paucī, -ae, -a, *a few* (4.26)

*paucitās, paucitātis, f., *small number* (4.30)

*paulātim, adv., *little by little, gradually* (4.30)

*paulum, -ī, n., *a little* (4.24)

   *paulō, adv., *by a little, a little* (4.32)

*pāx, pācis, f., *peace* (1.3)

pecūnia, -ae, f., *money* (6.17)

*peditātus, -ūs, m., *infantry, foot soldiers* (4.34)

pellō, pellere, pepulī, pulsus, *to push, strike; to drive off, rout* (1.7)

*pendō, pendere, pependī, pēnsus, *to weigh; to pay* (5.27)

per, prep. + acc., *through; with the help of* (1.6)

percurrō, percurrere, percucurrī, percursūrus, *to run through, run along* (4.33)

perdiscō, perdiscere, perdidicī, *to learn thoroughly* (6.14)

perdūcō, perdūcere, perdūxī, perductus, *to lead through, extend, prolong* (5.31)

perferō, perferre, pertulī, perlātus, *to bring through* (5.39)

*perficiō, perficere, perfēcī, perfectus, *to complete* (1.3)

perīculum, -ī, n., *danger* (1.5)

permaneō, permanēre, permānsī, permānsūrus, *to remain, continue* (6.14)

*permoveō, permovēre, permōvī, permōtus, *to move thoroughly; to influence, prevail upon, persuade* (1.3)

*perpetuus, -a, -um, *perpetual, everlasting* (4.34); in perpetuum, *forever*

persuādeō, persuādēre, persuāsī, persuāsus, *to make something* (acc.) *agreeable to someone* (dat.), *to persuade someone* (dat.) (1.2)

perterritus, -a, -um, *terrified, frightened* (4.24)

*pertineō, pertinēre, pertinuī, *to reach, extend; to pertain, refer; to tend* (1.1)

*perturbō, -āre, -āvī, -ātus, *to disturb, confuse, throw into confusion* (4.26)

*perveniō, pervenīre, pervēnī, perventūrus, *to arrive, come to* (1.7)

pēs, pedis, m., *foot* (4.25)

petō, petere, petīvī, petītus, *to head for, look for, seek* (4.27)

*pīlum, -ī, n., *spear, javelin* (5.40)

*Plancus, -ī, m., *Lucius Munatius Plancus* (one of Caesar's legates) (5.24)

plēbs, plēbis, f., *common people* (1.3)

plēnus, -a, -um, *full* (4.29)

*plērīque, plēraeque, plēraque, *most, very many, a great many* (6.13)

*plērumque, adv., *generally, mostly* (4.24)

plūrimus, -a, -um, *most, very much* (5.27)

plūs, plūris, n., pl., plūrēs, *more* (4.26)

*polliceor, pollicērī, pollicitus sum, *to promise* (4.27)

pōnō, pōnere, posuī, positus, *to put, place* (5.29)

*pōns, pontis, m., *bridge* (1.6)

populus, -ī, m., *people* (1.3)

portō, -āre, -āvī, -ātus, *to carry* (1.5)

possum, posse, potuī, irreg., *to be able, can* (1.2)

post, prep. + acc., *after* (1.5, 4.28, 4.30)

*posteā, adv., *later on, afterwards* (4.30)

*posterus, -a, -um, *following, next* (5.38)

postquam, conj., *after* (5.32)

*postrēmō, adv., *at last, in the end, finally* (5.28)

*potēns, potentis, *powerful* (1.3)

*potestās, potestātis, f., *power; opportunity* (5.41)

*potior, potīrī, potītus sum + abl. or gen., *to get possession of, get control of* (1.2) *praeda, -ae, f., *loot* (4.34)

*praedicō, -āre, -āvī, -ātus, *to declare publicly, report, announce* (4.34)

*praeficiō, praeficere, praefēcī, praefectus, *to put someone* (acc.) *in command of something* (dat.) (5.24)

praemittō, praemittere, praemīsī, praemissus, *to send ahead* (4.27)

*praemium, -ī, n., *reward* (5.40)

*praesentia, -ae, f., *presence* (5.37)

*praesertim, adv., *especially, particularly* (5.27)

*praesidium, -ī, n., *protection* (5.41)

*praestō, praestāre, praestitī, praestitus + dat., *to stand out, surpass; to bestow; to fulfill, perform* (1.2)

*praesum, praeesse, praefuī, praefutūrus, irreg. + dat., *to be charge of, be in command of* (5.24)

*praetereā, adv., *in addition* (5.33)

*premō, premere, pressī, pressus, *to press, press upon, press hard* (4.32)

prīmus, -a, -um, *first* (4.25)

prīmō, adv., *first, at first* (4.33)

*prīnceps, prīncipis, *leading, chief;* as substantive, *important man, leader, chieftain* (1.7)

*prīncipātus, -ūs, m., *leadership* (1.3)

*prīstinus, -a, -um, *former, original; previous* (4.26)

prīvātus, -a, -um, *private* (1.5)

prō, prep. + abl., *for, on behalf of; in return for; as; in front of; in proportion to, relative to* (1.2)

*probō, -āre, -āvī, -ātus, *to approve; to prove, demonstrate, show* (1.3)

*prōcēdō, prōcēdere, prōcessī, prōcessūrus, *to go forward, advance* (4.32)

*procul, adv., *far off, in the distance* (5.34)

prōcurrō, prōcurrere, prōcurrī, prōcursūrus, *to run forward* (5.34)

*prōdō, prōdere, prōdidī, prōditus, *to hand over, hand down; to betray* (4.25)

*proelium, -ī, n., *battle* (1.1)

*profectiō, profectiōnis, f., *departure* (1.3)

proficīscor, proficīscī, profectus sum, *to set out* (1.3)

prōgredior, prōgredī, prōgressus sum, *to go forward, advance* (4.24)

*prohibeō, prohibēre, prohibuī, prohibitus, *to keep someone* (acc.) *away from something* (abl.); *to prohibit, prevent, stop* (1.1)

prōiciō, prōicere, prōiēcī, prōiectus, *to throw forward* (4.25)

*prōnūntiō, -āre, -āvī, -ātus, *to proclaim, announce* (5.31)

*prōpellō, prōpellere, prōpulī, prōpulsus, *to drive forward; to drive away* (4.25)

*propinquus, -a, -um, *nearby;* as substantive, *relative* (6.14)

*propius, adv. + acc., *nearer* (4.28)

*propter, prep. + acc., *because of, on account of* (4.24)

*proptereā, adv., *for this reason, therefore;* **proptereā quod**, *because* (1.1)

*prōvideō, prōvidēre, prōvīdī, prōvīsus, *to foresee; to provide against, provide for; to fulfill, discharge, perform* (4.29)

*prōvincia, -ae, f., *province;* specifically, *the Roman province* in southern Gaul controlled by Rome before Caesar's conquests. (1.1)

proximus, -a, -um, *nearest (to);* of time, *most recent* (1.1)

pūblicus, -a, -um, *belonging to the people, public* (4.25)

rēs pūblica, reī pūblicae, f., *state, government*

*pugna, -ae, f., *fight, battle* (4.24)

pugnō, -āre, -āvī, -ātus, *to fight* (4.24)

*Pullō, Pullōnis, m., *Titus Pullo* (a centurion) (5.44)

pulsus: see **pellō**

putō, -āre, -āvī, -ātus, *to think* (1.7)

Q

*quā: see **quī**

*quadringentī, -ae, -a, *four hundred* (1.5)

*quaestor, quaestōris, m., *quaestor* (a financial official) (5.24)

quam, adv., *than, as* (5.27)

quam, adv. + superlative adj. or adv., *as . . . as possible* (1.3) *quantus, -a, -um, *how much, how great, what a great* (4.34)

quārtus, -a, -um, *fourth* (4.28)

-que, enclitic conj., *and* (1.1)

quī, quae, quod, *who, which, that*; after a period or semicolon, *he, she, it, this*; after sī, nisi, num, nē = aliquī (1.1)

*quā, *where, by what route, along which* (1.6)

quod, *the fact that* (4.31)

*quīcumque, quaecumque, quodcumque, *whichever, whatever* (4.26)

quīdam, quaedam, quoddam, *a certain*; in pl., *certain, some* (5.27)

quidem, adv., *indeed, in fact* (5.29)

nē . . . quidem, *not even* (5.40)

quiētus, -a, -um, *quiet* (5.24)

*quīn, conj. + subj., *but that, that* (1.3)

quīndecim, *fifteen* (5.26)

quis, quid, interrogative, *who, what* (5.29) after sī, nisi, num, or nē = aliquis (5.27)

*quispiam, quaepiam, quodpiam, indef. adj., *any* (5.35)

*quisquam, quisquam, quicquam, *someone, something, anyone, anything* (5.41)

*quisque, quidque, indef. pron., *each person, each one, every one* (1.5)

quisque, quaeque, quodque, indef. pron. and adj., *each one, every one*

quod, conj., *because*; after a verb expressing emotion, *that* (1.1)

quoque, adv., *also* (1.1)

R

*ratiō, ratiōnis, f., *reckoning, account; care, concern* (5.27)

rebelliō, rebelliōnis, f., *rebellion, revolt, renewal of war* (4.30)

recipiō, recipere, recēpī, receptus, *to take back, recover; to receive, accept* (1.5)

*sē recipere, idiom, *to take oneself back, return, withdraw, retreat* (4.33)

*reddō, reddere, reddidī, redditus, *to give back, give* (6.13)

redeō, redīre, rediī or redīvī, reditūrus, irreg., *to return, go back* (5.48)

redūcō, redūcere, redūxī, reductus, *to lead back* (4.34)

referō, referre, retulī, relātus, irreg., *to bring back, carry back* (4.28)

*reficiō reficere, refēcī, refectus, *to make again, restore, repair* (4.29)

refugiō, refugere, refūgī, *to flee back, draw back* (5.35)

regiō, regiōnis, f., *area, region* (6.13)

*rēgnum, -ī, n., *royal power, rule; kingdom* (1.2)

regredior, regredī, regressus sum, *to go back, return* (5.44)

*religiō, religiōnis, f., *piety, religion*; in pl., *religious matters* (6.13)

*relinquō, relinquere, relīquī, relictus, *to leave behind, abandon* (5.31)

reliquus, -a, -um, *the rest, the remaining, other* (1.1)

remaneō, remanēre, remānsī, remānsūrus, *to stay behind* (4.32)

remittō, remittere, remīsī, remissus, *to send back* (4.27)

removeō, removēre, remōvī, remōtus, *to remove* (4.25)

repellō, repellere, reppulī, repulsus, *to drive back, drive away, repulse* (5.42)

*repentīnus, -a, -um, *sudden* (5.26)

reportō, -āre, -āvī, -ātus, *to carry back, bring back* (4.29)

rēs, reī, f., *thing, event, matter, situation, affair* (1.2)

rēs pūblica, *state, government* (4.25)

reservō, -āre, -āvī, -ātus, *to reserve* (5.34)

resistō, resistere, restitī + dat., *to resist* (5.27)

respiciō, respicere, respexī, respectus, *to look back* (5.43)

respondeō, respondēre, respondī, respōnsus, *to reply* (1.7)

revertor, revertī, reversus sum, *to return* (1.7)

*Rhēnus, -ī, m., *the Rhine River* (1.1)

*Rhodanus, -ī, m., *the Rhône River* (1.1)

rogō, -āre, -āvī, -ātus, *to ask* (1.7)

Rōmānus, -a, -um, *Roman* (1.3)

rumor, rumōris, m., *rumor* (6.20)

*rūrsus, adv., *again* (4.30)

S

*Sabīnus, -ī, m., *Quintus Titurius Sabinus* (one of Caesar's legates) (5.24)

sacrificium, -ī, n., *sacrifice* (6.13)

saepe, adv., *often* (1.1)

*salūs, salūtis, f., *safety* (5.27)

*Samarobrīva, ae., f., *Samarobriva* (capital city of the Ambiani) (5.24)

satis, adv., *enough* (1.3)

sciō, scīre, scīvī, scītus, *to know* (5.46)

scrībō, scrībere, scrīpsī, scrīptus, *to write* (5.46)

sē or sēsē, *himself, herself, oneself, itself, themselves* (1.1)

sed, conj., *but* (5.27)

senātus, -ūs, m., *senate* (1.3)

*sententia, -ae, f., *feeling; opinion* (5.29)

*sentiō, sentīre, sēnsī, sēnsus, *to perceive, notice, realize* (5.27)

septimus, -a, -um, *seventh* (4.32)

*Sēquanī, -ōrum, m. pl., *the Sequani* (a Gallic tribe) (1.1)

sequor, sequī, secūtus sum, *to follow* (1.4)

*sermō, sermōnis, m., *speech, conversation* (5.37)

*servitūs, servitūtis, f., *slavery* (5.27)

*servō, -āre, -āvī, -ātus, *to save, preserve* (4.26)

servus, -ī, m., *slave* (5.45)

sēsē, alternative form of sē (1.3)

sī, conj., *if* (1.7)

sī quis (= aliquis), *if anyone* (5.27)

*sīc, adv., *thus, in this way, so* (5.31)

*sīcutī, adv., *as if, as, just as, just as if* (5.43)

*signum, -ī, n., *sign, signal; standard* (4.26)

silva, -ae, f., *woods, forest* (4.32)

similis, -is, -e + dat., *similar (to)* (5.47)

simul, adv., *at the same time* (4.24)

simul atque, *as soon as* (4.27)

*simulācrum, -ī, n., *image, figure* (6.16)

sine, prep. + abl., *without* (1.7)

*singulāris, -is, -e, *single, one at a time, individual; unusual, exceptional* (4.26)

*socius, -ī, m., *ally* (1.5)

*spatium, -ī, n., *space, distance; period of time, interval* (1.7)

spectō, -āre, -āvī, -ātus, *to watch, look at; to face* (1.1)

*spērō, -āre, -āvī, -ātus, *to hope* (1.3)

*spēs, speī, f., *hope* (1.5)

*sponte, *voluntarily, of one's own accord* (5.28)

stabilitās, stabilitātis, f., *stability, steadfastness* (4.33)

statim, adv., *immediately* (4.27)

stō, stāre, stetī, status, *to stand* (5.35)

*studium, -ī, n., *enthusiasm, zeal* (4.24)

sub, prep. + abl. or acc., *under* (5.24)

*subdūcō, subdūcere, subdūxī, subductus, *to draw up from below, raise, haul up* (4.29)

subitō, adv., *suddenly* (4.28)

sublātus: see tollō

submittō, submittere, submīsī, submissus, *to send* (as reinforcements) (4.26)

*subsequor, subsequī, subsecūtus sum, *to follow closely, follow* (4.24)

*subsidium, -ī, n., *assistance, aid* (4.26)

*subveniō, subvenīre, subvēnī, subventūrus + dat., *to come to the aid of* (5.35)

*succēdō, succēdere, successī, successūrus, *to go under, enter; to follow, take the place of* (4.32)

*succendō, succendere, succendī, succēnsus, *to set on fire, burn* (5.43)

sum, esse, fuī, futūrus, irreg., *to be* (1.1)

summus, -a, -um, *greatest, very great; highest, the top of . . .* (4.24)

*superior, superiōris, *higher; of time, previous* (4.28)

*superō, -āre, -āvī, -ātus, *to overcome, defeat* (4.27)

*supplicium, -ī, n., *punishment, execution* (6.16)

*suprā, adv., *above; previously* (4.27)

suspiciō, suspiciōnis, f., *suspicion* (1.4)

*suspicor, -ārī, -ātus, *to suspect* (4.31)

*sustineō, sustinēre, sustinuī, sustentus, *to sustain, endure, withstand, hold out* (4.32)

sustulī: see tollō

suus, -a, -um, *his, her, one's, its, their (own)*; as substantive, *their men* (1.1)

T

tamen, *however* (1.7)

tandem, adv., *finally, at last* (5.31)

tantus, -a, -um, *so great, so much* (4.25)

*Tasgetius, -ī, m., *Tasgetius* (a prince of the Carnutes) (5.25)

*tēlum, -ī, n., *spear; weapon* (4.24)

*tempestās, tempestātis, f., *weather; storm* (4.28)

tempus, temporis, n., *time* (4.29)

teneō, tenēre, tenuī, tentus, *to hold* (1.7)

terra, -ae, f., *earth, ground* (5.42)

terreō, terrēre, terruī, territus, *to frighten, terrify* (5.30)

terror, terrōris, m., *fear, terror* (4.33)

*tertius, -a, -um, *third* (1.1)

*testūdō, testūdinis, f., *tortoise; mobile shelter* (for attackers) (5.42)

timeō, timēre, timuī, *to be afraid, fear* (5.29)

timidus, -a, -um, *timid, fearful* (5.33)

timor, timōris, m., *fear* (4.34)

Titūrius: see Sabīnus

*tollō, tollere, sustulī, sublātus, *to lift, raise; to pick up, take away* (1.5)

*tormentum, -ī, n. *catapult; torture* (4.25)

*tot, adv., *so many* (5.29)

tōtus, -a, -um, *all, the whole* (1.2)

*trādō, trādere, trādidī, trāditus, *to hand over, hand down* (5.25)

*trāgula, -ae, f., *spear* (of a type used by the Gauls) (5.35)

*trāiciō, trāicere, trāiēcī, trāiectus, *to throw through, pierce* (5.35)

trāns, prep. + acc., *across* (1.1)

trānseō, trānsīre, trānsiī or trānsīvī, trānsitūrus, *to go through, cross* (1.5)

trānsferō, trānsferre, trānstulī, trānslātus, *to carry across, bring over* (6.13)

trānsportō, -āre, -āvī, -ātus, *to bring across* (4.29)

trēs, trēs, tria, *three* (1.1)

*Trēverī, -ōrum, m. pl., *the Treveri* (a Gallic tribe originally from Germany) (5.24)

*tribūnus, -ī, m., *tribune* (a title given to several Roman officials); tribūnī mīlitum, *military tribunes* (5.28)

*tribūtum, -ī, n., *taxes, taxation* (6.13)

tū, *you* (sing.) (5.30)

tum, adv., *then* (4.25)

*turpis, -is, -e, *disgraceful, shameful* (5.28)

*turris, turris, f., *tower* (5.40)

*tūtus, -a, -um, *safe* (5.27)

tuus, -a, -um, *your* (5.44)

U

ubi, adv., conj., *where, when* (1.7)

*ūllus, -a, -um, *any* (1.7)

*ultrō, adv., *beyond, furthermore; voluntarily, without being asked* (4.27)

*ūnā, adv., *together* (1.5)

*unde, adv., *from where* (4.28)

*undique, adv., *from all sides, in all directions* (1.2)

*ūniversus, -a, -um, *all together* (4.25)

ūnus, -a, -um, *one; only* (1. 1)

*ūnā, adv., *together* (1.5)

*ūsus, -ūs, m., *use* (4.25)

ūsuī esse, *to be of use, be useful*

ut or utī, conj. + indic., *as, how, when;* + subjunct., *so that, that, in order to;* with clause of fearing, *that . . . not* (1.2)

*uter, utra, utrum, *which one, which* (of two) (5.44)

*uterque, utraque, utrumque, *each* (of two), *both* (4.26)

*ūtor, ūtī, ūsus sum + abl., *to use, make use of* (1.5)

uxor, uxōris, f., *wife* (6.19)

V

*vādum, -ī, n., *shallow place, ford* (1.6)

*vāllum, -ī, n., *wall, rampart* (around a camp) (5.26)

veniō, venīre, vēnī, ventūrus, *to come* (4.27)

*ventitō, -āre, -āvī, -ātūrus, *to come often, keep coming* (4.32)

ventus, -ī, m., *wind* (4.28)

*vereor, verērī, veritus sum, *to fear* (5.25)

*vērō, *in truth, truly, indeed; however* (4.26)

*versō, -āre, -āvī, -ātus, *to turn around, handle, deal with;* in passive, *to be involved with, engaged with* (5.44)

via, -ae, f., *road* (5.40)

victor, victōris, m., *winner, victor* (5.39)

victōria, -ae, f., *victory* (5.29)

videō, vidēre, vīdī, vīsus, *to see;* in passive, *to be seen, to seem; to seem good/ best/advisable* (4.28)

*vigilia, -ae, f., *wakefulness, sleeplessness. lack of sleep; watch* (one of the four divisions of the nighttime) (5.31)

*vinculum or vinclum, -ī, n., *chain* (1.4)

vincō, vincere, vīcī, victus, *to conquer, overcome, defeat; to prevail* (5.30)

vir, virī, m., *man* (5.35)

*virtūs, virtūtis, f., *courage.* (1.1)

*vīs, acc., vim, abl., vī, pl., vīrēs, f., *violence, force, power* (1.6)

vīta, -ae, f., *life* (6.16)

*vīvus, -a, -um, *alive, living* (6.16)

*vix, adv., *with difficulty, scarcely* (1.6)

vocō, -āre, -āvī, -ātus, *to call* (5.43)

volō, velle, voluī, irreg., *to wish, want* (4.25)

*voluntās, voluntātis, f., *wish, will; good wishes, goodwill* (1.7)

*Vorēnus, -ī, m., *Lucius Vorenus* (a centurion) (5.44)

vōs, *you* (pl.) (5.30)

vōx, vōcis, f., *voice* (4.25)

*vulgus, -ī, n., *crowd* (5.33)

*vulnerō, -āre, -āvī, -ātus, *to wound* (5.40)

*vulnus, vulneris, n., *wound* (5.28)

Index of Reading Notes

This page lists all the Cultural Content, Forms, Reading Strategies, Structure, Text, and Vocabulary notes. Reading Strategy notes that deal with a specific topic are listed separately, while those that show how an experienced reader of Latin would deal with a complex sentence are grouped together under "complex sentence." Likewise, all notes that discuss textual problems in specific passages are grouped together.

* * * * * * * * *

Illustrations, diagrams, and maps are listed on page vi.

* * * * * * * * *

Acknowledgments

Maps
All maps created by XNR Productions.

Photographs
Note: Every effort has been made to secure permission and provide appropriate credit for photographic material. The publisher deeply regrets any omission and pledges to correct errors called to its attention in subsequent editions.

Unless otherwise acknowledged, all photographs are the property of Pearson Education, Inc.

Photo locators denoted as follows: Top (T), Center (C), Bottom (B), Left (L), Right (R), Background (Bkgd).

Cover Shutterstock
3   The Art Gallery Collection/Alamy Images
29   Ancient Art & Architecture Collection Ltd/Alamy Images
72   Lebrecht Music and Arts Photo Library/Alamy Images
81   (R, L) Courtesy of the American Numismatic Society
87   Andrew Palmer/Alamy Images
101 Art Resource, NY
131 Arterra Picture Library/Alamy Images
157 DeAgostini/SuperStock
167 PjrStudio/Alamy Images

174 Detail Heritage/Alamy Images
193 Mary Evans Picture Library/Alamy Images
208 Caroline Switzer Kelly
209 Alamy Images
242 Alamy Images

Text
Grateful acknowledgement is made to the following for copyrighted material:

50–71   Penguin Books, Ltd. (UK) "Book 1: The Expulsion of Intruders" by Julius Caesar from *The Conquest of Gaul*. Used by permission.

75–180,   Penguin Books, Ltd. (UK) "Book
198–207   6: Operations Near the Rhine" by Julius Caesar from *The Conquest of Gaul*. Used by permission.

210–247   Penguin Books, Ltd. (UK) "Book 7: The Rebellion of Vercingetorix" by Julius Caesar from *The Conquest of Gaul*. Used by permission.

Note: Every effort has been made to locate the copyright owner of material reproduced in this book. Omissions brought to our attention will be corrected in subsequent editions.